Managing People, Finance and Marketing

VOLUME 1

Second Edition

PEARSON
Custom
Publishing

We work with leading authors to develop the strongest educational materials bringing cutting-edge thinking and best learning practice to a global market.

Under a range of well-known imprints, including Financial Times/Prentice Hall, Addison Wesley and Longman, we craft high quality print and electronic publications which help readers to understand and apply their content, whether studying or at work.

Pearson Custom Publishing enables our customers to access a wide and expanding range of market-leading content from world-renowned authors and develop their own tailor-made book. You choose the content that meets your needs and Pearson Custom Publishing produces a high-quality printed book.

To find out more about custom publishing, visit
www.pearsoncustom.co.uk

A Pearson Custom Publication

Managing People, Finance and Marketing

VOLUME 1

Second Edition

Compiled from:

Management: An Introduction
Fourth Edition
by David Boddy

Organising and Managing Work
Second Edition
by Tony Watson

PEARSON
Custom Publishing

Pearson Education Limited
Edinburgh Gate
Harlow
Essex CM20 2JE

And associated companies throughout the world

Visit us on the World Wide Web at:
www.pearsoned.co.uk

First published 2007

This Custom Book Edition © 2009 Published by Pearson Education Limited

Compiled from:

Management: An Introduction Fourth Edition
by David Boddy

ISBN 978 0 273 71106 3

Organising and Managing Work Second Edition
by Tony Watson

ISBN 978 0 273 70480 5

ISBN 978 1 84776 409 6

Printed and bound in Great Britain by 4edge Limited, Hockley. www.4edge.co.uk

Contents

Part 1

Organisational context, management and leadership

Week 1

Introduction to the Module

Week 2

Organisational Structure and Strategic Environment

Chapter 10
Organisation structure

Aim

To introduce terms and practices that show the choices managers face in shaping organisational structures.

Objectives

By the end of your work on this chapter you should be able to outline the concepts below in your terms and:

1. Outline why the structure of an organisation affects performance
2. Give examples of management choices about dividing and coordinating work, with their likely advantages and disadvantages
3. Compare the features of mechanistic and organic structures
4. Use the 'contingencies' believed to influence choice of structure to evaluate the suitability of a form for a given unit
5. Summarise the work of Woodward, Burns and Stalker, Lawrence and Lorsch and John Child, showing how they contributed to this area of management theory
6. Explain and illustrate the features of a learning organisation.

Key terms

This chapter introduces the following ideas:

organisation structure
organisation chart
formal structure
informal structure
vertical specialisation
horizontal specialisation
formal authority
responsibility
delegation
span of control
centralisation
decentralisation
formalisation
functional structure
divisional structure
matrix structure
network structure
mechanistic structure
organic structure
contingencies
technology
differentiation
integration
determinist
structural choice

Oticon www.oticon.com

CASE STUDY

This Danish company is the world's second largest producer of hearing aids with about 1,200 staff in Denmark (the parent company, William Demant Holdings, has about 4400 employees worldwide). Oticon has research and production facilities that help ensure the high-quality design and manufacture of its products. Competition intensified during the 1980s and the company began to lose market share to larger rivals such as Siemens. Lars Kolind was appointed chief executive in 1988. In 1990 he concluded that a new approach was needed to counter the threats from larger competitors that were becoming stronger. Oticon's only hope for survival and prosperity was to be radical in all aspects of the business. Kolind intended the changes to turn Oticon from an *industrial* organisation producing hearing aids into a *service* organisation with a physical product.

He organised product development work around projects. The project leader was appointed by the management team and recruited people to do the work. Employees chose whether or not to join – and could only do so if their current project leader agreed. Previously most people had a single skill; they were now required to be active in at least three specialties – one based on professional qualification and two others unrelated to the first. A chip designer could develop skills in customer support and advertising, for example. These arrangements allowed the company to respond quickly to unexpected events and to use skills fully.

Previously Oticon had a conventional hierarchical structure, and a horizontal structure of separate functional departments. The only remnant of the hierarchy is the ten-person management team, each member of which acts as an 'owner' to the many projects through which work is done. Kolind refers to this as 'managed chaos'. The company tries to overcome the dangers of this by developing a strong and clear mission – 'to help people with X problem to live better with X'; and a common set of written values. Examples include: 'an assumption that we only employ adults (who can be expected to act responsibly)', and 'an assumption that staff want to know what and why they are doing it', so all information is available to everyone (with a few legally excepted areas).

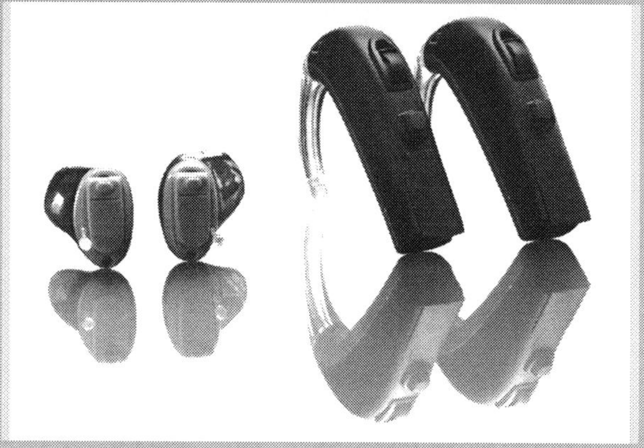

Oticon

There are no titles – people do whatever they think is right at the time. The potential for chaos is averted by building underneath the flexible organisation a set of clearly defined business processes, setting out essential tasks: 'The better your processes are defined, the more flexible you can be.' The absence of departments avoids people protecting local interests and makes it easier to cope with fluctuations in workload.

Oticon was one of the earliest companies to redesign the workplace to maximise disturbance. This was most visible in the 'mobile office', in which each workstation was a desk without drawers (nowhere to file paper). There were no installed telephones, though everyone had a mobile. The workstations were equipped with powerful PCs through which people worked (staff had a small trolley for personal belongings that they wheeled to wherever they were working that day). Although common today, this arrangement was revolutionary at the time.

Source: Based on Bjorn-Andersen and Turner (1994); Rivard *et al.* (2004): and company website.

Case questions 10.1

- What factors persuaded management to change the structure at Oticon?
- How would you expect staff to react to these changes?

10.1 Introduction

Managers at Oticon had to adapt its structure to survive new competition. This required not only lower costs, but also an ability to respond more quickly to the needs of individual customers and to broader changes in technology and in the market.

Senior managers of companies that have not been performing well frequently announce structural changes. When Shell was trying to recover from the 2004 oil reserves crisis the board first dismissed the three senior executives involved in the failure – and then started to change the structure to prevent a recurrence. In 2007 Cadbury Schweppes announced that it would split the drinks and confectionery parts of the business into separate companies, in the belief that this would allow both to perform better. Management at Philips, the Dutch electronics group, has been working to ensure that the fiercely independent units in the company cooperate more closely with each other to improve performance.

When an owner-manager is running a small business he or she decides what tasks to do and coordinates them. If the enterprise grows the entrepreneur usually passes some of the work to newly recruited staff, though the division will probably be flexible and informal. Owner and staff can easily communicate directly with each other, so coordination is easy. If the business continues to grow, new structural questions arise about how best to use available resources. Managers divide the enterprise into distinct units of activity – which brings the possibility of misunderstanding between people in separate units with less direct contact: they need to establish some mechanisms to ensure coordination. How they do this reflects their theory about organisation structure.

This chapter outlines the structural issues that managers in all organisations need to resolve, and which Figure 10.1 illustrates. Managers create a formal structure when they decide how to divide and coordinate the work of the organisation. These decisions in part reflect their interpretation of contingencies affecting the business, and in part the views of stakeholders. Together with many informal arrangements, these decisions create a structure that balances mechanistic and organic forms, which affect organisational performance.

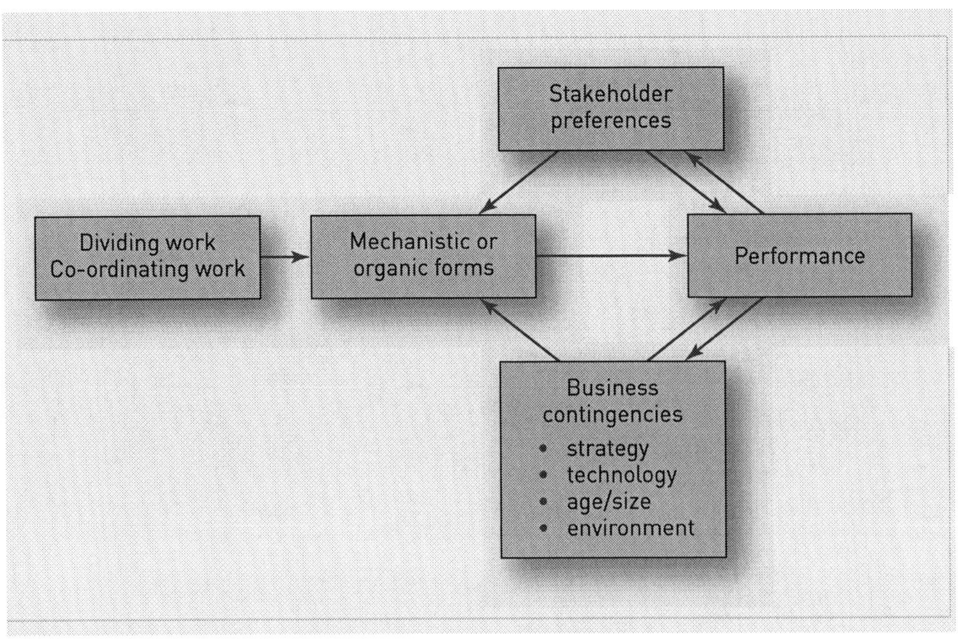

Figure 10.1
Alternative structures and performance

10.2 Designing a structure

Organisation structure describes the way work is divided, supervised and coordinated. When people join a department or take a job within the structure this gives a fairly clear signal about what they should do. The director of marketing is expected to deal with marketing, not finance. Various 'operating policies' reinforce the signal from the basic structure. These cover matters such as recruitment, selection, appraisal and reward (Chapter 11) which managers design to influence employees to act in ways that support wider objectives.

Organisation structure 'The structure of an organisation [is] the sum total of the ways in which it divides its labour into distinct tasks and then achieves co-ordination among them' (Mintzberg, 1979).

The organisation chart

The **organisation chart** shows the structure as a picture. It shows the main departments and positions, with lines linking senior executives to the departments or people for whose work they are responsible. It shows who people report to, and clarifies four features of the **formal structure**:

An **organisation chart** shows the main departments and senior positions in an organisation and the reporting relations between them.

1 tasks – the major tasks or activities the organisation undertakes;
2 subdivisions – how the major tasks are further divided;
3 levels – the position of each post within the management hierarchy;
4 lines of authority – the lines linking the boxes show who has formal authority over whom, and to whom people report.

Formal structure is the official guidelines, documents or procedures setting out how the organisation's activities are divided and coordinated.

Organisation charts give a convenient (though transient) summary of the current allocation of tasks and who is responsible for them. Figure 10.2 shows the chart for an aircraft factory within what is now BAE Systems, a UK defence contractor. The chart shows it has six main departments – design, production engineering, purchasing, inventory, production and human resources. It also shows the chain of command within the plant and the tasks of the respective departments (only some of which are shown). In this case the chart includes direct staff such as operators and engineers, and shows the lines of authority throughout the factory. It does *not* show the **informal structure** – the many patterns of work and communication that are part of organisational life.

Informal structure is the undocumented relationships between members of the organisation that inevitably emerge as people adapt systems to new conditions and satisfy personal and group needs.

Work specialisation

'Job specialisation ... is an inherent part of every organisation, indeed every human activity' (Mintzberg, 1979, p. 69). Management divides work into smaller tasks, with people or departments specialising in one or more of these. They become more expert in one task than they could be in several and are more likely to come up with improved ideas or methods. Taken too far specialisation leads to the negative effects noted in Chapter 15.

Figure 10.2 shows the specialisation of work in the BAE factory. At the top is specialisation between design, production, purchasing and so on. It shows a **vertical specialisation** in that people at different levels deal with distinct sets of activity. It also shows a **horizontal specialisation**. Within production engineering some specialise in electrical problems and others in mechanical, within which groups specialise in structures, systems and fittings. Although Multi-show Events is still a very small company, they too have begun to create a structure showing who is responsible for what.

Vertical specialisation refers to the extent to which responsibilities at different levels are defined.

Horizontal specialisation is the degree to which tasks are divided among separate people or departments.

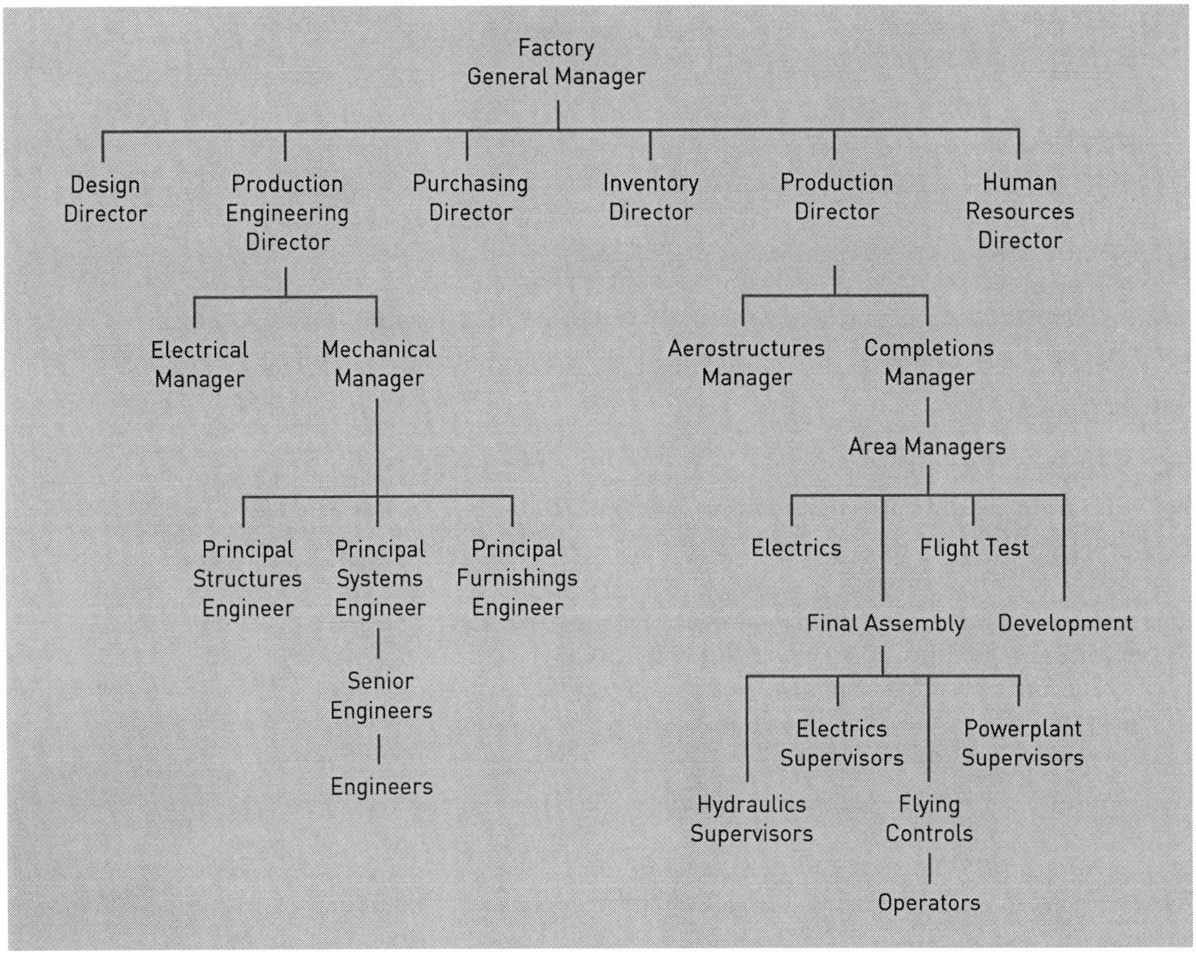

Figure 10.2 The structure within a BAE aircraft factory (www.baesystems.com)

management in practice

Multi-show Events

Multi-show Events employs 11 people providing a variety of entertainment and promotional services to large businesses. When Brian Simpson created the business in 1990 with a full-time staff of 2 the company obviously had no formal structure. He reflected on the process of growth and structure:

> **While the company was small thinking about a structure never occurred to me. It became a consideration as sales grew and the complexity of what we offered increased. There were also more people around and I believed that I should introduce a structure so that clear divisions of responsibility would be visible. It seemed natural to split sales and marketing from the actual delivery and production of events as these were two distinct areas. I felt that by creating 'specialised' departments we could give a better service to clients as each area of the company could focus more on their own roles.** [Figure 10.3 shows the structure.]

We had to redesign the office layout and introduce a more formalised communication process to ensure all relevant information is being passed on – and on the whole I think this structure will see us through the next stage of business growth and development.

Source: Private communication.

Chain of command

The lines of authority show the links between people – who they report to and who reports to them. It shows who they can ask to do a piece of work, who they can ask for help – and who will be expecting results from them. In Figure 10.2 the production director can give instructions to the aerostructures manager, but not to the electrical manager in production engineering. Figure 10.3 shows the lines of authority in Multi-show Events. In both there are many informal contacts in the course of normal human activity, which bring the organisation to life and help people cope with unplanned events.

The lines of authority show the allocation of **formal authority** within the organisation – the right a person has to make decisions, allocate resources or give instructions. It is based on the position, not the person. The production engineering director at BAE has formal authority over a defined range of matters – and anyone else taking over the job would have the same amount of formal authority.

Formal authority is the right that a person in a specified role has to make decisions, allocate resources or give instructions.

Subordinates – those below someone else in the hierarchy – comply with instructions or requests because they accept the person has the formal (sometimes called legitimate) authority to make them. An operator in the hydraulics area of final assembly would accept an instruction from the hydraulics foreman, but probably not from the power-plant foreman (he or she may help them as a personal favour, but that is different from accepting formal authority). If managers attempt to give instructions beyond their area of formal authority they are likely to meet resistance.

Responsibility is a person's duty to meet the expectations associated with a task. The production director and the hydraulics foreman are responsible for the tasks that go with those positions. To fulfil those responsibilities they require formal authority to manage relevant resources.

Responsibility refers to a person's duty to meet the expectations others have of them.

Accountability means that people with formal authority over an area are required to report on their work to those above them in the chain of command. The principal systems engineer is accountable to the mechanical manager for the way he or she has used resources: have they achieved what was expected as measured by the cost, quantity, quality or timeliness of the work?

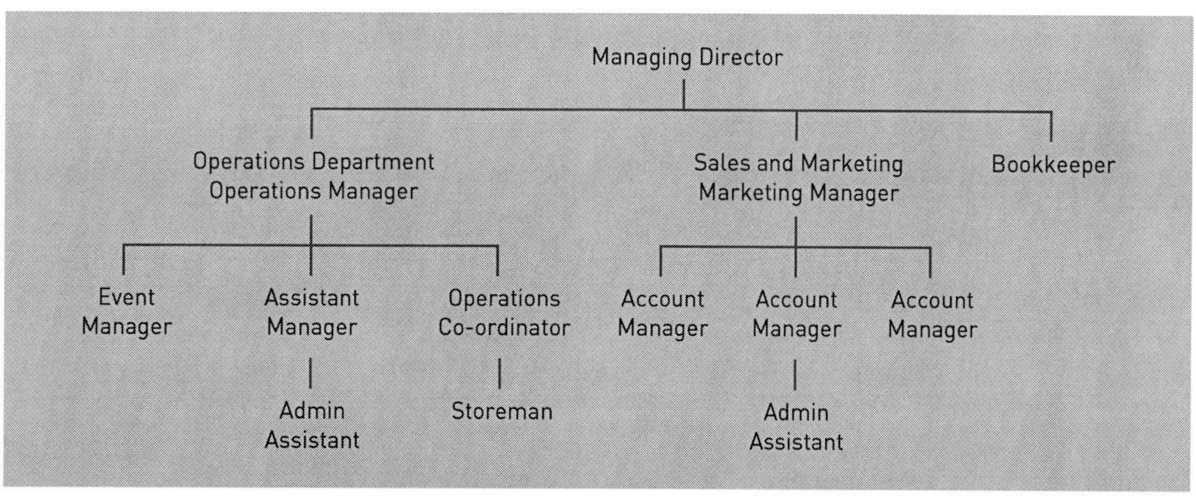

Figure 10.3 The organisation structure at Multi-show Events

Oticon – the case continues – hierarchy and rank www.oticon.com

CASE STUDY

Before the change the company had six distinct hierarchical levels, with privileges based on rank:

Not only was there a specific company car assigned to each management level, but other material signs existed ... prestige and reward were very apparent: in the length of the curtains, the type of carpet ... the size of people's desks. It all gave status. And that was what people strove for. (Rivard *et al.*, 2004, p. 181)

Horizontal boundaries were also strong, as the two main divisions – Electronics (product development) and International (sales) communicated poorly. Within these divisions work was organised round specific departments and tasks: 'People were locked into specific roles and responsibilities and were rewarded only for those – nobody took initiatives' (Rivard *et al.*, 2004, p. 180).

Source: Based on Bjorn-Andersen and Turner (1994); and Rivard *et al.* (2004).

Delegation occurs when one person gives another the authority to undertake specific activities or decisions.

Delegation is the process by which people transfer responsibility and authority for certain parts of their work to people below them in the chain of command. While the production director is responsible and accountable for all the work in that area, they are only able to do this by delegating. They are still accountable for the results, but they pass the responsibility, and the necessary authority, to subordinates – and this continues down the hierarchy. If managers delegate more to their subordinates this enables quicker decisions and more rapid responses to new conditions – though some managers are reluctant to delegate in case it reduces their power (Chapter 14).

The span of control

A **span of control** is the number of subordinates reporting directly to the person above them in the hierarchy.

The **span of control** refers to the number of subordinates reporting to a supervisor. Where staff are closely supervised there is a narrow span of control – as shown in the top half of Figure 10.4. If staff have more autonomy and responsibility they need less direct supervision, so more can report to the same manager – the span of control becomes wider, and the structure flatter.

key ideas

Joan Woodward's research

Joan Woodward's study of 100 firms in Essex found great variety amongst them in the number of subordinates managers supervised (Woodward, 1965). The number of people reporting directly to the chief executive ranged from 2 to 18, with the median span of control being 6. The average span of control of the first line supervisors varied from 10 to 90, with a median of 37. Woodward explained the variation by the technological system used (discussed more fully in Section 10.6).

Centralisation and decentralisation

When an organisation grows beyond the smallest operation management divides work vertically, as those at the top delegate more of their work to those below them – and so begin to create a hierarchy such as that shown in Figure 10.4. As the business grows the hierarchy becomes more complex, but it is often possible to see three levels – corporate, divisional and operating – such as at Cadbury Schweppes ( ).

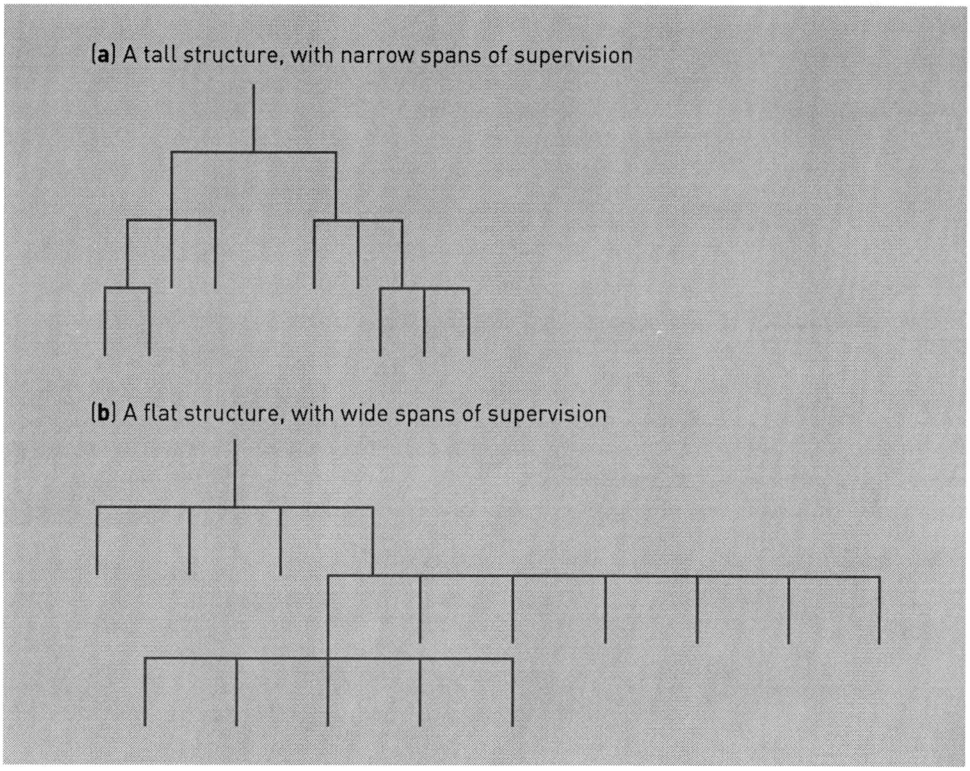

Figure 10.4
Tall and flat organisation structures

- *Corporate* The most senior group, such as the board of Cadbury Schweppes, who are responsible for managing the overall direction of the organisation. This includes not only guiding and monitoring the performance of the organisation but also maintaining links with significant external institutions such as banks and political bodies.
- *Divisional* Responsible for implementing broad areas of policy and for allocating budgets and other resources. Cadbury Schweppes is organised geographically so the managers in, for example, the Europe, Middle East and Africa (EMEA) division are responsible for meeting the targets which the board sets for that division. Divisional managers represent the division's interests to the board and also monitor and control the performance of the operating units.
- *Operating* The level responsible for the technical work of any organisation – making products, catching thieves, caring for patients or delivering services. Within EMEA at Cadbury's there is a team responsible for the Dairy Milk brand in the United Kingdom – ensuring it is produced and sold successfully in that market; other teams look after other products.

Centralisation is when a relatively large number of decisions are taken by management at the top of the organisation.

Decentralisation is when a relatively large number of decisions are taken lower down the organisation in the operating units.

The vertical hierarchy establishes what decisions people at each level can make. **Centralisation** is when those at the top make most decisions, with managers at divisional level ensuring those at operating level follow the policy.

Decentralisation is when a relatively large number of decisions are taken in the divisions or operating units. Branch managers in ATMays, a chain of retail travel agents (now part of Going Places) had considerable freedom over pricing and promotional activities, but were required to follow very tight financial reporting routines.

management in practice **Philips** www.philips.com

After a period of heavy losses during the 1990s Philips, the Dutch electronics company, appointed a new chief executive in 2001 – Gerard Kleisterlee. He acted quickly to restructure the company, including reducing staff by 25 per cent. The company has a rich 113-year history of innovation and pioneered electric shavers, medical X-rays and compact disks: it symbolised European technical prowess.

But the same engineering culture has also produced failures (such as an early rival to the now-standard VCR) and revenues today are little higher than they were 10 years ago. To pick up the pace, Kleisterlee has reorganised the company – selling unprofitable areas, outsourcing much electronics manufacture (see Section 10.6). Now he is refocusing the company around the most profitable sectors, especially medical systems, and pushing all products to a digital format. This focus is backed up by breaking down the walls separating the fiercely independent divisions and getting them to communicate. 'We're transforming ourselves into a single company', says Mr. Kleisterlee. Under the 'One Philips' slogan, he is centralising functions such as marketing and human resources to eliminate duplication.

Source: *Business Week*, 3 May 2004.

management in practice **Johnson & Johnson** www.jnj.com

This leading health care products company has three divisions – drugs, medical devices and consumer products. Although widely known for products such as Band-Aid and baby powder, its deeper strength lies in scientific research and innovation.

> **J&J's success has hinged on its unique culture and structure ... Each of the far-flung units operates pretty much as an independent enterprise. Businesses set their own strategies; they have their own finance and human resources departments, for example. [While this is costly] Johnson & Johnson has been [successful] precisely because the businesses it buys, or the ones it starts, are given near-total autonomy. That independence fosters an entrepreneurial attitude that has kept J&J ... competitive as others around it have faltered.**

Source: *Business Week*, 5 May 2003.

In practice, organisations display a mix of both. Many have moved towards a more decentralised structure in the belief that those closest to the action will make better decisions. Others limit the power of divisions and operating units by taking more decisions at the centre. Hewlett-Packard had a tradition of local autonomy ('The HP Way'). The company founders believed that 'smart people will make the right choices if given the right tools and authority' and so pushed strategic decisions down to the managers in each business. The company appointed a new CEO, Carleton Fiorina, in 1999. She created a strategy council to advise her on strategy and to allocate resources – a big change from 'The HP Way'.

There is always a tension between centralisation and decentralisation. The profile at any point reflects the shifting power of these forces, as managers weigh the benefits of a move in one direction or the other (including career interests). Table 10.1 summarises these.

Factor	Advantages	Disadvantages
Response to change	Thorough debate of issues	Slower response to local conditions
Use of expertise	Concentration of expertise at the centre makes it easier to develop new services and promote best practice methods	Less likely to take account of local knowledge
Cost	Economies of scale in purchasing Efficient administration if use common systems	Local suppliers may be better value than corporate suppliers
Policy implications	Less risk of local managers breaching legal requirements	More risk of local managers breaching legal requirements
Staff commitment	Backing of centre ensures wide support	Staff motivated by greater local responsibility
Consistency	Provides consistent image to the public – less variation in service standards	Local staff discouraged from taking responsibility – can blame centre

Table 10.1
Advantages and disadvantages of centralisation

Formalisation

Formalisation is the practice of using written or electronic documents to direct and control employees. Documents include rule books, procedures, instruction manuals, job descriptions – anything that sets out what people must do in designated circumstances. They include the scripts that operators in most call centres must use to guide their conversation with a customer. The intention of these formal methods (consistent with the ideas of Max Weber discussed in Chapter 2) is to bring consistency and predictability to organisational work.

Formalisation is the practice of using written or electronic documents to direct and control employees.

There is always tension between formality and informality. If people want to respond to individual needs or local conditions, they favour informal arrangements with few rules, as this seems the best way of meeting those needs. Other requirements, such as those of industry regulators or consumer legislation, pull towards more formality. They may specify detailed procedures and guidelines to protect customers against unsuitable selling methods or to protect staff against unfounded complaints. This leads to formal systems and recording procedures.

Activity 10.1 Critical reflection on structures

Select an organisation with which you are familiar, or one of those mentioned in this text. Gather information about aspects of the structure, such as:

- Does the organisation chart look tall, or flat?
- What evidence is there of high or low levels of formality?
- Which decisions are centralised, and which are decentralised?

Share your information with colleagues on your course, to increase your awareness of the range of ways in which people have designed structures.

10.3 Grouping jobs into functions and divisions

While work specialisation divides the tasks of the enterprise into smaller jobs for individuals, an opposite process groups jobs together in functional, divisional or matrix forms. Two other forms use teams and networks as the basis of structure. Figure 10.5 shows these alternatives.

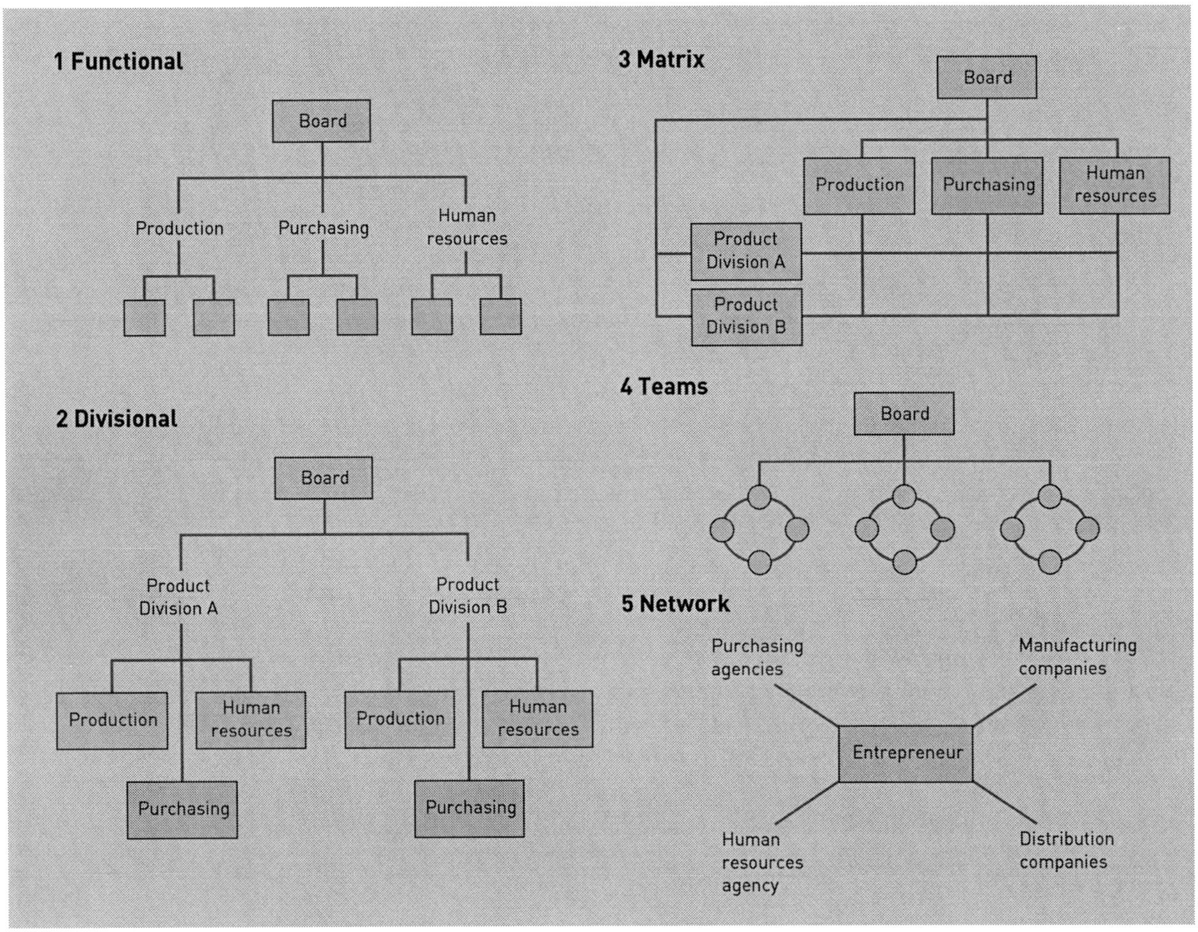

Figure 10.5 Five types of structure

Specialisation by function

A **functional structure** is when tasks are grouped into departments based on similar skills and expertise.

In a **functional structure** managers group activities and staff according to their profession or function – such as production, finance or marketing. The BAE chart shows design, production engineering, purchasing, inventory, production and human resources functions. Figure 10.6 shows a hospital chart, with a functional structure at senior level.

The functional approach can be efficient as people with common expertise work together, sharing and seeing a professional career path. A difficulty is that it may be a source of conflict (Nauta and Saunders, 2001) if the separate functions develop different perceptions of organisational goals. The same may happen as an organisation grows and diversifies into a range of different products, markets or geographical areas. Managers

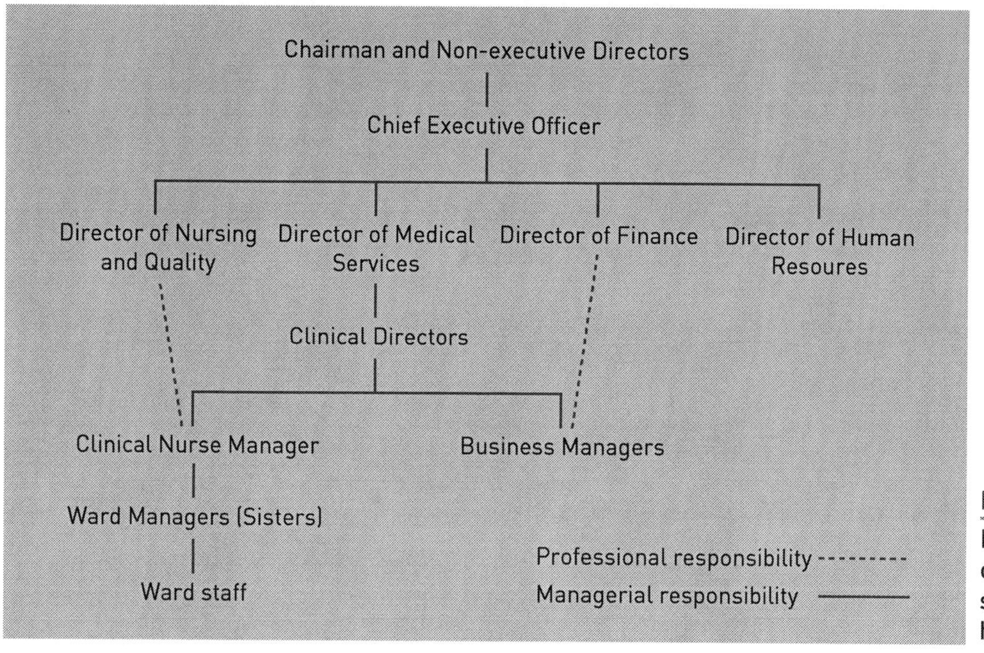

Figure 10.6 Partial organisation structure in a hospital

responsible for these areas expect functional staff to give them priority – leading to competition between business units for functional services.

Specialisation by divisions

Managers create a **divisional structure** when they arrange the organisation around its main products, services or customer groups. In a divisional structure senior managers give each unit the authority to design, produce and deliver the product or service. Functions within the division are likely to cooperate as they depend on satisfying the same set of customers, though duplicating functions make it expensive.

A **divisional structure** is when tasks are grouped in relation to their outputs, such as products or the needs of different types of customer.

Product or customer

Divisional structures enable staff to focus on a distinct group of customers. Banks know that wealthy clients have different needs from other people – and have created divisions to focus on meeting those needs. Hospitals can use what they term the 'named-nurse' system, in which one nurse is responsible for several identified patients. That nurse is the patient's point of contact with the system, managing the delivery of services to the patient from other (functional) departments. Figure 10.7 contrasts the approaches.

Geographic divisions

Here managers group tasks by geography – a common approach in companies with many service outlets – supermarkets, hotels or pub chains. It allows people to focus on identifying and meeting different customer requirements in the region, and it is also easier for divisional managers to monitor and control the many outlets – see Table 10.2.

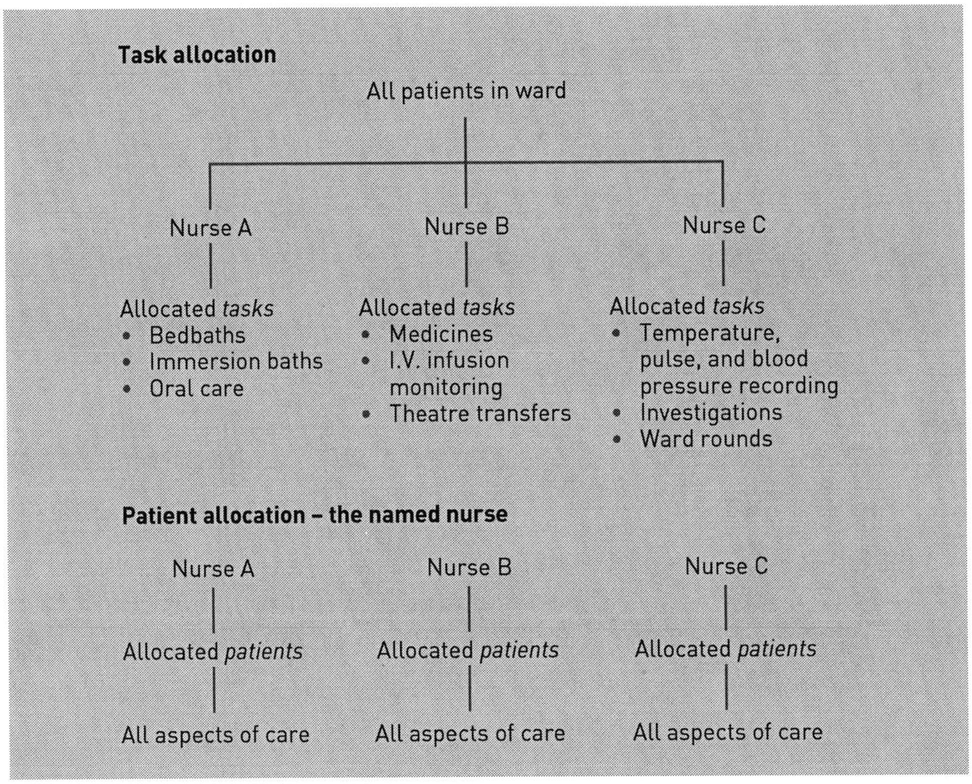

Figure 10.7
Task and named-nurse structures

Table 10.2
Advantages and disadvantages of functional and divisional structures

Structure	Advantages	Disadvantages
Functional	Clear career paths and professional development Specialisation leads to high standards and efficiency Common professional interests support good internal relations	Isolation from wider interests damages promotion prospects Conflict over priorities Lack of wider awareness damages external relations
Divisional	Functional staff focus on product and customer needs Dedicated facilities meet customer needs quickly Common customer focus enables good internal relations	Isolation from wider professional and technical developments Costs of duplicate resources Potential conflict with other divisions over priorities Focus on local, not corporate, needs

Activity 10.2 Choosing between approaches

Go to the website of a company that interests you, and gather information about the structure of the company.

- Gather evidence to decide whether it has a functional or divisional structure – and if the latter, is that based on products or geography?
- If it has international operations, how are they shown in the structure?

Compare your research with colleagues on your course, and prepare a short presentation summarising your conclusions.

10.4 Grouping jobs in matrices, teams and networks

Matrix structure

A matrix structure combines functional and divisional structures: function on one axis of the matrix and products or projects on the other. Functional staff work on one or more projects, moving between them as required. They report to two bosses – a functional head and the head of the current project.

A **matrix structure** is when those doing a task report both to a functional and a project or divisional boss.

management in practice

Product development at Toyota www.toyota.com

Toyota used to organise its product development in a matrix form. The product planning division employed about 7000 people working on 16 current projects. Each represented a new model and employed a chief engineer and several hundred staff. There were also 16 functional engineering divisions.

> A chief engineer had to co-ordinate people in 48 departments in 12 divisions to launch a new product ... In addition, relatively young chief engineers did not always get sufficient co-operation from senior functional managers ... For their part, functional managers found it difficult to spend the time on managing details on so many projects. Most of these managers had to oversee work for about 15 different projects at the same time.

Source: Cusumano and Nobeoka (1998, pp. 22–24).

Teams

In their search for more flexibility, lower costs and faster response some companies organise work into teams – most evident in companies that depend on a steady flow of new products – such as Johnson & Johnson or Philips. Management delegates significant responsibilities and authority not to individual workers but to an identifiable team, which is then accountable for the results (Chapter 17).

Networks

Network structures refer to situations in which organisations remain independent but agree to work together to deliver products or services. Sometimes this happens when managers arrange for other companies to undertake certain non-core activities on their behalf. The remaining organisation concentrates on setting strategy direction and managing the core units. Abbey (a Spanish-owned UK bank) has an agreement with computer services company Unisys to manage the 1.5 million insurance policies it has sold. Large electronics producers such as Dell or Sun Microsystems have their products made under contract by companies that specialise in such work. The arrangement is becoming common in personal services – such as when Care UK runs schools for disturbed children on behalf of local government.

A **network structure** is when tasks required by one company are performed by other companies with expertise in those areas.

A similar structural form is when managers sell one of their services to another company, but still deliver the service to customers under their own name. Abbey sold its credit card business to MBNA as the cost of updating its systems to compete effectively in the card business was too high. The company continues to offer cards with the Abbey logo, but MBNA operates the service.

Mixed forms

Large organisations typically combine functional, product and geographical structures within the same company – the structure of Unilever, the Anglo-Dutch conglomerate that produces a vast range of consumer products throughout the world, is an example – see Management in Practice.

management in practice **Mixed structure at Unilever** www.unilever.com

During the year ended 31 December 2005 Unilever's top management team consisted of regional, category and functional presidents, and was headed by the group chief executive. He was accountable for all aspects of Unilever operations, managing business performance and overall profit responsibility for the group.

The three regional presidents (the Americas, Asia/Africa and Europe) are responsible for profit, implementing proven brand mixes in their region, and single-mindedly focusing on growth through excellent go-to-market execution.

The categories presidents (Food and Home and Personal Care) are responsible for category strategy and brand development (including R&D and innovation): 'The interdependence between the regions and the categories allows us to capitalise on our global scale while building on our deep roots in local markets.'

Finance and HR presidents ensure excellence in their functional areas and provide support to the regions, categories and corporate centre.

Source: Extracts from *Unilever Annual Report*, 2005.

The counterpart to the task of dividing work is that of coordinating it – without which there will be confusion and poor performance.

Activity 10.3 **Comparing structures**

Think of an organisation you have worked in, or about which you can gather information.

- Which of the five structural forms did it correspond to most closely?
- What were the benefits and disadvantages of that approach?

Compare your conclusions with colleagues on your course, and use your experience to prepare a list of the advantages and disadvantages of each type of structure.

10.5 Coordinating work

There are five ways to coordinate the activities of people working on different tasks.

Direct supervision

This is where a manager ensures coordination by directly supervising his or her staff to ensure they work together in line with company policy. The number of people whom a manager can effectively supervise directly reflects the idea of the span of control – that beyond some (variable) point direct supervision is no longer sufficient.

Hierarchy

If disputes or problems arise between staff or departments, they can be reconciled by putting the arguments to their common boss in the hierarchy. It is the boss's responsibility to reach a solution. At BAE (Figure 10.2), if the engineer responsible for structures has a disagreement with the systems engineer, they can ask the mechanical manager to adjudicate. If that fails they can escalate the problem to the production engineering director. The weakness of this is that it takes time to get a response, and meantime the issue is unresolved. In rapidly changing circumstances the hierarchy cannot cope with the volume of issues requiring attention, and becomes slow at making decisions.

Standardising inputs and outputs

This involves making sure that what goes into the system, and what managers expect it to produce, are standardised. If the purchaser of components specifies accurately what is required, and the supplier meets that specification, coordination between users will be easier. If staff work to precise specifications that helps coordination with the next stage. If they receive the same training they will need less direct supervision, as their manager can be more confident that they will be working consistently.

Rules and procedures

Another coordination method is to prepare rules or procedures, such as that shown in the Management in Practice feature. Organisations have procedures for approving capital expenditure. To compare proposals on a common basis they set strict guidelines on the questions a bid should answer, how people should prepare a case, and to whom they should submit it. Companies developing computer software have coordination problems if several designers are working on a project, so use strict change control procedures to ensure that the sub-projects fit together.

Safety procedures in a power station

management in practice

The following instructions govern the steps that staff must follow when they inspect control equipment in a nuclear power station:

1 Before commencing work you must read and understand the relevant Permit-to-Work and/or other safety documents as appropriate.
2 Obtain keys for relevant cubicles.
3 Visually inspect the interior of each bay for dirt, water and evidence of condensation.
4 Visually inspect the cabling, glands, terminal blocks and components for damage.
5 Visually check for loose connections at all terminals.
6 Lock all cubicles and return the keys.
7 Clear the safety document and return it to the Supervisor/Senior Authorised person.

Information systems

Information systems help to ensure that people who need to work in a consistent way have common information, so that it is easier to coordinate their activities. The Internet offers a radical way of moving information and knowledge between organisations, as the Siemens example shows.

management in practice

Internet coordination at Siemens www.siemens.com

Mr von Pierer, chief executive of Siemens, is enthusiastic about the way the company is using the Internet to coordinate different parts of the company. One example is online purchasing, which enables the company to save huge amounts of money by pooling the demands of several purchasing departments, using a company-wide system called click2procure.

Another is encouraging customers to buy online. They can click on 'buy from Siemens' on the website home page and place orders for most Siemens products. The automation and drives division, for example, generates some 30 per cent of its sales online. The strategy also helps to improve internal administrative processes – such as by handling 30,000 job applications a year online, or expecting employees to book their business travel arrangements over the Internet.

> **There is more to this than paperless administration. The idea is to make sure that the whole supply chain – from customers, through Siemens, and then on to its suppliers – runs smoothly.**

Von Pierer also wants customers to have a single, coordinated view of the company:

> **I don't think that in the future customers will tolerate four or five different views about Siemens. They want one view of our capabilities. Even if a customer is buying things from several different Siemens divisions, it should deal directly with only one, which should act as a lead manager within the company. Inside Siemens, the customer should be identified by only one code.**

However he acknowledged that reorganising all the internal processes would be a major task.

Source: Boddy *et al.* (2005) and company website.

Many companies now conduct their purchasing over the Internet, ensuring that new instructions to hundreds of suppliers flow almost automatically as the manufacturing programme changes to match current orders. This was previously a laborious task in which people easily made mistakes: the Internet makes it tightly coordinated.

Direct personal contact

The most human form of coordination is when people talk to each other. Mintzberg (1979) found that people use this method in both the simplest and the most complex organisation. There is so much uncertainty in the latter that information systems cannot cope – only direct contact can do this, by enabling people to making personal commitments to each other across business units (Sull and Spinosa, 2005).

Coordination in a social service

management in practice

The organisation cares for the elderly in a large city. Someone who had worked there for several years reflected on coordination:

> Within the centre there was a manager, 2 deputies, an assistant manager, 5 senior care officers (SCOs) and 30 officers. Each SCO is responsible for 6 care officers, allowing daily contact between the supervisor and the subordinates. While this defines job roles quite tightly, it allows a good communication structure to exist. Feedback is common as there are frequent meetings of the separate groups, and individual appraisals of the care officers by the SCOs. Staff value this opportunity for praise and comments on how they are doing.
>
> Contact at all levels is common between supervisor and care officers during meetings to assess the needs of clients – for whom the care officers have direct responsibility. Frequent social gatherings and functions within the department also enhance relations and satisfy social needs. Controls placed on the behaviour of the care officers come from senior management, often derived from legislation such as the Social Work Acts or the Health and Safety Executive. Performance is measured – outsiders regularly assess how the Quality of Practice code is working – and there are internal measures of absenteeism and lateness.

Source: Private communication.

Activity 10.4 Comparing coordination

Think of an organisation you have worked in, or about which you can gather information.

- Which forms of coordination did it use?
- What were the benefits and disadvantages of that approach?

Compare your conclusions with colleagues on your course, and use your experience to prepare a list of the advantages and disadvantages of each method of coordination.

The accumulation of decisions on the division and coordination of work lead to organisations that can be analysed in terms of how closely they correspond to mechanistic or organic forms.

10.6 Mechanistic and organic structures

The purpose of structure is to encourage people to act in ways that management hopes will support its objectives. Some organisations have a structure that emphasises the vertical hierarchy, by defining responsibilities clearly, taking most decisions at the centre, delegating tightly defined tasks and having rigorous reporting requirements. This enables those at the centre to know what is happening, and ensuring that staff apply policies consistently. This enables them to present a uniform image, to ensure that customers receive consistent treatment and that best practices are shared. Communication is mainly vertical, as the centre passes down instructions and staff send queries to those above them. Burns and Stalker (1961) called this a **mechanistic structure**.

A **mechanistic structure** means there is a high degree of task specialisation, people's responsibility and authority are closely defined and decision making is centralised.

Others develop a structure with broadly defined, flexible tasks, many cross-functional teams, and base authority on expertise rather than position. Management accepts

An **organic structure** is one where people are expected to work together and to use their initiative to solve problems; job descriptions and rules are few and imprecise.

that those at the centre must depend on those nearest the action to find the best solution. Communication is likely to be horizontal amongst those familiar with the task. There may not be an organisation chart, so fluid is the division of work. Burns and Stalker (1961) called this an **organic structure**. Table 10.3 compares mechanistic and organic forms.

Table 10.3
Characteristics of mechanistic and organic systems

Mechanistic	Organic
Specialised tasks	Contribute experience to common tasks
Hierarchical structure of control	Network structure of contacts
Knowledge located at top of hierarchy	Knowledge widely spread
Vertical communication	Horizontal communication
Loyalty and obedience stressed	Commitment to goals more important

Source: Based on Burrns and Stalker (1961).

management in practice

A more organic structure at Philips www.philips.com

The Dutch group Philips is the world's third largest consumer electronics company – renowned for its innovative products. It has faced many crises in recent years, and in 2002 was trading at a heavy loss. Gerard Kleisterlee became chief executive in 2001 and has made radical changes in the company's structure. He reduced the many separate divisions to just five, and is breaking down long-established internal divisions' barriers to communication, so that expertise in one can be used in another. For example the lighting group is working with the consumer electronics division to produce a room lighting system that changes colour according to what is being shown on the TV.

Source: *The Economist*, 12 June 2004.

Within a large organisation some units will correspond to mechanistic forms and others to organic. A company may have a centralised information system and tightly controlled policies on capital expenditure – while also allowing divisions considerable autonomy on research or advertising.

Case questions 10.2

- What was the role of strategy and technology in encouraging the change at Oticon?
- What features of the present form correspond to the organic model?
- How does management hope that the new structure will support their strategy?

Contingencies are factors such as uncertainty, interdependence and size that reflect the situation of the organisation.

Why do managers favour one form of structure rather than another? A widely held (though disputed) view is that it depends on certain **contingencies**:

> the essence of the contingency paradigm is that organizational effectiveness results from fitting characteristics of the organization, such as its structure, to contingencies that reflect the situation of the organization. (Donaldson, 2001, p. 1)

Successful organisations appear to be those in which managers maintain a good fit between contingent factors (such as strategy, technology, size/life cycle and environmental uncertainty) and the structure within which people work. Figure 10.1 illustrated these contingent factors – strategy, technology, age/size and environment.

Strategy

Chapter 8 outlined Porter's view that firms adopt one of three generic strategies – cost leadership, differentiation or focus. With a cost leadership strategy managers concentrate on increasing efficiency to keep costs low. A mechanistic structure is likely to be the best support for this strategy, with closely defined tasks in an efficient functional structure. There is likely to be a hierarchical chain of command to ensure that people work to plan and vertical communication to keep the centre well informed. PowerGen, a privatised electricity utility, initially took a cost–leadership approach and adopted a tight functional structure with detailed rules and performance measures.

A differentiation strategy focuses on innovation – developing new products rapidly and imaginatively. An organic structure is most likely to support this, by enabling ideas to flow easily between people with something to contribute, regardless of their function. Oticon moved towards this team-based structure, as has Microsoft in its efforts to maintain high levels of innovation in its research organisation. As PowerGen diversified into different businesses it supported this with a structure of autonomous product divisions, able to respond quickly to new demands. Hill and Pickering (1986) showed that companies in which business units had relatively high decision-making authority were more successful than those that were centralised. The Management in Practice feature shows how GlaxoSmithKline (GSK) followed this approach when the board restructured its R&D activities into six autonomous, but tightly focused, units.

management in practice

GlaxoSmithKline www.gsk.com

In February 2001 Tachi Yamada, head of R&D at GlaxoSmithKline (GSK), set out the company's plan to split the company's research organisation ('the engine room of any pharmaceutical company') into six 'internal biotechnology companies'. These units will compete for resources. Divided along therapeutic lines, they will operate autonomously. GSK is the world's second largest drugs company, and employs 15,000 scientists with an annual budget of £2.5 billion. Jean-Paul Garnier, chief executive, said that organising this research group required a radical new structure. Early research, where scarce skills and expensive equipment are applied across a range of diseases, needed to stay big. So did late-stage development where huge dossiers of clinical trial data were prepared for regulators. However, the section in the middle, where bright ideas were honed into drugs, would work best as competing, autonomous units: 'We start big, we move to small and then back to big again. Nobody has attempted this before.'

The job of the six autonomous units is to deliver drugs with 'proof of concept' – after small-scale clinical tests on patients – to GSK's development organisation. That will put drugs through full clinical trials, aimed at winning regulatory approval and maximising sales potential.

The business units, called Centres of Excellence for Drug Discovery (CEDDs), can deliver molecules invented at GSK or brought in from academia or external biotech groups. Dr Yamada said: 'They have complete autonomy. They can have 100 chemists per project, or 5. It doesn't matter to me how they do it, so long as they produce drugs.'

Clinical trials are undertaken on a massive scale, often across continents, and must comply with strict regulatory conditions. Thus corporate control, uniformity and economies of scale are pre- ▶

eminent. The other area where scale will be leveraged is early research, where hundreds of millions of pounds are spent on platform technology. Two divisions, Genetics Research and Discovery Research, will work on understanding basic biology and on producing leads to set drug discovery units on their way. Figure 10.8 illustrates the new structure.

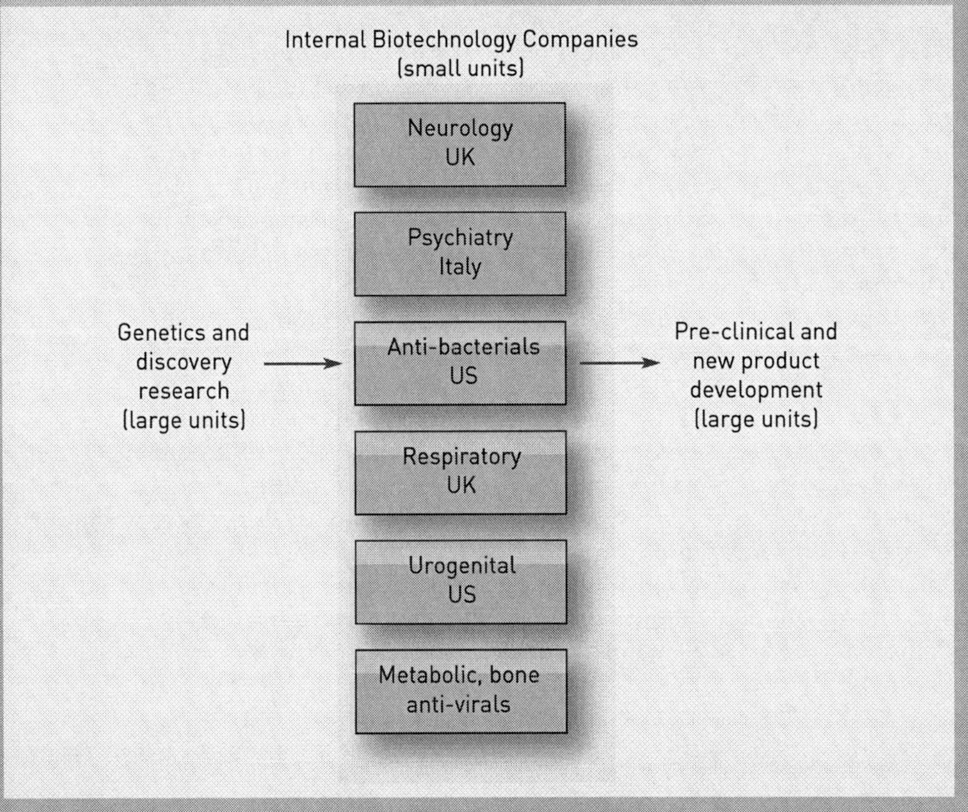

Figure 10.8 The structure introduced at GlaxoSmithKline

In 2007 Jean-Pierre Garnier was able to report that the change in structure was paying off – the company now had a strong pipeline of new drugs, and was planning five major product launches during the year. It was also creating additional CEDDs for inflammatory diseases and infection.

Source: Based on *Financial Times*, 24 October 2002 and 9 February 2007.

Figure 10.9 expresses the idea that different strategies require different structures. The more the strategy corresponds to cost leadership, the more likely it is that managers will support it with a functional structure. If the balance is towards differentiation, the more likely there will be a divisional, team or network structure.

Technology

Technology is the knowledge, equipment and activities used to transform inputs into outputs.

Technology includes the knowledge, tools and techniques used to transform organisational inputs into outputs. It includes buildings, machines, computer systems and the knowledge and procedures associated with them. Some technologies seem to be better supported by some structures than others.

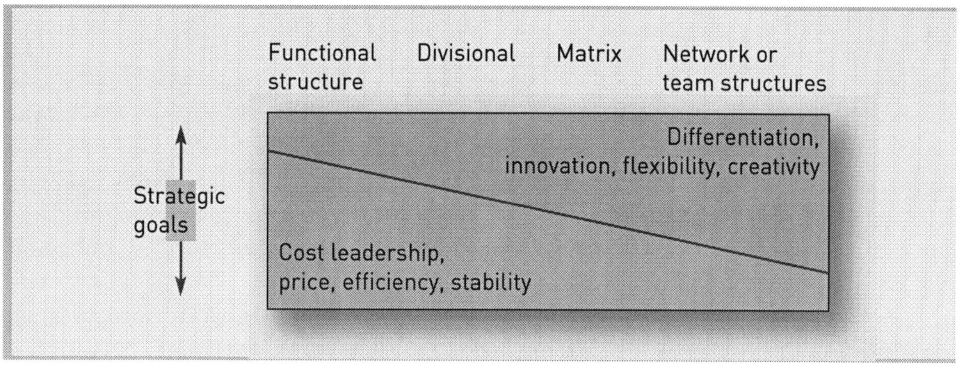

Figure 10.9 The relationship between strategies and structural types

Joan Woodward's study of organisations and their structure (1965) had a great influence on thinking about management. She gathered information from 100 British firms to establish whether structural features such as the span of control or the number of levels in the hierarchy varied between them. The researchers could see no pattern until they analysed the companies by their manufacturing process, which they grouped into 11 categories, of three broad types. These formed a scale of increasing technical complexity. The researchers then noticed a relationship between the degree of technical complexity and company structure.

- *Unit and small batch production* Firms in this group produce goods in small numbers, often to a customer's unique order. It is similar to craft work, as people and their skills are deeply involved in the process – custom-built cycles, designer furniture, Aston Martin sports cars or luxury yachts.
- *Large batch and mass production* This form is typified by the production of large quantities of standard products. The physical products move along an assembly line, with people complementing the machinery – mobile phones, Ford cars or Electrolux washing machines.
- *Continuous process* Here the entire workflow is mechanised, in a sophisticated and complex production technology. The machinery does the production work, with operators monitoring it, fixing faults and generally overseeing the process – a Guinness Brewery, a Shell oil refinery or a Mittal steel plant.

Woodward concluded that the different technologies impose different demands on people. Unit production requires close supervision to ensure that staff meet the customer's unique requirements. Supervisors can communicate directly with those working on different parts of the task and so manage the uncertainties and changes involved in producing 'one-off' items. On an assembly line the work is routine and predictable, so a supervisor can monitor more staff: there is a wide span of control. Commercially successful firms were those where the structure provided the right kind of support to the technology.

Technology also helps to deliver services, and managers create structures to shape the way staff interact with customers. Staff at banks used to handle many cash transactions, and sat behind secure glass screens that made them seem remote and unwelcoming. Technology means that little cash is now handled in branches – which have been redesigned to bring staff and customers closer together. The Part 4 Case – Royal Bank of Scotland – traces structural changes in that service business, including its centralised manufacturing division.

Environment

Chapter 3 showed how environments vary in terms of their complexity and dynamism. Research by Hage and Aiken (1967), Gerwin (1979) and Hill and Pickering (1986) shows that a firm's performance depends on having a structure that is suitable for its environment. Burns and Stalker (1961) compared the structure of a long-established rayon plant in Manchester with the structures of several new electronics companies then being created in the east of Scotland. Both types of organisation were successful – but had different structures.

The rayon plant had clearly set out rules, tight job descriptions, clear procedures, and coordination was primarily through the hierarchy. There was a high degree of specialisation, with tasks divided into small parts. Managers had defined responsibilities clearly and discouraged people from acting outside of their remit. They had centralised decisions, with information flowing up the hierarchy, and instructions down.

The small companies in the newly created electronics industry had few job descriptions, while procedures were ambiguous and imprecise. Staff were expected to use their initiative to decide priorities and to work together to solve problems. Communication was horizontal, rather than vertical (see Table 10.3).

Burns and Stalker (1961) concluded that both forms were appropriate for their circumstances. The rayon plant had a stable environment, as it was the production unit of a larger business, and its sole purpose was to supply a steady flow of rayon to the company's spinning factories. Delivery schedules rarely changed, the technology of rayon manufacture was well known and fully documented. In contrast, the electronics companies were in direct contact with their customers, mainly the Ministry of Defence. The demand for commercial and military products was volatile, with frequent changes in delivery requirements. The technology was new, often applying the results of recent research. Contracts were often taken in which neither the customer nor the company knew what the end product would be: it was likely to change during the course of the work.

Oticon – the case continues – communication and technology www.oticon.com

CASE STUDY

Lars Kolind knew that the dramatic change in structure he proposed would not be achieved without pain: he was attacking the established culture, privileges tied to seniority and titles, and on work processes. In moving to an organisation in which there would be only project members, project leaders and project owners, many would not easily accept losing the power they derived from controlling information. He used his power to drive the change, announcing:

> **I am 100 per cent sure that we will try this. There's enough time so that you can make a choice – whether you are going to try it with us or whether ... you find another job** (quoted in Rivard *et al.*, 2004, p. 174).

While the company used advanced information systems (IS) for many functions Kolind believed that dialogue is better than e-mail, and designed the building to support face-to-face dialogue between staff. The problem owner will usually use e-mail or personal contact to bring two or three people together and have a stand-up meeting. Decisions are noted in the computer (accessible by everyone).

By 1994 the company had halved product development time and more than doubled sales. It employed half as many administrative staff as in 1990, but double the number on product development. Financial performance improved dramatically in the years following the change. Lars Kolind said, 'Hardware companies have organisations that look like machines: a company that produces knowledge needs an organisation that looks like a brain, i.e. which looks chaotic and is unhierarchical.'

Source: Based on Bjorn-Andersen and Turner (1994); Rivard *et al.* (2004).

Case questions 10.3

- Oticon has had both mechanistic and organic structures: what prompted the change?
- Why has the new structure improved business performance?

Burns and Stalker (1961) concluded that neither mechanistic nor organic structures were appropriate in all situations. Stable, predictable environments were likely to encourage a mechanistic structure. Volatile, unpredictable environments were likely to encourage an organic structure. This recognition that environmental conditions place different demands upon organisations was a major step in understanding why companies adopt contrasting structures – an idea illustrated in Figure 10.10.

		Structure	
		Mechanistic	*Organic*
Environment	*Uncertain (unstable)*	**Incorrect Fit:** Mechanistic structure in uncertain environment Structure too tight	**Correct Fit:** Organic structure in uncertain environment
	Certain (stable)	**Correct Fit:** Mechanistic structure in certain environment	**Incorrect Fit:** Organic structure in certain environment Structure too loose

Figure 10.10 The relationship between environment and structure

Activity 10.5 Comparing mechanistic and organic forms

Think of a department you have worked in, or about which you can gather information.

- Was it broadly mechanistic or organic?
- Why has that form evolved, and is it suitable?
- How does it compare to other departments in the organisation?

management in practice: Organic problem solving in a mechanistic structure

The organisation I work for has just come through a short-term cash-flow crisis. The problem arose because, while expenditures on contracts are relatively predictable and even, the income flow was disrupted by a series of contractual disputes.

The role culture permeates the head office, and at first the problem was pushed ever upwards. But faced with this crisis all departments were asked for ideas on how to improve performance. Some have been turned into new methods of working, and others are still being considered by the 'ideas team', drawn from all grades of personnel and departments. This was a totally new perspective, of a task culture operating within a role culture – that is, we developed an organic approach. What could be more simple than asking people who do the job how they could be more efficient?

To maintain the change in the long run is difficult, and some parts have now started to drift back to the role culture.

Source: Private communication.

Differentiation The state of segmentation of the organisation into subsystems, each of which tends to develop particular attributes in response to the particular demands posed by its relevant external environment.

Integration is the process of achieving unity of effort amongst the various subsystems in the accomplishment of the organisation's task.

Organisations do not face a single environment. People in each department try to meet the expectations of players in the wider environment, and gradually develop structures that help them to do that. A payroll section has to meet strict legal requirements on, amongst other things, salary entitlements, taxation and pensions records. Staff must follow strict rules, with little scope for using their initiative: they work in a mechanistic structure. The product development or advertising departments face quite different requirements – and so will have evolved a structure that encourages creativity and innovation: they work in an organic structure.

An important implication of this is that coordination between such departments will be difficult, as they will work in different ways. Paul Lawrence and Jay Lorsch explored this issue, and their contribution is in the Key Ideas feature.

key ideas: Lawrence and Lorsch: differentiation and integration

Two American scholars, Paul Lawrence and Jay Lorsch, developed Burns and Stalker's work. They observed that departments doing different tasks face a separate segment of the environment – some relatively stable, others unstable. Lawrence and Lorsch predicted that to cope with these varying conditions departments will develop different structures and ways of working. Those in stable environments would move towards mechanistic forms, those in unstable environments would move towards organic.

Empirical research in six organisations enabled Lawrence and Lorsch to show that departments did indeed differ from each other, and in ways they had predicted. Those facing unstable environments (research and development) had less formal structures than those facing stable ones (production). The greater the **differentiation** between departments the more effort was needed to integrate their work. Successful firms achieved more **integration** between units by using a variety of integrating devices such as task forces and project managers with the required interpersonal skills. The less effective companies in the uncertain environment used rules and procedures.

Source: Lawrence and Lorsch (1967).

Size and life cycle

Small organisations tend to be less formal with less division of labour – people take part in a wide range of tasks and coordination is achieved informally by face-to-face contact or direct supervision. Weber (1947) noted that larger organisations tended to have more formal, bureaucratic structures, and research by Blau (1970) and Pugh and Hickson (1976) showed that as organisations grow they develop more formal structures, hierarchies and specialised units. Like the head of Multi-show Events, as managers divide a growing business into separate units they need more controls such as job descriptions and reporting relationships.

Growth and structure in a housing association

management in practice

A manager in a housing association, which was created to provide affordable housing for those on low incomes, describes how its structure changed as it grew.

> Housing associations have to give tenants and their representatives the opportunity to influence policy. In the early days it had few staff, no clear division of labour and few rules and procedures. It was successful in providing housing, which attracted more government funds, and the association grew. Managing more houses required a more formal structure to support the work. The association no longer served a single community, but several geographical areas. Staff numbers grew significantly and worked in specialised departments. The changes led to concerns amongst both staff and committee that the organisation was no longer responsive to community needs and that it had become distant and bureaucratic.

Source: Private communication from the manager.

This implies that organisations go through stages, with structures adapting to suit. The entrepreneur creates the business alone, or with a few partners or employees. They operate informally with little division of labour – tasks overlap (for a discussion of the unique structural issues facing entrepreneurs in high technology industries, see Alvarez and Barney (2005)). There are few rules or systems for planning and coordination. The owner makes the decisions, so they have a centralised structure. If the business succeeds it will need to raise more capital to finance growth. The owner no longer has sole control, but shares decisions with members of the growing management team. Tasks become divided by function or product, creating separate departments and more formal controls to ensure coordination. Many small companies fail when they expand rapidly but fail to impose controls and systems for managing risks – as an executive of a publishing company that got into difficulties recalled: 'We were editors and designers running a large show, and we were completely overstretched. Our systems were simply not up to speed with our creative ambitions.' This observation is consistent with a study by Sine *et al.* (2006), which shows how successful Internet companies were those that were able to balance the essential creative spirit of their companies with a degree of formalisation, specialisation and administrative intensity. They survived, while those that lacked even the most rudimentary structures failed.

If a business continues to grow it takes on more of the features of a bureaucracy. There is more division of responsibilities and more rules to ensure coordination. There are more professional and specialist staff in areas such as finance or human resources, with systems for budgeting, financial control and rewards. Mature, established firms tend to become mechanistic, with a strong vertical system and well-developed controls.

More decisions are made at the centre – bringing the danger of slow response to new conditions. To overcome these barriers to innovation and to encourage cross-functional communication managers may change the structure. One approach is to decentralise the organisation by creating separate divisions with profit responsibility – as Microsoft did when it created seven business units with a high degree of autonomy.

Oticon – the case continues – limiting risks

CASE STUDY

www.oticon.com

While the changes at Oticon had spurred creativity, the board of the firm also became concerned about profitability in the early years, as the new structure was creating so many initiatives and new products that it was difficult to manage them all effectively. They therefore appointed Neils Jacobsen as co-chief executive in 1992, to place more emphasis on financial discipline and performance. Jacobsen took over from Kolind as chief executive in 1998.

In 1996 more controls were introduced, to balance some of the risks of the new form. A competence centre was established that took over some of the rights previously held by project managers. It alone now had the right to initiate projects and appoint project managers – thus restraining the earlier principle that anyone could start a project. It also took over the task of negotiating salaries that had initially been delegated to project managers.

These changes were intended to overcome some of the costs associated with the radical structure. When there was no limit to the number of projects, nor to the number of projects on which a person could work, it had become hard to ensure completion: the most capable staff were spread over too many projects. There was also some concern that staff and teams were not always sharing knowledge as fully as expected. Despite these adjustments, the company remains a radically different form of organisation.

Source: Based on Foss (2003).

Contingencies or managerial choice?

Contingency approaches to organisation structure propose that the most effective structure will depend (be contingent) upon the situation in which the organisation is operating:

> The organization is seen as existing in an environment that shapes its strategy, technology, size and innovation rate. These contingent factors in turn determine the required structure; that is, the structure that the organization needs to adopt if it is to operate effectively. (Donaldson, 1996, p. 2)

Determinism is the view that an organisation's structure is determined by its environment.

Structural choice approaches emphasise the scope management has for deciding the form of structure, irrespective of external conditions.

Effective management involves formulating an appropriate strategy and developing a structure which supports that strategy by encouraging appropriate behaviour. The emphasis is **determinist** (the form is determined by the environment) and functionalist (the form is intended to serve organisational effectiveness) (Donaldson, 1995). Management's role is to make suitable adjustments to the structure to improve performance as conditions change – such as by increasing formality as the company grows. Others, such as GSK, introduce greater divisional autonomy to encourage creativity or responsiveness to local conditions.

John Child (1972, 1984) disagreed with this view, arguing that contingency theorists ignore the degree of **structural choice** which managers have. The process of organisational design is not only a technical, rational matter but one shaped by political processes. These political considerations (reflecting the values and interests of influential groups) are able to influence the structure that emerges for these reasons:

- The standards of performance against which organisational performance is assessed are not always rigorous. Some degree of under-performance caused by an inappropriate structure may be tolerated if there is sufficient 'slack' within the system.
- To some extent structures will reflect the interests of powerful groups within the organisation. They will try to secure structures that protect or advance their positions, even if this reduces performance to some degree.

Overall, writers of this view argue that contingency theory reduces managers almost to automatons, or puppets, able to exercise little influence on their own actions. In practice, they argue, managers do have choice over the structure they design. The contrasting ways in which leading grocery companies have used the Internet seems to support that view.

Retailers' response to the Internet

management in practice

The Internet makes it possible for supermarket chains to create a website on which customers can order their shopping, which the company then delivers to their home. Sainsbury's responded by creating a new division to handle this business, with a separate management structure, warehouses and distribution system. Tesco chose to integrate its Internet shopping business with existing stores – staff pick the customer's Internet order from the shelves of a conventional store. Other chains, such as Somerfield and Morrisons do not (in 2007) offer an online service. So while the technology is available to all, only some have chosen to use it and they manage it with different structures.

Activity 10.6 Critical reflection – contingency or choice?

Recall some significant changes in the structure of your organisation. Try to establish the reasons for them, and whether they had the intended effects. Do those reasons tend to support the contingency or management choice perspectives?

Case questions 10.4

- Does the Oticon example support contingency or management choice approaches?
- Gather specific examples of management actions in the case which illustrate each theory.

Another consideration is that the direction of causality is not necessarily from strategy to structure. It is also possible that an organisation with a given structure finds that that makes it easier to embark on a particular strategy.

10.7 Learning organisations

Innovation is the main reason why many advocate the development of 'learning organisations', since organisations that operate in complex and dynamic environments can only be successful innovators if they develop the capacity to learn and respond quickly to changing circumstances. The term 'learning organisation' is used to describe an organisation that has developed the capacity to continuously learn, adapt and change. In a learning organisation the focus is on acquiring, sharing and using knowledge to encourage innovation.

According to Nonaka and Tageuchi (1995) the ability to create knowledge and solve problems has become a core competence in many businesses. In their view, everyone is a knowledge worker – someone dealing with customers, for example, quickly finds out about their likes and dislikes, and their view of the service. Because they are typically in low-paid jobs far from corporate headquarters, this valuable intelligence is overlooked.

Table 10.4
Features of a learning organisation

Feature	Explanation
A learning approach to strategy	The use of trials and experiments to improve understanding and generate improvements, and to modify strategic direction
Participative policy making	All members are involved in strategy formation, influencing decisions and values and addressing conflict
Informative	Information technology is used to make information available to everyone and to enable front-line staff to use their initiative
Formative accounting and control	Accounting, budgeting and reporting systems are designed to help people understand the operations of organisational finance
Internal exchange	Sections and departments think of themselves as customers and suppliers in an internal 'supply chain', learning from each other
Reward flexibility	A flexible and creative reward policy, with financial and non-financial rewards to meet individual needs and performance
Enabling structures	Organisation charts, structures and procedures are seen as temporary, and can be changed to meet task requirements
Boundary workers as environmental scanners	Everyone who has contact with customers, suppliers, clients and business partners is treated as a valuable information source
Inter-company learning	The organisation learns from other organisations through joint ventures, alliances and other information exchanges
A learning climate	The manager's primary task is to facilitate experimentation and learning in others, through questioning, feedback and support
Self-development opportunities for all	People are expected to take responsibility for their own learning, and facilities are made available, especially to 'front-line' staff

Source: Based on Pedler *et al.* (1997).

Table 10.4 (based on Pedler *et al.*, 1997) presents a view of the features of an ideal learning organisation – features to which managers can aspire. These features cluster under five headings, shown in Figure 10.11.

In a learning organisation members share information and collaborate on work activities wherever required – including across functional and hierarchical boundaries. Boundaries between units are either eliminated (as at Oticon) or are made as porous as possible to ensure that they do not block the flow of ideas and information. Learning organisations tend to emphasise team working, and employees operate with a high degree of autonomy to work as they think will best enhance performance. Rather than directing and controlling, managers act as facilitators, supporters and advocates – enabling their staff to work and learn to the greatest degree possible.

Learning depends on information, so there is an emphasis on sharing information amongst employees in a timely and open manner. This too depends on managers creat-

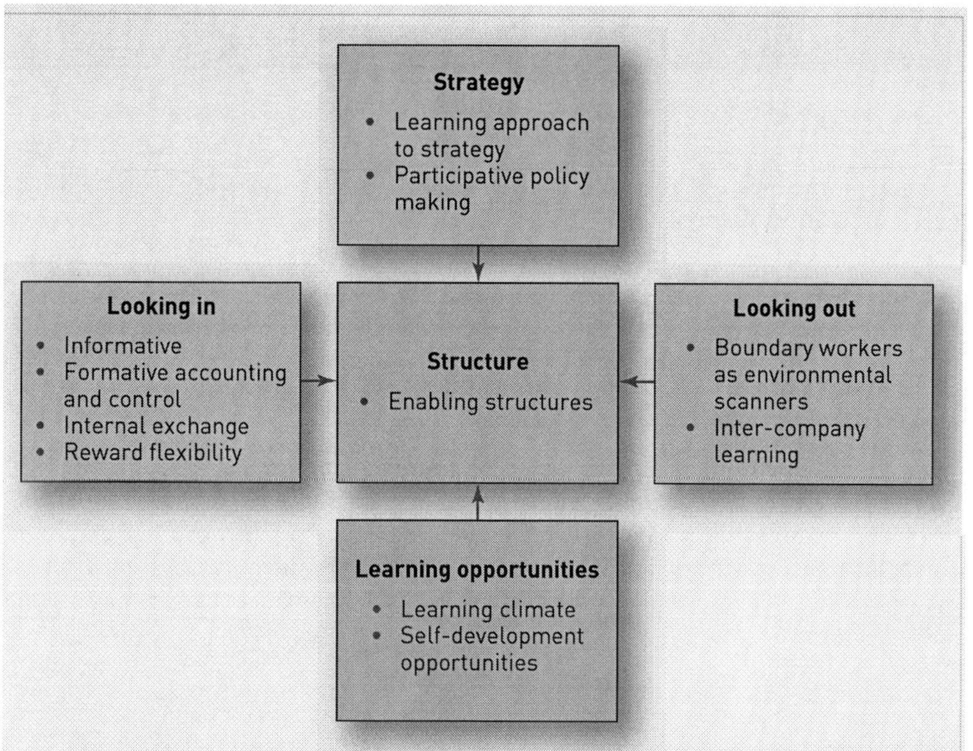

Source: Pedler *et al.* (1997).

Figure 10.11 Clusters of learning organisation features

ing a structure that encourages people to pass information in this way. Leadership is also important in the sense that one of their primary roles is to facilitate the creation of a shared vision for the business, and ensuring employees are enabled to work continually towards that. Finally the culture is one in which all agree on a shared vision and understand how all aspects of the organisation – its processes, activities, environment – are related to each other. There is a strong sense of community and mutual trust. People feel free to share ideas and communicate, share and experiment – able to learn without fear of criticism or punishment.

Argyris (1999) distinguished between single-loop and double-loop learning. The classic example of single-loop learning is the domestic thermostat which, by detecting temperature variations, takes action to correct deviations from a predetermined level. In single-loop learning, the system maintains performance at the set level, but is unable to learn that the temperature is set too high or too low. Learning how to learn involves double-loop learning – challenging assumptions, beliefs and norms, rather than accepting them and working within their limitations. In single-loop learning, the question is 'How can we better achieve that standard of performance?' In double-loop learning the question becomes: 'Is that an appropriate target in the first place?' In the context of developing the skills to cope more effectively with change, the aim is to enhance the ability of members to engage in double-loop learning.

10.8 Current themes and issues

Performance

Changes in the business environment are encouraging managers to experiment with new forms of organisation:

> During the 1990s the transition from an economy based on the processing of materials to one based on flows of information became ever more apparent, especially in the developed economies. The transition unfettered many aspects of organization from their former physical constraints, permitting, for example, activities in dispersed locations to be as effectively integrated as those gathered on the same site. Increased information intensity is today the fundamental development to which new organizational designs must respond. (Child, 2005, p. 27)

These trends encourage many to advocate a move from bureaucratic, hierarchical, mechanistic structures to smaller, more organic units with more emphasis on personal discretion and creativity. They argue that arrangements which encourage empowerment, flexibility, learning, innovation and teamwork are the only ways to survive in many sectors of the economy, and Table 10.5 contrasts some features of conventional and 'new' forms.

Table 10.5
Contrasts between conventional and new forms of organisation

Structural elements	Conventional organisation	New organisation
Initiative and authority	Centralised	Distributed
Control	Centralised, rule based	Decentralised, cultural
Basis of reward	Individual's position	Group performance
Roles	Specialised, defined	Fuzzy, loosely defined
Systems	To reduce uncertainty	To signal need for change
Coordination	By rules and procedures	By direct contact and IS
Networking	Only major stakeholders	Integral to the value chain
Outsourcing	Little	Much (non-core activities)
Alliances	Avoided	Extensive

The Oticon case in this chapter, and the examples of Semco (Chapter 14) and W.L. Gore (the Part 5 Case) illustrate how some managements have responded to these conditions.

However, these decentralised structures also expose the organisation to the danger that actions by managers in the autonomous units damages the business as a whole. BP has suffered because staff in its US subsidiary were careless about safety, and Siemens has exposed cases of bribery in one of its divisions. In both cases, the companies have decentralised decision making to local managers.

Responsibility

Many companies respond to competitive pressures by granting significant autonomy to local subsidiaries, or joining a network structure of suppliers contributing to the final product. This often enables them to outsource the production of many goods and services to poor regions of the world, which in turn is one of the main drivers of globalisation. These structural choices add to local incomes, and many governments compete for this work.

However many criticise the policies and behaviour of subsidiaries and suppliers – especially when they adopt labour and/or environmental standards that would be unacceptable in the companies' home country. The structural changes do not, in the view of their critics, absolve the organisation from responsibility for what happens in their suppliers. Nike suffered bad publicity for years after the conditions experienced by staff producing Nike products in Indonesia were revealed. The company responded by further structural measures, such as a requirement that all suppliers would be regularly monitored and inspected to ensure they met adequate labour standards. Coca-Cola is currently receiving similar criticism over the practices of some of its overseas joint ventures.

Reconciling demands for greater accountability and control with the performance benefits of decentralisation is a challenge for those shaping organisational structure.

Internationalisation

Internationalisation makes it possible for a firm to extend its operations into many other countries, and so be able to produce more cheaply by spreading costs over a larger volume. At the same time it may face pressure to vary the design of its products and services to suit local tastes. So managers may need to create a structure that is able to achieve both more standardisation and more flexibility within the same organisational structure.

The same process exposes a firm to greater external complexity, by expanding the number of organisations – customers, competitors, suppliers, governments, non-governmental organisations (NGOs) and many more – whose actions may be relevant to it. Many more events in the external world are relevant to the global firm, which needs to enter into more intensive dialogue with external parties. This greater external complexity has to be matched by suitable structural arrangements – more specialists in relevant fields, and more attempts to influence a wider constituency of stakeholders.

Summary

1 Outline why the structure of an organisation affects performance

- People create structures to signify people's tasks and responsibilities towards the current objectives, and to provide incentives for work that supports them. The structure signals what people are expected to do within the organisation, and is intended to support actions that are in line with performance goals.

2 Give examples of management choices about dividing and coordinating work, with their likely advantages and disadvantages

- Managers divide work to enable individuals and groups to specialise on a limited aspect of the whole, and then combine the work into related areas of activity. Task division needs to be accompanied by suitable methods of coordination.
- Centralisation brings consistency and efficiency, but also the danger of being slow and out of touch with local conditions. People in decentralised units can respond quickly to local conditions but risk acting inconsistently.

- Functional forms allow people to specialise and develop expertise and are efficient; but they may be inward looking and prone to conflicting demands.
- Divisional forms allow focus on particular markets of customer groups, but can duplicate facilities thus adding to cost.
- Matrix forms try to balance the benefits of functional and divisional forms, but can again lead to conflicting priorities over resources.
- Networks of organisations enable companies to draw upon a wide range of expertise, but may involve additional management and coordination costs.

3 Compare the features of mechanistic and organic structures

- Mechanistic – people perform specialised tasks, hierarchical structure of control, knowledge located at top of hierarchy, vertical communication, loyalty and obedience valued.
- Organic – people contribute experience to common tasks, network structure of contacts, knowledge widely spread, horizontal communication, commitment to task goals more important than to superiors

4 Use the 'contingencies' believed to influence choice of structure to evaluate the suitability of a form for a given unit

- Strategy, environment, technology, age/size and political contingencies are believed to indicate the most suitable form, and the manager's role is to interpret these in relation to their circumstances.

5 Summarise the work of Woodward, Burns and Stalker, Lawrence and Lorsch and John Child, showing how they contributed to this area of management theory

- Woodward: appropriate structure depends on the type of production system ('technology') – unit, small batch, process.
- Burns and Stalker: appropriate structure depends on uncertainty of the organisation's environment – mechanistic in stable, organic in unstable.
- Lawrence and Lorsch: units within an organisation face different environmental demands, which implies that there will be both mechanistic and organic forms within the same organisation, raising new problems of coordination.
- John Child: contingency theory implies too great a degree of determinism – managers have greater degree of choice over structure than contingency theories implied.

6 Explain and illustrate the features of a learning organisation

- Learning organisations are those that have developed the capacity to continuously learn, adapt and change. This depends, according to Pedler *et al.* (1997), on evolving learning-friendly processes for looking in, looking out, learning opportunities, strategy and structure.

Review questions

1 Draw the organisation chart of a company or department that you know. From discussing it with people in one or more of the positions shown, compare their account of the structure with that shown on the chart.

2 What factors are encouraging companies to (a) centralise, (b) decentralise organisational functions?

3 Several forms of coordination are described. Select two that you have seen in operation and describe in detail how they work – and how well they work.

4 How does the structure of an organisation support or hinder its strategy?

5 Explain the difference between a mechanistic and an organic form of organisation.

6 Explain the term 'contingency approach' and give an example of each of the factors that influence the choice between mechanistic and organic structures.

7 If contingency approaches stress the influence of external factors on organisational structures, what is the role of management in designing organisational structures?

8 What is the main criticism of the contingency approach to organisation structure?

9 What examples can you find of organisational activities that correspond to some of the features of a learning organisation identified by Pedler *et al.* (1997)?

Concluding critical reflection

Think about the structure and culture of your company, or one with which you are familiar. Review the material in the chapter, and perhaps visit some of the websites identified. Then make notes on these questions:

- What examples of the themes discussed in this chapter are currently relevant to your company? What type of structure do you have – centralised or decentralised; functional or divisional, etc? Which of the methods of coordination identified do you typically use? What structural issues arise that are not mentioned here?
- In responding to issues of structure, what **assumptions** about the nature of organisations appear to guide your approach? If the business seems too centralised or too formal, why do managers take that approach? What are their assumptions, and are they correct?
- What factors in the **context** of the company appear to shape your approach to organising – what kind of environment are you working in, for example? To what extent does your structure involve networking with people from other organisations – and why is that?
- Have you seriously considered whether the present structure is right for the business? Do you regularly compare your structure with that in other companies to look for **alternatives**? How do they do it?
- What **limitations** can you identify in any of the ideas and theories presented here? For example how helpful is contingency theory to someone deciding whether to make the organisation more or less mechanistic?

Further reading

Woodward, J. (1965), *Industrial Organization: Theory and practice*, Oxford University Press, Oxford. Second edition 1980.

Burns, T. and Stalker, G.M. (1961), *The Management of Innovation*, Tavistock, London.

Lawrence, P. and Lorsch, J.W. (1967), *Organization and Environment*, Harvard Business School Press, Boston, MA.

These influential books are short and accessible accounts of the research process, and it would add to your understanding to read at least one of them in the original. The second edition of Woodward's book (1980) is even more useful, as it includes a commentary on her work by two later scholars.

Donaldson, L. (2001), *The Contingency Theory of Organizations*, Sage, London.

A comprehensive and up-to-date account by one of the leading scholars of contingency theory. Outlines the underlying principles of the theory and the controversies surrounding it, as well as offering valuable guidance on emerging research possibilities.

Rivard, S., Benoit, A.A., Patry, M., Pare, G. and Smith, H.A. (2004), *Information Technology and Organizational Transformation*, Elsevier/Butterworth-Heinemann, Oxford.

As well as being the source of some information on the Oticon case, this book includes other examples of the way in which information technology is enabling managers to develop new forms of organisation. A coherent theoretical structure makes the book a useful addition to this area.

Weblinks

These websites have appeared in the chapter:

www.oticon.com
www.baesystems.com
www.cadburyschweppes.com
www.philips.com
www.jnj.com
www.toyota.com
www.unilever.com
www.siemens.com
www.gsk.com

Visit two of the business sites in the list, and navigate to the pages dealing with corporate news, investor relations or 'our company'.

- What organisational structure issues can you identify that managers in the company are likely to be dealing with? Can you find any information about their likely culture from the website?
- What kind of environment are they likely to be working in, and how may that affect their structure and culture?

Annotated weblinks, multiple choice questions and other useful resources can be found on www.pearsoned.co.uk/boddy

Week 3

Management Theory and Practice

CHAPTER 1

Organising and managing work: study, critique and practice

Objectives

Having read this chapter and completed its associated activities, readers should be able to:

- Appreciate the value of a 'management of work', rather than a 'management of people' or a 'management of systems' approach as a starting point for thinking about work organisations and their management.
- Understand the contribution which various social science disciplines make to the academic study of the organising and managing of work.
- See how the study of work organisation and management relates to associated studies like those of strategy, human resource management, organisation theory, management learning and critical management studies.
- Recognise continuity between social science thinking and a critical form of common sense.
- Understand the value of studying the organising and managing of work in a critical way.
- Discriminate between frameworks, perspectives, theories and research findings in terms of how useful (or 'true') they are when it comes to relating theory and practice.
- Use concepts in a social scientific way in the analysis of organisational and managerial practices.
- Distinguish between two broad ways of 'framing' human behaviours and organisational patterns: the systems-control and the process-relational.

The management of work

To create the goods, services and quality of life that people look for in the modern world, rather complex patterns of cooperative human behaviour have to be orchestrated or 'managed'. The academic study of the organising and managing of work involves taking a step back from our day-to-day involvement in these patterns of behaviour and trying systematically to understand how they come about. Such a study can also help us achieve a better quality of productive cooperation than we typically manage in contemporary work organisations.

We study work organisation and its management because we are interested in the various individual human motivations, interests, values and meanings which play a part in bringing about the patterns of behaviour we see in workplaces ranging from shops, offices and factories to schools, hospitals and universities. But the study also has to concern itself with the ways in which these human activities and meanings themselves come to be an influence on the people that are involved in them. Once human beings create institutions and structures, like work organisations and managerial practices, their lives become significantly shaped by them. One of the things which makes the study of the organising and managing of work so challenging is that it has to understand how individual choices and initiatives, on the one hand, and already existing and *emerging* organisational and societal structures and patterns, on the other, both play their parts in social life. And these two influences – of human action and structural context – do not work separately. They are inextricably intertwined. This means that we must be careful not to overemphasise either the 'people' side of work organising and managing or the 'organisational systems' aspect of work patterning. The intention of *Organising and Managing Work* is to go beyond the tendency, seen in both academic programmes and the everyday thinking of organisational practitioners, to oversimplify these issues by treating organising in a one-sided manner as primarily a matter of, to put it very simply, either 'managing people' or 'managing systems'.

The notion of 'managing people' is widely and popularly used in the organisational world. There are, however, three major problems of thinking about organising and managing work in such terms. First, there is the problem of whether it is realistic even to contemplate the possibility of managing people. Is it at all reasonable, especially in a modern democratic society, to assume that there are people about who are willing to be 'managed' – to subjugate themselves to the wills of 'bosses' at work? Surely not. In fact, it can be argued that one of the main ways that members of the human species differ from other animals is that they are active agents in the shaping of their lives. However meek or submissive particular individuals might be, each human being is nevertheless always the owner and shaper of their own identity, to some degree. As far as the historical record can tell us, no human group in the history of the human species has yet found another group over which it could exert complete control. And this applies even in the extreme conditions of slave societies or extermination camps, where human beings have still demonstrated what looks like an

FIGURE 1.1 Managing people is like trying to herd cats

inherent tendency of the species: to be recalcitrant; to resist being managed. There is a very popular cliché that one hears day after day in work organisations to the effect that 'managing people is like trying to herd cats'.

One hears engineering managers say that 'managing engineers is like trying to herd cats'; health service managers saying 'managing medical workers is like trying to herd cats'; retail managers saying 'managing shop workers is like trying to herd cats' and university faculty deans saying 'managing academics is like trying to herd cats'. There is probably no sphere of work where this cliché has not been applied (it is nearly as common as 'You need to be mad to work here'!). But there is an important insight behind the cat herding cliché: human beings are indeed inherently 'unmanageable' in the same way that cats are inherently 'un-herdable'.

A second problem with the idea of managing people is a rather important ethical one. It can be argued that a manager does not have the moral right to direct, manage or 'boss' any individual in their area of responsibility *as a whole person* or in *the totality of their workplace behaviour*. Instead, they have a limited authority to give instructions to employees in tightly prescribed and limited areas of activity. The moral basis of that authority lies in its purpose – to fulfil those work tasks in which the employees have contractually agreed to participate. Employees in modern democratic societies do not sign a contract of employment on the assumption that managers appointed by their employer will have the right to manage them as a person. The manager is appointed to manage the work tasks – and as part of this has limited rights to instruct people.

But these rights only exist as means to specific organisational ends and not because of any 'right to command' over the person as a whole. It is thus morally improper to encourage a view of managerial and organisational work based on a principle of 'managing people'.

The third problem with the people management idea is that a focus on people or indeed on 'organisational *behaviour*' tends to leave blurred the part played by structures, systems, cultures, processes and the rest. It is, in effect, to focus on human behaviours at the expense of paying attention to the performance of the systems within which those behaviours occur.

It has perhaps been in recognition of the problems inherent in shaping work activities by directly focusing on people, rather than structures and processes, that we see an alternative emphasis in managerial thinking and organisation theory existing alongside the people management emphasis. This is what is often called 'systems thinking'; a way of looking at patterns of activity which has some significant virtues, but which has some considerable weaknesses too. Identifying those weaknesses, and going beyond them, is to be a key theme of Chapter 2. But what we can say, for the moment, is that replacing the idea of 'managing people' with the idea of 'managing systems' is rather problematic. Just as with the 'management of people' approach, the 'management of systems' approach founders on a fundamental problem with one of its key assumptions. This is the assumption that once a sensible and coherent system of operating has been devised by systems designers, the people who are to be employed to operate those systems will unquestioningly fulfil the roles in the systems allocated to them. Once again the issues of human self-expression and the universal tendency of people to resist the power of others arises. Of course, people will go along *up to a point* with the instructions of 'people managers' and, of course, people will go along *up to a point* with the requirements of the working systems within which they undertake employment. But their willingness to 'go along' with the requirements of others or fit into the demands of systems is tightly bounded. Recognition of the extent of that boundedness is vital to any realistic understanding of how work organisation and management can realistically be achieved – especially in societies whose cultures emphasise concepts of political freedom, personal expression and social and economic choice.

How do we get away from these two rather limited ways of thinking about the organising and managing of work? The suggestion is that we turn away from a focus on both the management of people and the management of systems and adopt a focus on the management of work itself. The most helpful starting point for any consideration of organisational and managerial behaviour is neither the 'people' nor the 'systems'. It is, instead, the work tasks that are to be carried out and the working relationships associated with those tasks that are managed. It is tasks and relationships which are organised and 'managed', not the people who carry out the tasks. It is the tasks and relationships which have to be shaped, in a relatively predictable and therefore relatively systematic way, not systems as such. And an important insight which follows from the adoption of this management of work focus is the recognition that work tasks are always *to an extent managed by everyone involved in those tasks*. Work management is not simply what people formally designated as 'managers' do. To say this is not, however, to play down the significance of the work done by people holding managerial posts. This immensely important type of work is closely examined in Chapter 3. And careful examination of what managers actually do makes it clear that effective managers recognise that much of the shaping or managing of work tasks is done by those nominally under the control of designated managers – albeit to different degrees in different circumstances.

Studying the organisation and management of work

The field of study covered in *Organising and Managing Work* is broader than that which is typically covered by traditional 'Organisational Behaviour' programmes taught in schools of business and management and, as was explained earlier, it is very different in its emphasis from courses in 'people management'. It can usefully be labelled 'work organisation and management studies' – an activity which is treated here as a social scientific form of activity.

Work organisation and management studies *Concept*

The analysis of the human aspects of work organisation and its management which draws on the social sciences to develop insights, theories and research findings with a view to informing the choices, decisions and actions of people who have a practical involvement with organisations.

We need to note several things about this way of characterising our field of study.

- What is studied is the 'human aspects of work organisation and its management'. This language is not meant to imply that attention is only paid to 'human aspects' at the level of the human individual. The focus is on work *organisation* and management, which means that patterns of human activity and thinking going beyond the level of the individual are as important as thinking about the human individual. The concern is with the interplay of factors at the level of human initiative and choice and factors at the level of social, political and economic context, or structure.
- The subject *informs* the choices, decisions and actions of people involved in practices in organisations. There is no question of developing an academic study which can tell people what they should do in the complex area of work management. The area is far too complex for there to be any basic rules or even sets of guidelines about 'how to do management'. Not only this but, given the moral factors which must come into every human situation where power and authority are involved, it would be quite wrong for a textbook to attempt to provide guidance in this way. What it can do, however, is to provide insights into the range of factors and issues which are relevant to any particular choice (of, say, job design or planning an organisational change programme). The actual choice or decision that is made is a matter for those

involved in the particular organisational situation – with all the political, moral and specific local considerations coming into play alongside the insights which can be derived from academic study of the managing and organisation of work.

- Reference is made to 'organisational practitioners' rather than 'managers' as the potential 'users' of the subject. This is done in recognition of the fact that people other than those formally designated as managers are closely involved in the way work tasks are managed. If there are social scientific ideas which would be helpful to a manager in an organisational situation wishing to have their understanding enhanced by academic thinking then surely those ideas are going to be equally relevant to anyone else concerned with that situation. This would be the case regardless of the person's formal authority in the organisation or, for that matter, their degree of commitment to official organisational policies.
- The social sciences are 'drawn on' in the study. 'Organising and managing work' is not seen as a social science in its own right. A variety of social science disciplines can be turned to to provide research findings, theoretical resources or insights that might be helpful in understanding organisational issues. This does not mean, however, that we simply turn in a random or *promiscuous* manner to the vast bank of social science materials every time we wish to analyse a particular situation. Each individual is likely to build up their set of preferred social science concepts as their learning proceeds. They then turn to the books and journals for further insight, as the need arises, and incorporate the new learning into their ever-developing personal framework of understanding.

The social scientific study of the organising and managing of work has tended to draw primarily on the social science disciplines of sociology, psychology and social psychology. And it supports the contributions of the main disciplines with insights from economics, political science and anthropology. The key concerns of each of these are outlined in Table 1.1.

All of these disciplines can be seen as providing resources which can be drawn upon when wishing to understand the organising and managing of work in general or any particular organisational situation or problem in particular. Many of the human issues that can arise in the organisational context do not fall into any one obvious disciplinary territory and many of them might use ideas from more than one discipline. Bearing this in mind, see how you get on with Activity 1.1.

Activity 1.1

Read the story about Rose Markey taking over as the manager of The Canalazzo restaurant (Case 1.1), thinking about the issues which Rose is going to have to deal with to satisfy her employers. Following the characterisations of the six social sciences set out in Table 1.1, note the factors or issues that you think might be identified as, respectively, psychological, social-psychological, sociological, economic, political and anthropological.

Table 1.1 Focal and supporting social science disciplines for studying the organising and managing of work

Focal social science disciplines	Supporting social science disciplines
Psychology focuses on individual characteristics and behaviour and on such matters as learning, motivation and individual ('personality') differences	**Economics** supports the sociological concern with the economic context and, also, the psychological concern with decision making (through its attention to 'rational' decisions made by economic actors)
Social psychology focuses on group characteristics and behaviour, on roles, attitudes, values, communication, decision making and so on	**Political science** supports the sociological concern with power and conflict and the social–psychological concern with decision making (through its concern with the state and other institutions handling matters of power and difference of interest)
Sociology focuses on structures, arrangements or patterns and how these both influence and are influenced by individual and group behaviour. It is concerned with the structure of the social and economic system as well as with the organisational structure and issues of technology, conflict, power and culture	**Anthropology** supports the social–psychological concern with norms, values and attitudes and the sociological concern with cultures (both organisational and societal) with insights taken from the study of non-industrial or 'less advanced' societies about such things as rites, rituals, customs and symbols

Rose takes over The Canalazzo restaurant

Case 1.1

Rose Markey had been working for a national chain of restaurants for only a couple of years when they asked her to take over a restaurant which they had recently acquired. They had bought The Canalazzo restaurant from the Italian family which had established the business some 20 or so years previously. The family had decided to return to Italy and to warmer summers. The company had originally put in one of their older managers to run the newly acquired restaurant. However, they were very disappointed with what was being achieved. Their Director of Finance argued that the turnover of the business simply did not justify the investment that had been made in the purchase of the business and in the redecoration of the premises. When they challenged the first manager they had put in, he talked of his resentment at being asked to move to a new part of the country at the age of 55. He persuaded the company to give him an early retirement settlement so that he could return to the part of the country he had lived in for most of his life. They were pleased to do this because it was clear, the human resources manager told Rose, that this man's poor motivation and attitude to customers was increasingly being reflected in the way the staff of the restaurant went about their work.

When Rose arrived at the restaurant she soon learned that her predecessor had clashed on several occasions with local police officers about serving late drinks. This was likely to get back to the magistrates and the restaurant would be in danger of failing to have its drinks licence renewed when it was next due for review. The manager's defence was that he was simply following local customs in the town whereby customers would have a night out that would bring them into the restaurant only after spending most of the evening in a public house. It was not his fault, he said, that the police officers and the magistrates all lived outside of the town and did not know about this.

When it came to the problems with the staff, Rose found that her predecessor had set up a strongly hierarchical set of relationships among them. This seemed to be accepted, albeit grudgingly, by the people who worked in the kitchen. But it was resented by the waiting staff who were largely part-time workers studying at the local university. Not only this, but the group of waiters – who all knew each other from the university – and the kitchen workers, all of whom had left school at 16, tended only to speak to members of their own group.

The chef, who was a middle-aged Italian, regularly fell out with the headwaiter – a woman a dozen years younger than him. Their respective ideas about how young female staff should be treated were poles apart and these differences led to frequent arguments. Overall there was very little coordination between the kitchen and the restaurant. All of this, Rose decided, seriously affected the quality of service the customers received.

Perhaps psychological factors will be the first to suggest themselves here, ranging from issues of differences of personality and temperament among different employees of the restaurant to ones of motivation and personal commitment. The varying sets of attitude in the restaurant are clearly a matter of social–psychological interest, as are the problematic patterns of communication and the way the two groups of kitchen and restaurant staff have developed to create a division among the junior staff as a whole. All of this feeds into the sociological factors and issues. There is a power structure within the restaurant and this has elements which relate to sociological variables such as age, gender and ethnicity – all of which relate to the way society as a whole is organised. But there are also sociological factors about the way the restaurant fits into the local economy and community, both as a provider of services and a source of employment. Here there is a clear overlap with economic issues of market organisation and this, in turn, relates to the most obvious economic issues of financial performance, turnover (and, by implication, profitability) and investment. Issues of a formal political nature (i.e. relating to issues of the role of the state) are present with regard to the police and magistrates, and there are obvious informal 'political' issues running right through the whole set of relationships in the restaurant. This is in addition to whatever the 'informal' politics of the relationship between local police officers and restaurant managers might be. Anthropological issues of informal customs might also be involved but, more obviously, the anthropological notions of custom and ritual are highly relevant to the patterns of restaurant use which influence the pattern of work that has to be managed by Rose Markey and the rest of the staff of The Canalazzo.

Work organisation and management studies and associated fields of study

We have now distinguished between, on the one hand, social science disciplines like sociology, social psychology, economics and anthropology and, on the other hand, the field of study that we are calling the organising and managing of work. But there are other fields of study which draw on the social science disciplines to study aspects of work organisation and its management. In fact, the field of study with which *Organising and Managing Work* is concerned brings together material and ideas from several of these. In the traditional curricula of business and management schools we will come across the subjects of Strategy (or 'strategic management'), HRM (Human Resource Management),

Organisational Behaviour (OB), Organisation Theory (OT, or Organisation Studies, OS), Critical Management Studies (CMS) and Management Learning. There are courses or modules in all of these, there are academic journals focusing on each of them and there are textbooks dealing with each one of them.

The field of study covered by the present text incorporates elements of all of these. But this is not done in a spirit of scholarly imperialism. It is done in order to provide a broader base for subsequent study than OB courses have tended to do. OB programmes often form part of the foundational level of business and management studies programmes. And they should thus provide ideas that can be built upon later than in broad strategic management or HRM modules or in more focused modules in such areas as management learning or critical management studies. But they typically do little bridging over into these areas. *Organising and Managing Work* tries to provide precisely this kind of bridging. It does this by actually incorporating into itself as a field of study some of the ideas and materials of strategy, HRM, OT, CMS and management learning.

Figure 1.2 shows the relationship between the 'organising and managing of work' field of study and the fairly standard business school subjects of OB, Strategic Management and HRM and the other fields of Organisation Theory/ Organisation Studies, Management Learning, and Critical Management Studies. OB tends to focus on the human behaviours associated with the internal functioning of organisations, with an eye on what will be helpful to managerial practitioners in this area. Organisation Studies (or 'Organisation Theory') looks at some of the same issues but with greater attention to how organisations relate to their societal contexts. It also has a primarily academic focus – concerning itself first and foremost with scholarly understanding rather than with the

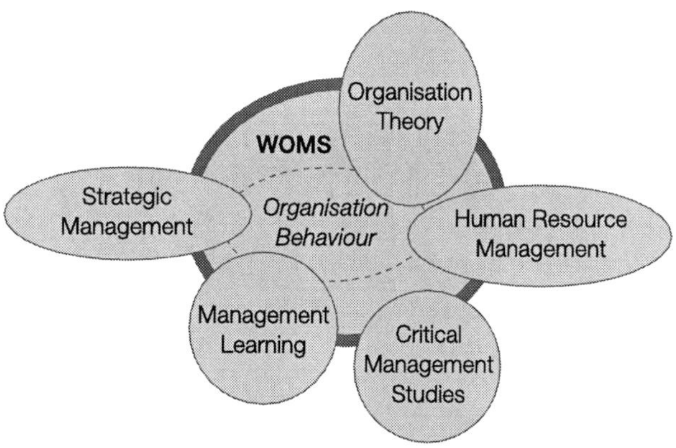

FIGURE 1.2 Work Organisation and Management Studies (WOMS) and associated fields of study

implications of such understandings for practice. The OS and OT materials are to be found in journals such as *Organisation Studies* and books like Tsoukas and Knudsen (2003), Vibert (2004) and Hatch (2006). Organisation Studies/Theory has also been more concerned with taking a critical stance than OB, something which has also informed the emergence of Critical Management Studies – in effect an application of the more critical ideas of Organisation Theory directly to issues of managerial activity (see the Further Reading on critical approaches in organisation and management studies p. 32).

Management Learning is another emergent field of specialist study with its own academic journal, *Management Learning*, and a concern to bring together theoretical developments in the understanding of human learning processes with issues of both educating and 'developing' managerial practitioners. *Organising and Managing Work* is informed by this development in its recognition of the central importance of issues of learning to all aspects of the organisation and management of work. And this is learning which, it is argued, needs to go beyond simple or 'everyday' common sense.

Common sense and social science in the study of work organisation

One of the first thoughts occurring to anyone trying to make sense of the problems we saw earlier arising with regard to The Canalazzo restaurant might be that 'common sense' is likely to be just as helpful as ideas from psychology, sociology or anthropology. It has, nevertheless, been a tradition of social science teachers to contrast social science thinking with common-sense thinking and to argue that social science analysis is to be preferred to common sense. But an alternative response might be to say, 'It all depends on what you mean by common sense.' This is necessary, in fact, because there are two quite different usages of the term 'common sense' that often get muddled up. It is useful to distinguish between *everyday common sense* and *critical common sense.*

Everyday common sense *Concept*

Analysis based on unthought-out, taken-for-granted, immediately 'obvious', everyday assumptions about the world and human activity within it.

Everyday common sense is necessary for 'getting by' in our daily lives. We all make quick assumptions about what is going on around us, drawing on all kinds of stereotypes, half-remembered experiences and simplistic cause–effect connections. This is necessary to cope with our daily lives. We would not cope with life if we stopped, sat back and deeply pondered on every eventuality that faced us between getting up in the morning and going to bed at night. But perhaps we can see why social scientists claim that their more analytical style of thinking has advantages over this. In the work context, for example, individuals frequently offer woefully simplistic generalisations such as 'People only go to work for the money' – typically adding, 'It stands to reason' or, 'It's obvious' or, 'It's common sense isn't it?' This is a good example of everyday common sense, based as it is on easy, unthought-out, taken-for-granted assumptions. Assumptions like these make life simpler – at first sight, anyway. But such assumptions are often dangerous guides to action on matters of any importance or complexity such as designing a pay system or 'reward structure', for example.

We therefore turn to critical common sense as a style of thinking which involves being deliberately logical or rational about things in the way that is common to all human beings when they are alertly and critically putting their mind to whatever matter is in hand.

Critical common sense

Concept

Analysis based on the basic logic, rationality, hard-headedness to be found in human beings whenever they step back from the immediate situation and critically put their minds to an issue or problem.

This is the kind of common sense that we can more reliably use as a guide to action when more complex matters of work organisation and management arise. It is an activity of the same order as that in which the scientist engages. Science, in this view, is essentially a formalised version of critical common sense. Scientific thinking – in principle if not always in practice – is the more formal, systematic and painstakingly analytical application of critical common sense.

Critical common sense analysis tends to start from a consideration of the most obvious or likely explanation of what is going on; the everyday common sense explanation in fact. But it then goes on to ask whether things are really as they seem at first. Alternative explanations are considered and attention is paid to available evidence in judging the various rival explanations. We can see the two types of common sense compared in Table 1.2 and the managerial implications of applying each of them, in this case in deciding for or against a performance-related pay system.

Table 1.2 Two types of common sense in practice

Everyday common sense and pay	Critical common sense and pay
If you pay employees in proportion to their output they will produce more than if they get the same wage whatever they turn out	Pay for output might work. But employees might prefer the comfort of a steady work rate and the security of a steady wage. They might resent the pressures of a bonus system on group relations
They will clearly work better under a performance-related pay system	It would be wise to find out what particular employees' requirements are before deciding for or against a performance-related pay system

The considerations about performance-related pay connected in Table 1.2 to a critical common sense way of thinking about work behaviour are indeed similar to ones which have emerged from social science research and theorising about the relationship between pay and behaviour. See, in particular, the 'expectancy' theory of work motivation explained in Chapter 8. Similar arguments to these critical common sense ones were developed in the light of one of the famous Hawthorne experiments – the Bank Wiring Observation Room experiment – by Roethlisberger and Dickson (1939).

The critical study of organising and managing

A critical common sense frame of mind is obviously relevant to any kind of practical human endeavour. But it has particular relevance to academic work – and especially to studies that claim to be scientific. Scientific analysis, as has already been suggested, can be understood as an especially rigorous or systematic application of critical common sense. And this would suggest that we could not do social science at all without being critical in the sense of constantly questioning taken-for-granted ideas and practices. However, there has been a growing trend of questioning the extent to which social science study of work behaviour and managerial practice has been sufficiently critical.

The crux of the problem that all writers and researchers interested in managerial issues have to face up to is the fact that managerial activities are always and inevitably implicated in issues of power and relative advantage and disadvantage between human groups and human individuals. Everyone engaged in management research and management education is therefore faced with a dilemma. How do they reconcile providing knowledge that might help improve the effectiveness of work activities with the fact that in doing so they might help some people ('managers' and the employers of managers, say) more than others ('the managed', for example)? Helping make work organisations more efficient or more effective is not a politically neutral matter.

In a world where valued resources tend to be scarce and there is continuous competition for the goods, services and rewards provided by work organisations, any intervention can involve one in taking sides between the relatively advantaged and the relatively disadvantaged. The social scientist is in danger of becoming a 'servant of power', as an early polemic on such matters put it (Baritz, 1960, p. 39). A desire to avoid this problem is something shared by all of those associated with the emergent 'critical management studies' movement (see the Further Reading on critical approaches in organisation and management studies p. 32). A radical strategy adopted by some critical management thinkers amounts, in effect, to 'going on the attack' against managerial ideologies and activities that are felt by the critical scholar to be 'wrong' or 'harmful'. Critical research and writing would, for example, offer its students 'an appreciation of the pressures that lead managerial work to become so deeply implicated in the unremitting exploitation of nature and human beings, national and international extremes of wealth and poverty, the creation of global pollution, the promotion of "needs" for consumer products etc.' (Alvesson and Willmott, 1996, p. 39). Such a critical management study is committed to exposing the political implications of managerial work with an ambition of helping achieve 'emancipatory transformation' – the transformation of both people and society. And, in the workplace itself, a 'critical' version of the concept of empowerment is called for, 'empowering employees to make more choices and to act more effectively to transform workplace relations' (Thompson and McHugh, 2002, p. 18).

These advocates of critical management studies, critical management education and critical organisation studies want their work to help change the balance of power in the worlds of work and employment. But they are not just critical of the existing patterns of power prevailing in organisations and society at large. They also aim their critical fire at the type of writing and teaching which constitutes the orthodoxy in contemporary business and management schools. And the main thrust of this critique is against the assumption behind much of this orthodoxy that success in managerial and organisational work comes from acquiring, developing and applying *skills* and *techniques* – skills and techniques which are neutral and 'innocent' in a political sense. Issues of power, inequality, conflict (at interpersonal, group and class levels), gender and ethnicity are either ignored or treated as peripheral matters which, from time to time, get in the way of smooth organisational functioning. Sympathy with this latter criticism has been an important inspiration for the writing of the present text and it informs the critique of what is called the *systems-control* orthodoxy and its displacement by a more realistic and politically sensitive *process-relational* frame of reference. But the whole text is underpinned by a particular notion of a critical organisation and management study, which is summarised in Figure 1.3. It is a notion that shares much ground with the work being produced under the flag of 'critical management studies' but its overlap is only partial, as the earlier Figure 1.1 suggested.

The conception of a critical organisation and management study adopted in *Organising and Managing Work* differs from that taken by some of the critical thinkers whose ideas were looked at above. This is primarily with regard to the issue of arguing for 'transformation', at both the personal and the social levels. It is felt that the choices that these transformations would entail are a matter for political and moral debate in society generally and for contestation within organisations themselves. They are not transformations which social science can or should push people towards. What the social sciences can do is to illuminate or inform those debates with information and insights derived from both research investigations and theoretical reflections. And if these insights, research contributions and theories are going to have any real potential to *make a difference* to practices in the world outside the classroom and library, there has to be openness about the fact that all social science analysis is itself value-laden. To contribute to either societal or organisational debates about how work tasks are to be organised and managed as if this were simply a matter of deciding which power-neutral technique or procedure to adopt would be dishonest at the moral level and misleading at the level of informing practice.

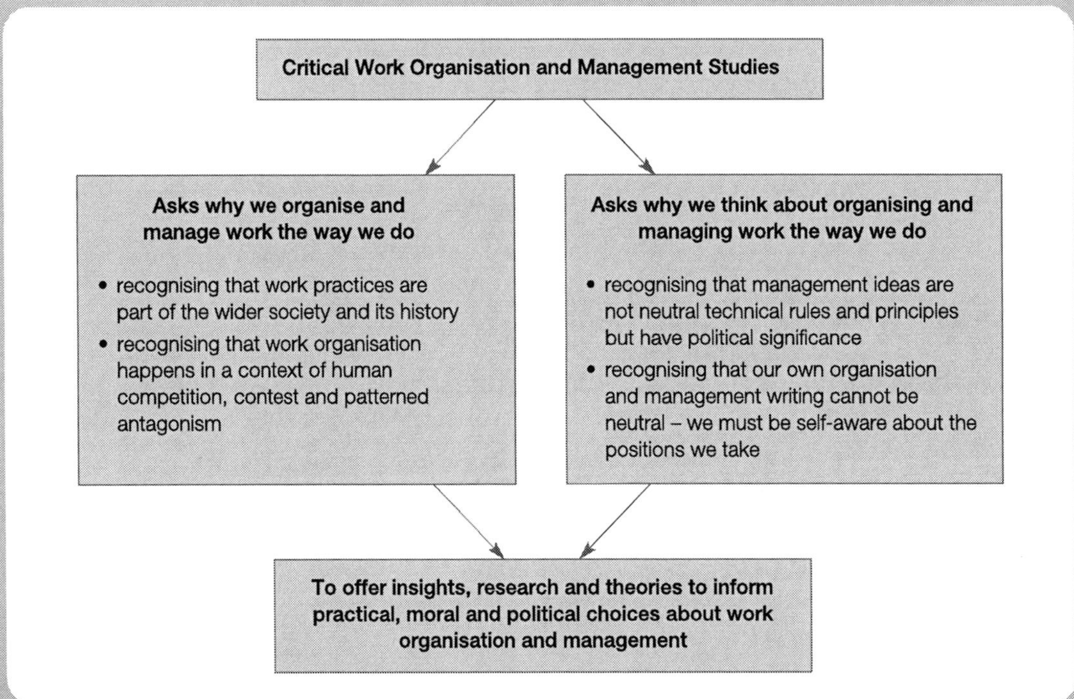

FIGURE 1.3 A critical study of work organisation and management

This means that no study of organisations and management can claim to be objective or in some sense 'value-free'. A critical study of organisation and management must keep asking questions of itself – as the words on the right-hand side of Figure 1.3 suggest. This entails recognising that the management and organisational ideas that are dealt with are not matters of technique or neutral principles, devoid of political significance. It also requires a degree of self-awareness in writing and teaching and a commitment to judiciously revealing our own biases and moral inclinations where this is necessary to help the reader or student take one's inevitable partiality into account. This principle was followed early in the present chapter where the notion of 'people management' was *engaged with* as a matter of morality as well as pragmatic realism.

The writing of the early part of this chapter was also relevant to the words on the left-hand side of Figure 1.3. The essence of critique is *questioning* and a critical study has to ask questions about the organisational activities that it is studying as well as constantly questioning what it is producing itself in its 'literature'. Accordingly we raised questions earlier in the chapter about the practice of speaking of organising work in terms of 'the management of people' or 'the managing of systems' as opposed to 'the management of work'. This argument will be built upon as *Organising and Managing Work* develops. And, as we ask questions about how and why work organisation practices are as they are, we will constantly bear in mind that work organisations are only in an extremely limited way a separate phenomenon from the economy and society of which they are part. They did not historically 'evolve' in the working out of some divine or abstract principle of increasing organisational efficiency. The hierarchy of jobs in today's organisations, for example, is both an outcome of and a contributor to the hierarchy of class and status which has developed in society as individuals and groups have competed with each other for advantage over the years. By the same token, markets do not exist 'out there' as part of the 'economic context' of business organisations. They are *made* by organisational initiatives as much as they are served by organisations. A critical perspective also requires us constantly to observe that differences of interest – and the frequent alignment and realignment of interests – are inherent in organisations. They permeate the managerial strata of organisations as well as underlying the basic tensions between employees and employers.

Activity 1.2

Quickly reread Case 1.1 and how Rose Markey 'took over' at The Canalazzo restaurant. Then read the sequel to that story (Case 1.2), 'Rose and The Canalazzo under threat'. Make a note of all the ways in which an understanding of both parts of The Canalazzo story would require attention to factors to which, it is argued above, a critical study of organisation and management draws attention. The wording on the left-hand side of Figure 1.3 is a starting point for your analysis.

Rose and The Canalazzo under threat

Case 1.2

After six months of managing The Canalazzo restaurant, Rose Markey prepared for her annual performance appraisal at the headquarters of the company which owned the restaurant. She was still finding her job quite a struggle. She had begun to adjust to living in the north of the country, having only ever lived in the south previously. She had established good relationships with the local police and the worry about losing the drinks licence had disappeared. However, she was having difficulties with the chef, who resented a woman being in charge of the restaurant. The problems with the chef were exacerbated by the fact that the kitchen staff seemed pleased to see her discomforted whenever she got into an argument with him. And the kitchen staff's uncooperative attitude towards the waiters had got worse. They knew that Rose was a university graduate and frequently mocked her southern middle-class accent in the same way they regularly mimicked what they called the 'posh' accents of the largely student waiting staff. They saw Rose and the waiters as people who were only in their present jobs as a means towards something better later on.

In spite of these difficulties, Rose felt sure she could succeed in improving the restaurant's popularity. She believed she could win over the chef in the long run, by encouraging him to develop some more adventurous menus and attracting a new clientele. This, she thought, would encourage him to discipline his kitchen staff more effectively – especially with regard to their relationships with the waiters.

Rose was excited about explaining all of this to the manager who was to do her appraisal. However, before she could even begin to talk about what she was doing, he told her that the company was considering closing the restaurant. A rival had ousted the chief executive of the company. The new managing director wanted, she said, to take the whole business 'up-market'. A restaurant in a northern town with a declining local economy did not 'fit into the new scheme of things'. Rose was to be offered redundancy – the terms of which she was invited to go and discuss with the human resources manager.

When Rose found the HR manager, he immediately invited her to go to a nearby wine bar for a drink. He explained that as an old friend of the former managing director he had felt it wise to seek a job with another business. He had been successful in this and therefore felt able, he said, to let Rose know that he believed she had been badly treated. He said that the possibility of closing the restaurant had arisen before Rose had been moved there. Rose had been chosen to take the Canalazzo job because one or two of the headquarter's managers felt that her 'face did not fit'. She was not only the one graduate trainee manager they employed. She was the only one with a black face.

The story of Rose and The Canalazzo involves many of the normal problems that someone is likely to face when trying to manage work – in a struggling restaurant or anywhere else. Alongside the obvious problems about the nature of the market for the particular services offered, and the need to achieve better coordination of the restaurant's division of labour, are a whole series of interpersonal and intergroup relationship problems. But most of these relate in some way to the patterns of conflict, inequality and discrimination existing in the wider culture and society. A critical organisation and management study would take all of this into account in an analysis of what was occurring. This would take it well beyond attention to orthodox issues of motivation, leadership and group relations. But it would also recognise the wider pattern of economic ownership which was relevant to issues in The Canalazzo and observe the way in which boardroom politics can affect what happens at a local workplace level in an organisation. There are politics at every level – workplace, organisation and society. A critical work organisation and management study would see these as centrally important matters, not merely as ones providing the 'context' in which the basic day-to-day application of managerial techniques and motivational skills have to be applied.

By now, after twice visiting The Canalazzo restaurant, two things should be apparent about analysing all the complexities of organisational and managerial behaviour as it occurs in 'real life' (as opposed to how it appears in the idealised world of standard management texts). First, as we saw in Activity 1.2, we have to look critically at facets of social, cultural, political and economic life that go way beyond a simple search for efficient management techniques. A whole series of moral issues arise in the Canalazzo story. Second, as we saw in Activity 1.1, we have to turn to a range of social science sources for help in analysing these matters. But each of these social sciences itself has a range of perspectives, models, concepts, theories and research studies on which we might draw when analysing whatever organisational or managerial issues interest or concern us. How do we choose between these?

Good, better and bad theories of organising and managing

One of the distinctive features of the present book (See Introduction, p. xix) is a concern with doing more than simply leaving readers more or less to decide for themselves which models, theories or ways of looking at organisations they prefer. However fair and reasonable this may seem at first, it avoids the issue of advising students of work organisation and management about what broad criteria they might apply to any piece of research or theorising they come across when trying to understand organisational or managerial practices. And this militates against taking a critical stance with regard to the study of work organisation and management itself. How do we make judgements about the relative value of one piece of analysis or knowledge compared with another?

To deal with this question we have to get involved with issues of *epistemology*. This is the branch of philosophy that deals with the relationship between the way the world is and the knowledge we have of that world. And it has a specific concern with the sort of truth claims that can be made for particular propositions or pieces of knowledge. This might seem a rather complex issue for us to get involved in here, something we can leave to philosophers while we get on with looking directly at organisations and their management. However, we really cannot duck the matter. It is vital to any understanding of how we relate 'theory and practice'.

Whether we like it or not, we all make epistemological judgements every day of our lives. We may have to decide, for example, 'how much truth there is' in the story we just read in our newspaper about an imminent business takeover. We might be concerned with 'how much truth there is' in the picture of society painted by the politician whose speech we have just listened to. Or we might be anxious about 'how much truth there is' in stories we have heard about a local school 'failing' and being closed down. Broadly speaking there are three approaches or 'theories' we can apply to such matters – approaches we can also take to the sort of accounts and analyses we come across when studying organisations and management. These are shown in Table 1.3.

In everyday life we apply all three ways of deciding the validity of a piece of knowledge. We do this in organisational contexts as much as we do in the other areas of life used in the examples in Table 1.3. But the approach to making judgements is obviously the most relevant to deciding what practices we are going to follow in any situation, in the light of the knowledge about that situation which is available to us. In the case of deciding which of the two tourist guides to trust, we would clearly be wise to apply the pragmatist 'theory of truth'. We would similarly be wise to apply this principle if we were considering taking a job with a particular organisation and had available to us, say, both the organisation's recruitment brochure and an article written by a researcher who had carried out participant observation research in that organisation. Which of these two 'pieces of knowledge' is the 'truer' one, we would tend to ask. And we would ask ourselves this question because we would be concerned to decide the most appropriate way to behave when entering the organisation. We would, in

Table 1.3 Three ways of deciding the 'truth' of knowledge

Three ways of deciding the 'truth' of an item of knowledge	For example . . .
Correspondence theories of truth judge an item of knowledge in terms of how accurately it paints a picture or gives a report of what actually happened or 'is the case'	A jury is asked to apply this principle (qualified by the notion of 'beyond reasonable doubt') when deciding between the accounts given by the prosecution and the defence. A judgement has to be made as to whether 'x' actually did or did not kill 'y'
Coherence/plausibility theories of truth judge an item of knowledge in terms of how well it 'fits in with' everything else we have learned about this matter previously	We might apply this principle when deciding whether a piece of gossip about somebody we know is true or false. We ask whether or not it fits with everything else we have seen of them and heard about them
Pragmatist theories of truth judge knowledge in terms of how effectively one would fulfil whatever projects one was pursuing in the area of activity covered by the knowledge, if we based our actions on the understanding of those activities which it offers	We might apply this principle when comparing what a promotional tourist brochure says about a foreign city we are going to visit and what is said in a book by an independent author drawing on their first-hand experiences. We have to decide which account of that city we are going to heed when deciding what to wear, how to address local people, how to find food that we like, or avoid being robbed

this respect, be applying a pragmatist theory of truth claims in the same way that we do when we compare the account of a product given in the manufacturer's advertisement and a report on the product published by an independent consumer association.

In the light of these examples, it is clear that a philosophical pragmatist approach to judging the sorts of material one comes across in studying organisations and management is invaluable. The wisdom of such an approach derives from two main things:

- It is impossible when looking at organisational issues to have enough information – free of interpretation, free of biased reporting, free of the tricks of human memory and free of ambiguity – to apply the correspondence theory of truth. This applies to social life in general as well as to organisations specifically. Because everything we are told about the world is mediated by language and interpretation, we can never receive an account which accurately reports or 'mirrors' that world.
- There are no absolute truths or 'final laws' which social scientific analysis can offer with regard to organisations or any other aspect of social life. One proposition, theory or research study can be judged to be truer than another, however. But this is only to the extent that it will tend to be a *more trustworthy, broad guide to practice* in the aspect of life it covers than the other. It cannot be wholly correct, totally true, or completely objective. One piece of knowledge is simply more useful than the other as an account of 'how things work' which we can use to inform our practices.

This pragmatist approach to judging the validity of the sorts of material we are going to study derives from a particular school of philosophy, the pragmatist philosophy of Charles Pierce, William James and James Dewey as well as, in part, the neo-pragmatist thinking of Richard Rorty (see Further Reading on epistemology and philosophical pragmatism, p. 32). It is important here to recognise that we are using the term 'pragmatist' in a more specific way than it tends to be used in everyday conversation, where it tends to mean 'expedient'. We are not using the word in the same way as the manager who says, 'Let's be pragmatic about this and get the job done, never mind what we ought to be doing in theory or according to the company's principles'. That manager was talking about doing something that was expedient or convenient, in the specific circumstances of the moment. This is not what we mean when we talk of philosophical pragmatism. What we talking about is something not dissimilar to the relatively straightforward notion of *critical common sense* looked at earlier. Pragmatist thinking leads us to the eminently sensible critical common sense practice of reading management and social science books (or considering any other kind of knowledge for that matter) and asking ourselves, 'To what extent should I take into account this knowledge when deciding what to do in practice?' If one theory, one research study, or even one piece of fictional writing, is thought to be more helpful in informing our practical projects than another, then it is a *better* theory, article or book. It is 'truer' in the philosophical pragmatist sense of 'true'. And note that this truth comes from the capacity to *inform practices*. It is in this that the truth lies. It is not a matter of a piece of knowledge or information being true because it is simply 'useful'. A lie can clearly be useful. To tell lies can be expedient. But where lies tend to fall apart is when one tries to base human practices on them. This is the sense in which lies are 'untrue' in philosophical pragmatist terms.

We also need to recognise that philosophical pragmatism avoids an absolute notion of truth. Instead, to put it simply, it regards some things as truer than others. One cannot produce a piece of academic research which presents the complete truth about an aspect of the world. The logic of science has to be understood as one of constantly looking for theories or explanations which are truer than those which preceded them (cf. Popper, 1963). But no absolute truth is achievable. In pragmatist terms, we will never have a body of knowledge upon which we can base our practices or projects in the world and which will give us complete success every time. However, there are some pieces of knowledge that will enable us to 'do better' if we take them as guides to action than if we utilise others. Truthfulness to the pragmatist is a relative matter.

To emphasise the relevance of pragmatist criteria for evaluating pieces of organisational and management knowledge is not to argue for completely turning our backs on the other criteria for judging truth. The concept of justice applied in many societies requires us to work with the correspondence theory of truth, for example, in courts of law or other types of judicial or bureaucratic enquiry. Yet even here, as we noted earlier, the ultimate impossibility of this is recognised in the acceptance that a judgement can only achieve a reliability which is 'beyond *reasonable* doubt'. We are therefore much safer, for most purposes, applying the more modest pragmatist criterion for judging truth claims. And we are certainly much safer applying this approach than making too much use of coherence or plausibility theories of truth. We apply these all the time – when, for example, we ask how one statement on some issue 'stacks up against' everything else we have heard on that matter. At the level of ordinary or everyday common sense we have to do this. But it is not good enough when we are engaged in the more rigorous and critical common sense type of thinking which we frequently have to do in the complex area of organising and managing work. Too many poor theories in the organisational and management sphere have an immediate plausibility, one that soon disappears when rigorous and critical common sense is applied to them.

The pragmatist style of thinking is also relevant, in a very basic way, to the arguments set out earlier for the *critical analysis* of work and organisational behaviours. Doing this, it was argued, involved appreciating that work organisation happens in a context of contest, inequality and conflict and that management ideas are more than neutral rules, principles or guides to action; they always have political significance. Knowledge of organisations and management which gives full recognition to these matters, according to the pragmatist principles, would be better – as a set of resources for informing practice – than knowledge which ignored them. This is because an organisational practitioner, managerial or non-managerial, would be better placed to succeed in whatever their purposes might be if they were informed in this way. We might go as far as to say that an individual who tried to undertake any kind of organisational task without a strong awareness of the political dimension of organisational life would be a fool! It follows from this that critical thinking is equally relevant to a manager, a non-managerial worker or someone wishing to challenge and undermine the whole enterprise. To put this another way, there cannot be 'managerially biased' knowledge – other than inadequate or misleading knowledge. If there is work organisation knowledge which helpfully informs the practices, projects and purposes of managers, then it is likely to be equally helpful to anyone else operating in that context – including someone wishing to oppose 'managerial' initiatives. The same principle applies to other spheres of human activity. Knowledge which helps a government rule can also help an opposition to bring it down, for example. Knowledge which helps a police force fight crime can equally help criminals carry out crimes more successfully, for example.

As far as *Organising and Managing Work* is concerned, everything in the book is intended to inform people involved in the management of work – whatever the nature of that involvement might be. The book should be helpful to those designated as 'managers'. But it should be equally relevant to someone whose 'project' is to have a quiet life at work, make an investment or customer decision about a work organisation or set out in some way to oppose the managers of an organisation. And, to put this style of 'active reading' into practice from the start, it can be useful to apply it to one of the most popular items ever taught to students of organisation and management: Maslow's hierarchy of needs theory.

Assessing a popular 'motivation theory' critically and pragmatically

A central place has been given for half a century or so in management education and organisational studies to certain thoughts of one particular mid-twentieth century American writer, Abraham Maslow (1943, 1954, 1968). Indeed, Maslow's 'hierarchy of needs' theory of motivation has come to play an iconic part in the study of organisational behaviour and courses on management. This is in spite of it having emerged from a body of work which is very much at odds with more recent thinking and values in psychological and social science research (Cullen, 1997). Countless teachers and students of areas of human endeavour ranging from organisation behaviour and supervisory management to nursing education and consumer behaviour have drawn and redrawn the triangle shown in Figure 1.4 – this being used to illustrate Maslow's at first sight plausible notion that human beings in their lives and activities generally work *upwards* through a particular sequence of 'needs'. People are said generally to seek to satisfy 'lower order' *physiological* and *safety* needs before moving upwards to satisfy 'higher order' *social* and *esteem* needs. At the top of the hierarchy is an idealised notion of perfect human fulfilment called '*self-actualisation*'. This is something that people allegedly seek to satisfy once they are well fed, safe, socially integrated and 'well thought of' by others.

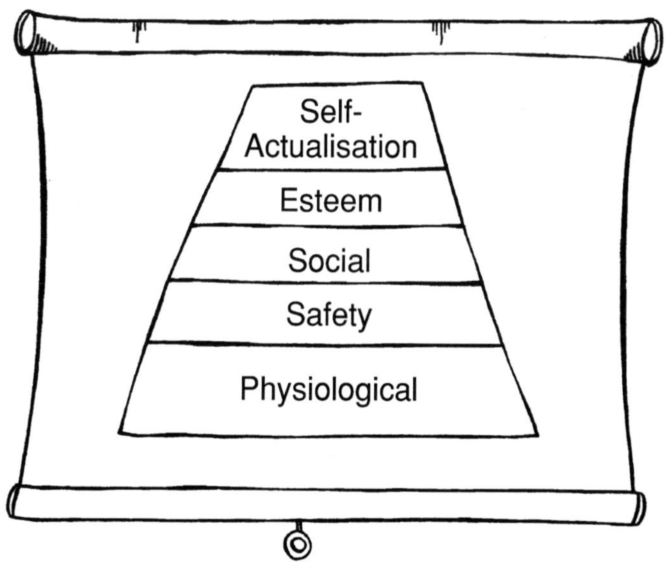

FIGURE 1.4 The ubiquitous hierarchy of needs model

At the level of everyday common sense (p. 10) there is some logic in this. If we wish to 'motivate' a starving worker running away from a hungry lion it is not unreasonable to consider chasing away the lion and giving them a loaf of bread in return for them performing as we require. Once the worker is getting plenty to eat and has had their 'safety needs' met, it seems equally reasonable to expect to have to offer some further incentives to gain worker cooperation: giving them the satisfactions of sociability with other human beings and making them feel esteemed or 'highly thought of'. Perhaps, beyond this, the only incentive that the worker can be offered is an opportunity to self-actualise or somehow to 'become everything that they would most want to be'.

The so-called 'hierarchy of needs' theory has some appeal at the everyday common sense level then. But before we turn to philosophical pragmatist criteria to help us reach a more critically commonsensical evaluation, let us first look at this theory in its social and political context in the way that fits with that requirement shown in Figure 1.2 whereby critical organisational and management studies 'asks why we think about organising and managing the way we do'. To understand why we think about 'motivation' in the hierarchy of needs way we have to note its origins in the particular setting in which Maslow was working. This was one, within the increasingly comfortable middle classes of the USA, where it was plausible to expect people who were 'doing well' to seek to 'get even more out of life'. The message from Maslow's popularisers to employers in the increasingly affluent sections of certain mid-twentieth-century societies was, in effect, 'if you want to get more out of your increasingly comfortable employees you had better think of some extra things to give them'. The ultimate 'extra' that successful industrial capitalism could offer people was the opportunity to achieve the total opposite of the 'alienation' that so many social commentators had worried about as a consequence of industrialism and capitalism. Maslow's message was corporate capitalism's answer to the Marxist fear of work under capitalism leading to dehumanising and the *alienation* of people (p. 448). Instead of people being separated from their essential humanity, as Marxists and other radical critics of capitalism feared, they could be rewarded not just with the material and social rewards of economic success but also with the chance to become everything that a human being could possibly become – the chance to realise their essential humanity, whatever that might be. This was self-actualisation.

Any critical study of organisational and managerial behaviour must pay attention to these ideological implications of what is probably the most frequently taught and most commonly remembered single 'theory' in the business and management studies curriculum.

Having identified the ideological roots of Maslow's thinking, we can move on to apply the normal social scientific critical rigour to the theory itself. Each of the three types of 'truth claim' that can be made for knowledge, set out above (p. 18) can be applied to the hierarchy of needs theory's claim that people only seek to satisfy 'higher order' needs once they have satisfied the lower level ones.

The *correspondence* criterion for judging the 'truth' of a theory might be applied by testing whether the sequence of 'need fulfilment' posited in the theory accords with what we see to 'be the case' if people are systematically studied meeting their needs in a research laboratory. Research psychologists have attempted to do this and found that people simply do not follow the sequence suggested by Maslow (Rauschenberger, Schmitt and Hunter, 1980). On these grounds, then, the theory fails.

On the *plausibility* criterion, which would judge the theory to be true if it fitted with everything else we know, we have already seen that there are some grounds for acceptance. But the plausibility of the theory soon drops away once we move beyond the everyday common sense mode of thinking (p. 10) in which truisms play an important part ('it's obvious isn't it?' we often say when thinking at the unreflective *everyday common sense* level). The *critical common sense* advocated earlier requires us to step back and critically put our minds to what at first seems credible.

So what about the *philosophical pragmatist* principle of judging truth claims? This requires us to ask how helpful the theory would be in informing our practices were we to find ourselves in the situation of trying to 'motivate' people at work. And here we can turn to the case of Campbell Toon, a manager and a management student whom we see in Case 1.3 applying, in effect, both critical common sense thinking and the philosophical pragmatist principle. He does not use these terms himself but the principles they represent are implicit in what he says to the researcher.

Activity 1.3

Read Campbell Toon's conversation with the researcher in Case 1.3 and his experience-based rejection of the Maslow theory of motivation and reflect on:

- why you think so many people seem to remember the 'hierarchy of needs' theory (or the triangular representation of it at least) and not the more complex theories that deal with 'motivation';
- the extent to which the hierarchical sequence of need satisfaction is followed in your own life (following the approach that Campbell takes to analysing the place of different aspects of need satisfaction in his personal life).

Campbell Toon confronts the Maslow triangle

Case 1.3

During a management class the researcher had reported the outcomes of some 'ethnographic experiments' he had done with other management students. During one of these events, a year or more previously, a student had uttered what the researcher took to be the very significant words, 'Motivation, that's Maslow isn't it?' (Watson, 1996a). Most of the current class reacted positively to the researcher's argument that these words perfectly captured the sort of 'surface learning' that can occur in management education when the topic of study becomes 'what this or that American professor wrote years ago' rather than how academic theorising relates to the actual practices of people involved in organising and managing work. Campbell Toon, however, was especially vocal in his attack on what he called 'Maslow's bloody magic triangle', arguing that he had been 'foolish enough to think that what he studied on management courses should be relevant to his practice as a manager'. When he visited the researcher's office after the class to collect a copy of the journal article reporting the study, he agreed to a tape recording of a conversation with the researcher. The researcher speaks first.

I hope, Cam, that I wasn't going too far in the class by asking the course members to be critical of both themselves and the material they have to study.

No, I don't think so. I think that you are right that too many lecturers and too many students simply go through the motions of drawing that dreaded triangle as an alternative to engaging with serious attempts to understand what it really means to have to motivate people at work. I'm not sure, though, whether you are right that people keep reproducing the triangle in their lectures and in their assignments as a magic ritual or a magic charm because they are actually frightened by – what was it you said?

'The frightening realities of managerial work', or some such thing, probably. No, I was just speculating that perhaps the endless drawing of the triangle by teachers and students is equivalent to people crossing themselves when they see a funeral pass by. You know, it's a sort of whistling in the dark when you are frightened because you don't really know what you are doing. But, leaving all that aside, I'm interested in your point that you did try to apply this thinking in your work.

Yes, I was facing some big problems in the packaging business where I work. It was made clear to me that the productivity levels in my part of the factory were not good enough. I knew I had to get more out of people. I had no sticks to beat people with – they were all doing a reasonable job, even if they rarely showed any kind of initiative and hardly ever helped each other out with problems. Generally, people seemed to me to be complacent. The firm was ostensibly doing well and people were reasonably paid and were secure in their jobs. When I tried exhorting people to speed up a bit, to work together a bit more when problems arose and to look for smarter ways of doing things, they just smiled at me and carried on in the same way. So you can see that when it came to the classes on motivation I was dead keen to see what these 'theories of motivation' would have to offer. The Maslow thing clicked with me when we covered it. The lower level needs of my people were all satisfied, I concluded, and therefore to motivate them to do more I had to offer them something at the 'higher order' level. I saw that Herzberg's job enrichment principle ('Herzberg spelled without a "t" ', I remember the lecturer saying) was a way of applying the Maslow theory. I therefore set about rearranging the jobs of my people so that there was more variety in their tasks and, by taking away a level of supervision, they were given more freedom to choose how to do the work. In introducing this I really played up the 'social needs' bit by pointing out that they would need to work more closely together and would find this socially rewarding. I gave even more emphasis to the 'esteem' need by making the point very strongly that I had a high opinion of my staff and that the firm had perhaps been insulting their abilities by supervising them so closely and prescribing every little detail of how to do things.

And did this work?

Did it hell. After only a week and a half I had to get some tight supervision back. The simple truth of the matter is that my people *did not want to have their jobs enriched*. Well, this is not entirely true. Two or three of them were persuaded by my arguments. I had a sort of post mortem talk with two of these. They told me that they agreed that people ought to find some of the fulfilment in their work that they tended to get with their families or in their hobbies. However, I inferred from what they told me that most of their work mates were happier getting their social, esteem and fulfilment needs satisfied outside of work and that they were happy 'cruising along' at work. But when I put it to them that 'money was not a motivator' they just laughed at me and said that had the new system lasted a little longer they were all going to put in a wage claim. When I expressed some shock they said, 'Sod money as a motivator. First, there's no way any factory worker is ever going to feel that they are paid enough. And, second, it would simply be unfair to leave people on the ordinary factory rate when they were now doing some of the old supervisor's job'.

One might argue that you had just been naïve here as a manager and that you can't really blame old Maslow for your naïvety.

I accept that. But your class last week made me think a lot about why, as management students, we often fail to test the material we are offered against our own work experiences, let alone common sense. Somehow, with me though, the confrontation with Maslow's magic triangle had encouraged me to *switch off* my common sense. When you think hard about the so-called hierarchy of needs, it doesn't stack up, does it? I am Jewish and I get a good deal of my self-esteem and an awful lot of the social rewards in my life from belonging to my culture. The meeting of these social and esteem needs, I have to say, comes before I meet my need to eat or my need to make love to whoever I fancy. The rules of my religion and my community define what and when I eat and who I can have sex with. If I was in the Israeli army, like my cousin recently was, I would put the need to belong to my community and my personal prestige needs, as a defender of my community, way before even my need for safety. Yet Maslow's simplistic scheme has us all working up through the satisfaction of the more basic physiological and safety needs towards the higher social or esteem ones. It is nonsense – there is simply no straightforward sequence to how people pursue their needs. And Maslow's whole notion of human beings seems to be one in which people live outside of culture. What I said about being Jewish would apply, in various ways, to members of any other culture of course.

Well, I'm sure he wasn't unaware of all of these things but the 'theory of motivation' that has been extracted from his writings and presented to generations of management students does seem to do just this. It reduces people, with all their choices, preferences, values and cultural influences to need-led little machines.

So this doesn't say a lot for business school education does it?

Well perhaps not. But, to be fair, I am sure that you covered other motivational theories that would be closer to your own commonsensical thinking and would helpfully, in my favourite phrase, 'inform your practice'. Do you not remember coming across something called 'expectancy theory' – an approach which stresses the importance of finding out just what your own particular employees actually want, rather than wasting time reflecting on human 'needs' in general? And did you not look at 'equity theories' and their emphasis on how ideas about fairness influence people's motivation (as happened with your people)? All of that would have been very useful to you as a manager, I suggest. And, of course, I would argue that the ideas about work orientations and implicit contracts that some of us use in this area are even more useful.

I confess that I just didn't take in these other theories – 'process theories' I think they called them. They just seemed to be more complicated – and more difficult to remember.

Well, you're not alone there. In the research paper you will see evidence that the vast majority of the three hundred or so students who took part in the events covered in the project, one year on, could remember practically nothing of the 'process theories' they studied.

For them motivation was Maslow?

Something like that.

On pragmatist grounds, then, it would seem that only very weak truth claims can be made for Maslow's theory. What Campbell Toon has to say, however, has a significance way beyond the hierarchy of needs theory specifically or to motivational theories generally. The conversation raises serious questions about the role that traditional management education plays in the management learning processes of those who take the courses and use the standard textbooks. This connects back to the earlier arguments for applying critical common sense to the questions that surface whenever we really want to understand the complex issues that arise with organising and managing work. Both parties to the conversation reflect on why the particular motivational theory of which they are so critical should be given such massive attention within management education. Cam recognises the relevance of information (and images) being easy to remember. The researcher speculates, at an anthropological level, about a possible symbolic role for the 'magic triangle' as some kind of talisman that helps management tutors and management students alike cope with the ambiguities and anxieties involved in studying something as complex and daunting as managerial practice (see Watson, 1996a). This issue of 'managerial angst' and the 'controlling the uncontrollable' expectations that are put on managers will be returned to in Chapter 6 (pp. 229–34).

Campbell's thoughts about how he does not move through a sequence of need satisfaction that remotely resembles the hierarchical models in his own life are especially significant. As he points out, every one of us lives within a culture. This means that satisfying 'needs' that can be characterised in social, esteem or 'self-actualisation' terms could be seen as having precedence over the satisfaction of so-called lower order ones – contrary to the hierarchical model. Is there anyone who could say that they regularly satisfy their physiological needs for food, drink, sex or to urinate without first considering the norms of the social groups to which they belong or prior to reflecting on what sort of esteem they will be held in if they prioritise their hunger, thirst, lust or full bladder over a need to 'belong' or a need to be admired? Of course not. One's 'motivations', in work or elsewhere, are matters of one's cultural location, personal identity, work orientation, values and life priorities and how these lead to exchanges in particular circumstances – like the exchange that people make through an implicit contract with a particular employer at a particular time.

Furthermore, it is unlikely that any of us would be able to point to any kind of sequential pattern at all in the way we go about managing our lives and handling our 'needs'. Maslow's desire to impose a particular order on people's need satisfaction behaviour is an example of the type of *linearity* in theorising about human behaviour that we will critically examine in Chapter 3. And, as we will also see in Chapter 3, matters of work motivation and orientation simply cannot be reduced to something as simple as 'needs'. While it is reasonable to talk of people 'needing' food and water, it becomes much more difficult to use the language of needs when considering matters like pursuing promotion to a high status position or trying to obtain a company car. 'Wants' would be a more realistic notion here, as would be the concepts of *expectancy* and *equity* that are used in some of the more process-oriented motivational theories that we shall meet in Chapter 8. But what are 'concepts' and how might we most effectively use them in our study of the organising and managing of work.

Concepts, perspectives and two ways of framing reality

Concepts

Concept

Concepts are the working definitions that are chosen or devised to make possible a particular piece of scientific analysis. They are the way scientists define their terms for the purpose of a specific investigation. They therefore differ from dictionary definitions which tend to have a much more general applicability.

In our everyday lives, we often look for *correct definitions* of phenomena, ones that will be generally helpful to us when communicating within a broad public language. If we wish to analyse phenomena with the greater degree of rigour and focus that distinguishes scientific analysis, however, we find ourselves having more carefully to *conceptualise* phenomena. This means devising working definitions which are helpful to us in trying to analyse and understand some aspect of the world. Thus an economist will conceptualise money more rigorously than the person in the street will 'define' it. Psychologists will do similarly with regard to 'intelligence' – working with different concepts of intelligence at different times. What this means is that in engaging in an enterprise like writing *Organising and Managing Work*, one develops concepts that are useful to one's purposes. One does not turn to a dictionary for the universally 'correct' definition. Thus, every time there is a 'defining of terms' in this book (usually using the device of a 'concept box'), it is done to be *helpful* to the purposes of the book – and *useful* to the readers who are interested in improving their understanding of how work is organised and managed. The whole enterprise of the book is based on the notion that some ways of conceptualising, 'management' or 'organisation', say, are more useful than others. The intent is not to find a 'correct' definition of what 'management' or 'organisation' is but to use concepts that help us critically engage with the world.

Although in the subsequent chapters we will be offering conceptualisations of management and of organisations that are helpful in analysing and thinking about work activities and their shaping, it is important to stress that concepts should not be seen as free-standing entities that can be used without being made consistent with other concepts being used in that same analysis. To analyse any area of human life we need 'bundles' or sets of concepts that are all compatible with each other, logically and in terms of the deeper assumptions underlying the concepts (Watson, 1997a). Thus, for any given analysis, one develops a conceptual framework or theoretical perspective that is appropriate to the purpose in hand. Thus a psychologist studying certain types of problem will want a set of linked concepts of, say, intelligence, personality, learning, motivation and so on.

Whilst it is the case that the individual social scientist will choose concepts appropriate to the particular piece of research that they are engaged in at any particular time, it is nevertheless true that each of us – both in our formal analytical endeavours and in our general thinking about life – tend to build up bundles of concepts that we find most helpful, these adding up to the personal analytical frames of reference that we take through life. These are, in the broadest sense of the word, 'theories' (systematic ideas about how the world works, we might say). These schemes are often and very usefully referred to as ways of 'framing reality'.

Framings of reality

Concept

These are broad ways of looking at the world that people adopt to make sense of various aspects of human life – work organisation and management being one of these. The framework that we use with regard to any particular aspect of life will incorporate:

- basic general assumptions about human beings ('people's characters are decided before birth', for example);
- conceptualisations of various dimensions of the specific area being considered (concepts of organisational culture or work identity, for example);
- broad ideas about how these various dimensions relate to each other (how organisational cultures relate to organisational structures, for example).

The notion of 'discursive framing' in human life will be examined in Chapter 3 (p. 102). For the moment we need simply to emphasise that the way we 'frame' reality influences how we both think and act in the world. We might, for instance, 'frame' *management* as essentially an activity in which intelligent and trained individuals decide how work should be done and then instruct less able and knowledgeable individuals to act accordingly. If we do this, we are likely to act differently when we get into management situations (as either the 'boss' or the 'worker') than we would if we 'framed' management as a process involving the bringing together of different types of knowledge, understanding and priorities to get work tasks done.

To help organise the present book, all the time applying the philosophical pragmatist principle of developing frameworks which better inform human practices, a basic distinction between *systems-control* and *process-relational* ways of framing the realities of human life generally and organisational activities specifically is used. These two framings will be unfolded in the next two chapters. For the moment, however, it is useful to see these two broad ways of thinking about human beings and about work organisations set out alongside each other. The first two columns of Table 1.4 (p. 30) derive from the thinking to be set out in Chapter 2 and the third and fourth columns relate to Chapter 3. The broad shape of the thinking behind these two chapters is presented here in part to offer a road map of the terrain over which we are about to travel. But it is also offered to show the parallels that exist between the issues to be covered at the organisational level and the issues to be covered at the level of the human being. This is not to say that organisations can be treated as if they were people. It is, instead, to recognise that there are clear parallels in the way we think about human beings on the one hand and work organisations on the other.

The most important point to stress before we move on is that, whilst it is *not* being argued that the systems-control way of framing is wrong or untrue and the process-relational framework is right or true, it will be argued, in pragmatist terms, that there are real and practical advantages in moving beyond systems-control ways of framing reality towards process-relational ones. This is fully in line with the intention behind *Organising and Managing Work* not to duck the issue of whether some ideas, theories or frames of reference relating to the organising and managing of work might be *better* than others. It is to be argued that all of us will be better placed to cope in the world of work management if we adopt thinking that can be broadly conceived of as part of a process-relational way of framing reality than if we follow the more traditional or orthodox systems-control style of thinking.

Table 1.4 is something that can helpfully be referred back to after Chapter 2 and 3 have been read. In the next chapter we will see how the systems-control way of framing organisational and managerial activities derives from modernist and universalistic aspirations to maximise control over human circumstances and does this through encouraging a notion of organisations as large goal-based controllable mechanical systems and individuals as small need-oriented systems. It will be argued that a more useful way of framing organisational realities – and indeed the broader human realities that we will consider in Chapter 3 – is to focus instead on the processes of emergence in the patterning of relations between people, organisations and the wider social world.

Summary

In this chapter, the following key points have been made:

- The most helpful way to think about issues of work organisation and management is not to focus on either the management of people or the management of systems but to focus on the management of work tasks and the relationships involved in fulfilling those tasks. This involves looking at all those activities which contribute to the management of work tasks, only then considering how such activities are divided up between people who have the title of 'manager' and those who do not.
- The field covered in the present text is the study of the human aspects of work organisation and its management which draws on the social sciences to develop insights, theories and research findings with a view to informing the choices, decisions and actions of organisational practitioners.
- This field of study is linked to, and incorporates elements of, several other established and developing academic subjects, including management learning, critical management studies, strategic management and human resource management.

Table 1.4 Systems-control and process-relational ways of framing organisations and people

Systems-control framing of organisations	Process-relational framing of organisations	Systems-control framing of people	Process-relational framing of people
The organisation is an *entity*: a system of managerially designed rules and roles existing on its own terms	Organisations are *relational* phenomena: sets of relationships and associated understandings	The individual person is an *entity* which exists on its own terms with an essential or 'true' self	People are *relational* beings: their individuality only becomes possible as a result of relating to others
The organisation is based on an *organisation design* with a set of structural and cultural characteristics	Organisations are *emergent patterns* resulting from processes of exchange, negotiation, conflict and compromise	The individual possesses a more or less fixed set of *personality* traits	People are always in a process of 'becoming': they have *emergent identities*
The organisation operates to ensure the completion of the *organisational goals* it was designed to fulfil	Organisations are *strategically oriented* in the sense that those in charge of them strive to ensure that they survive in the long term	People have sets of needs which create *motives* propelling them towards particular behaviours	People are *sense making* and *project oriented* rather than need led: in the light of how they interpret their situation they make *exchanges* with others to deal with their material and emotional circumstances
The organisation is a rational *system of rules and procedures* which ensures the completion of tasks that ensure corporate goal fulfilment	Organisations operate with *both reason and emotion*: the feelings of managers, workers and customers are as relevant to their behaviours as is their rational pursuit of material interests within formal corporate procedures	People at work are capable of suppressing emotions so that their engagement in *rational analysis* and decision making is unaffected by feelings and values	People are *simultaneously rational and emotional*: their feelings about the world and their reasoning capacities mutually influence each other
The organisation is an expression of universally applicable organisational and managerial principles	Organisations all follow modernist bureaucratic principles, but their functioning also reflects the economic, cultural and political circumstances of their societal setting	People, regardless of the society in which they live, play the role of worker, manager or whatever according to the logic of modern systems of employment and work organisation	People are cultural animals: they make sense of the world and their work activities in the light of the culture and values of the society and communities of which they are a part

- The social science disciplines drawn upon by *Organising and Managing Work*, and their analytical styles, are not essentially different from 'common sense' thinking. In fact, they have a close continuity with what can be called 'critical common sense'.
- In the spirit of 'critical common sense', the style of work organisation and management studies adopted here can be identified with certain aspects of the emergent tradition of 'critical management studies'. This entails continually asking, first, why

work is organised and managed in the way it is and, second, why we think about and study work and its management in the ways we do. It also involves continuous recognition of the extent to which work organisation happens in a context of human competition, context and patterned antagonism as well as recognising that management ideas are not neutral technical rules and principles but always have political significance.

- To be able to relate what we study to issues of practice in the organisational and managerial world we need some criteria for judging the relative merits of the theories, research studies and other materials that are available to us. The most useful criterion we can apply to judging theories, and the rest, is one derived from pragmatist philosophy. There is no way of judging absolute truth or validity. But some accounts can be seen as 'truer' than others. It is suggested that one piece of material may be judged to be 'truer' than another to the extent to which it better informs human practices or 'projects' in the aspect of human activity with which it deals.
- In spite of a growing interest in processual thinking, an almost fetishistic level of attention is given to 'motivation theories' in business and management education and, especially to Maslow's 'hierarchy of needs' theory. This latter theory has enormous weaknesses and has little value as a guide to human practice. But it nevertheless has an important ideological significance in how employment relationships have been thought about in more affluent societies over the past half century. It may also have a symbolic role in the handling of managerial angst.
- Concepts are vital tools for social scientific analysis and are different from dictionary definitions in that they are devised for the specific purpose of a given analysis. Concepts are drawn together into conceptual or theoretical frameworks. Such frameworks are, again, devised for specific studies. But all of us develop personal ways of looking at the world which are broadly of a similar nature: they help us make sense of the world around us and influence how we act in the world. These perspectives can be understood as ways of 'framing realities'. There are two basic ways of framing the realities of the organising and managing work: a systems-control framing and a process-relational framing. The latter has greater promise as a frame of reference that will inform the practices of anyone involved in organisational situations.

Recommended reading

A stimulating and accessible overview of a critical style of thinking about organising and managing is provided by Chris Grey in his *A Very Short, Fairly Interesting and Reasonably Cheap Book about Studying Organization* (London: Sage, 2005). This book is nicely complemented by the collection of pieces edited by Mats Alvesson and Hugh Willmott, *Studying Management Critically* (London: Sage, 2003). For a coverage of the variety of different theoretical positions on organisations that gives useful background to the systems-control/process-relational scheme used in *Organising and Managing Work* see the book written by Mary Jo Hatch with Ann Cunliffe, *Organization Theory: Modern, symbolic and postmodern perspectives, 2nd edition* (Oxford: Oxford University Press, 2006). And for a fuller explanation of how one can apply pragmatist thinking to research on managing and organising see the Tony Watson article 'Theorising managerial work: a pragmatic pluralist approach to interdisciplinary research' (*British Journal of Management*, 8: 3–8, 1997).

Further reading

Further reading Critical approaches in organisation and management studies

Alvesson, M. and Deetz, S. (1999) *Doing Critical Management Research*, London: Sage

Alvesson, M. and Willmott, H. (1996) *Making Sense of Management: A critical introduction*, London: Sage

Alvesson, M. and Willmott, H. (eds) (2003) *Studying Management Critically*, London: Sage

Fournier, V. and Grey, C. (2000) 'At the critical moment: conditions and prospects of critical management studies', *Human Relations*, 53(1): 7–32

Grey, C., Knights, D. and Willmott, H. (1996) 'Is a critical pedagogy of management possible?' in R. French and C. Grey (eds) *Rethinking Management Education*, London: Sage

O'Connor, E.S. (1999) 'The politics of management thought: a case study of Harvard Business School and the human relations school', *Academy of Management Review*, 24(1): 117–131

Perriton, L. (2000) 'Verandah discourses: critical management education in organizations', *British Journal of Management*, 11(3): 227–237

Prasad, P. and Capruni, P.J. (1997) 'Critical theory in the management classroom: engaging power, ideology, and praxis', *Journal of Management Education*, 21(3): 284–291

Reynolds, M. (1997) 'Towards a critical management pedagogy' in J. Burgoyne and M. Reynolds (eds) *Management Learning: Integrating perspectives in theory and practice*, London: Sage

Reynolds, M. (1998) 'Reflection and critical reflection in management learning', *Management Learning*, 29(2): 183–200

Reynolds, M. (1999) 'Grasping the nettle: possibilities and pitfalls of a critical management pedagogy', *British Journal of Management*, 10(2): 95–184

Sotorin, P. and Tyrell, S. (1998) 'Wondering about critical management studies', *Management Communication Quarterly*, 12(2): 303–336

Steffy, B.D. and Grimes, A.J. (1986) 'A critical theory of organisational science', *Academy of Management Review*, 11(2): 322–336

Watson, T.J. (1994) 'Towards a managerially relevant but non-managerialist organisation theory' in J. Hassard and M. Parker (eds) *Towards a New Theory of Organizations*, London: Routledge

Willmott, H. (1997) 'Critical management learning' in J. Burgoyne and M. Reynolds (eds) *Management Learning: Integrating perspectives in theory and practice*, London: Sage

Wilson, F. (2004) *Organizational Behaviour and Work: A critical introduction, 2nd edition*, Oxford: Oxford University Press

Further reading Epistemology and philosophical pragmatism

Davidson, D. (1986) 'A coherence theory of truth and knowledge' in E. Lepore (ed.) *Truth and Interpretation*, Oxford: Blackwell

Gallie, W.B. (1952) *Pierce and Pragmatism*, Harmondsworth: Penguin

Haack, S. (1996) 'Pragmatism' in N. Bunnin, and E.P. Tsui-James (eds) *The Blackwell Companion to Philosophy*, Oxford: Blackwell

James, W. (ed. D. Olin) (1992) *Pragmatism in Focus*, London: Routledge

Mounce, H.O. (1997) *The Two Pragmatisms*, London: Routledge

Putnam, H. (1995) *Pragmatism*, Oxford: Blackwell

Rorty, R. (1980) *Philosophy and the Mirror of Nature*, Oxford: Blackwell

Rorty, R. (1982) *Consequences of Pragmatism*, Brighton: Harvester

Rorty, R. (1989) *Contingency, Irony, and Solidarity*, Cambridge: Cambridge University Press

Tsoukas, H. (1989) 'The validity of idiographic research explanations', *Academy of Management Review*, 14: 551–561

Tsoukas, H. (1998a) 'Forms of knowledge and forms of life in organized contexts' in R. Chia (ed.) *In the Realm of Organization*, London: Routledge

Tsoukas, H. (1998b) 'The word and the world: a critique of representationalism in management research', *International Journal of Public Administration*, 21(5): 781–817

Urmson, J.O. (1989) 'Truth' in J.O. Urmson and J. Rée (eds) *The Concise Encyclopedia of Western Philosophy and Philosophers*, London: Routledge

Watson, T.J. (1997) 'Theorising managerial work: a pragmatic pluralist approach to interdisciplinary research', *British Journal of Management*, 8 (special issue): 3–8

Week 4

From Management to Leadership

Chapter 14

Influence and power

Aim

To examine how people influence others by using personal skills and/or power.

Objectives

By the end of your work on this chapter you should be able to outline the concepts below in your own terms and:

1 Distinguish leading from managing, and explain why each is essential to performance

2 Explain why leading and managing both depend on being able to influence others

3 Compare trait, behavioural and contingency perspectives on influencing

4 Outline theories that focus on power (both personal and organisational) as the source of influence

5 Contrast the style and power perspectives, and explain why sharing power may increase it

6 Outline a model of the tactics people use to influence others, including the use of cooperative networks.

Key terms

This chapter introduces the following ideas:

influence
leadership
traits
the big five
transactional leaders
transformational leaders
behaviour
initiating structure
consideration
situational models
power
political behaviour
networking

Semco http://semco.locaweb.com.br/ CASE STUDY

Semco is a Brazilian company that in 2007 employed about 2500 people in three countries, working in manufacturing, professional services and software. The main offices are in São Paolo, where Antonio Semler founded the company in 1953 to make industrial equipment such as pumps and centrifuges. He ran it in a traditional way, but in 1982 his son Ricardo Semler took over as chief executive. The company has survived a turbulent Brazilian economy, and the annual revenue of what is in effect a federation of about ten companies exceeds $200 million.

Ricardo Semler has unusual ideas about business and has gradually dismantled the management structure he inherited, moving Semco towards a very flexible form with profit sharing, employee participation and a free flow of information. Under the profit-sharing plan employees (known as associates) receive one-quarter of the profits of their respective division. The scheme is run by an elected committee, which reflects Semler's trust in his employees' abilities to make decisions.

Employees are free to agree their working hours with their co-workers – coming in and leaving work at times to suit their domestic or other commitments. Many were sceptical of this innovation – but Semler argues that provided people are committed to their job and the company, they will (and do) manage their time responsibly –

they're the best judges of the amount of time and the proper place necessary to get the work done . . . do we really believe that responsible adults . . . would simply not show up after promising to do so? That a journalist who understands the urgency of deadlines would go to the movies while the presses are standing still, waiting for his submission? (Semler, 2003, pp. 27–28)

The Brazilian economy was in poor shape during the early 1990s, with many companies going bankrupt. Semco survived, though only by cutting costs sharply. The workers themselves proposed the solutions, such as having people do several jobs rather than one. This developed a workforce that was cross-trained in several skills, and with a deep knowledge of the business. Most work is now done by units that perform all the necessary support functions such as marketing and finance themselves. For many years the company has organised work in self-managed teams, whereby groups of six to eight manufacturing employees take responsibility for all aspects of a production task. They set their targets and production goals, and decide what they should be paid. The teams vote on hiring and firing members and managers.

Corbis: James Leynse.

The management structure is like three concentric circles. The inner core has six counsellors who determine general policy and strategy, each acting as CEO for six months. Two seats at meetings are reserved for employees – the first there take the seats. The second circle consists of partners – the leaders of each division. All remaining associates make up the outer circle. Team leaders are within this outer circle – such as engineers, marketers and production supervisors. Associates are encouraged to openly oppose and reject proposals by upper management.

Sources: Based on material from Thunderbird, The American School of International Management, Case A15-98-0024, *Ricardo Semler and Semco S.A.;* Semler (2003); and other published material.

Case questions 14.1

- What examples are there of senior managers influencing associates?
- What examples are there of associates influencing senior managers?
- What assumptions about people lie behind Semler's management style?

14.1 Introduction

When Ricardo Semler took over Semco from his father he faced challenges typical of many managers today. The Brazilian economy was in trouble, and employee morale was threatened by the danger of losing their jobs or of not earning an adequate wage. While he could have used conventional means of authority and control to influence his staff, he took a radically different approach of delegating increasing amounts of power to employees, later commenting that:

> Semco managers are concerned with the essence of what employees do for the company, nothing more. (Semler, 2003, pp. 28–29)

All managers face this challenge of influencing others – such as when Sari Baldauf became head of Nokia's network division, and built it up to become one of the world's leading suppliers of network equipment. When the market collapsed in 2000, she had simultaneously to cut back that division (reducing staff by 7500 in three years) while still influencing the company and its staff to invest for future growth in other areas. Willie Walsh at British Airways faces these issues as he seeks to change the way people work, to reduce the company's costs in the face of competition from low-cost airlines.

management in practice

Deanna Oppenheimer of Barclays and Carlos Ghosn of Renault

Deanna Oppenheimer became chief executive of retail banking at Barclays in 2005 after a successful banking career in the United States. She was instrumental in growing the insurance business for which she worked from a relatively small player to the seventh largest insurer in the United States.

Carlos Ghosn, now CEO of Renault (see Chapter 16), faced the challenge of influencing staff at Nissan (which is part-owned by Renault) to make unprecedented changes in the way they worked – changes that transformed it from a loss-making to a profitable business. He now faces a similar challenge at Renault.

Both have shown their ability to influence others (staff, unions, customers, colleagues or investors) of the wisdom of their policies.

Influence is the process by which one party attempts to modify the behaviour of others by mobilising power resources.

Whatever their role, people only add value to resources by influencing others. The tasks of planning, organising, leading and controlling depend on securing the cooperation of other people within a web of mutual **influence**. Everyone's performance depends on how well they do this, and the targets of their attempts at influence will often be in more senior positions.

In that sense the work of the manager is not that of the careful analyst, working out precisely the best solution to a problem. It is closer to that of an entrepreneur, determined to get things done in an often hostile, indifferent or political setting. Managers typically operate across established functional or departmental boundaries, working with many different people who have other priorities and interests.

This chapter explores the topics shown in Figure 14.1. It begins by clarifying what influence means in the context of managing and then presents three perspectives on the topic – traits, behavioural and contingency. It then examines theories on how people can use their power to influence others, power that can come from both personal and organisational sources. Finally it presents a model of the tactics people can use to influence, including that of networking. The figure also indicates that the outcomes of an influence attempt depend not only on the choice of method but on the circumstances in which it is used. Those outcomes in turn affect the influencer's power – a successful result is likely

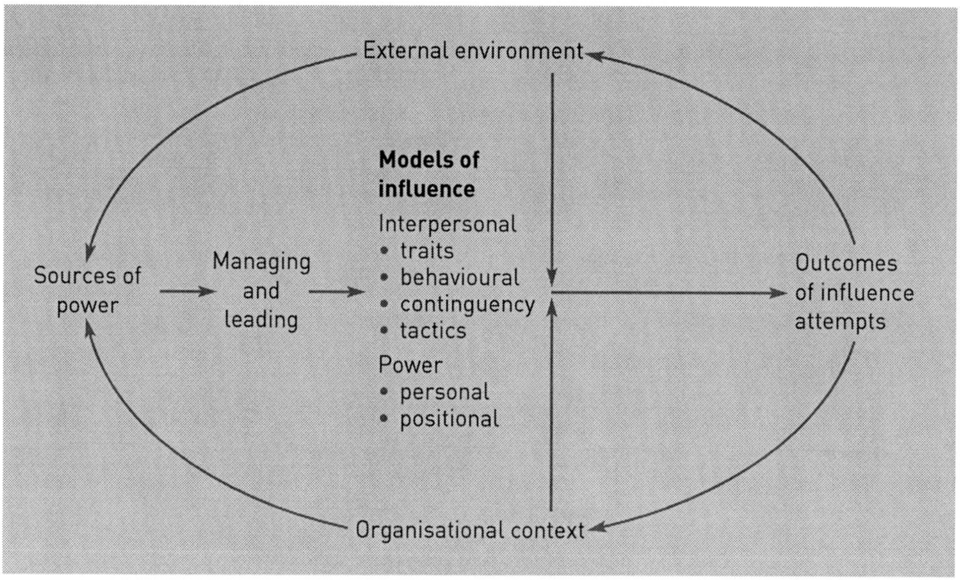

Figure 14.1
A model of the influencing process

to further increase it, and vice versa. The chapters on motivation, communication and teams are closely linked to influence and power.

14.2 Managing and leading

Research and commentary on influencing use the terms 'manager' and 'leader' (and their derivatives) interchangeably, as there is no definitive distinction. It is worth briefly clarifying the meanings that some attach to them.

Chapter 1 defined a manager as someone who gets things done with the support of others. Most commentators view an 'effective manager' as one who 'gets things done' to ensure order and continuity. They maintain the steady state – keeping established systems in good shape and making incremental improvements. People generally use the term 'effective leader' to denote someone who brings innovation, moves an activity out of trouble into success, makes a worthwhile difference. They see opportunities to do new things, take initiatives, inspire people.

Leif Beck Fallesen, chief executive of Borsen http://borsen.dk

management in practice

Borsen is a Danish business newspaper, equivalent to the *Financial Times*. During the early 1990s circulation and profitability declined. In 1996 the board appointed Leif Beck Fallesen as chief executive, with a brief to improve the position. The paper's circulation has grown by about 15 per cent a year since 1997, while that of similar papers has remained static or declined. The leadership actions he took included creating:

- regular features aimed at growing market segments (such as small businesses, family-owned businesses and younger readers);
- a joint venture providing business content to Danish television;
- an innovative online version of the paper.

Source: Company presentation and other sources.

Leadership refers to the process of influencing the activities of others toward high levels of goal setting and achievement.

Peter Drucker (1999) writes of the leader's ability to generate unusual or exceptional commitment to a vision, and of **leadership** being 'the lifting of people's vision to a higher sight, the raising of their performance to a higher standard, the building of their personality beyond its normal limitations'. And Anita Roddick wrote that:

> [People] are looking for leadership that has vision ... You have to look at leadership through the eyes of the followers and you have to live the message. What I have learned is that people become motivated when you guide them to the source of their own power and when you make heroes out of employees who best personify what you want to see in the organization. (1991, p. 223)

key ideas — John Kotter on leading and managing

Kotter (1990) distinguishes between the terms leadership and management – while stressing that organisations need both, and that one person will often provide both. He regards good management as bringing order and consistency to an activity – through the tasks of planning, organising and controlling. He observed that modern management developed to support the large companies which developed from the middle of the nineteenth century. These complex enterprises tended to become chaotic, unless they developed good management practices to bring order and consistency. The pioneers of management (such as Robert Owen, Chapter 2 Case) created the discipline

> to help keep a complex organization on time and on budget. That has been, and still is, its primary function. Leadership is very different. It does not produce consistency and order . . . it produces movement.

Individuals whom people recognise as leaders have created change – whether for the better or not. Good leadership is that which

> moves people to a place in which they and those who depend on them are genuinely better off, and when it does so without trampling on the rights of others.

Leaders succeed by establishing direction and strategy, communicating it to those whose cooperation is needed, and motivating and inspiring people. Managing and leading are closely related, but differ in their primary functions – the one to create order, the other to create change. Organisations need both if they are to prosper.

Source: Kotter (1990).

Many people work to create change and to create order in varying degrees, so there is no value in a sharp distinction between managing and leading (John Adair quotes a Chinese proverb: 'What does it matter if the cat is black or white, as long as it catches mice' (Adair, 1997, p. 2)). Managing and leading both depend on being able to influence others to put effort and commitment to the task – whether that is to create order or to create change.

People at all levels who want to get something done need to influence others. The effectiveness of senior managers in influencing others has the most visible effect on performance. They shape the overall direction of the business, moving it into new areas or changing the way it operates. Yet they depend on people lower down the organisation also being able and willing to exercise influence – whether to bring stability or to initiate change and creativity in their areas of responsibility.

Managers (and leaders) often influence people who are equally powerful – as the first woman to take the top management job at a leading City of London legal practice observed:

> The hardest things in management ... are complicated people issues. Sometimes you realise you can't solve everything. Our assets are the brains and personalities of some highly intelligent people, so there are a huge number of relationship issues. Most of these 250 people are very driven. If you get it right, the commitment is already sorted out. But you've got to take a lot of people with you a lot of the time. (*Financial Times*, 15 February 2001, p. 17)

So managing and leading require people to influence colleagues on the same organisational level, those formally above them in the hierarchy and people outside the organisation. Figure 14.2 illustrates this.

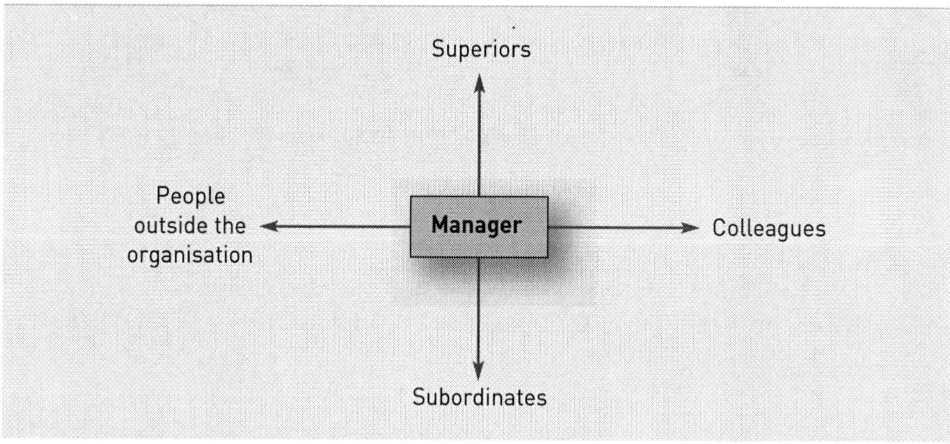

Figure 14.2 Influencing in four directions

How do managers and leaders try to ensure that others do what they want them to do? The following sections present answers to that question, beginning with trait theories.

14.3 Traits models

Many people have tried to identify the personal characteristics associated with effective leaders. They observed the personalities of prominent figures, and distinguished what they believed were enduring aspects of their personality, which they displayed in a variety of settings, and that appeared to influence them to behave in a particular way. Early work on personality and leadership identified numerous such **traits** – and this in itself hindered the development of a practically useful theory, as the lists of potentially valuable traits grew longer.

A **trait** is a relatively stable aspect of an individual's personality that influences behaviour in a particular direction.

The big five

A major advance in this area of study came when researchers noted that they could group the many observed traits into a much smaller number of clusters or 'super traits' (McCrae and John, 1992). These have become known as **the big five**: Table 14.1 shows the label for each cluster, and adjectives that describe the extreme positions on each.

The big five refers to trait clusters that appear consistently to capture main personality traits: openness, conscientiousness, extraversion, agreeableness and neuroticism.

McCrae and John (1992) show that each of the big five super traits contains six traits. Using these in personality assessments enables researchers to identify the pattern of traits an individual displays, which may then be linked to aspects of behaviour: in the present context the focus would be on which traits appear to affect the ability of people to influence others.

Table 14.1
The big five trait clusters

Openness	Explorer (O+): creative, open-minded, intellectual	Preserver (O–): unimaginative, disinterested, narrow-minded
Conscientiousness	Focused (C+): dutiful, achievement oriented, self-disciplined	Flexible (C–): frivolous, irresponsible, disorganised
Extraversion	Extravert (E+): gregarious, warm, positive	Introvert (E–): quiet, reserved, shy
Agreeableness	Adapter (A+): straightforward, compliant, sympathetic	Challenger (A–): quarrelsome, oppositional, unfeeling
Neuroticism	Reactive (N+): anxious, depressed, self-conscious	Resilient (N–): calm, contented, self-assured

The *Financial Times*/PwC annual survey of the world's most respected companies continues the tradition of identifying the traits of effective leaders. Common traits included vision, ability to forecast trends, speed, decisiveness, courage, tenacity, optimism and enthusiasm. Table 14.2 indicates the characteristics of the leaders of companies that regularly feature in the survey.

Table 14.2
Traits of those leading some of the world's most respected companies

Leader	Company	Traits
Jurgen Schremp	DaimlerChrysler	'daring behaviour'
Michael Dell	Dell Computers	'listening to customers and employees'
Richard Branson	Virgin	'a maverick, encouraging people to do things differently'
John Browne	BP (until 2007)	'taking lead on environment and social responsibility'

James Burns: transactional and transformational leaders

A **transactional leader** is one who treats leadership as an exchange, giving followers what they want if they do what the leader desires.

A **transformational leader** is a leader who treats leadership as a matter of motivation and commitment, inspiring followers by appealing to higher ideals and moral values.

James Burns (1978) distinguished between **transactional** and **transformational leaders**. Transactional leaders influence subordinates' behaviour through a bargain. The leader enables followers to reach their goals, while at the same time contributing to the goals of the organisation. If subordinates behave in the way desired by the leader they receive rewards – transactional leaders tend to support the status quo by rewarding subordinates' efforts and commitment.

Burns contrasted this approach with that of transformational (sometimes called charismatic) leaders. They are thought to change the status quo by infusing work with a meaning that encourages subordinates to change their goals, needs and aspirations. Transformational leaders raise the consciousness of followers by appealing to higher ideals and moral values. They energise people by, for example, articulating an attractive vision for the organisation, reinforcing the values in that vision, and empowering subordinates to come up with new and creative ideas. They also articulate

> transcendent goals, demonstration of self-confidence and confidence in others, setting a personal example for followers, showing high expectations of followers' performance, and the ability to communicate one's faith in one's goals. (Fiedler and House, 1994, p. 112)

What do charismatic leaders do to gain support?

key ideas

Conger and Kanungo (1994) note that people often use the terms 'charismatic' and 'transformational' leadership interchangeably, but go on to suggest that the first term directs attention to measurable leader behaviours, while the second focuses on the effects on followers: 'In essence the two formulations of charismatic and transformational are highly complementary, and study the same phenomenon only from different vantage points' (p. 442).

They then develop a set of behavioural scales to measure charismatic leadership, with 25 items in six groups:

1 vision and articulation e.g. 'consistently generates new ideas';
2 environmental sensitivity e.g. 'recognises barriers that may hinder progress';
3 unconventional behaviour e.g. 'uses non-traditional methods';
4 personal risk e.g. 'takes high personal risk for the sake of the organisation';
5 sensitivity to member needs e.g. 'shows sensitivity to needs and feelings of others';
6 not maintaining the status quo e.g. 'advocates unusual actions to achieve goals'.

The full scales have been validated and used widely in research on charismatic leadership (see for example Groves, 2005).

One limitation of the traits model is that a trait that is valuable in one situation is not necessarily valuable in another. Whatever traits Phillip Watts had that led to his appointment as head of exploration at Shell were still there when he resigned in 2004 after a scandal over the way the company reported their oil reserves. Having certain traits is probably necessary for effective leadership, but will not be sufficient – which may explain the inconclusive results of research that attempts to relate traits to performance (Bono and Judge, 2004). Their relative importance may depend on other factors in the situation. For example, De Hoog *et al.* (2005) found that while four of 'the big five' had a positive effect on both transactional and charismatic (transformational) leadership in a stable environment, they were negatively associated with charismatic leadership in a dynamic environment. Different conditions seem to need different traits.

Despite these limitations the traits model may help to explain why some people get to positions of great influence and others do not. Baum and Locke (2004) note a revival of interest in the personal characteristics of potential leaders, such as entrepreneurs creating new ventures. Management selection practices reflect this belief, and the criteria often include traits that are thought to be relevant for success. Table 14.3 lists the traits that the UK National Health Service Leadership Qualities Framework identifies as distinguishing 'effective and outstanding leaders'.

Table 14.3
NHS Leadership Qualities Framework

Personal qualities	Setting direction	Delivering the service
Self-belief	Seizing the future	Leading change through people
Self-awareness	Intellectual flexibility	Holding to account
Self-management	Broad scanning	Empowering others
Drive for improvement	Political astuteness	Effective and strategic influencing
Personal integrity	Drive for results	Collaborative working

Source: Based on Department of Health (2002), *NHS Leadership Qualities Framework*, NHS Leadership Centre, London.

As two of the foremost scholars of leadership concluded:

> There is no one ideal leader personality. However, effective leaders tend to have a high need to influence others, to achieve; and they tend to be bright, competent and socially adept, rather than stupid, incompetent and social disasters. (Fiedler and House, 1994, p. 111)

Activity 14.1 Which traits do employers seek?

Collect some job advertisements and recruitment brochures. Make a list of the traits that the companies say they are looking for in those they recruit.

14.4 Behavioural models

Another set of theories sought to identify the behavioural styles of effective managers. What did they do to influence subordinates that less effective managers did not? Scholars at the universities of Ohio State and Michigan respectively identified two categories of **behaviour**: one concerned with interpersonal relations, the other with accomplishing tasks.

Behaviour is something a person does that can be directly observed.

Ohio State University model

Researchers at Ohio State University (Fleishman, 1953) developed questionnaires that subordinates used to describe the behaviour of their supervisor, and identified two dimensions – 'initiating structure' and 'consideration'.

Initiating structure is a pattern of leadership behaviour that emphasises the performance of the work in hand and the achievement of production or service goals.

Initiating structure refers to the degree to which a leader defines people's roles, focuses on goal attainment and establishes clear channels of communication. Those using this approach focused on getting the work done – they expected subordinates to follow the rules and made sure they were working to full capacity. Typical behaviours included:

- allocating subordinates to specific tasks
- establishing standards of job performance
- informing subordinates of the requirements of the job
- scheduling work to be done by subordinates
- encouraging the use of uniform procedures.

Consideration is a pattern of leadership behaviour that demonstrates sensitivity to relationships and to the social needs of employees.

Consideration refers to the degree to which a leader shows concern and respect for followers, looks after them and expresses appreciation (Judge *et al.*, 2004). Such leaders assume that subordinates want to work well and try to make it easier for them to do so. They place little reliance on their formal position and power, typical behaviours including:

- expressing appreciation for a job well done
- not expecting more from subordinates than they can reasonably do
- helping subordinates with personal problems
- being approachable and available for help
- rewarding high performance.

Surveys showed that supervisors displayed distinctive patterns – some scored high on initiating structure and low on consideration, while others were high on consideration and low on initiating structure. Some were high on both, others low on both. Research into the effects on performance were often inconclusive, but a recent review of over 130 such studies (Judge *et al.*, 2004) concluded that there was evidence that consideration tended to be more strongly related to follower satisfaction, while initiating structure was slightly more related to measures of leader performance.

University of Michigan model

Researchers at the University of Michigan (Likert, 1961, 1967) conducted similar studies and found that two types of behaviour distinguished effective from ineffective managers: job-centred and employee-centred behaviour.

- *Job-centred supervisors* ensured that they worked on different tasks from their subordinates, concentrating especially on planning, coordinating and supplying a range of support activities. These correspond to the initiating structure measures at Ohio.
- *Employee-centred supervisors* combined the task-oriented behaviour with human values. They were considerate, helpful and friendly to subordinates, and engaged in broad supervision rather than detailed observation. These behaviours were similar to what the Ohio group referred to as considerate.

From numerous studies, Likert (1961) concluded that:

> Supervisors with the best records of performance focus their primary attention on the human aspects of their subordinates' problems and on endeavouring to build effective work groups with high performance goals. (p. 7)

Managerial grid model

Blake and Mouton (1964, 1979) developed the managerial grid model to extend and apply the Ohio State research. Figure 14.3 shows various combinations of concern for production (initiating structure) and concern for people (consideration).

The horizontal scale relates to concern for production, which ranges from 1 (low concern) to 9 (high concern). The vertical scale relates to concern for people, also ranging from 1 (low concern) to 9 (high concern). At the lower left-hand corner (1,1) is the impoverished style: low concern for both production and people. The primary objective of such managers is to stay out of trouble. They merely pass instructions to subordinates, follow the established system, and make sure that no one can blame them if something goes wrong. They do only as much as is consistent with keeping their job.

At the upper left-hand corner (1,9) is the country club style: managers who use this style try to create a secure and comfortable family atmosphere. They assume that their subordinates will respond productively. Thoughtful attention to the need for satisfying relationships leads to a friendly atmosphere and work tempo.

High concern for production and low concern for people is found in the lower right-hand corner (9,1). This is the produce or perish style. These managers do not consider subordinates' personal needs. All that matters is achieving the organisation's objectives. They use their formal authority to pressure subordinates into meeting production quotas. They believe that efficiency comes from arranging the work so that employees merely have to follow instructions.

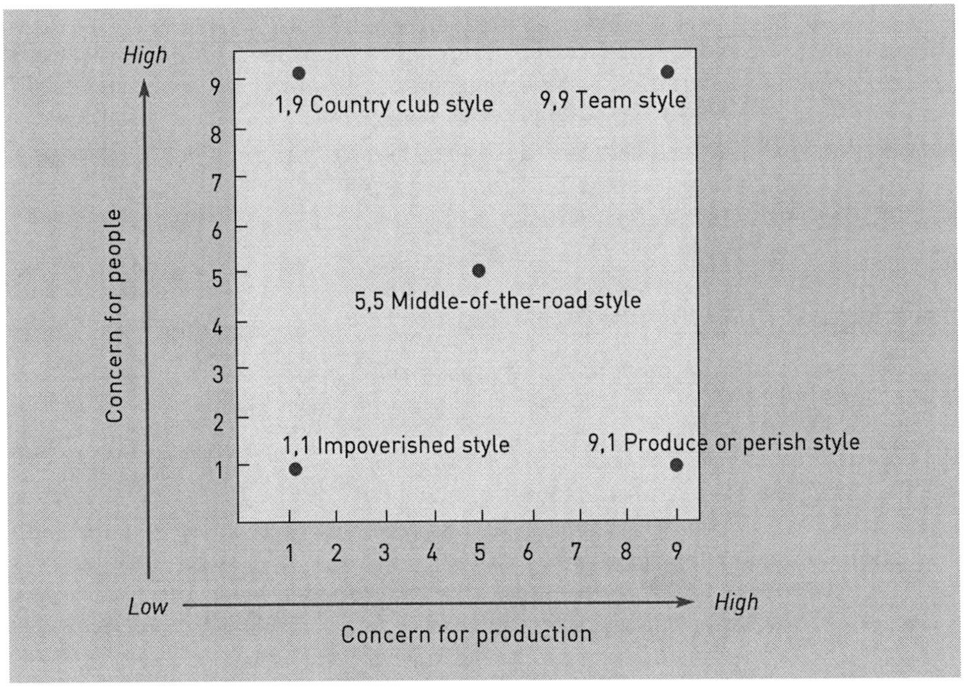

Figure 14.3
The managerial grid

In the centre (5,5) is the middle-of-the-road style. These managers obtain adequate performance by balancing the need to get the work done with reasonable attention to the interests of employees. In the upper right-hand corner (9,9) is the team style which, according to Blake and Mouton, is the most effective approach, aiming for both high performance and high job satisfaction. The manager fosters performance by building relationships of trust and respect.

Activity 14.2 Critical reflection on the managerial grid

- Reflect on two managers you have worked with, one effective and one ineffective from your point of view.
- Which of the positions in the Blake and Mouton grid most closely describe their style? Note some of their typical behaviours.
- What were they like to work for? Does your reflection support or contradict the model? If the latter, what may explain that?

management in practice Two leaders' styles

Jeroen Van der Veer, CEO of Shell

Good leadership ... means being clear about what is weak and what is strong, and where you want to go in the longer term, and having the ability to put it into clear words. The best way for a leader to take a company forward is to have some very simple words about how you would like to change it and the culture of the company.

Source: *Financial Times*, 2 February 2007, p. 19.

David Michels, chief executive of Hilton Hotels
Argument is an essential part of the success of any business, he says:

> You have to talk to staff and you can't insulate yourself by getting in first-class limos all the time. You have to get on the Tube and you have to get people to argue with you. I argue so much with my staff I sometimes wonder who is in charge. I enjoy [life as chief executive], I really do. But sometimes I sit back and think 'bloody hell, this is difficult'.

Source: *Financial Times*, 6 June 2003.

Many trainers use the Blake and Mouton model to help managers develop towards the '9,9' style. Implicit in the approach is the idea of flexibility. Others question whether showing a high level of concern for both production and people is always the best approach. Sometimes a concern for production may be more important than concern for people – such as in a sudden crisis that requires swift action. Situational or contingency models offer a possible answer.

Semco – the case continues

http:///semco.locaweb.com.br/

CASE STUDY

Employees have gradually taken greater responsibility over everything from cafeteria menus to new product designs and plant relocations. They are always free to develop new skills in other areas of the business, and to transfer to different units if they are accepted by their new colleagues. Another innovation is that workers set their own production quotas and come in on their own time to meet them if necessary, without pressure from management and without overtime pay. Their managers have considerable autonomy over the strategy for their business unit, including setting levels of pay.

Employees can see all company financial information, and Semco developed a unique way of presenting financial information in a clear, simplified way. They also developed a course to teach everyone to read balance sheets and cash-flow statements. Employees in each business group use this financial information to develop their business plan for the next six months, deciding what staff they will need and fixing their salaries. There are 11 compensation options (such as fixed salaries, royalties or stock options), which employees can choose between.

> **Anyone who requests too large a salary . . . runs the risk of being rejected by their colleagues. So self-interest almost always prevents them from asking for excessive paycheques. We also encourage people to set their own salaries without creating a deficit in their departments. That's why monthly revenue reports, budgets, costs, salaries, profit sharing, and transparent numbers [publishing salaries] are so important at Semco. If workers understand the big picture, they'll know how their salaries fit. (Semler, 2003, p. 197)**

All meetings, including those of the counsellors, are open to all employees who wish to attend. This gives staff the information they need to make informed decisions, and reinforces the democratic nature of the decision-making process.

> **Moving an organization or business ahead by virtue of what its people stand for means removing obstacles like official policies, procedural constraints and relentless milestones, all of which are set up in the pursuit of quarterly or otherwise temporary success. It means giving up control, and allowing employees to manage themselves. It means trusting workers implicitly, sharing power and information, and celebrating true democracy. (Semler, 2003, pp. 112–113)**

Sources: Based on material from Thunderbird, The American School of International Management, Case A15-98-0024, *Ricardo Semler and Semco S.A.*; Semler (2003); and other published material.

▶

Case questions 14.2

- Where would you place Ricardo Semler on Blake and Mouton's managerial grid?
- Does the Semco story support or not the prescriptions of that model?

14.5 Situational (or contingency) models

Situational models of leadership attempt to identify the contextual factors that affect when one style will be more effective than another.

Situational (or contingency) **models** present the idea that managers influence others by adapting their style to the circumstances. Three such models are set out below (a fourth, developed by Vroom and Yetton (1973) featured in Chapter 7).

Tannenbaum and Schmidt's continuum of leader behaviour

Unlike the 'one best way' model implied by the behavioural models, Robert Tannenbaum and Warren Schmidt (1973) saw that leaders worked in different ways, which they presented as a continuum of styles, ranging from autocratic to democratic. Figure 14.4 illustrates these extremes and the positions in between. Which of these the leader uses should reflect three forces:

1 **forces in the manager:** personality, values, preferences, beliefs about participation and confidence in subordinates;
2 **forces in subordinates:** need for independence, tolerance of ambiguity, knowledge of the problem, expectations of involvement;
3 **forces in the situation:** organisational norms, size and location of work groups, effectiveness of team working, nature of the problem.

House's path–goal model

House (House and Mitchell, 1974; House, 1996) argued that effective leaders are those who clarify their subordinates' path to the rewards available, and ensure that rewards the subordinates value are available. They help subordinates to identify and learn behaviours that will help them complete the task and so secure the rewards for doing so. The model identifies four styles of leader behaviour:

1 **directive:** letting subordinates know what the leader expects; giving specific guidance; asking subordinates to follow rules and procedures; scheduling and coordinating their work;
2 **supportive:** treating them as equals; showing concern for their needs and welfare; creating a friendly climate in the work unit;
3 **achievement oriented:** setting challenging goals and targets; seeking performance improvements; emphasising excellence in performance; expecting subordinates to succeed;
4 **participative:** consulting subordinates; taking their opinions into account.

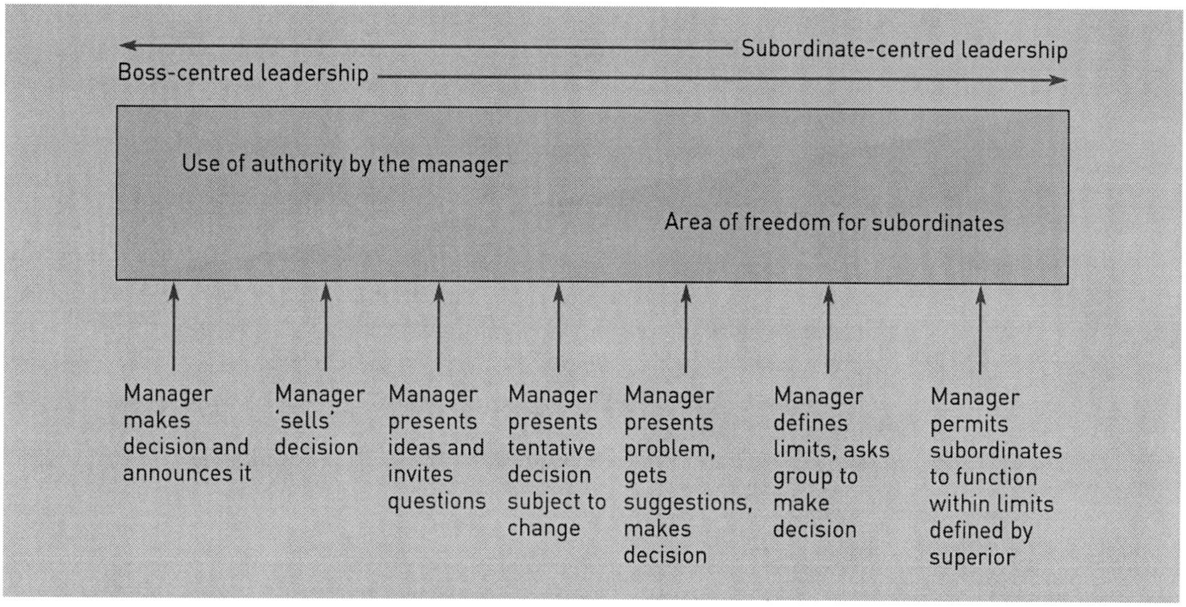

Figure 14.4 The Tannenbaum–Schmidt continuum of leadership behaviour

Source: Tannenbaum and Schmidt (1973), reprinted by permission of *Harvard Business Review*, © 1973 Harvard Business School Publishing Corporation; all rights reserved.

House suggested that the appropriate style would depend on the situation – the characteristics of the subordinate and the work environment. For example, if a subordinate has little confidence or skill then the leader needs to provide coaching and other support. If the subordinate likes clear direction they will respond best to a leader who gives it. Most skilled professionals expect to use their initiative and resent a directive style:

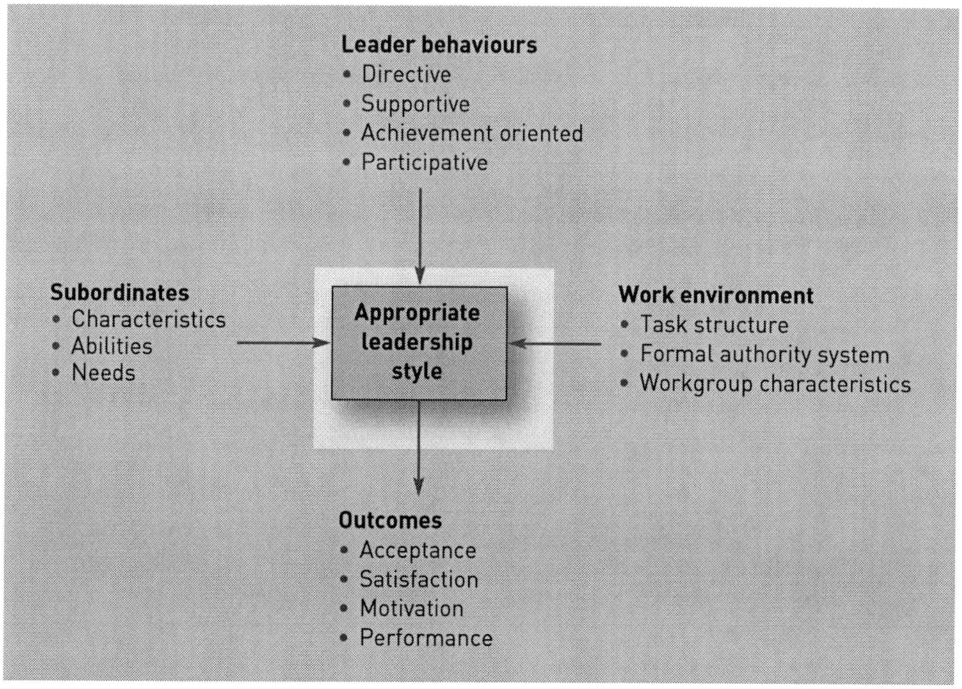

Figure 14.5
House's path–goal theory

they will respond best to a participative or achievement-oriented leader. The work environment includes the degree of task structure (routine or non-routine), the formal authority system (extent of rules and procedures) and the work group characteristics (quality of teamwork).

Figure 14.5 summarises the model which predicts, for example, that:

- a directive style works best when the task is ambiguous and the subordinates lack flexibility – the leader absorbs the uncertainty and shows the group how to achieve the task;
- a supportive style works best in repetitive frustrating or physically unpleasant tasks – subordinates respect the leader who joins in and helps;
- an achievement-oriented style works best when the group faces non-repetitive ambiguous tasks, which will challenge their ability – they need encouragement and pressure to raise their ambitions;
- a participative approach works best when the task is non-repetitive and the subordinate(s) are confident that they can do the work.

management in practice

Helmut Panke, chief executive of BMW www.bmw.com

Helmut Panke became CEO of Bavarian Motor Works (BMW) in 2002, since when he has overseen a rapid expansion of the model range. Sales, and the company's share price, rose strongly after he took charge of the company. Panke demands top performance from staff, and from himself. He first demonstrated his skills at building BMW's global business as head of North American operations in the mid-1990s, during which time the United States became BMW's largest market.

> Panke's management style could be called Socratic. He loves to pose questions and lead debates with groups of managers – a practice that reflects his academic training (he has a doctorate in nuclear physics) and gets results . . . By encouraging debate, Panke has forged a performance-driven culture that isn't afraid to send tough questions up the ranks. 'Panke takes a huge amount of time to discuss with people, then he lets them manage on their own. That way he gets 120% from everyone', says a manager who has seen Panke rise up the ranks over 20 years . . . 'My biggest challenge is saying "no" to projects that are exciting but don't fit BMW's strategy', comments Panke (p. 48).

Source: *Business Week*, 7 June 2004.

Such contingency models indicate that participative leadership styles are not necessarily the most effective, and that, as Table 14.4 shows, there will be situations where a directive style is appropriate.

Table 14.4
Conditions favouring participative or directive styles

Participative style most likely to work when:	Directive style most likely to work when:
Subordinates' acceptance of the decision is important	Subordinates do not share the manager's objectives
The manager lacks information	Time is short
The problem is unclear	Subordinates accept top-down decisions

John Adair and Action Centred Leadership

key ideas

Over 2 million people worldwide have taken part in the Action Centred Leadership approach pioneered by John Adair. He proposes that people expect leaders to fulfil three obligations – to help them achieve the task, to build and maintain the team and to enable individuals to satisfy their needs. These three obligations overlap and influence each other – if the task is achieved that will help to sustain the group and satisfy individual needs. If the group lacks skill or cohesion it will neither achieve the task nor satisfy the members. Figure 14.6 represents the three needs as overlapping circles – almost a trademark for John Adair's work. To achieve these expectations the leader performs the eight tasks in the figure.

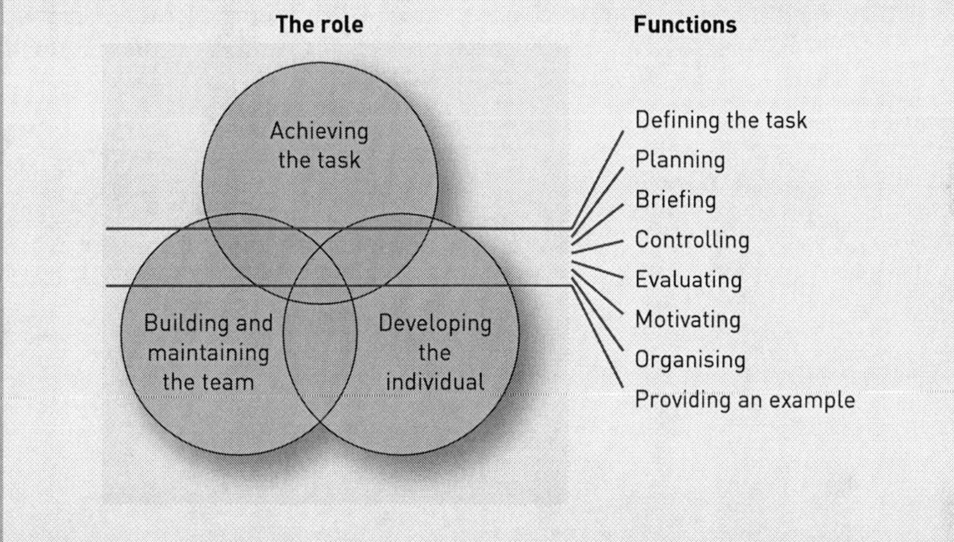

Figure 14.6 Adair's model of leadership functions
Source: Adair (1997, p. 21).

14.6 Sources of power to influence others

Earlier sections have centred on the personal skills that people can use to influence others, including their ability to adapt their methods to the situation in which they are working. Another perspective shows that people influence others by using **power**.

Power concerns 'the capacity of individuals to exert their will over others' (Buchanan and Badham, 1999).

Sources of power

What are the bases of one person's power over another? French and Raven's (1959) widely quoted classification identifies five sources of power:

1 **Legitimate power** flows from the person's formal position in the organisation. The job they hold gives them the power, for example, to make capital expenditures, offer overtime, choose a supplier or recruit staff.
2 **Reward power** is the ability to reward another if they comply with a request or instruction. The reward can take many forms – pay, time off or interesting work.

3 **Coercive power** is the ability to obtain compliance through fear of punishment or harm. It includes reprimands, demotions, threats, bullying language or a powerful physical presence.
4 **Referent power**, also called *charismatic* power, is when some characteristics in a person are attractive to others: they identify with them, which gives the charismatic person power.
5 **Expertise power** is when people acknowledge someone's knowledge and are therefore willing to follow their suggestions. This knowledge or skill may be *administrative* (how an organisation operates) or *technical* (how to do a task).

Table 14.5 develops the French and Raven list, by showing that each type of power can have both a personal and a positional source. The most significant change to the French and Raven model is to show that referent (charismatic) power is not just personal but can also have a positional source (Hales, 2001). Chapter 3 showed how organisations develop distinctive cultures and sub-cultures. When people refer to the prevailing culture in an attempt to influence behaviour ('what I'm asking fits the culture') they are drawing on a positional form of referent power.

Table 14.5
Personal and positional sources of power

Power resource	Personal	Positional
Coercive	Forcefulness, insistence, determination	Authority to give instructions, with the threat of sanctions or punishment available
Reward	Credit for previous or future favours in daily exchanges	Authority to use organisational resources, including the support of senior people
Expertise:		
Administrative	Experience of the business, whom to contact, how to get things done	Authority to use or create organisational policies or rules
Technical	Skill or expertise relevant to the task	Authority to access expertise, information and ideas across the business
Referent	Individual beliefs, values, ideas, personal qualities	Authority to invoke norms and values of the organisational culture

Source: Based on Hales (2001).

Someone who has little access to these sources of power will have less influence than someone with much access. People continually defend their power sources, and try to gain new ones.

Perceptions of power

Power is only effective if the target of an influence attempt recognises the power source as legitimate and acceptable. If they dispute the knowledge base of a manager, or challenge their positional authority over a matter, the influence attempt is likely to fail. Managers who are successful influencers ensure that their power sources are sustained, and take every opportunity to enhance them.

Marketing brand Me

management in practice

People should manage their reputation like a brand. The most effective candidates [for promotion] do not leave their image to chance. They work at it, and massage its growth. They know that the best publicists they can have are their immediate staff. They are aware that team members talk about them more than anyone else. So they provide evidence to feed that grapevine ... Staff need stories about their leader.

Another way to manage your reputation is to manage your boss ... People keen to manage their reputation should find out what motivates the boss and try to satisfy those goals. If your boss likes punctuality and conscientiousness, turn up on time and work hard. If he or she needs reassurance, give it. If it is power, respond as someone who is less powerful. Why irritate a person who can influence your career path?

Source: John Hunt, 'Marketing brand Me', *Financial Times*, 22 December 2000.

Responses to the use of power

People respond to influence attempts in three ways – resistance, compliance and internalisation. Table 14.6 describes the alternatives. Resistant staff will have no commitment to the work. They do what is required grudgingly, and without enthusiasm or imagination. While it may be possible to overcome resistance by using threats or coercion, this may not be the most useful reaction in the longer term. Compliance too has limitations, especially if long-term success depends on further innovation. Only when staff are fully committed because they have internalised the influencer's goals, and see themselves as part of the creative process, is the influencing task complete.

Table 14.6

Three outcomes of influence attempts

Outcome	Description	Commentary
Resistance	Target is opposed to the request and actively tries to avoid carrying it out	Target may make excuses or try to dissuade the influencer from persisting. May also seek support from higher authority or undermine the influencer's efforts
Compliance	Target willing to do what is asked, but is apathetic, unenthusiastic and makes minimal effort	For a complex task, an unsatisfactory outcome. For routine tasks it may be enough for the influencer to accomplish their goals
Internalisation	Target internally agrees with a decision or request and makes a geat effort to meet it successfully	Usually the most successful outcome from the point of view of the influencer, especially on a difficult task

Grudging compliance is unlikely to lead to satisfactory performance. The complexities of work processes often require people to work with imagination and flexibility. In service industries employee behaviour directly influences customer perceptions, such as whether they see employees working responsibly and with concern for what they are doing. This is not likely to happen if managers have used their power in ways that have secured only compliance, not the commitment that comes from internalisation.

Activity 14.3 Critical reflection on sources of power

- Try to identify at least one example of each of the personal and positional power sources. Examples could come from observing a manager in action (including people in your university or college) or from your reading of current business affairs.
- Can you identify what the person concerned has done to develop their power?
- Have other events helped to build, or to undermine their power?

Case questions 14.3

- Which of the sources of power in Table 14.5 has Ricardo Semler used?
- What has he done to increase his power in the eyes of those he is trying to influence?
- What other forms of authority has he acquired?
- Which of the sources of power in Table 14.5 could the associates use?

14.7 Using positional power to influence others

Those who want to be effective influencers can increase their chances of doing so by building up those sources of power that come from their position within the organisation. Kanter (1979) observed that people are more likely to be influenced by strong and powerful managers than by weak and isolated ones. She identified many ways in which a manager's position in the organisation affects their power, such as:

- approvals needed for non-routine decisions (fewer approvals means more power)
- relation of job to current organisational priorities (central relation means more power)
- external contact (more opportunities for this means more power)
- senior contact (more opportunities for this means more power).

The nature of the job and the pattern of contacts that come with it give the manager access to three 'lines of power':

- **supply:** money and other resources that can be used to bestow status or rewards on others in return for their support;
- **information:** being in the know, aware of what is happening, familiar with plans and opportunities that are in the making;
- **support:** able to get senior or external backing for what he or she wants to do.

Political behaviour is 'the practical domain of power in action, worked out through the use of techniques of influence and other (more or less extreme) tactics' (Buchanan and Badham, 1999).

The more of these lines of power the manager has, the more will subordinates co-operate. They do so because they believe that the manager has the power to engage in **political behaviour** and make things happen: they have 'clout' – weight or political influence in the organisation. A person's position in the organisation gives them access to one or more of the sources of power shown in Table 14.5.

Coercive

This is the ability to give instructions or threaten penalties, derived from a person's formal position in the hierarchy. Kramer (2006) observed how many 'Great Intimidators' work – often achieving great success for their organisation, at other times failing badly. Their tactics included:

- getting up close and personal – being directly confrontational, often using aggressive behaviour and language;
- being angry – often using a calculated loss of temper to strike fear into their opponent;
- keeping them guessing – revealing as little as possible about their plans, to increase opponents' anxiety;
- know it all – extensive preparation to be able to dominate any discussion; this includes being aware of weaknesses in the opponent's history or character.

Reward

This is the ability that position gives to use the financial and other resources of the organisation in return for support. Managers with large budgets and valuable networks of contacts use these resources, or the promise of them, to exert influence. Managers who choose to be remote and isolated in back-room work will not have that power – and so will have little influence on people or events.

Expertise

Administrative expertise

This is the power that the holder of a position has to create formal policies which support their influence attempts. They can create rules, procedures or positions that sustain their power – especially if they can also appoint loyal supporters, or those in their debt, to those positions. In this way they encourage others to act in the way they prefer – as when the new chief executive of Centrica persuaded his staff to improve customer service.

Structures and rewards at Centrica www.centrica.co.uk

management in practice

Centrica inherited severe customer relations problems when it demerged from British Gas, so restoring customer trust was an important part of the new chief executive's job. He changed the structure of Centrica to influence other managers to give it priority. Customer service satisfaction targets were included in an executive bonus scheme covering its top 200 people. Also, a senior board executive was made responsible for all customer services.

Source: Based on *Financial Times*, 24 February 2001.

key ideas

Sir John Harvey-Jones's leadership at ICI

In a classic study of ICI under Sir John Harvey-Jones, Pettigrew traced the link between the leadership of the company and the change process. Sir John implemented fundamental changes in what was then a very large company, but Pettigrew shows he did not achieve this by a few dramatic acts or decisions. Rather it depended on actions he took over many years to change the structure of the organisation so that managers had more access to sources of power with which to influence others to make radical change. For example, greater power was given to divisional directors to reward staff according to their performance.

Pettigrew concluded that studies of leadership should not focus only on the actions of individuals, important though they are. Rather they should view leadership within a context. The leader exerts influence by shaping that context and providing others with positional power to initiate change.

Source: Pettigrew (1985, 1987).

management in practice

Too much internal focus

A department of a local authority consisted of a director, 2 senior officers, 3 officers and 14 staff. The director's style was to involve himself in operational matters, and he rarely worked with other senior managers. He normally met only the senior officers in his department and rarely involved others, believing that officers should not be involved in policy. He saw himself as the only competent person in the department and was comfortable in this operational role.

Staff consider themselves to be capable and professional. They expect to be involved more fully and are used to taking initiatives. The director's involvement in operational detail annoyed staff as it showed that he did not trust their abilities. They were even more annoyed at the low status of their department, due to the director not being active externally and so lacking influence outside the department.

Technical expertise

This is the power a person gains from holding a position that gives them access to information, of being in the know, aware of what is happening and of opportunities which are emerging. They can use their position, and the contacts that go with it, to build their image as a competent person. This credibility adds to their power to influence others. It is a contentious area, since people compete for access to information, and the power that goes with it.

Referent

This is where managers use their position to influence others by showing that what they propose is consistent with the accepted values and culture of the organisation. They invoke wider values in support of their proposal. The effectiveness of the influence attempt depends on the other people having a similar view of the culture.

The more of these sources of power the manager has, the more others will cooperate. They do so because they believe that the manager has the power to make things happen. Such a manager has weight or political influence, which encourages others to cooperate.

'To increase power, share it'

Kanter (1979) also proposed that managers can increase their power by, paradoxically, **delegating** some of it to subordinates. As subordinates carry out tasks previously done by the manager, he or she has more time to build the external and senior contacts – which further boost power. By delegating not only tasks but also lines of supply (giving subordinates a generous budget), lines of information (inviting them to high-level meetings) and lines of support (giving visible encouragement), managers develop subordinates' confidence, and at the same time enhance their own power. They can spend more time on external matters, making contacts, keeping in touch with what is happening and so building their visibility and reputation. A manager who fails to delegate, and who looks inward rather than outward, becomes increasingly isolated.

Delegation occurs when one person gives another the authority to undertake specific activities or decisions.

Semco – the case continues

http:///semco.locaweb.com.br/

CASE STUDY

The offices are open plan (like those at Oticon – Chapter 10), and managers have none of the minor privileges often associated with the role, such as parking spaces, executive dining rooms or secretaries. There are very few rules, as Semler believes in treating employees like adults.

We have absolute trust in our employees . . . (and) we are proving that worker involvement doesn't mean that bosses lose power. What we do is strip away the blind, irrational authoritarianism that diminishes productivity. We're thrilled that our workers are self-governing and self-managing. It means that they care about their jobs and about their company, and that's good for all of us. (Semler, 1994, pp. 4–5)

A major innovation occurred when some engineers offered to develop new products and lines of business, working with Semco equipment and facilities in return for a share of the royalties or savings from their ideas. They would report to senior management after six months – who would extend or revoke the mandate. The group was successful, and senior managers have encouraged this 'satellite' system throughout the group. These have become highly innovative divisions within Semco, and some two-thirds of the company's new products come from satellites. Workers thrived on having complete accountability and responsibility, understanding that failure to perform would result in the unit being discontinued.

This way of growing the business has enabled it to develop from the original industrial machinery unit, which has evolved into high-tech mixing equipment used in, for example, the pharmaceutical industry. Another unit (SemcoBAC) makes cooling towers for commercial properties, and a third (Semco Johnson Controls) manages large properties such as hospitals and airports. Other units are in environmental consulting, inventory management, HRM outsourcing: in 2004 it entered a joint venture with Pitney-Bowes, the world leader in mail and document management solutions. The common theme is that they are all in markets in which the solutions are highly engineered (and therefore difficult) and in which Semco can be a market leader, able to charge a high price. Underlying all of the transformation that has taken place, Semler identifies a common core value:

If you ask people what Semco is, their answer will be the same as it was two decades ago . . . People will talk about shared ideas . . . and that comes from the freedom to ask, Why? (Semler, 2003, p. 8)

Sources: Based on material from Thunderbird, The American School of International Management, Case A15-98-0024, *Ricardo Semler and Semco S.A.*; Semler (2003); and other published material.

14.8 Choosing tactics to influence others

Another approach to the study of influence has been to identify directly how managers tried to influence others. An early example of this was work by Kipnis *et al.* (1980), who identified a set of influencing tactics that managers used in dealing with subordinates, bosses and co-workers. Yukl and Falbe (1990) replicated this work in a wider empirical study, and refined the categories – as shown in Table 14.7.

Table 14.7
Influence tactics and definitions

Tactic	Definition
Rational persuasion	The person uses logical arguments and factual evidence to persuade you that a proposal or request is viable and likely to result in the attainment of task objectives
Inspirational appeal	The person makes a request or proposal that arouses enthusiasm by appealing to your values, ideals and aspirations or by increasing your confidence that you can do it
Consultation	The person seeks your participation in planning a strategy, activity or change for which your support and assistance are desired, or the person is willing to modify a proposal to deal with your concerns and suggestions
Ingratiation	The person seeks to get you in a good mood or to think favourably of him or her before asking you to do something
Exchange	The person offers an exchange of favours, indicates a willingness to reciprocate at a later time, or promises you a share of the benefits if you help accomplish the task
Personal appeal	The person appeals to your feelings of loyalty and friendship towards him or her before asking you to do something
Coalition	The person seeks the aid of others to persuade you to do something, or uses the support of others as a reason for you to agree also
Legitimating	The person seeks to establish the legitimacy of a request by claiming the authority or right to make it or by verifying that it is consistent with organisational policies, rules, practices or traditions
Pressure	The person uses demands, threats or persistent reminders to influence you to do what he or she wants

Source: Based on Yukl and Falbe (1990).

The nine tactics cover a variety of behaviours that people can use as they try to influence others – whether subordinates, bosses or colleagues. Yukl and Tracey (1992) extended the work by examining which tactics managers used most frequently with different target groups. They concluded that managers were most likely to use:

- rational persuasion when trying to influence their boss
- inspirational appeal and pressure when trying to influence subordinates
- exchange, personal appeal and legitimating tactics when influencing colleagues.

Networking refers to 'individuals' attempts to develop and maintain relationships with others [who] have the potential to assist them in their work or career' (Huczynski, 2004, p. 305).

14.9 Influencing through networks

An important way to influence others is the ability to draw on a network of informal relationships. **Networking** refers to 'individuals' attempts to develop and maintain relationships with others [who] have the potential to assist them in their work or career' (Huczynski, 2004, p. 305). Table 14.8 shows several types of network.

Table 14.8
Types of network

Practitioners	Joined by people with a common training or professional interest, and may be formal or informal
Privileged power	Joined by people in powerful positions (usually by invitation only)
Ideological	Consisting of people keen to promote political objectives or values
People oriented	Formed around shared feelings of personal warmth and familiarity – friendship groups that people join on the basis of identity with existing participants
Strategic	Often built to help develop links with people in other organisations

The ability to influence can be greatly enhanced by being connected to many such networks, giving access to contacts and information. They help people to know what is happening in their business and to extend their range of contacts in other organisations. Strong anecdotal evidence that networking influences career progression was supported by Luthans' (1988) research described in Chapter 1, which showed that people who spent a relatively large amount of time networking received more rapid promotion than those who did not. As Thomas (2003) observed:

> in management what you know and what you have achieved will seldom be sufficient for getting ahead. Knowing and being known in the networks of influence, both for what you have achieved and for who you are, may be essential (p. 141).

Art Kleiner and Core Groups

key ideas

Kleiner suggests that organisations, despite the rhetoric about customers and stakeholders, exist to serve the interests of what he calls their Core Group – 'the people who really matter'. The nature of the Core Group varies from place to place – sometimes concentrated amongst senior managers, at others widely dispersed – but every organisation is continually acting to fulfil the perceived needs and priorities of its Core Group – the organisation goes wherever people 'perceive the core group needs and wants to go' (p. 8). 'If we are going to act effectively in a society of organisations, we need a theory to help us see organisations clearly, as they are' (p. 6).

Source: Kleiner (2003).

Kotter (1982) observed that general managers rely heavily on informal networks of contacts to get things done. This is especially necessary to influence those in other organisations – to make a sale, to gain access to a country's market or to set up a joint venture – though as Anand and Conger (2007) found, few people have the abilities required to be fully effective networkers. Hillman (2005) showed how senior managers increase their influence over the business environment by appointing ex-politicians to their boards of directors. Government policy and regulations are a major source of uncertainty in some industries, and one way to reduce that is to build close links with politicians and others with access to or influence over the government process. Hillman proposed that the value of doing this would be more pronounced in heavily regulated industries such as telecommunications, biotechnology or tobacco, than in industries such as consumer electronics or retailing, which face little regulation. She found that firms in heavily regulated industries did indeed have more directors with political experience, and that firms with politicians on their board were associated with better financial performance, especially in the heavily regulated industries.

management in practice **Influence in China and Taiwan**

Star TV (a subsidiary of Rupert Murdoch's News Corporation) developed close links with the Chinese authorities, in the hope of expanding the delivery of its entertainment channel on Chinese TV. This paid off in 2003, when it became the first foreign-owned company to receive permission for a limited nationwide service.

> Everything in China is about relationships and mutual benefit,' said Jamie Davis, head of Star TV in China. 'I think Rupert Murdoch has a very good relationship with the Chinese Government . . . and we work hard at it

FT

Source: *Financial Times*, 9 January 2003.

> The sudden elevation of Ho-chen Tan to the top job at Chunghwa Telecom last month was demonstration of the value of having friends in high places. He was in charge of transport in Taipei in the mid-1990s, when the Taiwanese President, Chen Shui-bian, was mayor of the city. Mr Ho-chen says his contacts in the administration will help Chunghwa to win a voice in how the government handles the company's privatisation: 'I hope our company can win the right to make suggestions. Perhaps my network in the current government and the faith put in me will help the company to get more opportunities.'

FT

Source: *Financial Times*, 21 February 2003.

Sparrowe and Liden (2005) note that informal networks are probably becoming more important as a means of influencing others:

> As traditional hierarchical structures have given way to flatter and more flexible forms, informal networks have become even more important in gaining access to valuable information, resources, and opportunities. The structure and composition of an individual's network allows him or her to identify strategic opportunities, marshal resources, assemble teams and win support for innovative projects ... Individuals who hold central positions in informal advice networks enjoy greater influence than those in peripheral positions (Brass, 1984) and receive more favorable performance ratings. (Sparrowe *et al.*, 2001, p. 505)

Whichever methods are used, the outcome of an influence attempt will depend not only on the tactics used but on how well the influencer is able to meet the needs of the person they are influencing – see Chapter 15.

14.10 Current themes and issues

Performance

The chapter has outlined what could be called interpersonal and structural ways of influencing others. The interpersonal methods include those based on trait and behavioural theories of influence, as well as those on tactics and networks. Structural approaches are those in which the influencer supplements their personal power sources with those that follow from their position within the organisation – the authority to promise promotion if a target is achieved, for example. While managers who develop high levels of interpersonal skills may be able to exert a great deal of influence, those who are able draw on structural sources of power are likely to be able to achieve much more.

Which of the many interpersonal and structural forms of influence are likely to be effective depends, as stressed in the chapter, on the situation in which the influence attempt is taking place. These can be distinguished on several dimensions, such as the people being influenced, the nature of the task, the dynamism or otherwise of the task environment, and the history of the relationships involved.

The essential influencing skill is that of being aware of the range of approaches, the conditions likely to favour the use of one approach rather than another, and the ability to diagnose to which of those conditions the current situation most closely corresponds. That enables the influencer to ensure that their attempts at influence enhance performance.

Responsibility

Influence is not an ethically neutral activity. The chapter has presented influencing as an essential element in the management task, being the means by which managers persuade others to act in ways that add value to resources. Both the content and the process of an influence attempt can reduce value for some stakeholders, at the same time as it may raise it for others.

Wealth can be created either by increasing the income from resources or reducing their costs. In either case it is possible that those responsible for an activity act in a way that others regard as irresponsible. This could include, for example:

- influencing customers to pay an unfairly high price because of an imbalance of power;
- influencing them to take a service or product that is inappropriate to their needs;
- influencing employees to accept less favourable or more stressful conditions to reduce costs;
- reducing costs by outsourcing or other means.

All of these could meet the criterion of adding value for the organisation, but destroying it for others.

The process by which someone influences others can also affect the distribution of wealth. Practices could include:

- using tactics that damage the target of influence, such as coercion or bullying;
- influencing through practices that may be illegal or unethical – such as bribery;
- deliberately using false or misleading information to support a case.

So although most discussion about corporate responsibility has focused on issues of customers or the environment, there are also issues about the processes of managing. Building a power base with which to influence others is an essential part of managing, but it may produce losers as well as winners. Awareness of this, and a willingness to act on it, is a mark of responsibility.

Internationalisation

The ability to manage internationally depends on being able to influence others in culturally mixed circumstances, where influence tactics that work in one place may be ineffective in another. Cross-cultural studies have found that cultural values (Chapter 4) affect the preferred influence tactics. For example Fu and Yukl (2000) found that Chinese managers rated coalition formation, giving gifts and favours, and personal appeals as more effective, and rational persuasion, consultation and exchange as less effective than did American managers. The authors noted that these preferences for influencing tactics were consistent with their respective cultural values: for the Chinese with their values of collectivism, feminism and a long-term orientation, and for the Americans with their values of equality, direct confrontation and pragmatism.

There is also evidence that styles of leadership vary between countries. Shao and Webber (2005) found that certain of 'the big five' personality traits associated with transformational leadership behaviour in North America are not evident in China. They attributed this to differences in the prevailing cultures:

> The Chinese culture, characterized as high power distance, high uncertainty avoidance and collectivism, fundamentally reinforces the hierarchical and conformist attributes of the top-down command structure. This structure emphasises a centralised authority and leadership, stability and predictability, which create barriers for the emergence of transformational leaders, who tend to challenge the status quo and raise performance expectations. (p. 943)

Summary

1 Distinguish leading from managing, and explain why each is essential to performance

- Although both are essential and the difference can be overstated, leading is usually seen as referring to activities that bring change, whereas managing brings stability and order. Many people both lead and manage in the course of their work.

2 Explain why leading and managing both depend on being able to influence others

- Achieving objectives usually depends on the willing commitment of other people. How management seeks to influence others affects people's reaction to being managed. Dominant use of power may ensure compliance, but such an approach is unlikely to produce the commitment required to meet innovative objectives.

3 Compare trait, behavioural and contingency perspectives on styles of influence

- Trait theories seek to identify the personal characteristics associated with effective influencing.
- Behavioural theories distinguish managers' behaviours on two dimensions, such as initiating structure and consideration.
- Contingency perspectives argue that the traits or behaviours required for effective influence depend on factors in the situation, such as the characteristics of the employee, the boss and the task.

4 Outline theories that focus on power (both personal and organisational) as the source of influence

- The more power a person has, the more they will be able to influence others. Table 14.5 identified sources of power as coercion, reward, expertise (administrative and technical) and referent – all of which can have both personal and organisational dimensions.

5 Contrast the style and power perspectives, and explain why sharing power may increase it

- Sharing power with subordinates may not only enable them to have more satisfying and rewarding work, but by enabling the manager to have more time to develop senior and external contacts, he or she can then enhance their power more than if they focused on internal matters.

6 Outline a model of the tactics people use to influence others, including the use of cooperative networks

- Yukl and Falbe (1990) identified these tactics in attempts to influence others: rational persuasion, inspirational appeal, consultation, ingratiation, exchange, personal appeal, coalition, legitimating and pressure. They have also found that effective influencers vary their tactics depending on the person they are trying to influence. A further line of research identifies the value of building collaborative networks as part of effective influencing.

Review questions

1 Why is the ability to influence others so central to the management role?

2 What evidence is there that traits theories continue to influence management practice?

3 What are the strengths and weaknesses of the behavioural approaches to leadership?

4 What is meant by the phrase a '9,9 manager'?

5 Discuss with someone how he or she tries to influence people (or reflect on your own practice). Compare this experience with one of the contingency approaches.

6 Evaluate that theory in the light of the evidence acquired in review question 5 and other considerations.

7 Explain in your own words the main sources of power available to managers. Give examples of both personal and institutional forms of each.

8 List the lines of power that Kanter (1979) identifies and give an example of each.

9 What does the network perspective imply for someone wishing to be a successful influencer?

Concluding critical reflection

Think about the ways in which you typically seek to influence others, and about how others in your company try to exert influence. Review the material in the chapter, and then make notes on these questions:

- What examples of the issues discussed in this chapter struck you as being relevant to practice in your company?
- Thinking of the people you typically work with, who are effective and who are less effective influencers? What do the effective people do that enables them to get their way? What interpersonal skills do they use? What sources of power, or what networks, do they use? Do the prevailing **assumptions** fit with Kanter's view that 'to increase power, share it'? On balance, do their assumptions accurately reflect the reality you see?
- What factors in the **context** – including the history of the company or your personal experience – have shaped the way you manage your attempts at influencing? Does your current approach appear to be right for your present position and company – or would you use a different approach in other circumstances? (Perhaps refer to some of the Management in Practice features for how different managers exert influence.)

▶

- Have people put forward **alternative** approaches to influencing, based on evidence about other companies? If you could find such evidence, how may it affect company practice?
- How do you and your colleagues react to the Semco approach, which appears to have helped create a successful, profitable business? What **limitations** can you see in it? Conversely what limitations does it expose in more conventional approaches to management?

Further reading

Yukl, G.A. (2004), *Leadership in Organizations* (6th edn), Prentice-Hall, Upper Saddle River, NJ.

Combines a comprehensive review of academic research on all aspects of organisational leadership with clear guidance on the implications for practitioners.

Buchanan, D. and Badham, R. (1999), *Power, Politics and Organizational Change: Winning the turf game*, Sage, London.

A modern approach to politics in organisations, offering a theoretical and practical guide, based on extensive primary research.

Huczynski, A.A. (2004), *Influencing Within Organizations* (2nd edn), Routledge, London.

Draws on a wide range of academic research to provide a practical guide to being an effective influencer – from how to conduct yourself at a job interview to coping with organisational politics.

Branson, R. (1999), *Losing My Virginity*, Virgin Books, London.

Roddick, A. (2000), *Business as Unusual*, Thorsons, London.

Semler, R. (2003), *The Seven Day Weekend: Finding the work/life balance*, Century, London.

Accounts of their approach to management by three charismatic leaders.

Kleiner, A. (2003), *Who Really Matters: The core group theory of power, privilege and success*, Doubleday, New York.

Absorbing perspective of the realities of corporate power, with many practical implications for career planning.

Adams, S. (1998), *The Dilbert Principle*, Boxtree, London.

Light relief from your studies.

Pedler, M., Burgoyne, J. and Boydell, T. (2004), *A Manager's Guide to Leadership*, McGraw-Hill, Maidenhead.

A highly practical book, based on the philosophy that leadership is defined by what people do when faced with challenging situations. The authors use their well-established self-development approach to encourage readers to act on situations requiring leadership, and then to reflect and learn from the experience.

Weblinks

Visit these websites (or others of similar companies of which you learn):

http://semco.locaweb.com.br/
http://borsen.dk
www.bmw.com
www.centrica.co.uk
www.thebodyshop.com
www.gore.com
www.oticon.com

Each of these organisations has tried to develop new approaches to managing and influencing staff, and have, despite periods of difficulty, survived and in most cases prospered. They are still quite rare, as relatively few entrepreneurs have successfully followed their example.

- Use the House model to analyse what conditions may explain their success.
- Why do you think so few others have adopted the same approach?

Annotated weblinks, multiple choice questions and other useful resources can be found on www.pearsoned.co.uk/boddy

Week 5

Management, Leadership, Change and Innovation

Chapter 13

Managing change and innovation

Aim

To outline theories of change in organisations and show how these relate to practice.

Objectives

By the end of your work on this chapter you should be able to outline the concepts below in your own terms and:

1. Explain the meaning of organisational change and give examples
2. Explain what the links between change and context imply for those managing a change
3. Compare life cycle, emergent, participative and political theories of change
4. Evaluate systematically the possible sources of resistance to change
5. Explain the meanings of organisational development and the learning organisation
6. Illustrate the factors believed to support innovation.

Key terms

This chapter introduces the following ideas:

external context
perceived performance gap
performance imperatives
organisational change
interaction model
receptive contexts
non-receptive contexts
life cycle
emergent model
participative model
political model
counterimplementation
organisation development
sensitivity training
process consultation
survey feedback
creativity
innovation
idea champions

Vodafone/Ericsson www.vodafone.com, www.ericsson.com CASE STUDY

In 2007 Vodafone offered mobile services to subscribers in 28 countries and was the world's largest mobile network operator, with about one-quarter of the market. Ericsson was the world's largest supplier of mobile network infrastructure, and Vodafone its largest customer. Vodafone has achieved its strong market position partly by internal growth and by acquiring other operators – such as AirTouch (USA) in 1998 and Mannesmann (Germany) in 2000. Many of these acquisitions also had shareholdings in other mobile operators, meaning that in some countries Vodafone operates through partially rather than wholly owned subsidiaries.

As demand for mobile services grew, Vodafone extended the network on a country-by-country basis, with local management teams running the business. They usually ordered network equipment from Ericsson, negotiating terms with Ericsson staff in their country. Although Vodafone's in-country managers communicated with their counterparts in other countries, Vodafone did not attempt to coordinate the way they operated. Ericsson operated in a more centralised fashion, though with some scope for local managers to establish terms of business that reflected their market or competitive environment.

This had the following consequences:

- Terms and conditions for purchasing network equipment varied between countries.
- Communication between the two companies in each country was direct, through meetings, telephones, letters, fax and e-mail.
- Communication about Ericsson products between Vodafone operators in different countries was *ad hoc*.
- Sharing of product information between Ericsson and Vodafone was in-country, mainly through written documents.
- Ordering and order tracking was done by local systems in each country.
- Configuration of network equipment varied between countries, as did service and support arrangements.

Before the merger with AirTouch, Vodafone management had begun to assess what synergies it could gain from the merger, especially in the supply of network equipment. The company expected to make big savings if it could aggregate its worldwide requirements for network equipment, and source this from common global suppliers. The later acquisition of Mannesmann increased the scope for synergy – and claims about the potential savings in this area were made to shareholders and the financial markets.

© Vodafone 2007.

Vodafone therefore began a project with Ericsson to develop new ways of managing the relationship. The intention was to find ways of aggregating Vodafone's global requirements so that the companies would manage their relationship in a unified way. They realised that managing a change of this scale would raise difficult issues about the:

- degree of planning to undertake
- scale and value of the synergies from a new global relationship
- attitudes of those managing Vodafone operations in the various countries
- resources that would be needed to manage the change.

Source: Based on material from Ibbott and O'Keefe (2004).

Case questions 13.1

- How may the structure of Vodafone's in-country operations affect the project?
- Will a new global relationship mean a more centralised or a more decentralised company?
- Should the two companies put significant resources into planning the change in advance?

13.1 Introduction

The manager whom Vodafone appointed to manage this change faces a problem that is familiar to many managers. The chief executive has put him in charge of implementing a major change that will affect many people, some of whom will be uneasy about how it will affect them. Changing from a country to a global structure will have implications for the way they run the business in their country, and change their relationship with their main equipment supplier.

Managers initiate or experience change so regularly that in many organisations change is seen as the normal state of affairs, interrupted by occasional periods of relative stability. In the most innovative areas of the economy some senior managers see one of their primary tasks as being to challenge current practices, hoping to foster a climate of exploration and innovation. They want people to see change as the norm – merely one further intervention in a continuing flow of events rather than something that will be followed by a return to stability. At BP, for example, the challenge to successive senior managers has been to continue transforming the business from a relatively small (for that industry), diversified business into the world's second-largest oil company. Mergers, such as that between Chrysler (USA) and Daimler (Germany), are usually followed by internal changes. Small businesses make radical changes too – as when Hindle Power, an engineering company with 30 employees, faced the loss of a valuable distribution contract unless it changed the way it worked. It embarked on a radical programme of change that returned the company to profit, and grew the business (*People Management*, 3 February 2000, p. 52).

The external environment described in Chapter 3 is the main source of change. The evolving PESTEL factors change what people expect of a business – which may encourage managers to alter their strategy or operations. Research by the Institute of Personnel and Development (IPD) into 151 large organisations found that major reasons for change were a need to create closer customer relationships, significant financial pressure to improve performance, or intensifying competition (IPD, 1999). Anecdotal evidence is that while most managers accept the need for change, many are critical of the way their organisations introduce it. Managers still experience great difficulty in implementing major organisational changes successfully.

This chapter presents theories about the nature of change in organisations. It begins by explaining current external pressures for change, and how these prompt internal change to one or more elements of the organisation. The chapter then outlines a model that shows how change depends on the interaction between the external and internal environments of the organisation. It then presents four complementary perspectives on

Activity 13.1 Recording a major change

From discussion with colleagues or managers, identify a major attempt at change in an organisation. Make notes on the following questions and use them as a point of reference throughout the chapter.

- What was the change?
- Why did management introduce it?
- What were the objectives?
- How did management plan and implement it?
- How well did it meet the objectives?
- What lessons have those involved taken from the experience?

how people try to manage that interaction, each with different management implications. Further sections deal with diagnosing the characteristics of a change, managing resistance, skills and structures, and organisation development.

13.2 Initiating change

Chapter 1 introduced the idea that managers work within a context that shapes what they do, and which they may also change. This chapter explains the interactive nature of that process, and Figure 13.1 illustrates the themes it will cover. A particular episode of change begins when enough people perceive a gap between desired and actual performance – usually because the internal context of the organisation is unable to meet the external demands upon it. Using their implicit or explicit theory of change, they initiate a project to change one or more aspects of the internal context in the hope of closing the performance gap. The outcomes of the change effort will be affected by practical issues of design and implementation – but whatever the outcomes they will in turn affect the subsequent shape of the external and internal contexts, providing the starting point for future changes.

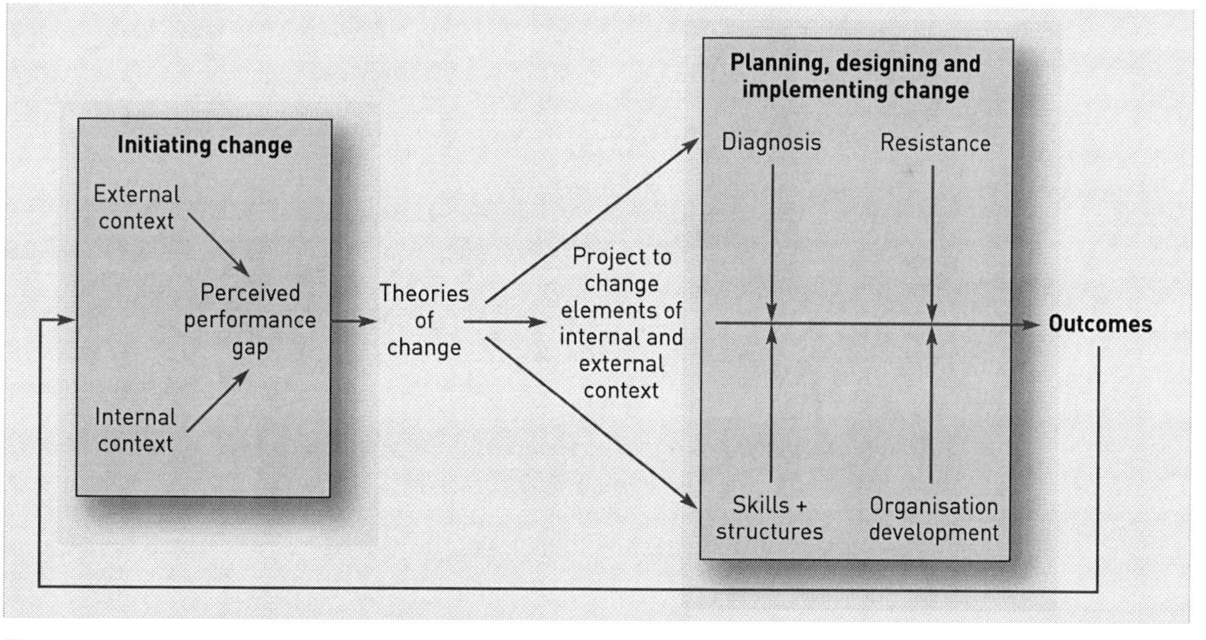

Figure 13.1 A model of the change process

The external context

Chapter 3 described the **external context** of business and successive chapters have illustrated the changes taking place, such as internationalisation, information technology and expectations about corporate responsibility. Together with deregulation and the privatisation of former state businesses these are transforming the competitive landscape in which firms operate. They face competition from unexpected quarters, threatening their prosperity or even their survival. Managers at British Airways and KLM have had to respond to the pressure of new competition from low-cost airlines such as Ryanair and

The **external context** consists of elements beyond the organisation such as competitors, or the wider PESTEL factors.

easyJet. Established banks face competition from new entrants such as retailers (Sainsbury's) or conglomerates (Virgin) offering financial services. The growth of the Internet has enabled companies offering high-value/low-weight products to open new distribution channels and invade previously protected markets.

management in practice **Successful change at GKN** www.gknplc.com

GKN is a leading global supplier to automotive, aerospace and off-highway manufacturers, employing 40,000 people in GKN companies and joint ventures. It was created by a series of mergers at the start of the twentieth century, creating Guest, Keen and Nettlefolds – then one of the largest manufacturing businesses in the world. It was involved in iron and coal mining, steel production and finished products such as nuts, bolts and fasteners.

Its present form reflects a small number of successful decisions made in the 1980s. The first was to abandon any thought of re-entering the steel industry (its interests there had been nationalised in the 1960s), and to focus instead on seeking growth in the motor components business. This decision was shaped by a piece of luck, in that in 1966 it had bought a UK engineering company and in doing so acquired a share in a German business which had worldwide patents for a unique constant velocity joint system for powering front-wheel drive cars.

A second decision was to cut back sharply on non-vehicle activities, into which the group had diversified in the 1970s. At that time unrelated diversification was a popular management strategy, but it soon became clear that unrelated businesses were best run independently: GKN soon disposed of most of that portfolio.

The third decision was to purchase Westland Helicopters – mainly because it gave GKN entry into the rapidly growing business of manufacturing aerospace components, which complemented the automotive business (Westland was sold in 2004).

In his book *Change Without Pain* Abrahamson (2004) identifies GKN as one of the most successful companies at managing significant strategic changes – not by disposing of skills, but by recombining them in ways that create even greater value – see Section 13.9 for more on Abrahamson's ideas.

Sources: *Financial Times*, 6 January 2004, 28 February 2007; *Independent*, 15 March 2007; company website.

These forces have collectively meant a shift of economic power from producers to consumers, many of whom now enjoy greater quality, choice and value. Managers wishing to retain customers need continually to seek new ways of adding value to resources if they are to retain their market position. Unless they do so they will experience a widening performance gap.

A **perceived performance gap** arises when people believe that the actual performance of a unit or business is out of line with the level they desire.

Performance imperatives are aspects of performance that are especially important for an organisation to do well, such as flexibility and innovation.

Perceived performance gap

A **perceived performance gap** arises when people believe that the actual performance of a unit or business is out of line with the level they desire. If those responsible for transforming resources into outputs do so in a way that does not meet customer expectations, there is a performance gap. Cumulatively this will lead to other performance gaps emerging – such as revenue from sales being below the level needed to secure further resources. If uncorrected this will eventually cause the business to fail.

In the current business climate, two aspects of performance dominate discussion – what Prastacos *et al.* (2002) call '**performance imperatives**': the need for flexibility and the need for innovation. In a very uncertain business world the scope for long-term planning is seriously limited. Successful businesses are likely to be those that develop a high degree of strategic and organisational flexibility, while also (Volberda, 1997) maintaining efficient and stable processes. This apparent paradox (combining flexibility and stability) reflects the fact that while companies need to respond rapidly they also need to respond efficiently. This usually depends on having developed a degree of stability and predictability in the way they transform resources into goods and services.

The other imperative identified by Prastacos *et al.* (2002) is innovation:

> to generate a variety of successful new products or services (embedding technological innovation), and to continuously innovate in all aspects of the business (p. 58).

In many areas of business, customers expect a constant flow of new products, embodying the latest scientific and technological developments: companies that fail to meet these expectations will experience a performance gap. Selling, say, an advanced mobile phone profitably depends not only on the quality of the applied research which goes into a better screen display, but also on turning that research into a desirable product *and* delivering the devices at a price which customers will pay. This depends on the organisation – the internal context of management.

The internal context

Chapter 1 introduced the internal context (Figure 1.3, repeated here as Figure 13.2) as the set of elements within an organisation that shape behaviour. Change begins to happen when sufficient influential people believe, for example, that outdated technology or a confusing structure is causing a performance gap, by inhibiting flexibility or innovation. They notice external or internal events and interpret them as threatening the performance that influential stakeholders expect. This interpretation, and their implicit theory of change, encourages them to propose a change to one or more aspects of the organisation, shown in Figure 13.2.

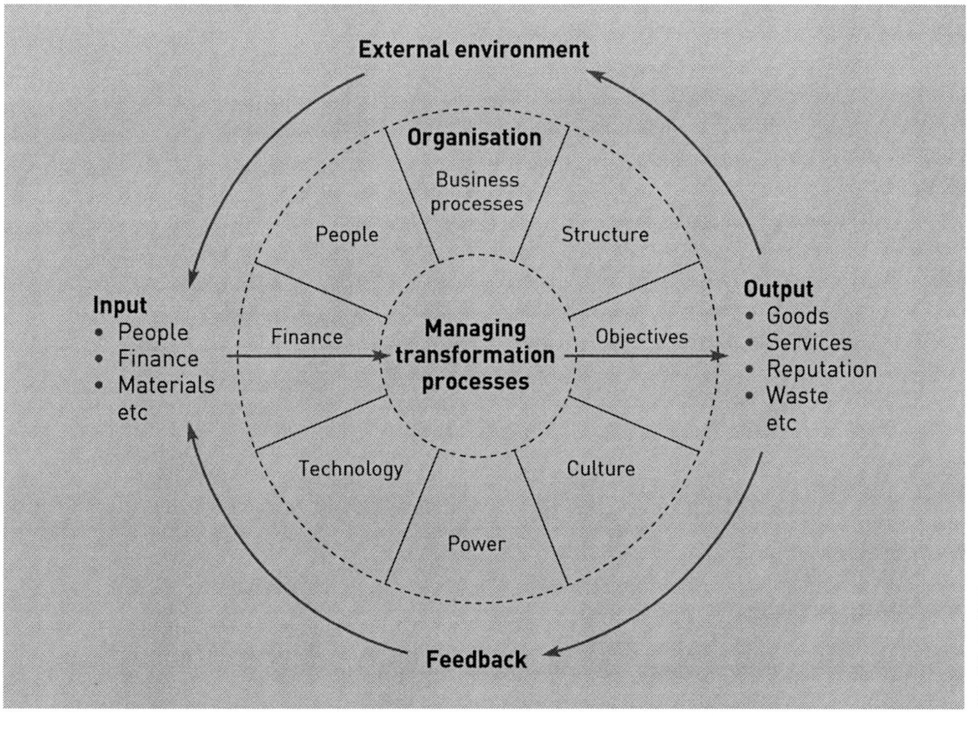

Figure 13.2
Elements of the internal context of management

They then have to persuade enough other people that the matter is serious enough to earn a place on the management agenda. People in some organisations are open to proposals for change, others tend to ignore them – BP faced new competitive pressures throughout the 1980s, but it was only around 1990 that sufficient senior people took the threats seriously enough to initiate a period of rapid change.

People initiate organisational change for reasons other than a conscious awareness of a performance gap – fashion, empire building or a powerful player's personal whim can all play a part. Employees or trade unions can propose changes in the way things are done to improve working conditions. The need for change is subjective – what some see as urgent others will leave until later. People can affect that process by managing external information – magnifying customer complaints to make the case for change, or minimising them if they wish to avoid change.

Organisational change is a deliberate attempt to improve organisational performance by changing one or more aspects of the organisation, such as its technology, structure or business processes.

Whatever the underlying motivations, **organisational change** is an attempt to change one or more of the elements shown in Figure 13.2. Table 13.1 illustrates specific types of change that people initiate under each element, including some which appear elsewhere in this book.

Table 13.1
Examples of change in each element of the organisation

Element	Example of change to this element
Objectives	Developing a new product or service Changing the overall mission or direction Oticon's new strategic objectives as a service business (Chapter 10 Case)
Technology	Building a new factory Creating a website on the Internet Pensco implementing a new computer system (see Section 13.4)
Business processes	Improving the way maintenance and repair services are delivered Redesigning systems to handle the flow of cash and funds Benetton's new system for passing goods to retailers (Chapter 20 Case)
Financial resources	A set of changes, such as closing a facility, to reduce costs New financial reporting requirements to ensure consistency The Royal Bank of Scotland reducing costs after the NatWest merger (Part 4 Case)
Structure	Reallocating functions and responsibilities between departments Redesigning work to increase empowerment Vodafone/Ericsson moving to a global structure (Chapter 13 Case)
People	Designing a training programme to enhance skills Changing the tasks of staff to offer a new service IKEA's policies to encourage high staff commitment (Chapter 15 Case)
Culture	Unifying the culture between two or more merged businesses Encouraging greater emphasis on quality and reliability GSK creating a more entrepreneurial research culture (Chapter 10)
Power	An empowerment programme giving greater authority to junior staff Centralising decisions to increase the control of HQ over operations

It is rare for any significant change to consist of only one element. The systemic nature of organisations means that a change in any of these areas is likely to have implications for others. When Tesco introduced its Internet shopping service alongside its established retail business the company needed to create a website (technology). In addition, managers needed to decide issues of structure and people (would it be part of the existing store business or a separate business unit with its own premises and staff?) and about business processes (how exactly would an order on the website be converted to a box of groceries delivered to the customer's door?). They had to manage these ripples initiated by the main decision. Managers who ignore these consequential changes achieve less than they expect.

Once they have perceived a need for change, those promoting it then use their implicit or explicit theory of change (Sections 13.3 and 13.4) to set up and implement change (Sections 13.5–13.8) in the relevant organisational unit. How well people manage the steps in this process determines the effect on the performance gap, which in turn feeds back to the context.

Case questions 13.2

Identify the possible ripple effects that may need to be managed in the Vodafone/Ericsson change, using the elements in Figure 13.2 as a guide.

- How may the move to a global relationship affect the structure area?
- What implications may that change have for other elements?
- Which of these are likely to cause most difficulty?

These begin to form the management agenda for this project. If possible compare your answers with others on the course, to see how many *alternative* possibilities you have identified.

13.3 The interaction of context and change

How managers implement change depends on their theory about its nature. This section presents an '**interaction model**', a theory of how a change interacts with its context. The following section outlines four complementary perspectives on managing that interaction.

The **interaction model** is a theory of change that stresses the continuing interaction between the internal and external contexts of an organisation, making the outcomes of change hard to predict.

People introduce change to alter the context

Management attempts to change elements of its context to encourage behaviours that close the performance gap. Vodafone wanted to change the context within which it worked with Ericsson. By moving from country relationships with Ericsson to a more unified global structure, management hoped to create a structure that enabled people in both companies to reduce the cost to Vodafone of expanding the network. When Tesco introduced online shopping management needed (at least) to change technology, structure, people and business processes to enable staff to deliver the new service. When people plan and implement a change they are creating new 'rules' (Walsham, 1993) that they hope will guide the behaviour of people involved in the activity.

People do not necessarily accept the new arrangements without question, or without adapting them in some way: in doing so they make further changes to the context. As people begin to work in new circumstances – with a new technology or a new structure – they make small adjustments to the original plan. As they use a new information system or website they decide which aspects to ignore, use or adapt.

As people become used to working with the new system their behaviours become routine and taken for granted. They become part of the context that staff have created informally. These new contextual elements may add to, or replace, the context that those formally responsible for planning the change created. These informally created aspects of the context may or may not support the original intentions of those who initiated the project. The interaction between people and context continues into the future.

management in practice **Sun Microsystems and a supplier** www.sun.com

Boddy *et al.* (2000) studied Sun Microsystems and one of their suppliers as they moved towards a more cooperative supply chain relationship. Managers in both companies introduced changes to the context of work – technology, processes and roles. These were designed to create a context that encouraged more cooperation, and closer interpersonal links, between people in the two companies. For example, the supplier's sales coordinator:

> There is a close relationship with my opposite number in Sun. We speak several times a day, and he tries to give me as much information as he possibly can.

Sun staff echoed this:

> What makes them different is that you're talking to them daily . . . The relationships are a bit different – it is a bit closer than an ordinary supplier where you don't have that bond. Dealings are more direct. People are becoming more open with each other.

Both groups came to appreciate the other's requirements and tried to make things easier for them. Sun staff learned about the supplier, and vice versa. Both spoke of 'harmonising expectations'.

Source: Boddy *et al.* (2000).

The context affects the ability to change

While people managing a project aim to change the context, the context within which they work will itself help or hinder that attempt. All of the elements of Figure 13.2 will be present as the project begins, and some of these will influence how people react. Managers who occupy influential positions in an existing structure will review a proposal to change it from the perspective of their careers, as well as of the organisation. At Tesco the existing technology (stores, distribution systems, information systems) and business processes would influence managers' decisions about how to implement the Internet shopping strategy.

The prevailing culture (Chapter 3) – shared values, ideals and beliefs – influences how people view change. Members are likely to welcome a project that they believe fits their culture or subculture, and to resist one that threatens it.

management in practice **Culture and change at a European bank**

While teaching a course to managers at a European bank, the author invited members to identify which of the four cultural types identified in Chapter 2 best described their unit within the bank. They were then asked to describe the reaction of these units to an Internet banking venture that the company was introducing.

Course members observed that colleagues in a unit that had an internal process culture (routine back-office data processing) were hostile to the Internet venture. They appeared to be 'stuck with their own systems', which were so large and interlinked that any change was threatening. Staff in new business areas of the company (open systems) were much more positive, seeing the Internet as a way towards new business opportunities.

Source: Data collected by the author.

Culture is a powerful influence on the success or failure of innovation – see Jones *et al.* (2005) for evidence of how it affected the acceptance of a new computer system. Some cultures support change: a manager in Sun Microsystems commented on that fast-moving business:

> A very dynamic organisation, it's incredibly fast and the change thing is just a constant that you live with. They really promote flexibility and adaptability in their employees. Change is just a constant, there's change happening all of the time and people have become very acclimatised to that, it's part of the job. The attitude to change, certainly within the organisation, is very positive at the moment.

Receptive contexts are those where features of the organisation (such as culture or technology) appear likely to help change.

Non-receptive contexts are those where the combined effects of features of the organisation (such as culture or technology) appear likely to hinder change.

At Sun (and many other companies such as Google or eBay) the culture encourages change, while elsewhere it encourages caution. Cultural beliefs are hard to change, yet shape how people respond:

> Managers learn to be guided by these beliefs because they have worked successfully in the past (Lorsch, 1986, p. 97).

Receptive and non-receptive contexts

key ideas

Pettigrew *et al.* (1992) sought to explain why managers in some organisations were able to introduce change successfully, while others in the same sector (the UK National Health Service) found it very hard to move away from established practices. Their comparative research programme identified the influence of context on ability to change: **receptive contexts** are those where features of the context 'seem to be favourably associated with forward movement. On the other hand, in **non-receptive contexts** there is a configuration of features that may be associated with blocks on change' (p. 268).

Their research identified seven such contextual factors, which provide a linked set of conditions that are likely to provide the energy around change. These are:

1 quality and coherence of policy
2 availability of key people leading change
3 long-term environmental pressure – intensity and scale
4 a supportive organisational culture
5 effective managerial–clinical relations
6 cooperative interorganisational networks
7 the fit between the district's change agenda and its locale.

While some of these factors are specific to the health sector, they can easily be adapted to other settings. Together these factors give a widely applicable model of how the context affects ability to change.

Source: Pettigrew *et al.* (1992).

The distribution of power also affects receptiveness to change. Change threatens the status quo, and is likely to be resisted by stakeholders who benefit from the prevailing arrangements. Innovation depends on those behind the change developing political will and expertise that they can only attempt within the prevailing pattern of power.

The context has a history, and several levels

The present context is the result of past decisions and events: Balogun *et al.* (2005) show how internal change agents adapted practice to suit aspects of their context, such as the degree of local autonomy, senior management preferences, rewards systems and financial reporting systems. Management implements change against a background of previous events that shaped the context. The promoter of a major project in a multinational experienced this in his colleagues' attitudes:

> They were a little sceptical and wary of whether it was actually going to enhance our processes. Major pan-European redesign work had been attempted in the past and had failed miserably. The solutions had not been appropriate and had not been accepted by the divisions. Europe-wide programmes therefore had a bad name. (Boddy, 2002, p. 38)

Beliefs about the future also affect how people react. Optimists are more open to change than those who feel threatened and vulnerable.

Vodafone/Ericsson – the case continues

CASE STUDY

www.vodafone.com, www.ericsson.com

Vodafone conducted business in each country in partnership with other operators, with Vodafone often having a minority shareholding in the company. For example, in the United Kingdom it owned 100 per cent of the equity, in Germany 99 per cent and in Australia 91 per cent. In The Netherlands, Portugal and Spain this fell to 70, 50 and 22 per cent respectively.

This meant that

> **considerable political skill and discussion was required to handle the attitudes of the various operating companies with regard to Ericsson's local in-country operations. Some countries had acquired very favourable terms and conditions that would not necessarily be matched by the global agreements, while others had key skills that would now be 'given up' to the global effort.**

Source: Ibbott and O'Keefe (2004), p. 226.

The context represented by Figure 13.2 occurs at (say) operating, divisional and corporate levels. People at any of these will be acting to change their context – which may help or hinder those managing change elsewhere. A project at one level may depend on decisions at another about resources, as this manager leading an oil refinery project discovered:

> One of the main drawbacks was that commissioning staff could have been supplemented by skilled professionals from within the company, but this was denied to me as project manager. This threw a heavy strain and responsibility on myself and my assistant. It put me in a position of high stress, as I knew that the future of the company rested upon the successful outcome of this project. One disappointment (and, I believe, a significant factor in the project) was that just before commissioning, the manager of the pilot plant development team was transferred to another job. He had been promised to me at the project inception, and I had designed him into the working operation. (Boddy, 2002, pp. 38–39)

Acting to change an element at one level will have effects at this and other levels, and elements may change independently. The manager's job is to create a coherent context that encourages desired behaviour, by using their preferred model of change.

Activity 13.2 Critical reflection on reactions to context

- What aspects of the contemporary context, shown in Figure 13.2, have had most effect on a project you are familiar with?
- How have historical factors affected people's reactions?
- Were the effects positive or negative for the project?
- To what extent is the context receptive or non-receptive to change?

Case questions 13.3

- How may the existing context of Vodafone and Ericsson affect how in-country managers react to the proposed change?
- How may that affect the way the project leader manages the change?

13.4 Four models of change

There are four complementary models of change, each with different implications for managers – life cycle, emergent, participative and political.

Life cycle models

Much advice given to those responsible for managing projects uses the idea of the project **life cycle**. Projects go through successive stages, and results depend on managing each one in an orderly and controlled way. The labels vary, but common themes are:

Life cycle models of change are those that view change as an activity which follows a logical, orderly sequence of activities that can be planned in advance.

1 Define objectives.
2 Allocate responsibilities.
3 Fix deadlines and milestones.
4 Set budgets.
5 Monitor and control.

This approach (sometimes called a 'rational–linear' approach) reflects the idea that a change can be broken down into smaller tasks, and that these can be done in some preferred, if overlapping, sequence. It predicts that people can make reasonably accurate estimates of the time required to complete each task and when it will be feasible to start work on later ones. People can use tools such as bar charts (sometimes called Gantt charts after the American industrial engineer Henry Gantt, who worked with Frederick Taylor), to show all the tasks required for a project, and their likely duration. These help to visualise the work required and to plan the likely sequence of events – as illustrated in Figure 13.3.

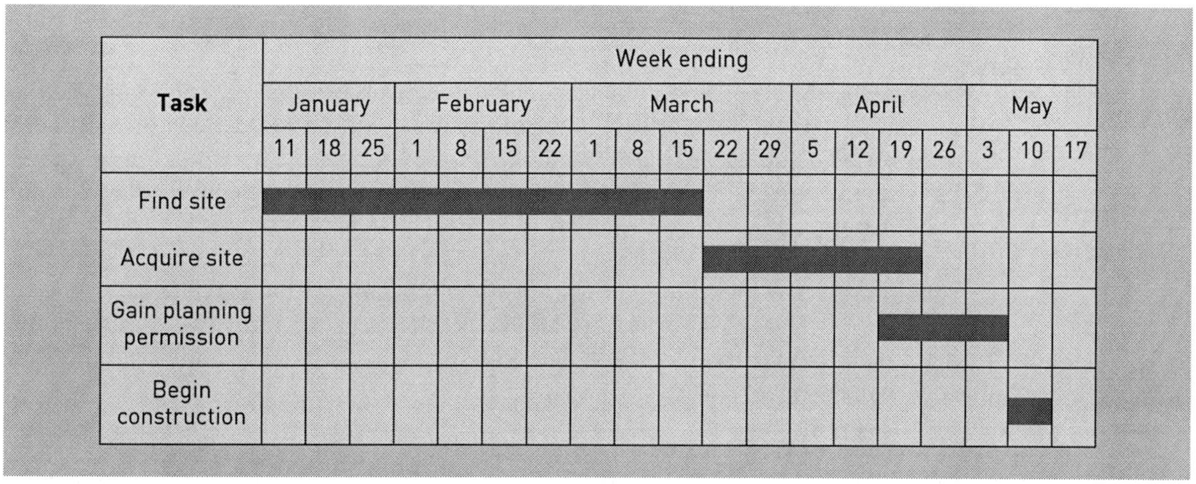

Figure 13.3 A simple bar chart

In the life cycle model successfully managing change depends on specifying these elements at the start and then monitoring them tightly to ensure the project stays on target. Ineffective implementation is due to managers failing to do this. Figure 13.4 shows the stages of a manufacturing project (Lock, 2003). He advises project managers to ensure that the stages are passed through in turn, 'until the project arrives back to the customer as a completed work package'. He emphasises the iterative, cyclical nature of the method:

> Clockwise rotation around the cycle only reveals the main stream. Within this flow many small tributaries, cross-currents and even whirlpools are generated before the project is finished (p. 26).

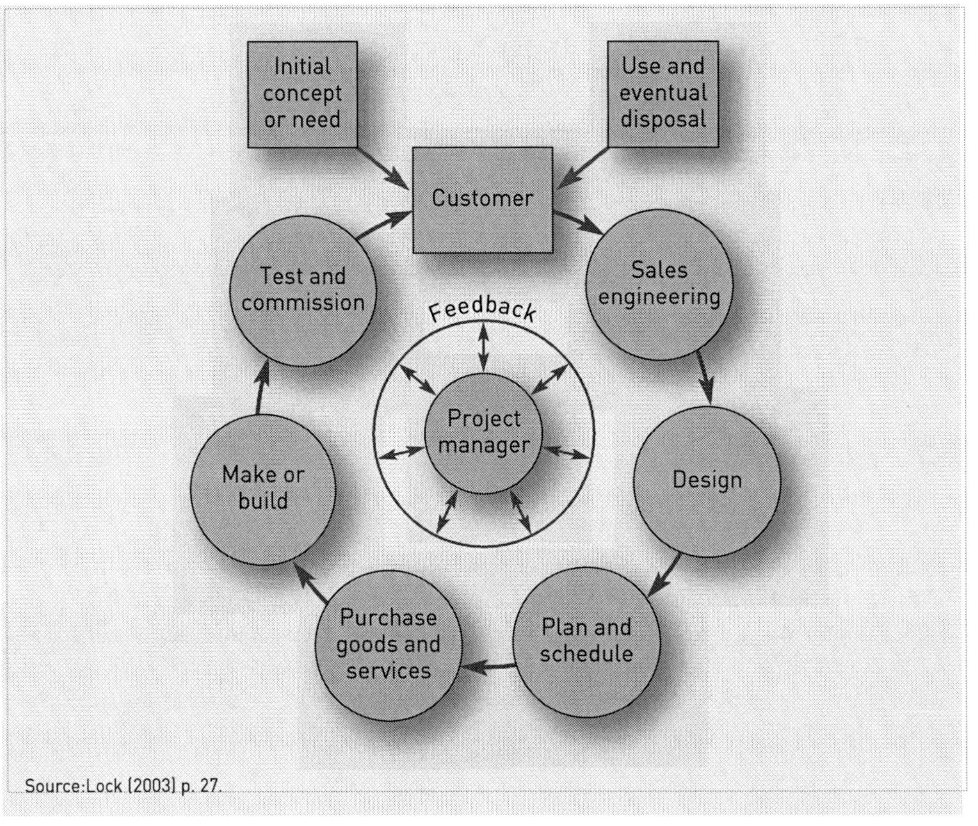

Figure 13.4
A project life cycle

Many books on project management, such as Woodward (1997) and Lock (2003), present advice on tools for each stage of the life cycle. Those advising on IS changes usually take a similar approach, recommending a variety of 'system development life cycle' approaches (Chaffey, 2003). For some changes the life cycle gives valuable guidance. It is not necessarily sufficient in itself, since people may not be able at the start to specify the end point of the change – or the tasks which will lead to that. In uncertain conditions it may make little sense to plan the outcomes in too much detail. It may be wiser to set the general direction, and adapt the target to suit new conditions that develop during the change. Those managing such change need an additional theory to cope with emergent change.

Activity 13.3 Critical reflection on the project life cycle

You may be able to gain some insight into the project life cycle by using it on a practical task. For example:

- If you have a piece of work to do that is connected with your studies, such as an assignment or project, sketch out the steps to be followed by adapting Figure 13.4; alternatively do the same for some domestic, social or management project.
- If you work in an organisation, try to find examples of projects that use this approach, and ask those involved when the method is most useful, and when least useful.
- Make notes summarising how the life cycle approach helps, and when it is most likely to be useful.

Emergent models

In Chapter 8 (Section 8.6) Barthélemy (2006) offers an insight into the strategy process at IKEA (Chapter 15 case), showing how many of its strategies have emerged from chance events or external conditions, rather than from a formal planning process. Evidence such as this led Quinn (1980) and Mintzberg (1994a, 1994b) to see strategy as an *emergent* or adaptive process. These ideas apply to change projects as much as they do to strategy. Projects are the means through which organisations deliver strategy. They take place in the same volatile, uncertain environment in which the organisation operates. People with different interests and priorities influence the means and ends of a project. So while the planning techniques associated with the life cycle approach can help, their value will be limited if the change is closer to the **emergent model.**

Emergent models of change emphasise that in uncertain conditions a project will be affected by unknown factors, and that planning has little effect on the outcome.

Vodafone/Ericsson – the case continues

www.vodafone.com, www.ericsson.com

CASE STUDY

The globalisation strategy was developed and implemented through the Global Supply Chain Management (GSCM) forum that first met in 1999. Initially it was attended by representatives from both companies in those countries where Vodafone had a majority shareholding in the local operating company, though membership gradually expanded to include most countries in which Vodafone operated. The initial meeting resolved that all joint activities should be conducted in an open and transparent way: 'It would be a process of learning through experience; there would be no requirement to produce plans that formed a rigid basis of change control' (Ibbott and O'Keefe, 2004, p. 224).

The members believed that a planned project approach would not have worked, as it was important to be able to cope with rapid change.

Both the end point and direction were uncertain, and fundamental process changes had to be agreed within and between companies. The acquisition of Mannesmann of Germany, unplanned at the start of the transformation, provided an opportunity for further benefits (p. 229).

The forum also recognised that the two sides would benefit in different ways, but there was no attempt to plan how to share the benefits – either party would retain whatever benefits they secured. Vodafone's equity-based structure in the different countries meant that those leading the project had to sell the concept of the global endeavour to the management teams of each entity. Ericsson's more unified structure of wholly owned subsidiaries gave them less scope for resisting proposals.

GSCM meetings set up several work streams that would move the relationship towards global collabora- ▶

tion. The leadership of each work stream was assigned to one or other of the participating countries. The teams leading them had to secure resources for the project from within their country operations, working as they saw fit. Examples of work streams were:

- creating a global price book for all products bought from Ericsson (UK team)
- agreeing a standard base station design (UK team)
- agreeing a common procedure for software design and testing (Australia)
- developing a computer-based information system linking the parties for information sharing – initially called groupware (The Netherlands).

While the groupware project was at first intended to support communications between the teams working on the globalisation project, it later evolved into a system through which both parties conducted routine transactions – such as ordering products. The simple communication system emerged, without any formal plan, into a system for handling all orders from Vodafone to Ericsson that had a global price.

Source: Ibbott and O'Keefe (2004).

Boddy *et al.* (2000) show how this emergent process occurred when Sun Microsystems began the partnering project described earlier. Sun's initial intention was to secure a UK source for the bulky plastic enclosures that contain their products, while the supplier was seeking ways to widen its customer base. There were few discussions about a long-term plan. As Sun became more confident of its supplier's ability it gave them more complex work. Both gained from this emerging relationship. They acknowledge that at first they did not foresee the amount and type of business they would eventually be undertaking. A sales coordinator:

> It's something we've learnt by being with Sun – we didn't imagine that at the time. Also at the time we wouldn't have imagined we would be dealing with America the way we do now – it was far beyond our thoughts. (Boddy *et al.*, 2000, p. 1010)

Mintzberg's point is that managers should not expect rigid adherence to 'the plan'. Some departure from it is inevitable, due to unforeseeable changes in the external environment, the emergence of new opportunities, and other unanticipated events. A flexible approach to change is one which recognises that

> the real world inevitably involves some thinking ahead of time as well as some adaptation en route (Mintzberg, 1994a, p. 24).

Case questions 13.4

- Were those leading the change taking a life cycle or an emergent view?
- Which of those views does the evidence of later events seem to support?

Participative models

The **participative model** is the belief that if people are able to take part in planning a change they will be more willing to accept and implement the change.

Those advocating **participative models** stress the benefits of personal involvement in, and contribution to, events and outcomes. The underlying belief is that if people can say 'I helped to build this', they will be more willing to live and work with it, whatever it is. It is also possible that since participation allows a wider range of views to be expressed the outcome will be of higher quality than if it takes account of a limited range of views. Empirical support for this was provided by the study by Ketokivi and Castañer (2004), cited in Chapter 6 (Section 6.4). They found that when employees participated in planning strategic change, they were more likely to view the issues from the perspective of the organisation, rather than their own position or function. Participation can be good for the organisation, as well as the individual.

Enid Mumford and participation

key ideas

A leading advocate and practitioner of participative approaches to change was Edith Mumford, who applied the principles of socio-technical systems in her work. This theory was outlined in Chapter 2 (Section 2.7) and is based on the idea that an organisation has both technical and social components. Mumford and her colleagues focused on change based on the introduction of computer systems, noting that IS development projects typically overemphasised the technical, and underestimated the social aspects. She sought, through the development of the ETHICS method (Mumford and Weir, 1979), to enable developers to give adequate attention to both. Advocates claimed that this approach would lead to systems that not only worked (from a technical perspective) but were also more attractive from a human point of view, enhancing motivation and job satisfaction.

The approach required a high degree of participation by users in the design, to ensure as much compatibility with the social system in which the technology would be set. This participative approach typically involved people in decisions about the design of the system, and in making decisions within a work team about its operation. Reflecting on the limited acceptance of participative systems in recent years, she concludes that a major barrier has been that of the cultural context. With many organisations retaining a hierarchical form, those in higher positions are frequently reluctant to give up power to the degree implied by participative approaches to change (Mumford, 1997, 2006).

Source: Mumford (1997, 2006).

Staff participation in planning the CGU merger

management in practice

One of the UK's biggest mergers in 1998 was that of Commercial Union and General Accident to form CGU. The merger involved many changes, and management decided to involve employees in planning these, mainly through three large meetings of hundreds of staff, nominated by their colleagues:

1 Two hundred staff conducted a culture survey of the two companies. They were paired, one from each company, and escorted each other into the other's company, where they used a set format to build a culture map – how the firms were similar and how they differed.
2 Five hundred managers and technical specialists attended a two-day conference to work in teams on the results of the culture survey and other data. Their task was to form a view about what would make CGU the 'best place to work'. Video cameras captured the action and displayed it overhead on giant television screens around the hall, giving the two days the feel of a vibrant sporting event. Amongst the priorities the delegates agreed were clear boundaries of authority, freedom to take decisions within those boundaries, clear expectations, feedback, access to opportunity, and support for development.
3 Eighty people attended a four-day structured design workshop. Their task was to start designing a new organisation to meet the needs of shareholders, customers, employees and business partners. They produced a design that included principles of access (ensuring all would have easy entrance to their new offices), size of business units (30 to 50 people), and size of teams (between 10 and 12).

▶

Tony Clarry commented:

The roll-out in the 51 locations so far has been smooth, which we attribute to the degree of commitment to the integration teams and to the conscientiousness of our people. Of course, there has been pain ... but involving people in decision making continues to be at the heart of what we do. We believe our approach has proved the value of real consultation.

Source: Based on an article by Tony Clarry, who led the integration of the two companies, in *People Management*, 2 September 1999.

While the approach is consistent with democratic values, it is not free. It takes time and effort, and may raise unrealistic expectations. It may be inappropriate when:

- there is already agreement on how to proceed;
- the scope for change is limited, because of decisions made elsewhere;
- those taking part in the exercise have little knowledge of the topic;
- decisions are needed urgently to meet deadlines set elsewhere;
- management has decided what to do and will do so whatever views people express;
- there is fundamental disagreement and inflexible opposition to a change.

Participative approaches assume that a sensitive approach by reasonable people will result in the willing acceptance and implementation of change. Other situations contain conflicts that participation alone cannot solve.

Activity 13.4 Critical reflection on participation

Have you been involved in, or affected by, a change in your work or studies?

If so

- What evidence was there that those managing the change agreed with the participative approach?
- In what way, if any, were you able to participate?
- How did that affect your reaction to the change?

If not:

- Identify three advantages and three disadvantages for the project manager in adopting a participative approach.
- Suggest how managers should decide when to use the approach.

Political models

The models described so far offer little guidance where a change challenges established interests, or where powerful players have opposing views. Change often involves people from several levels and functions who will pull in different directions, pursuing personal as well as organisational goals:

> Strategic processes of change are ... widely accepted as multi-level activities and not just as the province of a ... single general manager. Outcomes of decisions are no longer assumed to be a product of rational ... debates but are also shaped by the interests and commitments of individuals and groups, forces of bureaucratic momentum, and the manipulation of the structural context around decisions and changes. (Whipp *et al.*, 1988, p. 51)

Several analyses of organisational change emphasise a **political model** (Pettigrew, 1985, 1987; Pfeffer, 1992a; Pinto, 1998; Buchanan and Badham, 1999). Pettigrew (1985) was an early advocate of the view that change requires political as well as rational (life cycle) skills. Successful change managers create a climate in which people accept the change as legitimate – often by manipulating apparently rational information to build support for their ideas.

Political models reflect the view that organisations are made up of groups with separate interests, goals and values, and that these affect how they respond to change.

Tom Burns on politics and language

key ideas

Tom Burns (1961) observed that political behaviour in the organisation is invariably concealed or made acceptable by subtle shifts in the language that people use:

> Normally, either side in any conflict called political by observers claims to speak in the interests of the corporation as a whole. In fact, the only recognised, indeed feasible, way of advancing political interests is to present them in terms of improved welfare or efficiency, as contributing to the organisation's capacity to meet its task and to prosper. In managerial and academic, as in other legislatures, both sides to any debate claim to speak in the interests of the community as a whole; this is the only permissible mode of expression. (p. 260)

Pfeffer (1992a) also argues that power is essential to get things done, since decisions in themselves change nothing. It is only when someone implements them that anyone notices a difference. He proposes that projects require more than people able to solve technical problems. Projects frequently threaten the status quo: people who have done well in the past are likely to resist them. Innovators also need to ensure the project is on the agenda, and that senior managers support and resource it. Innovators also need to develop a political will, and to build and use their power. Buchanan and Badham (1999) consider why political behaviour occurs, and conclude that:

> Its roots lie in personal ambition, in organisation structures that create roles and departments which compete with each other, and in major decisions that cannot be resolved by reason and logic alone but which rely on the values and preferences of the key actors.
>
> Power politics and change are inextricably linked. Change creates uncertainty and ambiguity. People wonder how their jobs will change, how their workload will be affected, how their relationships with colleagues will be damaged or enhanced. (p. 11)

Reasonable people may disagree about means and ends, and fight for the action they prefer. This implies that successful project managers understand that their job requires more than technical competence, and are able and willing to engage in political actions.

Henry Kissinger on politics in politics

key ideas

In another work Pfeffer (1992b) quotes Henry Kissinger:

> Before I served as a consultant to Kennedy, I had believed, like most academics, that the process of decision-making was largely intellectual and all one had to do was to walk into the President's office and convince him of the correctness of one's view. This perspective I soon realised is as dangerously immature as it is widely held. (p. 31)

Source: Pfeffer (1992b).

management in practice — Politics and change in the public sector

These views of change as a fluid process find support in a contemporary account of project management in the public sector, based on research amongst a group of managers implementing major change projects:

> **The powerful influence of the political process on organisational and cultural change is transparent for local authorities, but this may also be relevant in other non-elected organisations. Competing values and interests between different stakeholders are often less overt but none the less powerful factors championing or blocking processes of change.**

Source: Hartley *et al.* (1997) p. 71.

The political perspective recognises the messy realities of organisational life. Major changes will be technically complex and challenge established interests. These will pull in different directions and pursue personal as well as organisational goals. To manage these tensions managers need political skills as well as those implied by life cycle, emergent and participative perspectives.

They need to be sensitive to the power and influence of key individuals, aware of how the change may alter those, and able to negotiate and sell ideas to indifferent or sceptical colleagues. They may have to filter information to change perceptions, and do things that make the change seem legitimate within the organisation.

management in practice — Political action in hospital re-engineering

Managers in a hospital responded to a persistent performance gap (especially unacceptably long waiting times) by 're-engineering' the way patients moved through and between the different clinical areas. This included creating multi-functional teams responsible for all aspects of the flow of the patient through a clinic, rather than dealing with narrow functional tasks. The programme was successful, but was also controversial. One of those leading the change recalled:

> **I don't like to use the word manipulate, but ... you do need to manipulate people. It's about playing the game. I remember being accosted by a very cross consultant who had heard something about one of the changes and he really wasn't very happy with it. And it was about how am I going to deal with this now? And it is about being able to think quickly. So I put it over to him in a way that he then accepted, and he was quite happy with. And it wasn't a lie and it wasn't totally the truth. But he was happy with it and it has gone on.**

Source: Buchanan (2001), p. 13.

management in practice — Pensco

Pensco was a life insurance business. Changes to legislation brought new opportunities in the market for personal and group pensions, and also more competition. The board appointed a new general manager who began to change the organisation towards a market-led, sales-maximising approach. He recruited a colleague from his previous company as head of information systems (IS), who had a reputation as an autocratic and aggressive manager. Changing the pensions products depended on new IS to process the new business.

The actuarial department (AD) proposed some new pension products. Staff in sales and marketing (S&M) interpreted the market differently, were dismissive of the AD proposals, and actively lobbied for their alternative ideas. S&M also believed that the IS department had

> **too much power in the organisation ... We are working to change that. S&M should drive the organisation ... But I can't get away from the view that IS still dictate what the company can and can't do.** (Knights and Murray, 1994, p. 187)

For their part, IS had trouble identifying the business requirements – partly because of unresolved conflicts between AD and S&M over the product range. The head of IS was seen to be seeking favour with the general manager by accepting all requests for systems developments – which staff were unable to deliver.

The company presented the project as a success. The authors of the case reported different views from the clerical staff who were processing new proposals (without adequate IS support). As a team leader commented:

> **They [the managers] don't have a grasp of what's going on. They just want the figures. They don't appreciate our problems. I wish they'd acknowledge there is one.** (p. 162).

Source: Based on Knights and Murray (1994).

These perspectives (life cycle, emergent, participative and political) are complementary in that successful large-scale change, such as that at Vodafone/Ericsson, is likely to require elements of each. Table 13.2 illustrates how each perspective links to management practice.

Table 13.2 Perspectives on change and examples of management practice

Perspective	Themes	Example of management practices
Life cycle	Rational, linear, single agreed aim, technical focus	Measurable objectives; planning and control devices such as Gantt charts and critical path analysis
Emergent	Objectives change as learning occurs during the project, and new possibilities appear	Open to new ideas about scope and direction, and willing to add new resources if needed
Participative	Ownership, commitment, shared goals, people focus	Inviting ideas and comments on proposals, ensuring agreement before action, seeking consensus
Political	Oppositional, influence, conflicting goals, power focus	Building allies and coalitions, securing support from powerful players, managing information

13.5 Driving and restraining forces – Kurt Lewin

Lewin (1947) observed that any social system is in a state of temporary equilibrium. Driving forces are trying to change the situation in directions they favour. Restraining forces push the other way to prevent change, or to move it in another direction. This equilibrium 'can be changed either by adding forces in the desired direction, or by diminishing the opposing forces' (p. 26). Figure 13.5 illustrates the idea: see Burnes (2004) for an appraisal of the influence and continued relevance of Lewin's ideas.

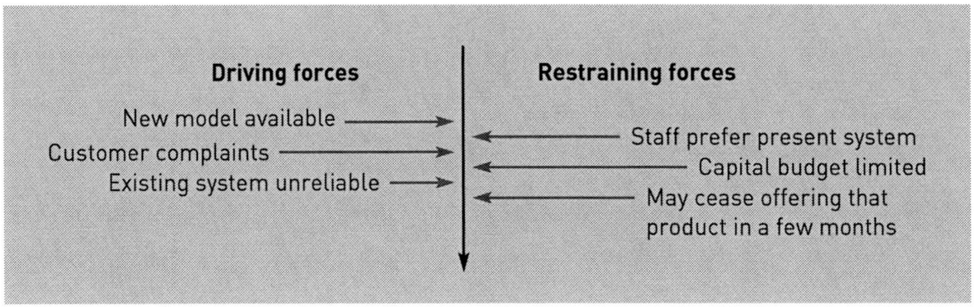

Figure 13.5 Driving and restraining forces

Driving forces encourage change from the present position. They encourage people and groups to give up past practice and to act in ways that support the change. They take many forms – such as a newly available technology, an inadequate business process or the support of a powerful player. Conversely factors such as the already-installed technology, shortage of finance, the opposition of powerful players or the company culture can be restraining forces. In many small companies, managers are said to be so absorbed in day-to-day matters that they are unable to put time and energy into major changes that would help the business to grow. They become committed to maintaining existing practice.

Those advocating a change can, in Lewin's terms, 'add forces in the desired direction' by stressing the advantages of the change, emphasising the threat from competitors or making the benefits seem more attractive. Mr Yun Jong-yon, chief executive of Samsung Electronics, was credited with transforming the company from a struggling producer of cheap electronics into one of the world's best-performing and most respected IT companies. He explained part of his approach:

> I'm the chaos-maker. I have tried to encourage a sense of crisis to drive change. We instilled in management a sense that we could go bankrupt any day. (*Financial Times*, 13 March 2003, p. 15)

Alternatively they can seek to 'diminish the opposing forces' by showing that the problems will not be as great as people fear, or pointing out that difficulties will be temporary.

Lewin observed that while increasing the driving forces could produce change in the desired direction, it could also increase tension amongst those 'forced' to change. The change may then be short-lived, or offset by the negative effects of the tension. Since these secondary effects may go against the interests of those promoting change, he suggested that trying to reduce the forces restraining change is usually the wiser route. The Management in Practice feature shows an alternative view – namely that increasing the driving forces can also work.

management in practice

The power of the visual image

Kotter and Cohen (2002) give several examples of the use of dramatic visual images to overcome inertia. In one case, showing a video of an angry customer to employees sparked a sense of urgency that helped to overcome long-standing resistance to improving the product. Another explains how a taskforce handling poor investment planning made a light-hearted video with spoof characters who mimicked the damaging behaviour of senior executives. The video apparently shocked the executives into changing their behaviour. Kotter believes that the main reason why change efforts of any size fail is that there is not a great enough sense of urgency about the need to change – and that visual shocks can help break that barrier.

Source: Kotter and Cohen (2002).

External events can trigger and drive change: new competition, a change in legislation, the activities of a pressure group, a chance conversation. Information from any of these sources can trigger change. People with sufficient power can use these and countless other external signs to justify a proposal.

In the same way, forces within the organisation – changing management priorities, the availability of funds, opposition from groups who see their privileges threatened – can drive change, or restrain it. The degree and direction of change in an organisation reflect the shifting balance and direction of the driving and restraining forces.

13.6 Forms and sources of resistance to change

Most managers are expected to implement change in the context in which they work. In doing so they use their power to influence others to act in a particular way. Chapter 14 outlines theories of power and influence, so this and the following sections examine just three aspects of this activity – understanding resistance to change, using front-stage and back-stage tactics, and supporting individual activity with formal structures.

Much of the management literature presents resistance to change in pejorative terms as something to be overcome, but this discussion takes a more neutral stance. There is anecdotal evidence of managers introducing change to further personal interests – to build a reputation or extend departmental influence. Since organisations comprise political and career systems as well as working systems, this is inevitable. Even when people intend to support organisational interests they may misinterpret the situation and propose misguided changes.

For all these reasons people at all levels will sometimes resist change, either as a threat to their interests or because they believe it will damage the organisation. Many change programmes fade from view – unless someone is able to make the change stick by creating a favourable context (Roberto and Levesque, 2005).

Forms of resistance

Overt and public resistance is often unnecessary. There are many other ways in which those opposed to a change can delay it, including:

- making no effort to learn
- using older systems whenever possible
- not attending meetings to discuss the project
- excessive fault finding and criticism
- deliberate misuse
- saying it has been tried before and did not work then
- protracted discussion and requests for more information
- linking the issue with pay or other industrial relations matters
- not releasing staff for training.

These delaying tactics come from anywhere in the organisation – they are as likely to come from managers who see a change as a threat to their interests as they are to come from more junior staff. Change creates winners and losers, and potential losers are apt to engage in what Keen (1981) termed the tactics of **counterimplementation**.

Counterimplementation refers to attempts to block change without displaying overt opposition.

key ideas Peter Keen on counterimplementation

Keen (1981) suggested that overt resistance to change is often risky, and may not in practice be necessary. He identified several ways in which those wanting to block a change can do so – even while appearing to support it. They include such tactics as:

- **Divert resources** Split the budget across other projects; give key staff other priorities and allocate them to other assignments; arrange for equipment to be moved or shared.
- **Exploit inertia** Suggest that everyone wait until a key player has taken action or read the report or made an appropriate response; suggest that the results from some other project should be monitored and assessed first.
- **Keep goals vague and complex** It is harder to initiate appropriate action in pursuit of aims that are multidimensional and specified in generalised, grandiose or abstract terms.
- **Encourage and exploit lack of organisational awareness** Insist that 'we can deal with the people issues later', knowing that these will delay or kill the project.
- **'Great idea – let's do it properly'** And let's bring in representatives from this function and that section, until we have so many different views and conflicting interests that it will take for ever to sort them out.
- **Dissipate energies** Have people conduct surveys, collect data, prepare analyses, write reports, make overseas trips, hold special meetings ...
- **Reduce the champion's influence and credibility** Spread damaging rumours, particularly amongst the champion's friends and supporters.
- **Keep a low profile** It is not effective openly to declare resistance to change because that gives those driving change a clear target.

Source: Based on Keen (1981).

Activity 13.5 Critical reflection on resistance

Discuss with someone who has tried to introduce change in an organisation what evidence there was of resistance.

- Which of the forms listed by Keen (in Key Ideas above) were in evidence?
- Can they identify any other forms?

Then consider these questions:

- Have you ever resisted a proposed change?
- What form did your resistance take?

Sources of resistance

Kotter and Schlesinger (1979) identified that sources of resistance included self-interest, misunderstanding and lack of trust: 'people also resist change when they do not understand its implications and perceive that it might cost them much more than they will gain' (p. 108). Employees assess the situation differently from their managers and may see more costs than benefits for both themselves and the company. Recardo (1991) made similar points from a study of new manufacturing systems. Change requires learning and exposure to uncertainty, insecurity and new social interactions, yet communication about the changes is often poor. Additional factors that Recardo identified as causing resistance were reward systems that did not reward the desired behaviour and a poor fit between the change and the existing culture.

These views can be enlarged by using the elements of the organisation shown in Figure 13.2. People can base their resistance on any of these contextual elements, as shown in Table 13.3.

Table 13.3 Sources of resistance to change

Element	Source of resistance
Objectives	Lack of clarity or understanding of objectives, or disagreement with those proposed
People	Change may threaten important values, preferences, skills, needs and interests
Technology	May be poorly designed, hard to use, incompatible with existing equipment, or require more work than is worthwhile
Business processes	As for technology, and may require unwelcome changes to the way people deal with colleagues and customers
Financial resources	Scepticism about whether the change will be financially worthwhile, or less so than other competing changes; lack of money
Structure	New reporting relationships or means of control may disrupt working relationships and patterns of authority
Culture	People likely to resist a change that challenges core values and beliefs, especially if they have worked well before
Power	If change affects ownership of and access to information, those who see they will lose autonomy will resist

In addition to these substantive or content reasons for resisting change, people may also resist because of the way others manage the change. They object to the process of change, irrespective of the specific change being made. Change is disturbing, and people are likely to resist if they do not feel they have been able to participate in discussions about the form it should take.

13.7 Organisation development

Organisation development (OD) is a comprehensive and widely used approach to managing change. It embodies a clear set of values about people and work, many of which relate to ideas on organisation culture (Chapter 3), human resource management (Chapter 11), and work design (Chapter 15).

Organisation development is a systematic process in which applied behavioural science principles and practices are introduced with the goal of increasing individual and organisational performance.

A common theme in managing is how to balance the needs of the individual with the behaviour required for high organisational performance. OD practitioners believe that

> with appropriate interventions based on social scientific understanding, the conflicting interests of organizations and their members can be diagnosed and reconciled. (Huczynski and Buchanan, 2007, p. 560)

Practitioners use OD to resolve conflicts within a single business unit or for the organisation as a whole, aiming for both individual development and organisational effectiveness. They try to achieve these mutually supporting goals through deliberate and systematic interventions, using knowledge from the social and behavioural sciences.

Robbins (2001, p. 553) outlines the values that underlie most OD activities:

- The individual should be treated with respect and dignity.
- The organisation climate should be characterised by trust, openness and support.

- Hierarchical authority and control are de-emphasised.
- Problems and conflicts should be confronted, not disguised or avoided.
- People affected by change should be involved in its implementation.

Some practitioners believe that this agenda is worth pursuing in its own right, though others stress that implementing practices based on these values will make a business more efficient and effective.

A common theme in OD is that bureaucracy is an obstacle to performance, and that an organisation in which staff have more freedom and flexibility in the way they work will also show a better financial performance. Table 13.4 summarises how OD practitioners tackle these problems in both private and public sector organisations (Bate, 2000).

Table 13.4
Bureaucratic diseases and OD cures

Bureaucratic disease	Symptoms	OD cures
Rigid functional boundaries	Conflict between sections, poor communications	Team building, job rotation, structural change
Fixed hierarchies	Frustration, boredom, narrow specialist thinking	Training, job enrichment, career development
Information only flows down	Lack of innovation, minor problems escalate	Process consultation, management development
Routine jobs, tight control	Boredom, absenteeism, conflict with supervisors	Job enrichment, job rotation, supervisory training

Source: Buchanan and Huczynski (2007), p. 563.

Common OD techniques are listed below, and more detail on each is contained in Huczynski and Buchanan (2007, pp. 568–572).

Sensitivity training is a technique for enhancing self-awareness and changing behaviour through unstructured group discussion.

- **Sensitivity training** Conducted in small groups, the aim of **sensitivity training** is to allow participants to discuss themselves, to observe and discuss how the members interact with each other and to exchange feedback on each other. The intention is that through such discussions participants become more sensitive to their behaviour, the effects they have on others, and how others see and relate to them.
- **Changing structure** OD projects often include efforts to decentralise organisations by giving more decision-making power to local units, or changing the horizontal structure of the organisation through business process redesign. Structural changes signify which areas of the organisation are becoming more significant, and which are in decline.

Process consultation is an OD intervention in which an external consultant facilitates improvements in an organisation's diagnostic, conceptual and action planning skills.

- **Process consultation** A consultant undertakes **process consultation** to help members of the organisation to develop a clearer insight into the problems facing the organisation, as distinct from an external consultant doing the analysis. It is consistent with core OD values that people are ultimately responsible for their development.

Survey feedback is an OD intervention in which the results of an opinion survey are fed back to respondents to trigger problem solving on the issues the survey identifies.

- **Survey feedback** This refers to the technique of conducting a survey of employee attitudes, and providing managers or supervisors with anonymous analyses of the results – hence the term **survey feedback**. Respondents may be invited to suggest themes or questions to include in the survey, and to take part in group discussions of the results.
- **Team building** Attempts to develop more effective teams using a wide variety of methods, such as that developed by Meredith Belbin (1993) in which members identify the distinctive team roles they play, and how different combinations affect performance (Chapter 17).

- **Intergroup development** This helps overcome the boundaries which can arise between groups that are expected to work together. Functional boundaries and diverse experiences lead groups to develop a strong internal identity – and possibly strong negative feelings towards other groups. Intergroup development helps to break down assumptions, and encourage more cooperative working across boundaries.
- **Grid organisation development** This is an application of Blake and Mouton's (1979) managerial grid, described in Chapter 14. The grid assumes that leadership styles vary on two dimensions – concern for production and concern for people. Managers can be assessed on the extent to which they are high, medium or low on each dimension. The prescription is that ideally they should be high on both, and the technique is intended to help managers reflect on their style, and move closer to the ideal type.

13.8 Stimulating innovation

An increasingly common aspect of managers' jobs is the pressure to stimulate innovation in the areas for which they are responsible. This covers being innovative in creating new products and services, and in the processes that deliver them. Some organisations have developed a reputation for being better able than others at sensing and satisfying consumer trends.

Lorne and Agnes Campbell and TravelCo

management in practice

TravelCo is an entrepreneurial travel company that specialises in delivering customised, luxurious holidays to US visitors interested in Scottish heritage. Employees must follow highly specified routines and systems in matters such as ticketing and scheduling: this is essential to ensure error-free reservations and other arrangements for their customers. However the same employees must be able to devise creative solutions to meet customers' individual requirements for their visit to Scotland – from where their ancestors often came. The company encourages employees to think laterally and creatively for this aspect of the work.

It does this by allowing them wide decision-making powers to come up with imaginative holiday ideas. An example was a US customer who wanted his itinerary to include an opportunity to meet some of his Clan Campbell ancestors. His guide, Abigail Forbes, was able to arrange for him to lunch with Lorne and Agnes Campbell, her 80-something grandparents in the ancient Scottish town of Inverary – which delighted the visitor as an imaginative and innovative way of achieving exactly what he wanted.

Source: Private communication.

Creativity and innovation

Creativity refers to the ability to combine ideas in a new way, or to make unusual associations between ideas. This helps people and organisations to generate imaginative ideas or ways of working: but that in itself does not ensure added value. That only comes when people turn the creative process into products or services that meet a demand, which they can meet profitably. In the public sector **innovation** is reflected in new ways of delivering services (such as the growing provision of online services); in the charities sector it could be a new way of raising funds, such as the RED brand associated with leading pop stars, which devotes a proportion of its profits to designated charities.

Creativity is the ability to combine ideas in a unique way, or to make unusual associations between ideas.

Innovation is the process of taking a creative idea and turning it into a useful product, service or method of operation.

Stimulating innovation

The systems model introduced in Chapter 1 helps to understand how organisations can become more innovative. Figure 13.6 shows that getting the desired outputs (more innovative products or work methods) depends on both the inputs and the transformation of those inputs.

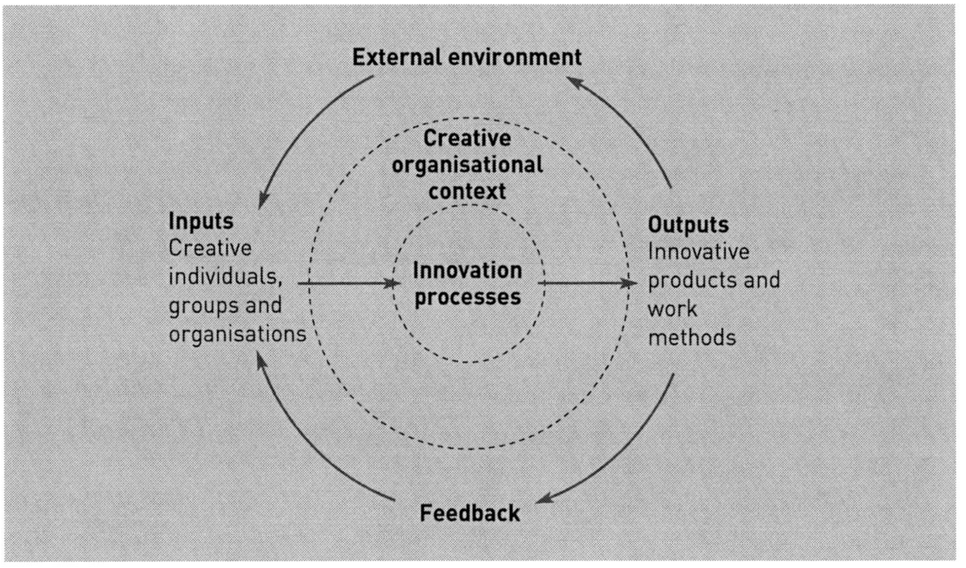

Figure 13.6
Systems view of innovation

Inputs include having creative people and groups who are able to generate novel ideas and methods, but creative people can only sustain their creativity in a favourable context. Figure 13.7 shows three significant elements of that context – cultures, HR policies and structures.

Cultures for innovation

Innovative organisations tend to have cultures that encourage experimentation, reward success and accept that some failures are inevitable – a source of learning rather than shame. Robbins and Coulter (2005, p. 329) suggest that an innovative culture is likely to have these features:

- *Acceptance of ambiguity* Too much emphasis on objective analysis and detailed planning constrains creativity.
- *Tolerance of the impractical* Individuals who offer impractical, even foolish, answers to speculative questions are not ridiculed. What at first seems impractical may lead to innovative solutions.
- *Low external controls* Rules, regulations and procedures are kept to a minimum.
- *Tolerance of risk* Employees are encouraged to experiment without fear of the consequence if they fail. Mistakes become opportunities for learning.
- *Tolerance of conflict* Diversity of opinions is encouraged. Harmony and agreement between people and sub-units is not taken as a sign of high performance.
- *Focus on end rather than means* Goals are clear, but individuals choose how to achieve them.
- *Open system focus* People are encouraged to monitor the business environment and to be ready to respond to change as it occurs.

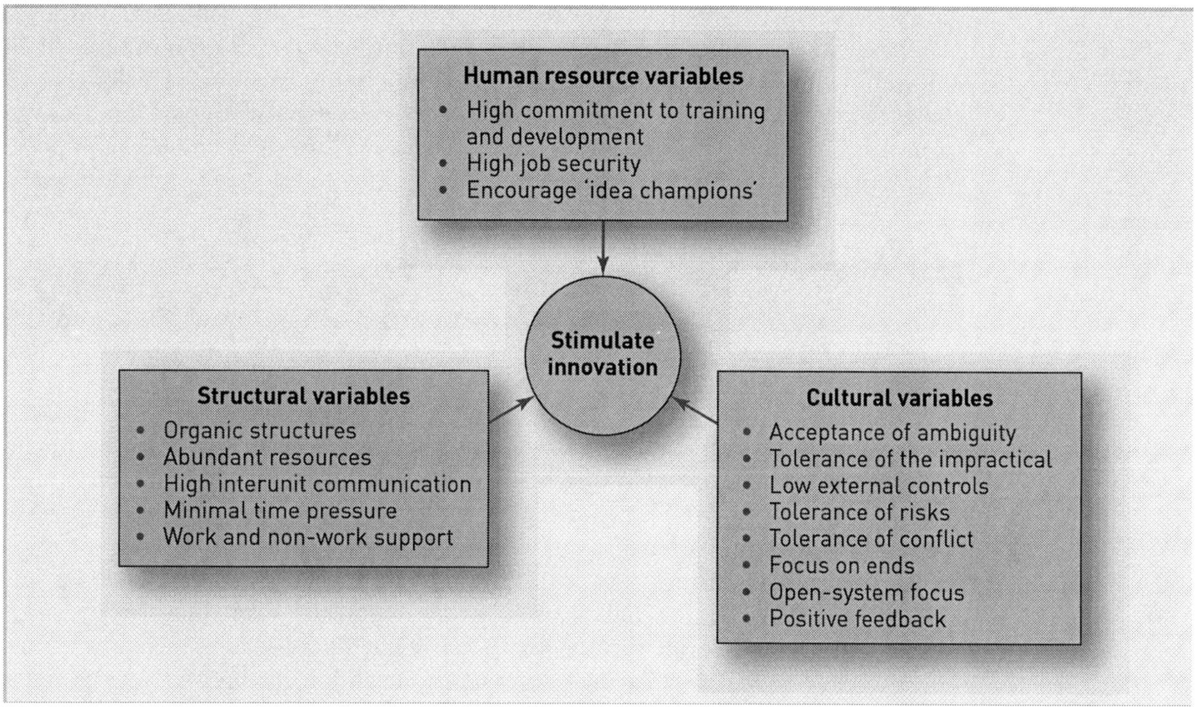

Figure 13.7 Innovation variables

- *Positive feedback* Managers provide positive feedback, encouragement and support so employees feel their creativity will receive attention.

HR policies for innovation

Innovative organisations actively promote the training and development of their members so that their knowledge remains current, offer job security to overcome the fear of making mistakes, and encourage people to become 'champions of change'. Such **idea champions** actively and enthusiastically support new ideas, build support, overcome resistance, and ensure that ideas are implemented. Idea champions tend to have similar personalities – high self-confidence, persistence, energy and a tendency to take risks. They also inspire and energise others with their vision of the potential of an innovation, and through their strong personal commitment to its success. They also need to be good at gaining the support of others – especially those at more senior levels of the organisation – which helps them overcome doubts elsewhere.

Idea champions are individuals who actively and enthusiastically support new ideas, build support, overcome resistance, and ensure that ideas are implemented.

Structures for innovation

Research into innovation has identified structural factors that encourage it, such as having an organic structure, encouraging horizontal communication, encouraging people to contribute ideas outside their loosely designed roles, having abundant resources, and frequent communication between units. Organic structures help because they have little formality, work in a decentralised way and encourage people to apply skills and knowledge to a wide range of tasks: this creates an atmosphere of cross-fertilisation and adaptability that in turn fosters innovation. Abundant resources help since they enable managers to purchase required expertise that may have developed in other companies, and also enables them to take risks by investing in new projects without too much anxiety that failure will damage the business. Frequent communication between units fosters the exchange of ideas and information, which can in turn stimulate combinations of knowledge, or its application, in unusual ways. Finally, there is evidence that when an organisation's structure provides explicit support for creativity from work and non-work activities, an employee's creativity is enhanced. Support includes encouragement, open communication, readiness to listen and useful feedback.

13.9 Current themes and issues

Performance

In a business world characterised by uncertainty and change, many advocate that organisations must change radically and relentlessly (see for example Foster and Kaplan, 2000). Managers are advised that to survive they must continually review all aspects of the way they do business. 'Change or perish' is the rationale of those who propose unrelenting change, who assume: 'that people naturally resist change and that leaders should destroy or cast aside the old ways in order to create a spanking new future' (Abrahamson, 2004). While the arguments may sometimes be valid, such as where an over-protected organisation suddenly faces new competition, disruptive change is costly, and does not necessarily improve performance (Barnet and Freeman, 2001).

Abrahamson (2004) identifies three symptoms of organisations suffering from excessive change – initiative overload, change related chaos and employee cynicism.

Initiative overload

An organisation in which managers become convinced of the need for radical change is likely to require more change than even they anticipate. Figure 13.2 reflects the systemic nature of organisations – a change in one area is likely to require complementary changes in others. An investment in IS may lead to further changes affecting, say, structures, people and business processes. They may or may not succeed – and if they fail then further changes follow. People experience 'initiative overload' and become dispirited and disinterested in whatever is proposed. Someone attempting to introduce a change in one area of a large business observed:

> There are so many changes taking place, they are more or less numb, and this is simply another change which they are just going to have to take on board. The result is that they are somewhat passive and neutral, and when I ask what their requirements might be, the response is usually 'you tell me'. (Boddy, 2002, p. 38)

Change related chaos

Major change inevitably means a period of overlap between old arrangements and the new, during which time there will be more than the usual scope for chaos. Abrahamson (2004) quotes the example of a bank that changed its cheque processing systems. Managers closed the previous system one Friday, opening the new one the following Monday. Things began to go badly wrong, as paper accumulated at all points in the system, which eventually collapsed:

> Why did the change fail so spectacularly? Because ... the new processes had not been fully tested and implemented. In the end, it became apparent to everyone that the change process had wreaked such chaos that it was almost destined to fail. (p. 17)

Employee cynicism

A succession of initiatives leading to change related chaos makes staff anxious and insecure. Communication failure will make this worse, leading to progressive alienation and dissatisfaction. Abrahamson (2004) refers to one senior banker he interviewed soon after a merger of the bank with a rival who told him that she was the only person left of the 60 people who had worked in her unit.

An alternative approach – change without pain?

Having taken a critical view of 'creative destruction', Abrahamson (2004) develops an alternative approach based on what he calls recombination. This takes the view that change will be a great deal less painful if managers take more time to analyse the positive aspects of the existing elements in the organisation. Taking these as the starting point, and basing change as far as possible on small adaptations to familiar arrangements will be much more acceptable to staff, and likely to produce better performance improvements than the radical alternatives.

Responsibility

The biggest challenge facing those implementing major change is that stakeholders will take different views of an organisation's problems, and will have varying degrees of commitment to changes intended to deal with them. Chapter 3 also quoted research by Nutt (2002) that half of the changes he studied produced poor results – in large part because decision makers failed to attend to interests and information held by key stakeholders.

An important step in influencing stakeholders is to assess their relative power and interest (Eden and Ackerman, 1998), which can be prepared to analyse the relative position of the stakeholders in an issue or project on two dimensions:

- their interest in the issue or activity being proposed, and
- their power to influence the outcomes of the issue or activity.

Those with both a high level of interest in the issue and high power to influence the outcome are the key players whom the organisation must seek to satisfy. Conversely those with low interest and power may require only minimal attention to ensure their acquiescence in a proposal.

A dilemma facing anyone with responsibility for implementing a change is how much attention they pay to different stakeholders. An instrumental approach would be to put most time and effort into meeting the needs of powerful stakeholders, as these are the ones who could cause most trouble if their needs are unmet. An alternative view would suggest that a responsible approach would take more account of the interests of those with less evident power – such as the disadvantaged, inarticulate or under-represented communities. Considerations of enlightened self-interest, as discussed in Chapter 5, could lead to a different approach to change management than one that only looked after the interests of the powerful.

International

The growing internationalisation of business has implications for the way international or global firms manage change. The issue here reflects one of the central themes within Chapter 4, namely the balance between a unified, global approach seeking to establish a common identity across all operations, or an approach that adapts the way the company operates to local conditions. Managers of local business units will have local priorities, and are likely to be unreceptive to change that the centre, or even another unit, appears to be imposing. The issues managers can face is illustrated by the experience of one who tried to introduce a new order processing system that would require compatible changes across seven European plants: see the Management in Practice feature.

management in practice — A Europe-wide change project

An individual needs to go out on a limb with an idea and be able to articulate that idea to a wider audience before they can get any interest, support and investment to go forward. In our company where the products and the business plan change very quickly it is enormously difficult to get people to focus on what is important rather than on what is urgent. We have seven sites all at different stages of development. We have in some way to make sure that each of them is positioned both in terms of resources, energy and commitment to support an integrated European programme. It is because we have a business which is fairly complex and so diverse that we have adopted the approach that basically says – generate a common level of understanding of what needs to be done, then allow each area to specify their unique requirements within this overall framework. It also allows each individual location to move at their own pace as long as they don't get too far out of line.

The team member from Valbonne wrote to me two weeks ago indicating that he's now been asked to do another European programme. Therefore because his particular group in Valbonne are very short of resources he will not be able to support this team. From my point of view as a programme manager that is totally unacceptable as his plant is a very big part of the order-fulfilment process. So without a representative from there any solution that we devise will only be partially successful.

Source: Boddy (2002), p. 172.

In this case, the manager was able to secure support for his role from European senior management, and was able to exert some influence over the individual plants. However, that influence was limited, meaning that the change introduced was less comprehensive, and less integrated, than would have been possible with a more centrally controlled structure. This balancing act faces all companies operating internationally.

Summary

1 Explain the meaning of organisational change and give examples

- Organisational change refers to deliberate attempts to change one or more elements of the internal environment, such as technology or structure. Change in one element usually stimulates change in other areas.

2 Explain what the links between change and context imply for those managing a change

- A change programme is an attempt to change one or more aspects of the internal context, which then provides the context of future actions. The prevailing context can itself help or hinder change efforts.

3 Compare life cycle, emergent, participative and political theories of change

- Life cycle: change projects can be planned, monitored and controlled towards achieving their objectives.

- Emergent: reflecting the uncertainties of the environment, change is hard to plan in detail, but emerges incrementally from events and actions.
- Participative: successful change depends on human commitment, which is best obtained by involving participants in planning and implementation.
- Political: change threatens some of those affected, who will use their power to block progress, or to direct the change in ways that suit local objectives.

4 Evaluate systematically the possible sources of resistance to change

- Reasons can be assessed using the internal context model, as each element (objectives, people, power, etc.) is a potential source of resistance. Analysing these indicates potential ways of overcoming resistance.
- The force field analysis model allows players to identify the forces driving and restraining a change, and implies that reducing the restraining forces will help change more than increasing the driving forces.

5 Explain the meaning of organisational development and the learning organisation

- OD refers to a set of techniques that practitioners use to reconcile the conflicting interests of people and organisations, both to satisfy human needs and to improve organisational performance. Typical values include treating individuals with respect, a trusting, open and supportive climate, flat rather than hierarchical structures, confronting conflict, and involving those affected by change in implementation.

6 Illustrate the factors believed to support innovation:

- Structural – organic form, abundant resources, high communication between units, and work and non-work support;
- Cultural – acceptance of ambiguity, low external controls, tolerance of risks, open systems focus, and positive feedback;
- Human resource policies – high commitment to training and development, high job security, and creative people.

Review questions

1. What does the term 'performance gap' mean, and what is its significance for change?
2. Explain what is meant by the inner context of management, and give examples of attempts to change one or more elements.
3. What are the implications for management of the systemic nature of major change?
4. Review the change that you identified in Activity 13.1 and compare its critical dimensions (Table 13.1) with those at the Royal Bank of Scotland.
5. Can managers alter the receptiveness of an organisation to change? Would doing so be an example of an interaction approach?
6. Outline the life cycle perspective on change and explain when it is most likely to be useful.
7. How does it differ from the 'emergent' perspective?
8. What are the distinctive characteristics of a participative approach, and when is it likely to be least successful?

9 What skills are used by those employing a political model?

10 Is resistance to change necessarily something to be overcome? How would you advise someone to resist a change to which he or she was opposed?

11 What are likely to be the benefits and disadvantages of using an OD approach to a major change project?

12 To what extent does the evidence from Google (Chapter 12) support the innovation theory implied by Figure 13.7?

Concluding critical reflection

Think about the way people handle major change in your company, or one with which you are familiar. Review the material in the chapter, and perhaps visit some of the websites identified. Then make notes on these questions:

- What examples of the themes discussed in this chapter are currently relevant to your company? What performance imperatives are dominant, and to what extent do people see a performance gap? What perspective do people have on the change process – life cycle, emergent, participative or political?
- In implementing change, what **assumptions** about the nature of change in organisations appear to guide the approach? Is one perspective dominant, or do people typically use several methods in combination?
- What factors in the **context** of the company appear to shape your approach to managing change – is your organisation seen as being receptive or non-receptive to change, for example, and what lies behind that?
- Has there been any serious attempt to find **alternative** ways to manage major change in your organisation – for example by comparing your methods systematically with those of other companies, or with the theories set out here?
- Does the approach typically used generally work? If not, do managers recognise the **limitations** of their approach, and question their assumptions?

Further reading

Pettigrew, A.M. and Whipp, R. (1991), *Managing Change for Competitive Success*, Blackwell, Oxford.

Pettigrew, A., Ferlie, E. and McKee, L. (1992), *Shaping Strategic Change*, Sage, London.

Both of these books provide detailed, long-term analyses of major changes – the first in four commercial businesses and the second in several units within the UK National Health Service. The theoretical approach of these works has informed the development of this chapter, emphasising the interaction of change and context. Although the cases are old, they still provide useful empirical insights into the task of managing change.

Lock, D. (2003), *Project Management* (8th edn), Gower, Aldershot.

An excellent source of information on conventional project management techniques.

Buchanan, D. and Badham, R. (1999), *Power, Politics and Organizational Change: Winning the turf game*, Sage, London.

A modern approach to politics in organisations, offering a theoretical and practical guide, based on extensive primary research.

Balogun, J., Gleadle, P., Hailey, V.H. and Willmott, H. (2005), 'Managing change across boundaries: boundary-shaking practices', *British Journal of Management*, vol. 16, no. 4, pp. 261–278.

An empirical study of the practices that change agents used to introduce major boundary-shaking changes in large companies, and how the context shaped their use. Many insights into practice in this valuable research.

Roberto, M.A. and Levesque, L.C. (2005), 'The art of making change initiatives stick', *MIT Sloan Management Review*, vol. 46, no. 4, pp. 53–60.

Another empirical study, this time in a single organisation, of how the context affected the willingness of people to change, and how senior managers needed to create a supportive context.

Weblinks

These websites have appeared in this and other chapters:

www.vodafone.com
www.ericsson.com
ww.gknplc.com
www.sun.com
www.siemens.com
www.ikea.com

Visit two of the business sites in the list, and navigate to the pages dealing with corporate news, investor relations or 'our company'.

- What signs of major changes taking place in the organisation can you find?
- Does the site give you a sense of an organisation that is receptive or non-receptive to change?
- What kind of environment are they likely to be working in, and how may that affect their approach to change?

Annotated weblinks, multiple choice questions and other useful resources can be found on www.pearsoned.co.uk/boddy

Part 2

Workplace Practices and Processes

Week 6

Motivation (1)

Week 7

Motivation and Organisational Change

CHAPTER 8

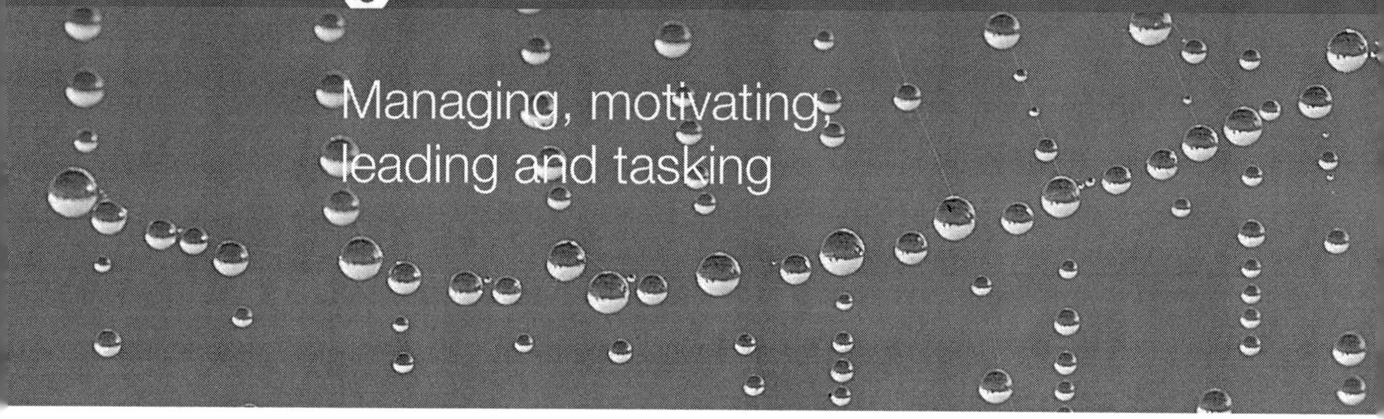

Managing, motivating, leading and tasking

Objectives

Having read this chapter and completed its associated activities, readers should be able to:

- Recognise that those aspects of the organisation of work at the level of basic task performance that are often treated as separate matters – motivation, leadership and job design – are better understood as closely related aspects of managerial task shaping and the winning of employee cooperation.
- See the advantages of considering organisational members' *orientations to work* and the *strategic exchanges* that occur in the context of the employment relationship rather than focus on people's general 'motivation to work'.
- Recognise the advantages of focusing on the managerial manipulation of employees' perceived *implicit contracts* rather than on managerial efforts to 'motivate' employees.
- Understand the extent to which there is negotiation and bargaining within the associated processes of 'motivation', 'leadership' and job design.
- Appreciate the importance of the *indulgency patterns* that arise – the implicit 'give-and-take' practices that can be observed in the relationships between workers and supervisors or managers.
- Appreciate that so-called 'process' theories of motivation like 'equity' and 'expectancy' theories nevertheless contain important insights that fit with the basic *strategic exchange* analysis developed in this chapter.
- Apply the concepts of *direct* and *indirect* managerial control attempts developed in the previous chapter to the *principles of work design* that have influenced the *job design practices* developed over the history of industrial capitalist economies.
- Understand how the application of different types of work design principles at different times can be related to the basic managerial problem of handling contradictions in the basic industrial and organisational system.

- Appreciate the ways in which values, choices and contingent circumstances influence the enactment of specific job designs – and are an element of the more general and strategic organisation-shaping processes that were identified in Chapter 7.

Linking motivation, leadership and job design

The organising and managing of work requires motivating organisational members to behave in certain ways, asking some organisational employees to play a more leading role than others in the workplace and deciding how tasks are to be allocated to people. The issues are always there and have to be tackled. However, it is important to avoid treating matters of motivating, leading and shaping tasks as separate and unconnected matters. This, however, is something that texts which treat 'motivation', 'leadership' and 'job design' as separate and discrete topics might encourage us to do. It is quite normal to find textbooks with separate chapters on 'motivation', 'leadership' and 'job design'. Yet ask any manager trying to direct the activities of an organisational section, department or function where the 'motivating' aspect of their work stops and 'leadership' starts. Even if they accepted the value of these concepts for understanding the work that they do, they would be hard pressed to explain how they differed in practice.

One might similarly ask any manager tackling issues of how tasks in an organisational department are going to be shaped and allocated whether this 'job design' work is simply a matter of the efficient sharing out of work tasks. No, they are likely to reply, a key consideration has to be how effectively different patterns of tasks and roles will 'motivate' or fail to motivate the people undertaking them. To choose whether, on the one hand, to ask employees to tackle the same simple task day in, day out or, on the other hand, to give each individual a variety of challenging tasks to do, requires giving thought to how those employees are likely to react in 'motivational' terms to such arrangements. If 'job designers' find themselves deciding to group people into work teams, it is unlikely to be long before they are talking about the need to design into the teamwork arrangements a role for a team *leader*. In practice, then, those matters that are typically treated as separate issues within orthodox managerial/academic discourses are closely interrelated.

The general meanings of the words that are used in this area would suggest this close interrelationship. When managers 'lead' people, our dictionaries suggest, they are getting people to follow or 'go along with them'. When they 'motivate' them, they are providing 'a stimulus to some kind of action'. These two things are clearly closely interrelated, and both are relevant to the work managers do when they design jobs – when they lay down the patterns of tasks that people are required to undertake. The cluster of tasks that any particular individual is asked to undertake will typically have been designed by managers to get their workers to 'go along with them' and to contain 'stimuli to action'. But managers do not do any of these things in their own departments or sections in isolation from what is going on more generally across the organisation in which they are involved. All of this motivating, leading and patterning of tasks happens in the context of the broader structural and cultural patterns that were looked at in Chapters 6 and 7. And, especially important, as we shall see, is the extent to which the structure and culture of the organisation tends towards the use of *direct* or *indirect* attempts to achieve managerial control. Managerial control is something that will never be completely achieved however hard managers work in *attempting* to achieve it. And the *productive cooperation* that managers are required to pursue will never be complete. Whatever productive cooperation is achieved has to be worked for. It has to be 'won'.

Motivating, leading and job designing are facets of this attempt to 'win cooperation' and they are often indistinguishable from each other in practice. We could say, though, that:

- when people speak of 'motivation' they tend to focus on the *people doing work tasks*;
- when people speak of 'leadership' they tend to focus on the *person trying to influence the carrying out of those tasks*;
- when people speak of 'job design' they tend to focus on the *tasks themselves* and in using the word 'design' are perhaps linking activities at the local level back to the way the organisation as a whole is structured, particularly in terms of either a *direct* or an *indirect* control emphasis.

In Chapter 5 attention was focused in Case 5.2 on Peter Brodie (pp. 177–8) as a manager who was working effectively to win the cooperation of a variety or people upon whom the long-term success of his enterprise depended. The focus there on the individual, however, brings to the fore the 'leadership' aspect of his managerial work. He was thus identified as an effective leader. This 'leadership' effectiveness cannot really be other than temporarily separated from the other aspects of what he was doing in his role as the chief executive of the charity he was shaping and running.

Motivation, leadership and job design need to be regarded as closely interrelated aspects of patterning of activities and understandings across the whole work organisation. And this means remembering that no manager works outside the basic structure and ethos of the organisation that employs them. The present chapter nevertheless tends to concentrate on activities at a more 'local' level within the organisation. It looks at those issues that are traditionally tackled under the traditional headings of motivation, leadership and work design as different facets of the overall processes that occur within task management practices and within the patterns of relationship, rivalry, adjustment and negotiated order that enable productive cooperation to occur to a level that allows the organisation to continue in existence into the future. The three Further Reading guides on leadership (Chapter 5, p. 196), motivation and work design (this chapter pp. 347–8) present material that is made available within the tradition of separating these aspects of managerial work from each other. The chapter itself, however, tries to minimalise this kind of separation.

Earlier, we questioned the value of the social science concept of 'motivation' as a tool for analysing and understanding why people do what they do at work – or anywhere else for that matter. The problems with an emphasis on motives and motivation in understanding human behaviour were discussed in Chapter 3 (pp. 89–90). 'Motivation' was shown to be a concept that is rooted in systems-control thinking about human beings and their behaviour in which the person is seen as 'a little machine-like system in which goals or "motives" operate as a motor "powering" the human entity so that it behaves in a particular way' (p. 86).

The story of Grant Park and his coffee drinking activities was used in Chapter 3 to demonstrate that motives are not usefully seen as things that people 'have' which *precede* behaviour (in the modernist tradition of dualism and linear thinking) (pp. 88–9). Instead, it was argued, 'motives' have to be seen as social rather than purely individual phenomena – often acting as justifications for a piece of behaviour made after the event rather than as causal springs of action or 'triggers' of behaviours. What people do (whether it be to commit a murder or to work hard at a desk all day to please a boss) is an outcome of a multiplicity of factors going way beyond the straightforward fulfilling of motives or the meeting of needs. Whereas systems-control thinking sees human behaviours occurring as individuals who are *motivated* to fulfil *needs* and *wants*, process-relational thinking sees actions taking place 'in the light of interpretations made about the world, to *enact* whatever *projects* individuals who are undertaking *strategically* to shape their lives and to manage *existential challenges*' (Table 3.1, p. 94). Thus, if we want to understand what is 'motivating' a particular individual to behave in a particular way at work we would look at their overall *work orientation* – the meaning that they currently attach to their work (see Chapter 4, pp. 116–24). And this orientation has emerged in the light of their idea of 'who they are' (their identity) and 'where they are going in life' (their personal *strategic shaping*). It is also an aspect of how they are handling life's anxieties and the pressures of their circumstances – matters ranging from how their family is to be fed to ones of values and, say, of conscience about what one 'ought to be doing with one's life'.

From 'worker motivation' to work orientations and strategic exchange

What all of this implies is that we need to stop focusing on people's 'motives' and look at what people are thinking and doing within the broader context of the *strategic exchange* relationships between employing organisations and employees. People going to work in organisations are involved in strategically shaping their lives, and organisations themselves have to be shaped strategically to trade with a whole range of constituencies. Employers and employees come together in an exchange that helps both parties fulfil their respective strategies. And the 'strategy' of the employee can be understood as their basic *orientation to work*. This is something much more subtle, much more complex and much more dynamic than 'motives'.

Activity 8.1

Reread the stories of Ravi Barr (Case 4.1, p. 119) and Sacha and her corporate affairs department (Case 4.2, p. 122):

- to remind yourself of the extent to which people's orientation to work (their overall 'work motivation' as it might be called) varies at different times of their life and in different circumstances;
- to recognise that the efforts of managers and supervisors in the workplace to 'motivate' their staff are only one factor in the resulting 'motivational' state of those staff.

In considering these two stories and what they tell us about the variations that can exist between how people are oriented to (or 'motivated within') their work it readily becomes apparent that we tend to use the notion of motivation in two ways when we look at work behaviour and meaning, as is noted in Table 8.1.

In the story of Ravi Barr in Case 4.1 we notice how a variety of factors in his life experience and his changing notion of identity led to changes in how he was broadly oriented towards work at different times. This could be expressed in terms of how his 'motivation' varied from circumstance to circumstance. The

Table 8.1 Two ways in which we talk about 'motivation' in the work context

Motivation as *the factors leading a person to behave in a certain way at work* (this is similar to the *strategic exchange* notion of a person's orientation to work)	Motivation as *managerial action to influence the people's behaviour at work so they perform as managers require* (in *strategic exchange* terms, this entails managerial manipulation of the implicit contract to get people to behave in a way that leads to productive cooperation)
We say, for example, that a person's 'motivation' has changed when their orientation to work has shifted from one where they sought to maximise their cash return from the employer while showing little interest in the employer's business to one where they concentrate on making a conscientious input to developing the business with a view to building up to a high salary level later in their career	We often say that part of a manager's job is to 'motivate' their staff: find a way of getting them to act in a way that fits with organisational requirements. A manager might observe that the staff are primarily interested in short-term cash reward and prefer to be told exactly what to do. However, the manager decides that it is necessary for these staff to involve themselves in finding new ways of doing the job. The manager might therefore talk of 'motivating my people differently'. This might involve persuading them they will find taking more initiative within their jobs rewarding

term 'orientation' is preferred, however, because it suggests the relevance of a wider variety of factors influencing the way an individual thinks and behaves at work than something as simplistic as a set of 'motives'. It might be reasonable to use the notion of motive to label a simple interest in maximising one's income. However, it is less helpful when it comes to considering such matters as the way in which one expresses one's identity in one's work or the way one develops a working career to fit into a changing set of life priorities or circumstances. We can see the same problem when we look at the staff who work in Sacha Boath's public relations department in Case 4.2. The original 'poor motivation' of Biffy Currie and Sniffy Gerardo, for example, simply cannot be put down to something as simple as 'motives'. Their problems appear to Sacha to be related to problems of identity arising from the loss of their jobs as journalists. Complex problems of marital disharmony and alcoholism were related to this. But their changed work orientations (to a 'positive motivation', as some would put it) seem to have come from changes that they made in their private lives rather than from direct managerial efforts to 'motivate them'. Sacha does claim a part in this change by pointing to her threat to them that they would have to 'ship out' if they did not 'shape up'. For all we know this might have been crucial in getting both men to reconsider what they were doing with their lives, but it can hardly be recognised as a case of a manager 'motivating' a member of staff. Sacha has made a significant managerial intervention, it would seem, but it was an intervention rooted in a subtle consideration of a range of factors influencing the men's lives. It was also risky: the men could have been alienated even more from their work as public relations officers and descended even faster into personal and work troubles.

Trying to influence employees' work orientations is a much more complex matter than simply seeking to 'motivate' them by trying to 'meet their needs' – as much of the standard motivational thinking has it (and to which we will return shortly). One reason for this complexity is the fact, demonstrated in Ravi's case as well as in the case of Smithy (Sacha's third public relations officer), that work orientations are highly influenced by aspects of people's lives outside the workplace. This is not to say that organisational influences are not themselves of enormous importance. And here, what might seem at first sight like fairly simple changes can have considerable effects. Sacha tells us how Snippy Spedale's approach to her work and to relationships in the office have changed significantly since her desk was moved from a relatively central position in the room. The office rearrangement can be understood as a matter of change in job design – the pattern of tasks and work roles and how these relate to each other is inevitably changed whenever one changes the physical layout of a workplace, however minor this may be. But this has changed the 'reward' side of the perceived implicit contract at the heart of Snippy's work orientation. The pleasure of being at the centre of the office's social life and being able to joke with everybody that entered the office has gone away. And Sacha is thinking about how she can intervene in this. We can infer that she is considering trying to bring something of this back into the informal contract with Snippy when she tells us that she is going to have to 'rethink the office layout'.

Motivating and leading people through the manipulation of implicit contracts

By manipulating Snippy Spedale's work orientation, Sacha is, in orthodox terms, trying to 'remotivate' her. But equally one could say she is attempting this shift in orientation by engaging in some minor job redesign. One might even say she is displaying a degree of subtle 'leadership'. The same might be said of the case of Sparky Learmonth. Sacha recognises that his job has changed – it has become more routine and is thus less intrinsically satisfying for him. But Sparky is happy with his salary and his job security. Such are the complexities and the multiplicity of factors that come into the work orientation of any individual and the implicit contract between them and the employer. Sacha has considered manipulating this by promoting him but, given that this is not feasible, she is talking of finding 'some exciting new project' that will turn him on. Again we can ask whether what is going on here is 'motivation', 'job design' or 'leadership'. It is hard to separate these out. And it is unnecessary. It is more helpful simply to recognise that:

- managerial work involves getting employees to do things that they might not otherwise do;
- to do this managers have to understand the complexities of employees' work orientations;
- any attempt to change these must involve making some adjustment in the individuals' perceived implicit contract – the way employees understand the relationship between what they are 'putting in' to the job and what 'they are taking out' of the employment relationship;
- to change an implicit contract there is bound to be a degree of bargaining, but all negotiations over the 'employment trade' always relate to all the *strategic exchanges* which both the individual and the organisation are making and occur within a relationship involving power differences. The managers, as the employer's agents, with all the organisation's resources behind them, typically have a power advantage over the employees.

Manipulating employees' perceived implicit contract *Concept*

This is at the centre of all motivational, leadership and job design work done by managers. Tasks are shaped and rewards are offered as part of a bargaining process in which managers try to persuade employees to work in the way they want them to work.

All motivational, leadership and work design efforts made by managers attempt to influence employee behaviours by influencing the employee's perception or understanding of the contract that is at the heart of the relationship between the organisation and the worker. How people behave in the workplace is fundamentally

Table 8.2 An 'input–reward' representation of how employees perceive their implicit contract with the employing organisation

Employee input	Employee reward
• physical effort	• money
• mental effort	• job satisfaction
• initiative	• personal 'growth'
• responsibility	• social reward
• impairment – *fatigue, risk of injury etc.*	• security
• compliance – *acceptance of a degree of managerial control*	• power
	• status
	• career potential

influenced by their understanding of the 'employment deal' which, following the analysis provided in Chapter 4 (pp. 115–25), is represented in Table 8.2.

Managers, in 'leading' or getting workers to go along with them, in 'motivating' or giving them incentives to act in a certain way and in shaping their tasks are necessarily involved in complex processes of negotiation. Recognition of this is central to process-relational thinking. It is not just a matter of negotiating with workers what tasks they do or how much they are to be paid for doing those tasks. It is a negotiation over the basic 'realities' of the employment relationship. In the power relationship within which the employment relationship is always set ('if, in the end, you do not do what we ask, you will lose your job') the manager has to establish a pattern of workplace relations and understandings. Within this, the employees have to be persuaded that there is a fair and reasonable return for the efforts and initiatives that they make, the risks to health and mental well-being that they take, and the degree of managerial authority over them that they accept. That return will be a complex mix of monetary, psychological and social rewards. It will be a mix of so much pay, so much security, so much opportunity for career advancement, so much social 'standing' and so on, that makes a fair balance, in the employees' mind, with what is being asked of those employees by the employer.

Activity 8.2

Read the story that Dal Cross tells in Case 8.1 about the foundry yard gang and:

- use as many as possible of the elements or 'headings' in the model of the general 'implicit contract' identified in Table 8.2 to make sense of the yard gang's perceived implicit contract with their employer – the one that prevailed before Dal Cross arrived;
- consider what actions Dal might consider, in terms of manipulating the perceived implicit contract, to change the yard gang's way of working, and stop it being necessary to have a foreman or manager sitting in the office all day turning requests from across the site into direct orders to be given to the 'yardies'.

Dal Cross and the recalcitrant yard gang

Case 8.1

I think I learned everything I know about the management basics from that six months when I was put in charge of the people who do the outdoor work in our foundries. I had only been with the company for about 18 months and was coming towards the end of the management training programme. My final 'attachment', as they called them in those days, was to work with the foundry works manager. This man turned out to be quite different from what I expected. He was a highly qualified metallurgist and he prided himself on being an educated and cultivated individual who, at the same time, had a 'common touch' when it came to his relationships with foundry workers. I'll never forget the words he used when I went to see him to discuss the assignment he was going to give me. He said, 'I can give you a job which, if you succeed with it, will teach you all the basics about managing in this sort of business', and he then used this unforgettable phrase, 'I want you to sort out my recalcitrant yardies'. That night, as you might guess, I looked up the word recalcitrant in my dictionary. It said something like 'not susceptible to control or authority'. What was I taking on?

I had not, in those days, heard of Jamaican 'yardy' gangs and immediately recognised who he was talking about when he pointed out of the window at a couple of men who were slowly – incredibly slowly – sweeping up a section of the factory yard opposite the works manager's office. Their foreman was about to retire and I was to take over from him for a six-month period. The brief was to 'sort things out' and recommend to the works manager what should be done about a permanent replacement for the foreman who, the works manager said, he was 'damned glad to see the back of'. I have to admit that I was rather nervous about taking this on. But I had been complaining to the training manager that I wanted a 'real management assignment' in which I would not only learn about doing management but 'prove myself' as a manager. I'd asked for everything I was going to get, hadn't I?

The foundry site had been developing over 30 to 40 years and it had become a complex jungle of buildings and workshops with all sorts of alleyways leading off the twisting main road that ran through the site. The role of the dozen or so yardmen was to keep these ways clear, clean and safe. They were also responsible for moving materials and 'work in progress' about between buildings on the various motorised trucks and hand-pushed carts that they controlled. The responsibility for scrap handling was also theirs.

The work was very hard and often very dirty. One minute they were shifting foundry sand, the next minute carting heavy castings from the furnace room to the fettling shop and soon after that they were having to sweep floodwater away after a heavy rainstorm or shovel snow or ice off the roadways. The work could be dangerous, especially given the cramped areas they often worked in and the heavy and awkward material they sometimes had to handle. And there was a degree of responsibility with this work. Some of the moulds or patterns that they moved about were very fragile, as were some of the ceramic cores that they handled. One slip with these items and not only was money lost but the production schedule could be completely blown. On top of that, the scrap was often quite valuable and the security people were always anxious that no one with a criminal record or with criminal contacts should be in the gang. Scrap thieving can be quite a lucrative activity around engineering works, you know.

What was obvious to me from the moment I began meeting members of the gang was that they took no initiative whatsoever. They wouldn't even sweep up a broken beer bottle in the middle of the car park without being instructed to do so, I discovered. The foreman had insisted that no work be done unless it was under his instruction. Members of the gang had to do exactly what he told them. If any one of them disobeyed him they would find themselves spending a disproportionate amount of time cleaning lavatories. When I looked at the wages that the blokes got they seemed fairly reasonable to me. They compared well with other manual workers who did not have a skilled trade. It seemed that the relatively dangerous and physically uncomfortable aspects of the job were well compensated for by the fairly high security of employment that the job gave them. The foreman might have been a bossy so-and-so but he made sure that his blokes stayed in work if they went along with him. Nevertheless I was quite puzzled at first that they were willing to put up with the heaviness of the control that he exerted. But after a few days I realised that this was balanced by the space he gave them for 'having a laugh together', as they put it. He allowed them longer tea breaks than any other workers took and he turned a blind eye to their practice of 'taking it easy' for the last half-hour of each working day. I knew that other supervisors across the site resented all of this, both because it undermined their own authority with their workers and because they often found themselves unable to get things moved towards the end of a shift or when the yardies were finishing off their card game during a protracted tea break. But few complained too loudly to the yard foreman because he would 'punish' them by ensuring that their 'breakages' increased for a few days or by saying that he had no truck available to move their goods.

There seemed few satisfactions for the yardies in the tasks that they did but I think they nevertheless enjoyed coming to work. And although, in one sense, their status was low as an unskilled group who had some pretty unpleasant tasks to do, they did carry a certain perverse status among the workforce. This was because of the informal privileges they enjoyed as a result of their foreman's power to protect them from any disciplines that might come from another direction. Nobody, including the works manager, dared question what went on. Too much boat-rocking would follow from upsetting the yardies.

Some of the other supervisors used to call the foreman the 'yard führer' and one of them, who had an Italian background, simply called him 'Il Duce'. This name-calling was obviously more than a matter of people with a knowledge of languages using the German or the Italian word for 'leader'! And if I was going to follow my own beliefs about good leadership in my six months with these men, I was going to have to make some big changes. I had to run things the old way at first, however. If I hadn't, the foundry would have ground to a halt. No man was willing to move from the rest room until he had an instruction from me. When I suggested that they all surely knew 'what needed doing on a Monday morning if they thought about it', they responded that they 'were not paid to think'. That was the foreman's job. But after a couple of days sitting at the old foreman's desk receiving phone calls from around the site asking for a truck here, a lavatory cleaner there, a bin emptied somewhere else and an oil leak cleared up outside the main waxroom – and then despatching the appropriate yardy for that job – I was even more convinced that I had to change things.

The implicit contract between the company and the yard gang members, as Dal Cross understands it, is as complex as one we might find with any group of workers. On the employee 'input' side of the trade there is clearly a high level of physical effort required and the yardies subject themselves to a degree of 'impairment' by getting quite dirty and risking accidents in some of the dangerous conditions they meet. They do not appear to make much input by way of initiative taking, however, and the responsibilities they bear are of a relatively passive kind. They simply have to take care not to damage fragile items that they are moving about. But this is a heavier responsibility than it might at first sound, since damage to some of these goods could harm the overall performance of the foundry as a business operation. We might imagine, though, that the foreman himself would take formal responsibility for such damage, given that he exerts so much direct control over the yard gang's work.

The approach he takes to his job means that anyone working in his gang has to surrender a significant amount of personal autonomy while at work. For the rewards that they receive, these men have to submit to a high level of direction from a 'boss'.

The pay that the yardies received, Dal infers, was not an issue. Taken together with the other rewards, an acceptable balance between the two sides of the effort bargain had been struck. Security of employment was clearly a significant factor on the reward side. There appeared to Dal to be little reward in terms of job satisfaction, personal growth or career potential. But we can imagine that they felt some degree of power through their being identified with the power that the foreman himself had over other supervisors and managers. Dal certainly notes a degree of 'perverse' status coming from certain advantages that the yardies had over other foundry workers. They had a greater opportunity to enjoy leisure at work than any other group, for example. It can be inferred that these lengthy card-playing tea breaks and the winding-down time provided the yardies with a degree of 'social reward' in the workplace. It was a fairly distinctive factor going into the mix or balance of 'inputs' and 'outputs' that makes up the implicit contract of this particular group of workers with the employing organisation. It was at the core of their work orientation and is thus something that anybody would need to appreciate – Dal Cross included – who wanted to understand why the yardies thought and behaved in the way they did with regard to their work.

The implicit contract has just been referred to as a trade that goes on between employees and the employing organisation. But, of course, 'the organisation' is not literally a trader itself. The bargain that we say, in a shorthand way, 'the organisation' is making with its employees is in fact made in the organisation's name by the various managers, personnel recruitment staff and supervisors with whom the individual deals at different stages of their entry to and continuing involvement in the organisation. And where there is a manager or supervisor directly involved in shaping the everyday activities of any individual or group of individuals there will necessarily be a degree of day-to-day negotiation or *give and take* about what work is done and how and when it is done. The works manager clearly saw the yard gang as an especially 'recalcitrant' group – clearly thinking of the yardies and the foreman together as a group that had managed to get itself in some ways 'above the law' that applied to other groups under the works manager's authority. However, we could say that all employees – all human beings indeed – are recalcitrant to a degree (see the earlier discussion of this, pp. 2–3). Every manager, schoolteacher or parent knows that the employees, pupils or children formally 'under their control' will never follow every instruction that they are given or submit totally to every rule that is meant to shape their behaviour. There has to be a degree of 'give and take' which allows the person in authority to get 'some of their own way' in return for allowing those subject to that authority to 'get away' with infringing some of the rules which, if followed in every detail, would turn the individual into a puppet or a robot rather than a human being with free will and personal autonomy. Gouldner, in a classic study of factory life (1954), conceptualised as an *indulgency pattern* the tendency he saw for supervisors to 'turn a blind eye' to certain rule-breaking activities. The supervisors did this as part of an implicit understanding that the workers would, reciprocally, indulge the supervisors when they sought compliance over matters that the workers might reasonably refuse to go along with.

Indulgency pattern *Concept*

The ignoring by supervisors or managers of selected rule infringements by workers in return for those workers conceding to requests that, strictly speaking, they could refuse.

The joiners' shop ritual reported in Chapter 7 (in Table 7.2, p. 286) whereby the joiners always used the first 20 minutes of their shift to take an 'illegal tea break' while the supervisors deliberately kept their backs to the working areas for the same period of time is an example of a ritualised expression of an indulgency pattern. In this case a particularly assertive manual work group is ritually demonstrating that it only cooperates with 'management' on its own terms, and the supervisors are ritually displaying their acceptance of this. A more typical indulgency pattern, however, is one in which a manager ignores their staff taking an extra long lunch break once a week to do their shopping, in return for those employees complying with the occasional short notice request to do some overtime or to cover for another worker who has not turned up for work. The yard foreman clearly indulges his staff by allowing them to take long breaks and to stop working well before the official finishing time. This, we can reasonably infer, is a trade. It is a conceding of free time during working hours in return for the workers allowing the supervisor to have an unusually high level of task control over them.

It is clear that implicit contracts have some very subtle aspects to them. The very fact that they involve a range of formally unstated agreements makes the managerial 'motivational' task quite a subtle and challenging one. The manager is constantly bargaining with the people that in traditional 'organisation behaviour' terms they are said to be 'motivating' or 'leading'. And, given that managers are frequently required to take initiatives to make changes in work behaviour, they face the considerable challenge of having to renegotiate the ongoing work exchange or *contract* with the people whose behaviours they are trying to change. Dal Cross refers to his foundry assignment as a 'change management' one and he uses the analysis of the yard workers' work orientations and perceived implicit contract that we have just reviewed to make the changes he sees as necessary. And the *processes* that he engages in to negotiate these changes are ones where, once again, we see the overlapping of so-called motivational, leadership and job design initiatives.

Activity 8.3

Read Dal Cross's continuing story in Case 8.2 about his managerial experiences with the yard gang in the foundry and:

- using Table 8.2 again (p. 316), analyse the new implicit contract that makes possible Dal's re-organising of the yard gang;
- consider the extent to which Dal has made changes to 'job design' in setting up the modified 'site services' function;
- consider whether you can see a 'theory of leadership' behind Dal's working towards these changes;
- identify the extent to which it might be said that there is now a new 'indulgency pattern' within these 'site services' arrangements.

Leadership in practice and a 'triumph of change management' Case 8.2

I had talked of 'proving myself' managerially by taking on this assignment with the foundry works manager and I knew that I was either going to fail miserably or that I was going to pull off a triumph of change management. I had been on a change management course and read all the stuff on choosing the 'right leadership style', motivating people, enriching jobs, empowering staff, quality circles and goodness knows what else. As I read through all this stuff again on the Monday evening after my first day with the yard gang, I struggled to make it all add up. I had to fall back on what I believed in about being a manager. When I had been interviewed for the management traineeship in the first place it seemed that I had said very much the right thing when I had argued that managers were going to have to initiate a lot of changes to make businesses successful in an increasingly competitive world. But managers would not be able to – nor should they morally – unilaterally impose these changes on the organisation's employees. The interviewing panel had been wary of my suggestion that this might involve negotiating work organisation changes with trade unions. But they warmed to my theme that managers and their staff had to 'work together' – with those being paid to be managers taking the lead – to find new ways of working that would give benefits to the organisation and the workers alike.

All these fine words came back to me on that Monday night. Although this was rather idealistic sounding, it did feel to me to be the only way I could *realistically* go about tackling the problem of the yard gang. The works manager was simply unwilling to allow the continuation of an operation led by a gang boss who bullied other managers and supervisors into a situation where they could neither question the level of service he gave them nor challenge the way he indulged his staff. What was clear to me was that I could not simply order the yardies to work differently and to start using their own initiative to provide the site with a fast and efficient service that didn't always have to be mediated by a gang boss.

Ever since my early reflections on what being a manager should mean, I knew that my preferred personal style of leadership would have to be one of establishing a relationship of trust with the men and then negotiating with them a new way of working. That Monday night I decided that I would 'give a lead' by proposing a working principle of 'providing a service to the site' and that this would entail treating people in the various foundry departments as 'internal customers'. I was fully aware that I could not simply foist these ideas onto the men as a cynical act of pushing management fads that I had heard about on a course. I was very tempted to use the 'empowerment' word in my discussion, for example. I think the word describes well what I wanted to do. But I thought that the pretentious overtones of this word would not go down well in the foundry context. If I was going to work with them in a trusting relationship I had to be subtle and establish with them that the 'new order' I had in mind would be one in which they would all be better off than under the old regime, in one way or another.

I called a meeting with all the men in their 'winding down' time on the Tuesday evening, promising overtime payment to cover time spent in this or subsequent meetings that might go beyond the end of the shift. I took time to listen to what each of the men felt about the good and the bad aspects of the job and I worked hard to get them to see where, as a bloke, I was 'coming from'. I think this worked out quite well, partly because I think I am quite good at presenting myself as a sincere sort of person. But it was equally because all of this was set within a promise that nobody would 'lose out' if they 'went along with me'. Pay would certainly not suffer and I would look into ways in which an 'improved service to the foundry' might lead to an improved pay level. As I pointed out, the company had a job evaluation scheme which would ensure that if they were to 'increase the thinking or initiative element' of their work then they should move to a higher pay band.

Above all, though, I argued that they would surely be much happier to be 'getting out from under the thumb' of the boss man who had pushed them around for so long. And surely it would be better to get proper job satisfaction from providing a service to people across the foundry that would be genuinely appreciated than to carry on taking whatever satisfaction they had been getting from long tea breaks and card games. Taking my managerial life into my hands – or so it felt at the time – I added to this that whatever pleasure they took in the 'fun time' that they had at work was surely undermined by the disgust that other workers felt at what they were 'getting away with'. A stony silence followed that particular input to the discussions. But I got out of the impasse that I had backed myself into by pointing out that if members of the new 'site services' department were to be given discretion over how they went about providing services then they would also obviously have to be given discretion over when they might need to rest or otherwise recover after carrying out a particularly onerous or exhausting task. All of this, I argued, would have to be part of the trust that would need to exist between the members of the department and whoever would be in charge of it.

I hope all of this doesn't sound too glib. It was all very hard work and I found myself fluctuating between elation and depression as I worked towards the new department that I wanted to establish. Without going into all the details, the 'gang' were now to be a 'team' who would meet each morning to allocate among themselves the areas in which each of them were to work through the day. Sections of the team would be allocated each day to an area of the foundry and the members of that section would themselves agree who would do what task – lavatory cleaning and bin clearing included – as the need for it arose within any given area of the site. I got the jobs upgraded and this was helped by a deal I did with the security department whereby the 'site services staff' carried out certain routine security tasks as part of their work. I also got the works manager to agree that it might be possible to appoint a team leader from within the group when I came to the end of my six months. I told the team that this was simply a possibility but that if any of them was interested in future promotion in the company they might like to talk to me about this idea. I felt it was important that the yard workers should have the incentive of personal development and a career available to them, just like elsewhere in the organisation. Site services, and everybody in it, were on the 'up and up', I was proud to say.

The new implicit contract does not involve any less physical effort or risk of impairment than the old one. The major changes are with regard to the increased degree of initiative that the men are being asked to show in organising their own work schedules and task allocations. This can be seen as an increased 'input'. Alongside this there is what might be seen as a reduced input: the removal of the old requirement to surrender a high degree of personal autonomy by submitting themselves to a foreman's tight and direct control. It is sometimes argued by managers in situations like this that the only change in reward that this requires is one that automatically follows from the workers being freed to take charge of their own working practices: the reward of increased job satisfaction. Such people argue that 'empowering' workers by giving them increased freedom to choose how to work is a reward in itself. However, it is far from unusual for employees to reject this line of bargaining. They are quite likely to respond in the way the yard workers did and raise the principle of 'being paid to think'. Employees are quite likely to observe that their 'empowerment' involves them taking on tasks that managers or supervisors previously carried out. They argue that taking on such work should be recognised with a higher rate of pay. Dal Cross is well aware of this type of argument, it would seem. Consequently he has sought ways of getting their pay increased: using the company's formal job evaluation scheme, one that incorporates the principle of paying for initiative and responsibility. To ensure that such an upgrading occurs he also adds a security guard dimension to their work. This has the potential tacitly to improve the status element of the reward side of the implicit contract. Dal also explicitly addresses the status issue by suggesting they will be better off without the rather questionable sort of status they gained by getting more leisure-in-work time than other employees.

Dal seems to be very aware that taking away the opportunity to enjoy unofficial social rewards in the extended tea breaks is not going to be easy. He therefore seeks to redefine it as implicitly a little shameful and unfair to other workers. It is not an untainted reward. But he goes even further to deal with this potentially tricky issue. In effect, he suggests his own version of the indulgency pattern that was part of the old regime. We can understand in this way his statement to the yard workers that they would 'obviously have to be given discretion over when they might need to rest or otherwise recover after carrying out a particularly onerous or exhausting task'. This offer is subtly connected to the principle of mutual trust that he speaks of as inherent in their generally increased discretion.

There is a lot of subtle 'motivational' work going on in the meetings of Dal and his staff and he shows considerable rhetorical skill in drawing on discursive resources like 'trust', 'service', 'internal customer' and 'team' to paint a very positive picture of the new world into which he wants to lead them. He was wary of using the discursive resource of 'empowerment', however. We might see this reluctance to use a possibly pretentious term as a reflection of Dal's skills of persuasion and leadership. He certainly seems to have worked out his own theory of leadership, one that incorporates a belief that one cannot impose changes on employees (or 'foist ideas' or 'management fads' on them). He sees negotiation as an important part of his 'personal style of leadership' and believes this should happen after establishing a trusting relationship with those with whom he is to negotiate. For Dal, this means allowing the men to get to know him personally and 'where he is coming from'. He also mentions taking time to listen to the views of the group before putting his ideas to them. To be a leader is nevertheless still a matter of initiating actions for Dal. He talks of 'giving a lead' by proposing the site service idea. However, that assertion of leadership is balanced with a clear recognition that is occurring within what is an essentially negotiated relationship of exchange – the employment bargain.

Dal is 'motivating' and 'leading' then, but he is also engaging is some significant job design work. By incorporating much of the foreman's old role into the work of the yard gang members themselves he is significantly redesigning the tasks away from the former *direct* control principles towards one in which control is much more *indirect*. Dal is not moving to a situation where the foundry management abandons control over the yard workers. It is asking them to control themselves, in the interests of the employing organisation as well as for their own benefit. He is utilising work design principles of *job enrichment, team-working* and the *semi-autonomous work group* (concepts we look at below, pp. 235–8). He does recognise, however, that the group might not satisfactorily work in an entirely 'leaderless' way when he ends his involvement with them in a few months' time. He therefore talks of the possibility of a team leader being appointed. And in talking of this he is making yet another adjustment to the implicit contract with the group – he is putting into the bargain for the first time a possibility of career advancement.

Equity, balance and expectancies in work orientations

Although it is now common for motivational theories that use ideas of equity or expectancy to be referred to as 'process theories' they go only a part of the way towards the full process-relational thinking that has been developed over the chapters of *Organising and Managing Work*. Their insights do parallel much of what has been said about orientations to work and implicit contracts however. An early process-oriented contribution to what has variously been referred to as 'balance', 'social comparison' or 'equity' theorising in this area was a classical study of American soldiers (Stouffer *et al.*, 1949). The researchers observed that there was a greater dissatisfaction with promotional opportunities in the Army Corps than in the Military Police. This was in spite of the fact that, objectively, there were better opportunities in the former part of the military than in the latter. The dissatisfactions and the 'de-motivating' influence of these were not the outcomes of what was objectively the case but arose out of the expectations of the people involved with regard to promotional opportunities. A general sense of unfairness had developed in large part as a result of individual soldiers comparing their own prospects with the way that others had been treated. Developments in this kind of thinking were pulled together into an 'equity theory of motivation' by Adams (1963, 1965). This sees people balancing what they put into their work with what they get out of it in the light of what they see other people putting in and taking out in similar situations.

Equity or balance theories of work motivation

Concept

These theories show how work behaviour is influenced by how people perceive their situation after comparing their work/reward exchange (or 'implicit contract') with the employer to that of other members of the organisation.

The basic insight of so-called 'equity theory' is a vital one and it is wholly consistent with how the *work orientation* and *implicit contract* concepts have been used here. The central attention given in strategic exchange thinking to how people perceive or understand the contract they make with an employer is the same as in balance and equity thinking. The stress on how this perception involves comparisons with other people is implicit but clear in, for example the earlier reference to employees having to 'be persuaded that there is a fair and reasonable return' for everything that those employees 'put into' their work (p. 00). None of us can decide as to how 'fair or reasonable' we can regard anything that we are asked to do or anything that we are offered without making comparisons with other people and their circumstances.

Activity 8.4

Consider how far matters of 'equity', 'balance' or perceived fairness come into the stories Dal Cross in Case 8.2 (p. 321) and Campbell Toon in Case 1.3 (p. 23) have to tell us about:

- the way Dal first analyses the work orientations and perceived implicit contracts of the yard gang and, later, enters negotiations with the men;
- Campbell's attempts to increase the productivity of the packaging workers in his part of the factory by 'enriching' their jobs.

When Dal Cross was trying to make sense of the work orientations of the members of the yard gang in his early involvement with them he looked at the balance between what they were 'putting in' and 'getting out' – as far as he could understand it as an observer. He is explicit about the fact that he is talking at this stage about his perception of their perceptions, so to speak, when he says that their wages 'seemed fairly reasonable to me'. In effect he tries to put himself in their position, and makes the sort of comparison with others that he thinks that they would make – with 'other manual workers who did not have a skilled trade'. Some more subtle thinking along these lines is done as he goes on to look at what he calls the 'perverse status' that they enjoy in the foundry. This analysis emerges from his trying to make sense in 'balance' terms of the fact that the yardies get more free time for their own leisure during working hours than do other workers. All of these complexities are later taken into account during the bargaining that he enters into with the gang as he works to move them towards a new implicit contract. He tries to get them to redefine this 'privilege' by effectively suggesting that it is not really a reward at all.

Dal is well aware that worker perceptions of inputs and outputs have an important economic dimension. He appreciates that a pay increase is going to be vital in shifting the exchange relationship. It is interesting that the company's 'job evaluation' scheme that he makes use of is a device similar to that which many employers use to deal openly with matters of comparison and perceived fairness in wages or salaries paid to different groups within an organisation. Job evaluation schemes are used in deciding pay relativities in many work organisations. They use measurements of work 'inputs' and 'outputs' that are believed to be acceptable to everyone as the basis for pay comparisons. Such a scheme could also be a help to Cam Toon if he wishes to try again to redesign the work tasks of the members of his department. He reports how his workers were comparing the new tasks that they were doing with what they believe supervisors do. In principle, a job evaluation scheme would enable their new jobs to be measured, compared to the work that a supervisor typically does in similar areas of the organisation and a 'fair' wage for the new employment trade identified.

Expectancy theories of work motivation

Concept

These theories show how work behaviour is influenced (a) by the particular wants and expectations which particular employees, in particular circumstances, bring to the organisation and (b) by the extent to which these are met by the employer.

The concept of *expectancy* has been utilised by various theorists to deal with these matters of employee perception or 'understanding'. The concept has played a central part in the turning away of motivation theorists from the focus on 'needs' towards use of the much more realistic 'wants' and expectations that employees bring to particular jobs. Instead of indulging in generalisations about the needs that human beings generally are said to bring to the workplace, it encourages managers to look at the specific work circumstances of whatever group of employees they are concerned with and at the specific expectations that they bring to their employment relationship with a particular employer. The 'expectancies' referred to by psychologists and motivation theorists like Vroom (1964) or Lawler (1971) correspond to some extent to the 'work orientations' notion that has emerged out of the industrial sociology tradition. We can draw out of expectancy thinking some highly commonsensical guidelines that can be applied to the various facets of work organisation and bear on the input–output bargain at the centre of the employment relationship management – from pay systems and promotional policies to job design and management style. For successful 'motivation' to occur several conditions have to be met.

- Employees must see that the effort they put in will, in fact, cause effective performance. It would be inappropriate for an individual output bonus to be paid to someone operating a machine that had a fixed rate or level of output, for example.
- Employees must see that appropriate performance will lead to their receiving the rewards claimed to be linked to them. Promotion would not be a good motivator, for example, if the individual either sees people being promoted for reasons other than effective performance or if they see cases of such performance failing to lead to promotion.
- The rewards available to employees must be ones in which they are actually interested – or can be persuaded to become interested in. The offer of the rewards of intrinsic job satisfaction (that Campbell Toon offered his staff, for example) or increased job status would be poor motivators for employees who simply wanted a quiet life at work in a secure job with a good level of pay to take home.
- Employees must have both the technical skills and knowledge to do the job.
- Employees must understand the broader implications of the role they are taking on – the sort of relationships they are expected to have with managers themselves and with other people in the organisation for example.

These practical managerial guidelines emerge from what textbooks label 'expectancy theories of motivation'. The theory behind these highly commonsensical recommendations is consistent with strategic exchange thinking and its emphasis on the interpretations and understandings that people bring to their employment. Expectancy thinking's focus is on the employees themselves, as we would expect from work emerging from the psychological tradition of 'motivational' theorising. In this respect, it is a more narrowly focused analysis than the strategic exchange one. Strategic exchange analysis is broader and deeper in its locating of managerial attempts to manipulate the implicit contract within both the social and cultural location and priorities of the employee and the strategic position and priorities of the employing organisation (whose exchanges with employees are just one resource exchange among many.

Strategic exchange analysis and the way it uses the concepts of work orientation and implicit contract is also broader (more fully process-relational we might say) than expectancy theory in its attention to the ongoing processes of negotiation and renegotiation that occur in the relationship between employers and employees. This is a relationship that exists within a political–economic context. And the nature of that context means that significant managerial efforts have to go into the constant handling of the basic tensions and contradictions that characterise the employment relationship in industrial capitalist societies. These tensions are always there in the background of every 'motivational' situation in the work organisation. Sometimes they are more obvious than at other times, however. They could be understood as manifesting themselves, for instance, when one of the two workers with whom Campbell Toon discusses the issue of whether or not 'money is a motivator' in Case 1.3 (p. 23) rejects the language of motivation and contextualises the proposed pay claim with the words, 'there's no way any factory worker is ever going to feel that they are paid enough'. Issues of social class and basic employer–employee conflicts are clearly playing a part here.

Work motivation, then, cannot be considered in isolation from a whole range of other issues that impinge on the negotiated relationship between the employing organisation and its employees. And there is no particular aspect of a manager's job that can be separated out from the rest of what they do as the 'motivational element' of their job. It has been clear throughout this chapter, not least in the reported managerial experiences of Dal Cross and Cam Toon, that to 'motivate' people (getting employees to do what they otherwise would not do) managers lead, build relationships, develop understandings, train people, devise promotional schemes and design jobs. Both Dal and Cam are, for example, engaged in a degree of job redesign work in their attempts to 'motivate' their staff to work more effectively. These were personal initiatives applying to their own departments. But, as was stressed earlier in the chapter, we cannot separate out what any manager does in their own department from the wider cultural and structural arrangements of the organisation as a whole. Each of these managers was attempting a move from a relatively *direct* approach to seeking managerial control to a relatively *indirect* one. In this, we can assume that they felt that such a move was not inconsistent with the broader cultural and structural trends in their companies. Broad considerations of job design are an important element in the strategic shaping of the organisation as a whole.

Direct and indirect control principles of work design

Organisational structures, and the task shaping and task allocation that is part of them, are very much 'emergent' phenomena – outcomes of the balance of managerial initiatives and employee acceptance. Process-relational thinking draws attention to the negotiated, political and emergent aspects of organisations. Organisations, as they emerge out of the processes of cooperation and conflict, rarely resemble their official managerial blueprint or organisation charts when we look at them in action. But this does not mean that managers are not continually working to design – or *re*design – the activities that are carried on in the organisation's name. To understand this, it is useful to look at certain work design principles that have played a part in shaping the practices of organisational managers throughout the history of the modern work organisation.

Work design/redesign principles *Concept*

General principles about how narrow or broad the tasks associated with jobs should be and the extent to which jobholders should use discretion in carrying out those tasks.

Job design/redesign practices *Concept*

The shaping of particular jobs, especially with regard to how narrow or broad the tasks associated with those jobs are and the extent to which jobholders exercise discretion in carrying out those tasks.

The terms 'job design' and 'work design' are often used interchangeably but, here, we will use them to represent two different but closely related ideas. The actual task pattern that emerges in any particular part of an organisation (the new version of the yard worker job introduced by Dal Cross in Case 8.2, for example) is referred to here as a matter of *job design* (or redesign). The broad principles that are drawn upon when designing or redesigning jobs are, however, referred to as *work design* principles. The former, then, are matters of actual practice and the latter matters of prescription or intent.

Work design is clearly something closely related to the broader structural and cultural 'design' of the organisation as a whole. It was argued in Chapter 7 that there is a basic choice that managers can make in trying to achieve managerial control through this design – through the shaping of the organisation as a whole. This is a choice between *direct* control attempts and *indirect* ones.

- An organisation leaning towards direct control principles would be a highly centralised one with a tightly bureaucratic structure and culture. There would be an emphasis on tight rules and closely prescribed procedures in which a relatively low level of psychological commitment would be sought from the employees. Because these arrangements imply that management is not putting a lot of trust in employees to do what is required of them of their own accord, a 'low trust' culture emerges in which relationships between employer and employees tend to be adversarial. Differences of interest between parties to the employment relationship thus become manifest and visible at a surface level.
- The organisation leaning more in the indirect control direction would be less centralised and have a loosely bureaucratic structure and culture. Rules would be relatively loose and procedures left flexible because employees would have discretion about how to carry out those tasks. They would, however, apply this discretion in a way that fitted with managerial requirements and the strategic priorities of the organisation because of their high level of psychological commitment to the organisation. This commitment is made possible, in turn, because of a culture of high trust between members of the organisation – one in which common or mutual interests between different parties to the employment relationship are emphasised. Differences of interest between parties to the employment bargain tend to remain below the surface of ongoing activities and are not expressed through overt confrontations.

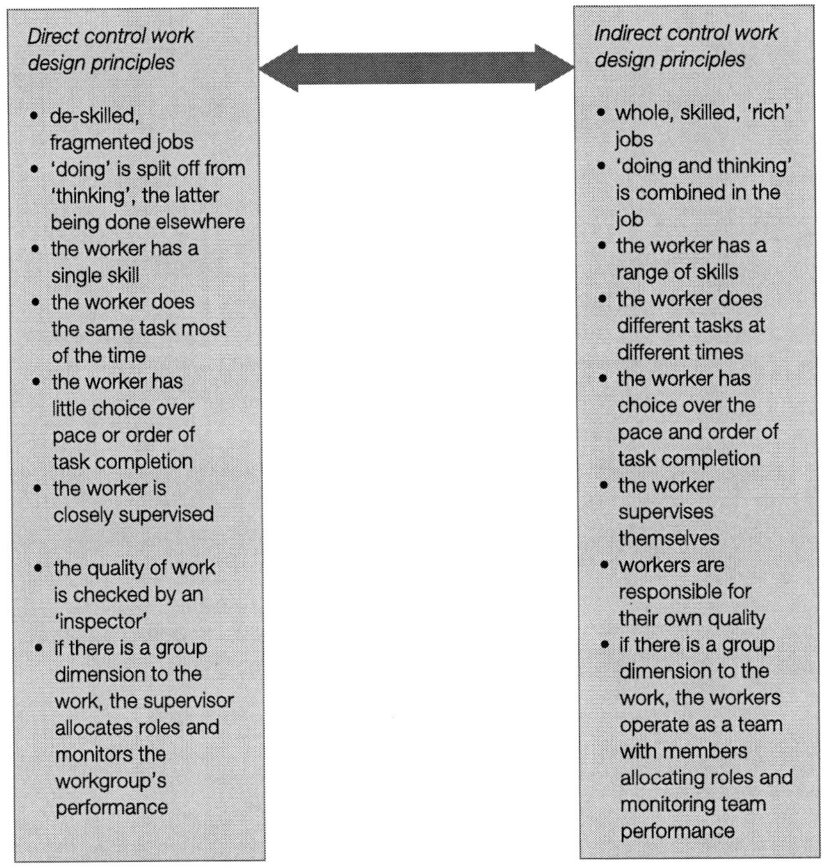

FIGURE 8.1 Direct and indirect control principles of work design

Within these two basic approaches to what we might call *organisational* design there are two basic sets of *work* design principles and these are outlined in Figure 8.1.

The two sets of work design principles outlined in Figure 8.1 are *ideal types* – constructs created by the social scientist to help make sense of the much more complex and potentially confusing picture that emerges when we go out into organisations to see what is happening 'on the ground' (as we saw with Weber's 'ideal type of bureaucracy' in Chapter 2, pp. 39–40). No actually observable job designs have ever fully followed the descriptions set out as two ends of the continuum in the diagram, and job designs can be found that are close to the basic work design principles set out in the two columns without following every element of the above characterisation. Within teamworking, to take an example from the 'indirect' side, it might be that the team allocates its own roles from day to day but is still subject to external monitoring of the resulting performance. Sometimes teamworking involves a 'team leader' who retains certain of the roles of the supervisor who plays an important role on the 'direct' side.

In practice, the actual job designs we are likely to come across in organisations will fall somewhere along the continuum outlined in Figure 8.1 and may even combine elements from both ends of it. The model is nevertheless valuable because it represents in a clear way the scope of choices open to managers when they embark on designing jobs in particular organisational settings. We might imagine some scheme like this having been in the minds of both Dal Cross and Campbell Toon when they set out to make changes in the designs of jobs for which they had managerial responsibilities. Both, as we noted earlier, were interested in making moves towards more *indirect* ways of controlling the work done in their departments. Each of these two managers were influenced by 'newer' work design ideas that they had come across. Dal tells us how he had been on a 'change management course' and amongst the 'stuff' that he had read was material on 'enriching jobs', 'empowering staff' and 'quality circles'. Cam refers to his 'classes on motivation', where one of the things he learned about was Herzberg's 'job enrichment principles'. Although these men mention different bits of 'management thinking', they do not closely follow any of the texts or manuals on any of these specific techniques. Instead, they pragmatically apply the basic principles that underlie all these specific innovations ('job enrichment', 'empowerment', 'quality circles', for example). These are the basic principles being characterised here as *indirect control* principles. Within these, Dal pragmatically devises his own form of 'teamworking', that in the longer run may or may not have a team leader role within it. Cam speaks of 'rearranging the jobs of my people so that there was more variety in their tasks'. He also tries to give them 'more freedom to choose how to do the work' by removing a level of supervision.

We shall shortly review some of the more significant managerial innovations and fashions that have been put forward in different guises and under different labels over the past half century. But it is more important to see what all of these have in common than to try to look for distinctions between, say, 'job enrichment', 'vertical task integration' and 'empowerment' or between 'semi-autonomous work groups' and 'teams'. Exactly that has been done here by clustering many of the features of these managerial innovations and identifying them as 'indirect control attempts' which, at the level of job design, are used to handle, in effect, the basic contradiction that all managerial work has to deal with. This is the contradiction whereby managers need to control what workers do while, at the same time, recognising that every managerial attempt at control is liable to be challenged. Organisational members, to varying degrees, will demand 'freedom' or autonomy in the workplace. But managers must make sure that this freedom is a freedom to do what, in the end, the managers want them to do. Loose control, in effect, is stronger than tight control. That is the basic principle of indirect control work design thinking.

Modernity, industrialism and the hesitant embracing of direct control work design

There is a powerful irony behind the fact that we typically treat the principles of *indirect* work design principles as managerial innovations, as 'new thinking', or in terms of progressive or enlightened management ideas. This is ironic because, in the larger historical scheme of things, it was the shift in industrialising societies towards *direct* forms of work control that was one of the fundamental innovations of the new industrial capitalist order. One has to take care not to romanticise the pre-industrial past but, generally speaking, the division of labour that operated in pre-industrial societies was a *social (or general) division of labour.*

Social or *general* division of labour — Concept

The allocation of work tasks across society, typically into occupations or trades.

The key work design principle was an occupational one: the working individual played their part in society as a farmer, brewer or shoemaker and would be expected to develop the cluster of skills that went with their particular craft or trade. They would be able to handle what work design experts later came to call 'whole tasks' – the planting, nurturing and harvesting of a crop or the production of a pair of shoes. In practice there were undoubtedly numerous people who did little more than sweep floors or carry trade workers' tools. However, something along the lines of what we have characterised as indirect work design principles were generally seen as desirable and at the centre of the pre-industrial social order. The rise of industrial capitalism, the growth of the institution of formal employment and the rationalising force of bureaucratisation saw a splitting down of many of the occupational roles within the old social division of labour into de-skilled jobs. There was now to be a *technical (or detailed) division of labour* whereby many work activities in factories and offices were split down so that individuals only did one specialised part of what had previously been the 'whole task' associated with an occupation.

Technical or *detailed* division of labour — Concept

The breaking down of 'whole' occupational roles into specialised and generally unskilled jobs.

We can envisage the seventeenth or eighteenth century violin maker working on each instrument all the way from the initial woodcarving stage to the varnishing and the adding of the bridge, pegs and strings. But we would find the typical worker in a modern violin factory only able to work the wood cutting machine, glue the front, sides and backs of the instrument together or varnish the violin when it reached the varnish shop. The work would have been de-skilled. Many more violins could be produced at a much higher rate of profit for the employer, but for this to occur, those with the expertise have to take on the role of instructing and monitoring the rest. The managers have to control the workers. Thinking is separated from doing (an important direct control design feature identified earlier in Figure 8.1) and the implications for human beings of this trend were recognised from the start. Adam Smith in his massively influential work *The Wealth of Nations* of 1776, in which the new industrial order was both chronicled and boosted further, provided an analysis of the splitting down of the process of making tacks ('pins' as he called them). This showed that if you fragmented the job of the craft pin maker, who was able to do every stage of pin making, so that each stage of the process became the specialised task of a different worker, a vastly greater number of pins could be produced per day. However, in an industrial order based on this principle, with all the increases of general wealth that would accompany it, these new specialised labourers would be serious 'losers'. 'Those who labour most get least', he observed. What he had in mind was what we might nowadays call the quality of their lives. Someone whose life 'is spent in performing a few simple operations', he observed has 'no occasion' to 'exert understanding' and hence 'becomes as ignorant as it is possible for a human creature to become'.

Smith's reservations about this aspect of modern industrialised labour have come forward and then retreated again at various times ever since he first expressed them. However, the growth of the de-skilling and direct control trend in the nineteenth century was significantly boosted by Charles Babbage (1832). Babbage powerfully demonstrated to employers just how much cheaper de-skilled labour was compared with skilled or craft-based labour. F.W. Taylor in the later part of the nineteenth century codified and systematised these direct control principles of work design and proselytised passionately for their introduction across the workshops of the fast growing industrial enterprises of that time (Taylor, 1911).

Scientific management (Taylorism) *Concept*

Work design principles that maximise the amount of discretion over task performance given to managerial experts, who calculate and precisely define how each job is to be carried out.

Taylor's so-called called *scientific management* entailed:

- managers and experts systematically or 'scientifically' analysing every work task;
- each job being fragmented to achieve the highest possible technical division of labour, on the basis of this analysis;

- the planning of work being separated from its execution;
- skill requirements and job-learning times being reduced to the minimum;
- materials handling by operators being minimised to avoid distraction from the worker's focal task;
- work performance being closely 'time-studied' and monitored;
- pay being tied directly to individual output to encourage each worker to maximise their efforts;
- the relationships between employers/managers and employees remaining formal and distant.

Although Taylor's principles were rarely followed in their entirety, the basic scientific management approach to work design was widely embraced in the industrial and industrialising world as it moved into the twentieth century. This included communist countries where one might have expected some resistance to what many saw as the de-humanisation of working people. But there was also controversy and resistance to the de-skilling and close control trend. We should perhaps note, however, that although Taylor can be seen as pointing to a way forward for large areas of industrial activity, his thinking was rooted in solving problems of workshops in the late nineteenth century American steel industry where much of the labour was unskilled and the workers unfamiliar with the English language. His system might have been more viable in that context than in others where workers might have expected more than monetary satisfactions from their employment. The same argument may apply to the innovations introduced into the car factories of Henry Ford where the 'robotising' of the worker implicit in Taylorism was extended by the placing of the worker on an assembly line. Ford was very conscious of the costs that could follow from treating workers in this way, however. He therefore departed radically from Taylorism in paying a fixed and relatively high wage and called for the worker to show a long-term loyalty to the employer and live a sober and responsible life fitting for a Ford worker. In this way, there was a shift away from the arm's-length type of employment relationship recommended by Taylor.

Fordism *Concept*

A combining of mass production de-skilled job design in the industrial workplace with employment and state welfare policies that develop workers as both fit workers and willing consumers of the products of industry.

Ford, we might say, set out to manipulate the work orientation of the industrial worker in the more sophisticated way called for by the changing circumstances of the twentieth century. But his innovations also actively influenced the way employment and indeed whole economies and societies were to develop. He recognised that industrial workers could also become the consumers of the products they made. The implicit contract was now to be one which might be expressed by managers as, 'Work hard in our factories in the way we direct you and in return for that you will be well paid and will be able to afford to buy one of the cars you make. And the more cars you buy, the more work there will be – and the better off you will become.' Fordism thus goes way beyond work design. As Fordist work design practices spread in industrialised societies they were supported by the state, whose economic, welfare and educational policies were increasingly aimed at developing a healthy workforce who would also be the consumers of the products and services they produced.

At the same time that Fordism was spreading, attention was beginning to be paid to the arguments of Roethlisberger and Dickson (1939) and Elton Mayo (1933) arising from the research in the Hawthorne plant in Chicago. This research was said to show the importance to them of people's social involvement at work and it was alleged that employees worked more effectively when managers 'showed an interest' in them. These arguments kept alive in some managers' minds an awareness that employees' expectations at work were complex and would not necessarily be straightforwardly satisfied by monetary rewards alone. Such awareness did not detract, however, from general managerial recognition of the immense benefits to employers that Taylorism and Fordism offered by way of both cost efficiency and the tightness of managerial control. A widespread recognition of these benefits meant, and continues to mean, that a powerful de-skilling logic runs through many work design efforts across a multiplicity of different types of employment. As Marxian analysis suggests, the *labour process* in a society based on capitalist principles is one where de-skilling is frequently the option that most effectively enables the employer to exploit the labour power of their employees (Braverman, 1974).

Capitalist labour process

Concept

In Marxian analysis this is the process whereby managers design, control and monitor work activities in order to extract surplus value from the labour activity of employees on behalf of the capital-owning class which employs them.

However, de-skilling always has its costs – as observers from Smith onwards had pointed out and as many managers themselves discovered. In some circumstances it was not the most effective way of utilising the efforts of employees (Friedman, 1977, Edwards, 1979).

Continuing doubts about de-skilled and tightly controlled work and the recognition of its inappropriateness to many work and labour market circumstances brings us back to Maslow and the significance we noted earlier of his recognition of the changing expectations that would be coming forward for workers in increasingly affluent sections of fast developing economies. As Cam Toon remembered from his management classes, Herzberg turned the Maslow principle into some specific job design practices: *job enrichment*.

Job enrichment

Concept

The expansion of the scope of jobs by such means as the re-integration of maintenance or inspection tasks; an extension of the work cycle; an increased degree of delegation of decision making by job holders.

Herzberg (1966) argued that what were frequently taken to be work incentives or 'motivators' – pay, good working conditions and good relationships with supervisors – were no longer motivators at all. They were, rather, 'hygiene factors' – conditions that had to be fulfilled before motivation would actually happen. And the rewards that would lead to this 'motivation' were ones such as achievement, recognition and, especially, the satisfaction coming from the job itself. Jobs should thus have more variety and responsibility built into them. Job enrichment would see the scope of jobs increased. The argument, in effect, was that managers should 'redesign' jobs along these lines to meet the rising expectations of modern employees.

But what about the social or group dimension of work design? The Hawthorne research referred to earlier (p. 12) had stressed the importance to employees of the social aspects of work and Maslow included 'social needs' in his scheme, albeit at a lower level than the rather idealised 'self-actualisation' notion that Herzberg tried to turn into something practicable. Mayo saw workers being 'tied into' the employing organisation via their location in meaningful groups of fellow workers. Maslow argued that people would look for social needs to be met at work once their lower level needs had been satisfied. However, other advantages of making groups or 'teams' central to work (re)design were stressed by British researchers working with the Tavistock Institute of Human Relations (Rice, 1958, Trist *et al.*, 1963). It was argued that work organisations should be regarded as *socio-technical systems*.

Socio-technical systems

Concept

An approach to work design in which the technical and the social/psychological aspects of the overall workplace are given equal weight and are designed at the same time to *take each other into account.*

The Tavistock researchers noted that, typically, the technical aspects of a work enterprise tended to be designed first: the buildings, hardware and the layout of both of these is 'blueprinted' first and a set of social arrangements then designed to slot into it. What would be more effective, the Tavistock writers argue, would be for the technical and the social components of the overall system to be designed simultaneously and for them to take each other into account.

Activity 8.5

Reread the story 'Walt and Roger develop a greenfield site' (Case 7.2, p. 262) and consider the extent to which it could be said that Roger is following socio-technical system principles in suggesting how he and Walt should go about designing both the physical/technical aspects of their new organisation and the social/cultural aspects.

Roger closely follows the principles that socio-technical thinking would suggest appropriate for both organisation and job design. He very effectively persuades Walt that organisation design should consider social and cultural factors, on the one hand, and technical and physical factors on the other hand, *at the same time* – the one taking the other into account. This would mean that when the 'system' is operating these two aspects of it – the 'socio' and the 'technical' – would *fit* with each other. Walt's approach of setting up the 'technical' aspect first and then 'adding people onto it' would lead to real difficulties once the site was operating, Roger persuaded him. At the level of job design, the same principles should be followed according to the Tavistock researchers. In setting up an office or workshop, the technical tasks (together with the desks or machines associated with the tasks) should be grouped together to form a logical 'whole task' that can then be performed by members of the group with minimal supervisory interference. We thus get a *semi-autonomous workgroup* in which a group of people possesses all the necessary skills and all the necessary equipment to manage themselves in, say, the assembly of a motor car. Or, we might see a group of staff take charge, as a team, of producing a company's in-house magazine. Members of the team would share out among themselves and jointly coordinate tasks ranging from the collection of stories to the assembling of the pages on a desktop publishing system.

Teamworking/semi-autonomous workgroups — *Concept*

The grouping of individual jobs to focus work activities on a *whole task*, with team members being fully trained and equipped so that they can be given discretion, as a group, over how the task is completed.

With this example of the 'self-managed' group of staff who produced their company's house magazine we see something that might be labelled 'a semi-autonomous workgroup' or put forward as an example either of 'teamworking' or 'high performance work design'. Labels change in the managerial world as fast as they do in the world of fashion clothing. Something close to what we see modern companies celebrate as highly innovative 'high performance teams' or 'cellular manufacture' might well have been seen in certain craft groups producing goods way back in the middle ages, albeit producing much simpler products or services. A detailed division of labour and tight direct control managerial supervision and surveillance has played a central part in the vast increases in wealth and welfare that industrial capitalism has brought about. But to de-skill and tightly control work task performance is to wield a double-edged sword. It can cut both ways: sometimes helping the managers of employing organisations to fulfil their agenda, sometimes hindering them because of the counterproductive 'de-motivating' or 'alienating' tendencies of de-skilled and directly controlled work.

Dilemmas and choices in shaping work tasks and gaining cooperation

Implicit in our review of changing work design principles and job design practices since the industrial revolution is a recognition that there may be circumstances in which certain work design principles are more successful, from a managerial point of view, than in others. For example, it is very likely that Taylor's scientific management practices would be more viable with the unskilled immigrant workers he came across in the nineteenth-century steel mills than they could ever be with well-educated and articulate workers in a modern aerospace company. Similarly, we are not too surprised to see principles very close to those articulated by Taylor proving satisfactory to the managers of a modern company hiring (and firing) relatively young and transient workers to serve hamburgers to a highly standardised recipe in fixed service format across the world (Ritzer, 1993, Royle, 2000). But we would be surprised to see the motivational and job design practices that prove profitable to the high street hamburger restaurant proving to be managerially successful in, say, a university or a city architect's department. There appear to be 'contingencies' that are relevant to managerial decision making in the job design area. These are the circumstances of the organisation, like its size, technology or environmental situation, which have a better 'fit' with certain types of organisational arrangement and culture than with others.

When we applied the contingency insight to general organisational arrangements earlier, it was emphasised that contingencies do not determine organisational arrangements. Managers take into account their interpretations of contingent circumstances when arguing about and negotiating what patterns of organisation they will work towards. So what are the contingent factors that might be relevant to managerial debate within any given organisation about the work design principles that are to be applied?

Activity 8.6

Review the model in Figure 7.4 'Choice and contingency in organisational shaping' (p. 275) and how this was explained in Chapter 7. How do you think the contingencies represented there might be built upon to bring out circumstantial factors directly relevant to job design issues?

The contingency of *organisational size* might be relevant to job design in that having a large number of employees increases the scope for making people's jobs more specialised, whether this is specialisation of the type that leads to the appointment of a company lawyer, say, or the de-skilling type of specialisation that fragments the job of a pin maker. However, the other two contingencies shown in the model are perhaps more significant – those of technology and environmental stability.

The organisation's *technology* is a key job design factor in two closely related ways. First, it defines the tasks that are to be done and the extent to which those tasks are amenable to fragmentation or de-skilling. The technology of brain surgery, for example, does not lend itself to a detailed division of labour in which a succession of single-skilled individuals take their turn at wielding different types of scalpel for different stages of an operation. The technology of high street hamburger cooking and serving, however, lends itself well to such an approach.

The nature of the *environment* within which the organisation operates is also immensely important. We saw in the last chapter that a fast-changing and highly competitive business environment, one that requires frequent innovative action on the part of employees to enable it to survive, finds an 'organic' or loose structure more appropriate to its situation than a tightly bureaucratic one. This clearly implies a need for job designs that do not involve the sort of tight prescription and standardisation that goes with direct control types of job design. There is a tendency therefore for managers to choose indirect control types of job design where there are environmental pressures requiring high levels of innovation or adaptability on the part of employees. There is an obvious incompatibility between asking people to apply high levels of discretion and innovation in their work and expecting them to take detailed orders from a manager and be continually checked up on by a supervisor.

A concept that is often used in this context is that of *flexibility*. It is frequently argued that a move towards indirect control job designs are necessary if workers are to perform flexibly so that an organisation can quickly change what it is doing to cope with competitive pressures. This, however, is only partly true. There are two types of flexibility that managers of organisations look for: flexibility for long-term adaptability and flexibility for short-term predictability.

Flexibility for long-term adaptability

Concept

The ability to make rapid and effective innovations through the use of job designs and employment policies that encourage people to use their discretion and work in new ways for the sake of the organisation – as circumstances require.

This fits with *indirect control* work design principles and high-trust relationships.

Flexibility for short-term predictability

Concept

The ability to make rapid changes through the use of job designs and employment policies that allow staff to be easily recruited and trained or easily laid off – as circumstances require.

This fits with *direct control* work design principles and low-trust relationships.

Sometimes organisations will have a predominant need for just one of these types of flexibility. A consultancy organisation would mainly need flexibility for long-term adaptability, for example, and would therefore tend to follow indirect control work design principles across the firm. An organisation in the sugar beet processing industry, with inevitably seasonal patterns of working, on the other hand, would need flexibility for short-term predictability. It would therefore find it more fitting to adopt predominantly direct control job designs. This would not only suit the seasonal need to hire at one time and fire at another; it would also fit with the generally low levels of skills required to apply the technology. And it would fit with the almost non-existent need to innovate and develop the product.

These two cases are relatively straightforward. But, in many organisations, managers find both types of flexibility are required. Sometimes one type of flexibility is relevant to one area of the organisation and the other to another area. This is a circumstance that will be considered later when we look at issues of how job design issues relate to overall issues of how an organisation is to be 'resourced' with inputs of human skill, knowledge and labour. Researchers on innovations in work design have frequently commented on the tendency for the managerial success of these initiatives at a local level to depend on whether or not they were supported by appropriate human resourcing policies at the level of the wider organisation (Buchanan and Preston, 1992). The possibility of organisations needing *dual human resourcing strategies* to cope with different types of flexibility being required in different parts of an organisation will be looked at in Chapter 10, (pp. 426–8).

Human resourcing policies inevitably have to cope with the fundamental contradiction that work design initiatives are always faced with. They must gain commitment and consent from the same employees that they need to 'exploit'. In recent decades of increasing international competition, we can see various employers desperately seeking new ways to handle this tension in order to stay in business – or rather to find new combinations of established work design principles. This has led to work design and human resourcing practices that incorporate novel mixtures of direct and indirect control principles. The *lean production* practices seen in the car industry are an example of this (Womack, Jones and Roos, 1990). 'Leanness' means that no time, effort, or resources are wasted and high psychological commitment to this ruthlessly tight regime is expected from a workforce that is expected to use its discretion in the spaces where this is allowed, always with the benefit of 'the customer' in mind.

Lean production *Concept*

The combining, typically within car assembly, of team working with automated technologies. Workers are required both to initiate 'continual improvements' in quality and to ensure that every task is got 'right first time' and completed to a demanding 'just-in-time' schedule.

A similar combining of direct and indirect control work design and human resourcing principles is seen with *business process re-engineering* (BPR) (Hammer and Champy, 1993; see Further Reading on work restructuring and re-engineering, p. 349). BPR has seen organisations across a range of industries restructured to focus on business *processes* (getting a product designed, manufactured and sold, say). This means turning away from an emphasis on business *functions* (where a design function focuses just on design, a manufacturing function focuses on production and a sales function concentrates just on selling, for example). A clear and integrated flow of processes is thus made possible by the use of advanced information technologies. Employees can be *empowered* and given new degrees of freedom to manage themselves in teams. They are no longer trapped in the separate boxes of functional organisation where managers, planners and schedulers have to direct and coordinate people's efforts to ensure that all the separate tasks and operations 'add up' to the provision of a successful product or service. The clearer logic of the basic process flow means that workers can 'make things add up' for themselves, as Roberto Auldearn's managing director put it when explaining the 'embracing of business process reengineering' at Dovecote Components in Case 8.3.

Business process re-engineering (BPR) *Concept*

The restructuring of an organisation to focus on business processes rather than on business functions. Advanced management control information technologies are used together with team working and employee 'empowerment'.

Activity 8.7

Read Roberto Auldearn's account in Case 8.3 of how Dovecote Components 'embraced' business process re-engineering.

After looking back once again at the model set out in Figure 7.4 (p. 275), note the ways in which a part was played in this exercise in 'organisational shaping' by:

- contextual political, economic and cultural patterns;
- enacted contingencies;
- managerial values, goals and interests;
- managerial argument, negotiation and choice.

Consider the extent to which we are helped to make sense of this story by the notion of a basic contradiction whereby managers have to gain commitment and consent from the employees at the same time as they are required to exploit and manipulate them.

Re-engineering Dovecote Components

Case 8.3

Dovecote Components has been an important employer in this town for a long time. Most people around here just call it 'The Doocot'. For over 20 years now the workforce has been steadily falling as we have increased investment in newer technologies and found a whole lot of ways of making the work less labour intensive. Productivity was steadily rising over this period and, as a management, we felt freer to make changes without having to fight with trade unions over every little detail. Government policies were partly responsible for this, but the unions – indeed the workforce generally – recognised that we were struggling in an increasingly difficult and increasingly international market place. Almost every year would see some redundancies and there was not a great deal of argument about this. I think people regarded these job losses as a sort of unfortunate fact of life and I don't think they affected morale within the company to any real extent. But people did not realise just how difficult things were going to get as we saw the auto companies that bought our components increasingly looking across the whole global economy to source their production.

About five years ago we realised that we needed to make radical changes in the business. We had been developing our technologies incrementally over the years and had introduced at different times a variety of innovations ranging from quality improvement groups to cellular and team working. A lot of our production is now done on a just-in-time basis. Components go out of the door just a few hours before the car plant 200 miles away needs them to stick in its cars. It was becoming clear to us, however, that there were increasing numbers of other suppliers who could get their products to the factories just as promptly. And not only could they supply at significantly lower prices but several of them were much faster than us at developing and improving their products. Our customers were facing increasing global competition just as we were and were constantly looking to improve the quality and functionality of the components they put in their vehicles.

At the first executive meetings where we talked seriously about making radical changes I put forward a plan to set up a completely new 'Research, Design and Manufacturing Innovation' department. This would be a crack team that I would recruit by head hunting from my quite extensive contacts across the engineering world. It would combine product development and the improving of production methods – making sure we designed for ease of manufacture as well as to delight our customers. Immediately I suggested this I was shot down. The first bloke to 'have a go' didn't bother me. As a management accountant, our finance man was right to look critically at my plans and question how we could possibly afford this. But, like every one else, I knew that he personally disliked me and would attack anything I put forward. It was the MD, Jerry Penick, who really put the boot in however. This did bother me. In the first place, he said, 'there is certainly no way we can afford to do that'. And, 'secondly', he went on, 'your whole philosophy is out of date'. That made me wild. I ranted on about how advanced my 'design for manufacturing' ideas were and that I would easily get a job with one of our competitors if he had so little respect for me. In fact I did slam out of the meeting at one point. I think it was when the Manufacturing Director – a blinkered and territorially minded idiot if ever there was one – made it clear that he wasn't keen for me to get involved in manufacturing issues. The MD came and found me puffing a cigar in the directors' lavatory and persuaded me to go back into the meeting and hear his thoughts on 're-engineering the Doocot'.

It turned out that the consultants that Jerry had brought in six months earlier, 'just to look over things' as he told us, had in fact come up with this scheme to 're-engineer' the processes in Doocot 'from top to bottom'. 'We have got to jump out of our functional boxes and our obsession with departmental boundaries,' he said, looking directly at me and then at my manufacturing colleague. 'Everything has got to be stripped down to the basics and everyone will make their contribution to the basic processes of getting ideas quickly and efficiently through from the drawing board to the customer's delivery bay. The bloke on the drawing board will be as interested in that customer's needs as the driver of the delivery wagon will – or as I will.'

At this stage we were all looking at each other a little shocked. Most of us had heard of this 'business re-engineering' thing, but had not really related it to our situation. Molly, our marketing woman, ventured to say that all the re-engineering cases that she had come across had been more exercises in 'blood letting' and 'axing people as well as departments' than improving processes. 'Well', came back Jerry, 'I don't want any talk like that. But the re-engineering exercise will mean taking quite a big axe to our management structures. Levels will be taken out.' He accepted that 'delayering' and 'becoming leaner' would be painful. The consultants, together with a small senior management team, would 'look at everybody's job' and nobody 'whose job doesn't serve our core processes' would survive. This would be hard and it would 'hurt everybody involved', Jerry said. But those who survived would be much better off. It wasn't just that their jobs would be more secure. Their 'prospects with the firm' would also be better. Above all, people would benefit by being 'more empowered'. He explained that, at present, all the efforts that people put in and all the operations across the plant had to be 'made to add up' by managers, supervisors and other 'functionaries'. By taking a lot of these out, people would be given the satisfaction of 'adding it all up' for themselves. And, he added, by 'taking away all the managerial buffers that exist between the workforce and the market place' people will see the need to 'work hard, conscientiously and cooperatively *for the business and not for their department* because they will know that if they don't we all go under'.

The whole thing seemed sensible, if rather terrifying. For six months the 'Re-engineering Action Group' (RAG), comprising four senior managers and four consultants, were to work 'day and night' with Jerry to 'completely reshape the business'. The business was to be more 'focused' than at present and this basically meant making it smaller. 'We have got too big and unwieldy', Jerry argued, 'so we'll cut the less profitable lines and try to stay at a size where a smallish top management team can keep their eyes on everything.' There would be a major investment in ICT, with the savings made on labour costs more than covering the 'costs of the new computer systems'. The 'software and hardware that are available now for management control', he insisted, 'were sophisticated enough now to cover the work of all the people who will be leaving us – and more'.

So, all of this went ahead. I was lucky to be kept on. But both my Finance Director and Manufacturing Director colleagues – and enemies – got the push. I was on the RAG – the action group charged with 'implementing' the re-engineering. At first I felt privileged. But this feeling soon went. I began to realise quite early on that the whole thing was doomed from the start. We had embraced business process re-engineering in a big way. But we had embraced a monster. In principle, I thought, it was wise. It was harsh. But harsh measures were necessary. And all of those who stayed with the business would experience a much higher level of empowerment and involvement with the core processes of the enterprise. They would clearly benefit. But as we all quickly learned, it wasn't to happen like that, and it's so easy to see why, in retrospect.

In one voice, we were saying that people were to be empowered, to be trusted and were to have their 'energies' released to do 'really meaningful work'. But in another voice we were asking people to kneel down to have their heads chopped off. This is where the massive catch in the whole thing lay. On the one hand we were asking people to be empowered, to manage themselves and be committed to the business. The logic of de-layering was one of saying that an empowered and committed workforce could, in many respects, manage things better than managers could. But on the other hand, we were a group of managers and consultants acting as if we were mighty gods who knew better than anyone how things should be done.

As you can imagine, the whole thing was treated with deep suspicion and bitter hostility from the beginning. And that's just among the managers! We RAG members were treated with utter disdain and mistrust as hypocrites and axe wielders. Because nobody would cooperate with us or give us any information we could trust, we simply could not do the work we were meant to do. But how could we back down? Consequently we made lots of cuts and we reorganised the place from top to bottom without really knowing what we were doing. And, yes, the business has survived. But we are running it through a regime of terror with most of the best staff we had having moved out to other jobs. I give the business a couple more years at most. And I shall be out of here well before that. When you see me next time, I'll have flown the Doocot.

These events at Dovecote Components would not have come about if there had not been major changes in the global economy. The most important contextual pressure is the growth of competition from producers of motor components across the world and the combination of this with car manufacturers choosing to 'source' themselves from a global market place. Relevant nationally is the state's role in reducing the ability of trade unions to resist managerial initiatives. And, at the local level, there appears to be a degree of goodwill towards 'The Doocot'. This goodwill might have helped managers make incremental changes which involved loss of employment over the years. Equally, it is possible that a sense of betrayal of this goodwill may have increased the level of resentment towards management when it came to the radical cuts associated with the business process re-engineering initiative.

These contextual matters influenced the particular *contingencies* that Dovecote managers *enacted* (interpreted and acted with regard to). The instability of the increasingly competitive business environment is obviously the major contingent factor. Jerry Penick has also acted on the basis of his view of technological contingencies. He believes that significantly more effective 'management control' hardware and software is now available to the company, and he has views about the contingency of organisational size, arguing that Dovecote is 'too big and unwieldy'.

Although the big decisions about how to handle the company's difficulties have largely been made by Jerry Penick alone, arguments taking place between the senior managers seem to reflect different value positions and interests among them. Roberto himself puts forward a solution that fits with his personal area of expertise and it is a solution that would have increased his personal influence in the company, we can reasonably infer. It was obviously one that clashed with the interests of the Manufacturing Director, an 'enemy' of Roberto who, apparently, was very 'territorial'. This individual was keen to 'fight his corner' as was Roberto's other 'enemy', the Finance Director. It is difficult to separate the values and the personal interests of the protagonists to these arguments. But it would appear that the Marketing Director brought certain values of concern for human beings into the discussions. It would seem that Jerry, in speaking of the inevitability of 'hurting' some people in order to benefit others, has gone through some internal value debate.

It is Jerry's choice, as the most powerful actor within the management team, to adopt business process re-engineering. However, the resistance to the way this was implemented, especially from other managers across the company, turned out to be so great that the initiative was seriously undermined. What Jerry Penick appears not to have realised was that strategic management has to cope with – or 'manage' – the basic contradictions that underlie all employing organisations. The contradiction between the requirement that managers must exploit or 'use' employees as resources and the requirement that they must win commitment and consent from employees as human beings is badly mismanaged here. The Dovecote management is saying that the changes will benefit the 'survivors' of business process re-engineering. People should therefore commit themselves to the changes. But it is making it clear at the same time that, for the moment, every individual is being considered for possible removal from the firm. Roberto expresses this by referring to the company as speaking with two voices. In one voice, he says, it talks of trust and empowerment, but with the other voice it is effectively asking every individual to 'kneel down' to allow the management to cut off their heads, should the 'Re-engineering Action Group' not see them as fitting into the new, re-engineered scheme of things.

Many organisations have in recent years reacted to the sorts of pressure faced by Dovecote Components by adopting business process re-engineering. And, even by the accounts of leading proponents of the practice, many of these have achieved nothing like the dramatic changes expected. Given the radical nature of the initiative and the way it tends to bring to the surface major underlying tensions this is not surprising.

Matters of the basic structure of economies and of global economic change cannot be separated from managerial efforts to 'motivate' and 'lead' people within organisations or from the initiatives they take to design or 'redesign' jobs – whether they involve minor initiatives or larger radical ones like business process re-engineering (see Further reading on Work restructuring and re-engineering, p. 349). Nevertheless, at the level of the individual manager doing the everyday routine managerial tasks that are the responsibility of the majority of managers across the range of work organisations in both the commercial and the public service sectors these bigger issues may not be at the front of their minds. However, one of the purposes of the present book – in the spirit of critical thinking discussed in Chapter 1 – is to enable everyone involved in organisations to be aware of the relevance of these broader factors. And this is vital for thinking in a strategic manner about how any particular organisation relates to its environment. It is to this aspect of the organising and managing of work that Chapter 9 turns.

Summary

In this chapter the following key points have been made:

- What are often seen as separate 'topics' in the study of organisations and their management – 'motivation', 'leadership' and 'job/work design' – can better be seen as closely related to each other and, also, as closely tied into the wider structural and cultural features of the organisation in which they occur and as influenced by the whole way in which modern societies and economies are organised.
- It is more helpful to look at people's general *orientations to work* rather than to consider their 'work motivation'. A focus on orientations allows a wider range of relevant factors to be taken into account and makes us more aware of how people think about their work, and what they are prepared to do, and can change as circumstances change.

- The very notion of a 'theory of motivation' is a questionable and potentially unrealisable one. Such a theory would, in effect, be a theory of 'why people do what they do'. However, useful insights have been developed about the role of perceptions of 'equity' and the role of 'expectancies' in shaping work behaviour under the 'motivation theory' banner. These insights can be incorporated into a process-relational way of thinking.
- There are two main principles of *work design* – direct control and indirect control principles – which can be drawn on when managers engage in specific *job design* work. These two sets of principles, the first of which operates with a logic of de-skilling and the latter with a logic of 'enriching' jobs in skill and responsibility terms, have been applied in different ways at different times across the history of industrialised societies.
- The application of these principles, and how it varies with circumstances and the ways in which managers 'enact' contingent circumstances, can be understood in terms of managerial attempts to cope with the underlying contradictions in the organisation of work and employment in modern societies. Managers need to control and manipulate employees as resources and, at the same time, win a degree of consent and commitment to the enterprise from them as human beings. Problems that can arise with the recently popular managerial initiative of *business process re-engineering* can be understood in terms of managerial struggles to handle these fundamental tensions.

Recommended reading

On the very specific matter of motivation theories and how students relate to them, the Tony Watson study, 'Motivation: that's Maslow, isn't it' (*Management Learning* 27(4): 447–464, 1996; also in C. Grey and E. Antonacopoulu (eds) *Essential Reading in Management Learning*, London: Sage, 2004) can, its author hopes, be entertaining as well as challenging to current teaching and learing practices. And on the broader matter of the trends occurring in the way work is organised and tasks designed, perhaps the most effective way to get an overview is to look at and read selectively from *The Oxford Handbook of Work and Organization* edited by Steve Ackroyd, Rosemary Blatt, Paul Thompson and Pamela Tolbert (Oxford: Oxford University Press, 2004). Also valuable here is David Knights' and Darren McCabe's *Organization and Innovation: Guru schemes and American dreams* (Maidenhead: Open University Press, 2003).

Further reading

Further reading Motivation theories

Adams, J.S. (1963) 'Towards an understanding of inequity', *Journal of Abnormal and Social Psychology*, 67: 422–436

Adams, J.S. (1965) 'Inequity in social exchange' in L. Berkovitz (ed.) *Advances in Experimental Social Psychology, Vol. 2*, New York: Academic Press

Ambrose, M.L. and Kulik, C.T. (1999) 'Old friends, new faces: motivation research in the 1990s', *Journal of Management*, 25(3): 231–292

Carter, P. and Jackson, N. (1993) 'Modernism, postmodernism and motivation, or why expectancy theory failed to live up to expectation' in J. Hassard and M. Parker (eds) *Postmodernism and Organisations*, London: Sage

Maslow, A. (1943) 'A theory of human motivation', *Psychological Review*, 50: 37–96

Maslow, A. (1954) *Motivation and Personality*, New York; Harper and Row

Maslow, A. (1968) *Towards a Psychology of Being*, Princeton, NJ: Van Nostrand

McGregor, D.C. (1960) *The Human Side of Enterprise*, New York: McGraw-Hill

Rauschenberger, J., Schmitt, N. and Hunter, T.E. (1980) 'A test of the need hierarchy concept', *Administrative Science Quarterly*, 25(4): 654–670

Vroom, V.H. (1964) *Work and Motivation*, New York: Wiley

Watson, T.J. (1996) 'Motivation: that's Maslow, isn't it?', *Management Learning*, 27(4): 447–464

Further reading Work design, empowerment and teams

Babbage, C. (1832) *On the Economy of Machinery and Manufacture*, London: Charles Knight

Barker, J.R. (1993) 'Tightening the iron cage: concertive control in self-managing teams', *Administrative Science Quarterly*, 38: 408–437.

Barker, J.R. (1999) *The Discipline of Teamwork*, London: Sage

Becker, B. and Huselid, M. (1998) 'High performance work systems and firm performance: a synthesis of research and managerial implications', *Research in Personnel and Human Resources*, 16(1): 53–101

Belbin, M. (1993) *Team Roles at Work*, Oxford: Butterworth-Heinemann

Benders, J. and Van Hootegem, G. (1999) 'Teams and their context: moving the team discussion beyond existing dichotomies', *Journal of Management Studies*, 36(5): 609–628

Braverman, H. (1974) *Labor and Monopoly Capital*, New York: Monthly Review Press

Buchanan, D.A. (1994) 'Cellular manufacture and the role of teams' in J. Storey (ed.) *New Wave Manufacturing Strategies: Organisational and human resource management dimensions*, London: Paul Chapman, 204–225

Buchanan, D.A. (2000) 'An eager and enduring embrace: the ongoing rediscovery of teamworking as a management idea' in S. Procter and F. Mueller (eds) *Teamworking*, Basingstoke: Macmillan

Buchanan, D. and Preston, D. (1992) 'Life in the cell: supervision and teamwork in a "manufacturing systems engineering" environment', *Human Resource Management Journal*, 2(4): 55–76

Burawoy, M. (1979) *Manufacturing Consent: Changes in the labour process under monopoly capitalism*, Chicago, IL: Chicago University Press

Edwards, R. (1979) *Contested Terrain*, London: Heinemann

Friedman, A.L. (1977) *Industry and Labour*, London: Macmillan

Guzzo, R.A. and Dickson, M.W. (1998) 'Teams in organizations: recent research on performance and effectiveness', *Annual Review of Psychology*, 49: 307–338

Hackman, J.R. and Oldham, G.R. (1980) *Work Redesign*, New York: Addison Wesley

Hampton, M.M. (1999) 'Work groups' in Y. Gabriel (ed.) *Organizations in Depth*, London: Sage, 112–138

Harley, B. (2001) 'Team membership and the experience of work in Britain: an analysis of the WERS98 data', *Work, Employment and Society*, 15(4): 721–742

Herzberg, F. (1966) *Work and the Nature of Man*, Chicago, IL: World Publishing Co.

Marchington, M. (1992) *Managing the Team*, Oxford: Blackwell

Parker, S. and Wall, T. (1998) *Job and Work Design: Organizing work to promote well-being and effectiveness*, London: Sage

Pollert, A. (1988) 'Dismantling flexibility', *Capital and Class*, 34: 42–75

Pollert, A. (ed.) (1991) *Farewell to Flexibility?*, Oxford: Blackwell

Procter, S. and Ackroyd, S. (2001) 'Flexibility' in T. Redman and A. Wilkinson (eds) *Contemporary Human Resource Management*, Harlow: FT Prentice Hall

Procter, S. and Mueller, F. (eds) (2000) *Teamworking*, Basingstoke: Macmillan

Procter, S. and Mueller, F. (2000) 'Teamworking, strategy, structure, systems and culture' in S. Procter and F. Mueller (eds) *Teamworking*, Basingstoke: Macmillan, 3–24

Royle, T. (2000) *Working for McDonald's in Europe: The Unequal Struggle*, London: Routledge

Sinclair, A. (1992) 'The tyranny of team ideology', *Organization Studies*, 13(4): 611–626

Smith, A. (1974) *The Wealth of Nations*, Harmondsworth: Penguin (originally 1776)

Smith, C. and Thompson, P. (1998) 'Re-evaluating the labour process debate', *Economic and Industrial Democracy*, 19(4): 551–577

Taylor, F.W. (1911) *The Principles of Scientific Management*, New York: Harper

Trist, E.L., Higgin, G.W., Murray, H. and Pollock, A.B. (1963) *Organisational Choice*, London: Tavistock

Watson, T.J. (1986) *Management, Organisation and Employment Strategy*, London: Routledge

Watson, T.J. and Rosborough, J. (1999) 'Teamworking and the management of flexibility: local and social-structural tensions in high performance work design initiatives' in S. Procter and F. Mueller (eds) *Teamworking*, Basingstoke: Macmillan

Womack, J.P., Jones, D.J. and Roos, D. (1990) *The Machine that Changed the World*, New York: Rawson

Wood, S. and Albanese, M. (1995) 'Can we speak of high commitment management on the shop floor?', *Journal of Management Studies*, 32(2): 215–247

Further reading Work restructuring and re-engineering

Ackroyd, S., Batt, R., Thompson, P. and Tolbert, P.S. (eds) (2004) *The Oxford Handbook of Work and Organization*, Oxford: Oxford University Press

Buchanan, D.A. (1997) 'The limitations and opportunities of business process re-engineering in a politicised organizational climate', *Human Relations*, 50(1): 51–72

Burke, R. and Cooper, C.L. (2000) *The Organization in Crisis: Downsizing, restructuring and privatisation*, Oxford: Blackwell

Champy, J. (1996) *Reengineering Management: The mandate for new leadership*, New York: Harper Business

Davenport, T. (1993) *Process Innovation: Reengineering work through information technology*, Boston, MA: Harvard Business School Press

Grey, C. and Mitev, N. (1995) 'Reengineering organizations: a critical appraisal', *Personnel Review*, 24(1): 6–18

Grint, K. and Willcocks, L. (1995) 'Business process re-engineering in theory and practice: business Paradise regained?', *New Technology: Work and Employment*, 10(2): 99–108

Hammer, M. and Champy, J. (1993) *Reengineering the Corporation*, London: Nicholas Brealey

Hammer, M. and Stanton, S. (1995) *The Reengineering Revolution: A handbook*, New York: Harper Business Press

Knights, D. and McCabe, D. (2003) *Organization and Innovation: Guru schemes and American dreams*, Maidenhead: Open University Press

Knights, D. and Willmott, H. (eds) (2000) *The Reengineering Revolution: Critical studies of corporate change*, London: Sage

Redman, T. and Wilkinson, A. (2001) 'Downsizing' in T. Redman and A. Wilkinson (eds) *Contemporary Human Resource Management*, Harlow: FT Prentice Hall

Storey, J. (ed.) (1993) *New Wave Manufacturing Strategies*, London: Chapman

Wilkinson, A. and Willmott, H. (eds) (1995) *Making Quality Critical: New perspectives on organizational change*, London: Routledge

Wilkinson, A., Redman, T., Snape, E. and Marchington, M. (1998) *Managing with Total Quality Management: Theory and practice*, Basingstoke, Macmillan

Willmott, H. (1994) Business process re-engineering and human resource management, *Personnel Review*, 23(3): 34–46

Willmott, H. (1995) 'The odd couple?: re-engineering business processes; managing human relations', *New Technology; Work and Employment*, 10(2): 89–98

Week 8

Team Working and Different Organisational Types

Chapter 17

Teams

Aim

To outline the significance of teams and how they develop.

Objectives

By the end of your work on this chapter you should be able to outline the concepts below in your own terms and:

1. Explain why organisations use teams for a wide range of tasks
2. Distinguish the stages of development through which groups pass
3. Explain Belbin's theory of team roles
4. Evaluate the effectiveness of a team and identify possible reasons for variations in performance
5. Outline the organisational factors that influence team performance
6. Describe the meaning of 'groupthink', and give some examples of its symptoms.

Key terms

This chapter introduces the following ideas:

structure
working groups
team
formal teams
informal groups
self-managing team
virtual teams
team-based rewards
preferred team role
observation
content
concertive control

Cisco Systems www.cisco.com

CASE STUDY

Courtesy of Cisco Systems, Inc. Unauthorised use not permitted.

Cisco Systems is a company at the heart of the Internet. It is a leading developer and supplier of the physical equipment and software that allow digital data to travel around the world over the Internet, and also provides various support services that enable companies to improve their use of the network. It was founded in 1984 by a group of scientists from Stanford University, and its engineers have focused on developing Internet Protocol (IP)-based networking technologies. The core areas of the business remain the supply of routing and switching equipment, but it is also working in areas such as home networking, network security and storage networking.

The company employs 34,000 staff working from 70 offices around the world, developing new systems and working with customers to implement and enhance their network infrastructure. Most projects are implemented by staff from several sites working as virtual teams, in the sense that they are responsible for a collective product but work in physically separate places.

The company created a team to coordinate the testing and release of a new version of Cisco's Element Management Framework (EMF), a highly complex piece of software that monitors the performance of large numbers of elements in a network. When the product was released a few months later, the members of the team were free to work on other projects. The team had eight members, drawn from four sites and three countries:

Name	Location	Role
Steve	Raleigh, North Carolina	Project coordinator
Richard	Cumbernauld, Scotland	Development manager
Graham	Cumbernauld, Scotland	Development engineer
Eddie	Cumbernauld, Scotland	Development engineer
Rai	Austin, Texas	Test engineer
Silvio	Austin, Texas	Test engineer
Jim	Raleigh, North Carolina	Network architect
Gunzal	Bangalore, India	Release support engineer

The role of the coordinator was to ensure the smooth operation of the team and to monitor actual progress against the challenging delivery schedule. The software was developed in Cumbernauld, by engineers writing the code and revising it as necessary after testing by the test engineers. They were responsible for rigorously testing all software and reporting all problems concisely and accurately to the development engineers.

The network architect has extensive knowledge of the network hardware that the software would manage, and supervised the development and testing of the software to ensure that it worked as efficiently as possible with the hardware. The release support engineer dealt with the logistics of software release, such as defining each version and ensuring deliverables are available to the manufacturing departments at the appropriate times.

Each member worked full-time on the project, though they never met physically during its lifetime. All members took part in a weekly conference call, and also a daily call attended by the coordinator, development manager and a member of the test team. Communication throughout the team was mainly by electronic mail, together with instant messaging.

Source: Communication from members of the project team.

Case questions 17.1

- What challenges would you expect a team that never meets will face during its work?
- In what ways may it need to work differently from a conventional team?

17.1 Introduction

Cisco is an organisation where management uses teams extensively to deliver its products and services to customers. The people with the skills it needs for a particular project will be widely dispersed around the organisation but need to work together to meet customer needs. Teams are a way of bringing them together for the duration of a project – they then disperse and re-form in different combinations to work on other projects. The company also uses teams for internal development projects, where staff from a variety of functions and geographical areas work together on a part-time basis to deal with a pressing management problem, such as improving a financial or marketing system.

People at work have always developed loyalties amongst small groups of fellow workers and there are well-documented examples of industries where work was formally organised in small, self-managing teams (Trist and Bamforth, 1951). This is now happening much more widely, with teams rather than individuals becoming the basic building block of many organisations. This is most evident in research-based organisations such as Microsoft (Cusumano, 1997), W.L. Gore and Associates or GlaxoSmithKline, where scientists or engineers from different disciplines come together to work on a common project and then disband when the work is complete. There are many cross-organisational teams – such as when Sun Microsystems and one of their major suppliers created a range of teams to manage the flow of components between the two businesses (Boddy *et al.*, 2000, and see Management in Practice in Section 13.3). Teams bring together people with different ideas and perspectives to solve difficult problems. Most economic and social problems require the contribution of several disciplines or organisations. Creating a team draws people from these areas together to work on the problem.

However, putting people together as a group does not in itself ensure either performance or satisfaction. Some teams, such as that at Cisco, work to very high standards and levels of achievement. They are conspicuously successful and achieve more than was expected. Others fail, wasting both time and opportunity. The differences in performance – in meeting business goals or in satisfying members – reflect how the members managed the team.

The diversity of backgrounds that makes a team worthwhile also makes it harder for the team to work. Creating a team (or 'group', 'section', 'task force' or 'working party') is only the start. Members then need to learn to work together collaboratively to reach a target. The greater the diversity, the greater the challenge it will be to make the team work.

This chapter examines the use of teams in organisations, and the management issues that they raise, as shown in Figure 17.1. The chapter begins by outlining why more organisations now use teams and introduces a way of evaluating how well a team performs. It then discusses the different types of teams and the stages through which an effective team must pass. This leads to a theory about the sources of team effectiveness, which forms the structure for the rest of the chapter – the motivation, composition and working methods of teams. For all their potential advantages, teams have costs as well as benefits, and are not appropriate for all kinds of work. Deciding to invest in teams should reflect a conscious evaluation of their potential costs as well as their potential benfits.

17.2 Benefits of teams

Those who decide to create a team probably do so in the hope that the members and the organisation will benefit.

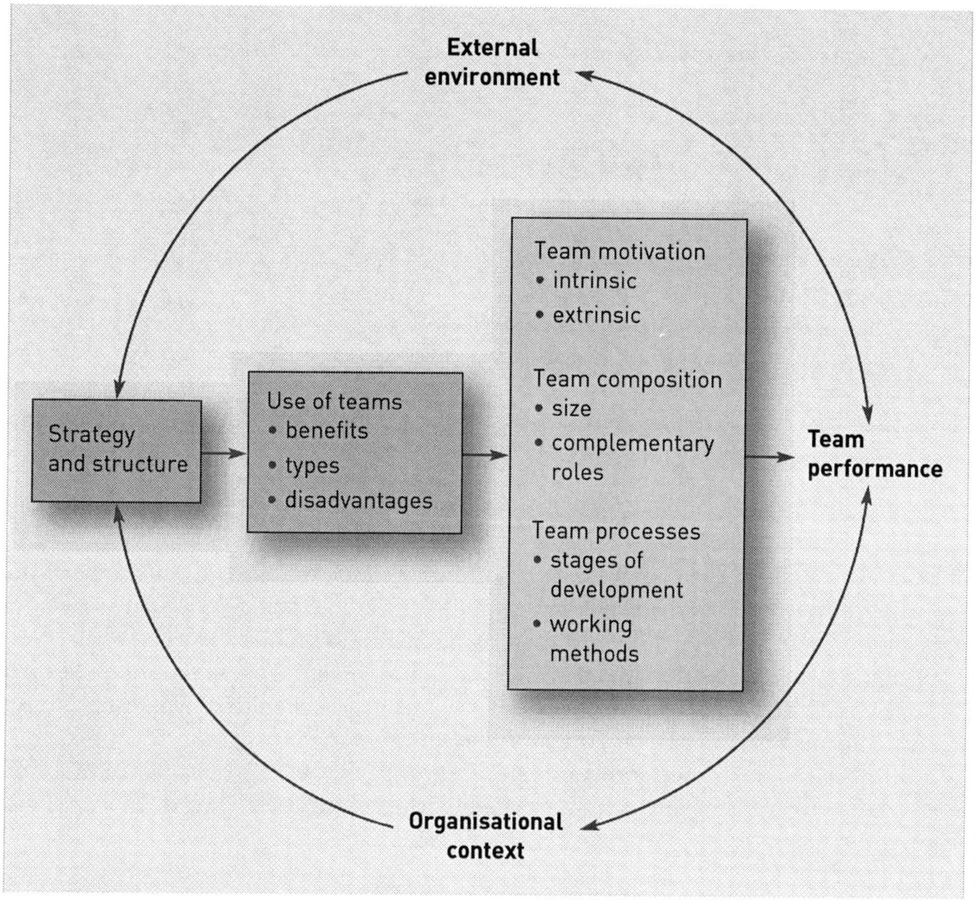

Figure 17.1
A model of team performance

Benefits to members

The Hawthorne studies described in Chapter 2 showed that a supportive work group had more influence on performance than physical conditions. People have social needs that they seek to satisfy by being acknowledged and accepted by other people. This can be done person to person (mutual acknowledgement or courteous small-talk on the train), but most people are also members of several relatively permanent cooperative groups. These provide an opportunity to express and receive ideas and to reshape one's views by interacting with others. Acceptance by a group meets a widely held human need.

Mary Parker Follett observed the social nature of people and the benefits of cooperative action. She saw the group as an intermediate institution between the solitary individual and the abstract society, and believed that it was through the group that people organised cooperative action. In 1926 Follett wrote:

> Early psychology was based on the study of the individual; early sociology was based on the study of society. But there is no such thing as the 'individual', there is no such thing as 'society'; there is only the group and the group-unit – the social individual. Social psychology must begin with an intensive study of the group, of the selective processes which go on within it, the differentiated reactions, the likenesses and the unlikenesses, and the spiritual energy which unites them. (Quoted in Graham, 1995, p. 230)

Likert (1961) developed this theme of organising work in groups. He observed that effective managers encouraged participation by group members in all aspects of the job,

key ideas Mary Parker Follett and Japanese management

According to Tokihiko Enomoto, Professor of Business Administration at Tokai University, Japan:

> Follett's work has become part of our teaching on management, and is well known to quite a number of ... managers in our government institutions and business organisations. Much of what Follett says about individuals and groups reflects to a substantial extent our Japanese view of the place of individuals in groups, and by extension their place in society ... She sees individuals not as independent selves going their separate ways, but as interdependent, interactive and interconnecting members of the groups to which they belong. This is something close to the Japanese ethos. We can fully agree with Follett when she writes that 'the vital relation of the individual to the world is through his groups'.

Source: Quoted in Graham (1995), pp. 242–243.

including setting goals and budgets, controlling costs and organising work. Individuals became members of a team who were loyal to each other and who had high levels of team-working skills. Likert maintained that these groups were effective because of the *principle of supportive relationships.* He agreed with Maslow that people value a positive response from others, which helps to build and maintain their self-esteem. Social relationships at work serve the same purpose, especially when people spend much of their time in a group. Managers in effective organisations had deliberately linked such groups to ensure people had overlapping membership of more than one group: 'each person ... is a member of one or more functioning workgroups that have a high degree of group loyalty, effective skills of interaction and high performance goals' (Likert, 1961, p. 104). Figure 17.2 shows the idea of supportive relationships.

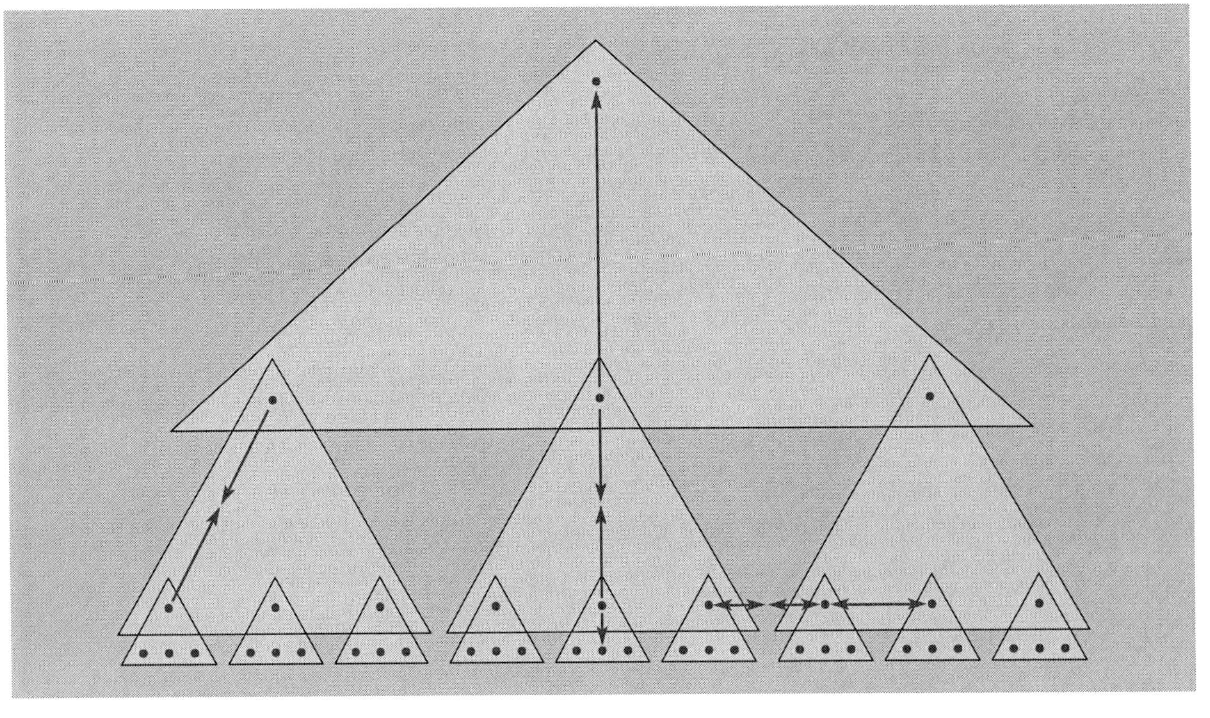

Figure 17.2 Likert's principle of supporting relationships

Note: The arrows indicate the linking pin-functions, both vertical and horizontal – as in cross-functional teams.

Source: Adapted from Likert (1967), p. 50.

These ideas continue to influence practice. Katzenbach and Smith (1993) observed that members of a team who surmount problems together build trust and confidence in each other. They benefit from the buzz of being in a team, and of 'being part of something bigger than myself'.

Benefits to performance

Scientific and technical knowledge is created by different professional groups, so solving many technical, production, social, health and other types of problem involve several disciplines working together. Even if staff remain within their separate hierarchical structures, managers create multidisciplinary teams to deliver a service or resolve some common problem. Teams can bring complementary skills beyond those of any individual.

In health care there is a growing interest in team working amongst those delivering care. One reason is the suffering caused when members of one group fail to pass information to others. Many also believe that encouraging different professions to work as multi-professional teams improves care and uses resources more effectively. Teams can also reduce costs and blur professional boundaries.

Other organisations seek similar benefits:

> When representatives from all of the relevant areas of expertise are brought together, team decisions and actions are more likely to encompass the full range of perspectives and issues that might affect the success of a collective venture. Multidisciplinary teams are therefore an attractive option when individuals possess different information, knowledge, and expertise that bear on a complex problem. (Van Der Vegt and Bunderson, 2005, p. 532)

The snag is that managers find it difficult to secure the benefits of multidisciplinary teams. The idea that diversity leads to performance is being replaced by one that examines how, and under what conditions this happens. For example, a team with a professionally diverse membership is more likely to bring performance benefits when the task is non-routine, and when there is a high degree of information sharing and sense of collective identity within the team (Van Der Vegt and Bunderson, 2005). Creating a team with appropriate authority gets talent working on organisational problems much more quickly than hierarchical structures could (Druskat and Wheeler, 2004).

Teamwork pays off at Louis Vuitton www.vuitton.com

management in practice

The French company Louis Vuitton is the world's most profitable luxury brand. The success of the company is attributed to a relentless focus on quality, a rigidly controlled distribution system and ever-increasing productivity in design and manufacture. Eleven of the 13 Vuitton factories are in France: although they could move to cheaper locations, management feels more confident about quality control in France.

Employees in all Vuitton factories work in teams of between 20 and 30 people. Each team, such as the ones at the Ducey plant in Normandy, works on one product, and members are encouraged to suggest improvements in manufacturing. They are also briefed on the product, such as its retail price and how well it is selling, says Stephane Fallon, a former manager for Michelin who runs the Ducey factory. 'Our goal is to make everyone as multi-skilled and autonomous as possible', says team leader Thierry Nogues.

The teamwork pays off. When the Boulogne Multicolour (a new shoulder bag) prototype arrived at Ducey, workers who were asked to make a production run discovered that the decorative metal studs were causing the zipper to bunch up, adding time and effort to assembly. The team alerted factory managers, and technicians quickly moved the studs a few millimetres away from the zipper. Problem solved.

Source: *Business Week*, 22 March 2004.

Teams can also cut costs, as the Management in Practice feature on Coats Ltd shows.

management in practice

Teams at Coats

Coats Ltd (a textile company) decided to introduce self-managed work teams into its manufacturing operations to improve quality and efficiency. The aim was to replace the traditional manufacturing set-up with teams of highly trained employees fully capable of managing themselves and completing a whole piece of work. The members of each team would be able to perform a wide variety of tasks, have more decision-making power and access to more information. They would perform roles traditionally performed by supervisors such as scheduling, setting priorities and monitoring quality. A manager:

> **We started with some pilot groups, and after some initial difficulties they are working well. The performance of the teams has reached, and in some cases exceeded, expectations, especially in three key performance measures of machine efficiency, wastage and absence.**
>
> **The role of individuals has also evolved. They are more flexible, committed and also willing to act in different team roles. A survey after six months showed that 85 per cent of staff prefer working in teams.**

Source: Communication from a manager in the plant.

Teams do not always work, and the next Management in Practice feature is a cautionary tale.

management in practice

A community mental health team

The management of a health care unit decided to reduce the number of hospital places and increase resources for community care. As part of the change a resource centre was established containing multidisciplinary teams, each with about 30 staff, to provide a 24-hour service for the severely mentally ill in the community. The service would use a team approach with a flattened hierarchy and greater mutual accountability, and this was supported by many team building and similar activities.

It soon became clear that many staff could not cope with the extra responsibility and shared decision making. The job is difficult and sometimes dangerous, since people's lives are at stake. Management therefore changed the system to clarify the role of each member of staff and to give a clearer structure of authority and management. It also recognised that, while team working may be an ideal, it needs to be supported by broader management structures and practices.

Source: Communication from a manager in the service.

Case questions 17.2

- What were the business reasons that led Cisco to use teams, especially virtual ones?
- On the information you have on the case so far, does the team meet the definition of a 'real team'? (See Table 17.1, p. 565.)

Why effective teams contribute to business performance

Teams can be a way of reaching a synthesis between high efficiency and high-quality jobs, since they can:

- provide a structure within which people with a range of skills and perspectives work together;
- provide a forum in which issues can be raised and dealt with – rather than being ignored;
- enable people to extend their roles, so possibly improving responsiveness and reducing costs;
- encourage acceptance and understanding by staff of a problem and the solution proposed;
- promote wider learning by encouraging reflection, and spreading lessons widely.

Activity 17.1 Gathering data on teams

Gather some original information on how at least two organisations have used teams to get work done, or where an organisation has abandoned teamwork. Use the questions below as a starting point for your enquiry. The data you collect may be useful in one of your tutorials, as well as adding to your knowledge of teams.

- What is the main task of the organisation or department?
- How are the staff in the area grouped into teams?
- Use the definition of a 'real team' (see Table 17.1) to describe the team.
- What type of team is it? (Use the ideas in Section 17.4 as a guide.)
- What do management and team members see as the advantages and disadvantages of team working in this situation?
- Have there been any recent changes in the organisation of the teams, such as members taking on new tasks? If so, why?

17.3 Crowds, groups and teams

A group (or team) is not just any collection of people. A crowd in the street is not usually a group: they are there by chance, and will have little if any further contact. Are 150 students in a lecture theatre a team? What about the staff in a supermarket? In a take-away restaurant? In the same section of a factory? They are not a crowd: they have some things in common, and people may refer to them as a group. Compare them with five people designing some software for a bank, each of whom brings distinct professional skills to their collective discussions of the most suitable design, or with seven students working together on a group assignment. They have a **structure** to handle the whole process, work largely on their initiative, and move easily between all the tasks, helping each other as needed.

Structure is the regularity in the way a unit or group is organised, such as the roles that are specified.

Activity 17.2 Crowds, groups and teams

Note down a few words that express the differences between the examples given. Do some sound more like a group than others?

One difference is in the extent to which they share a common purpose. Groups or teams aim to produce some outcome to which all members have contributed, and for which they share some collective responsibility. A second difference is in the extent to which members share ideas and activities to get the job done. Teams can add value to individual work by exchanging ideas, information and effort. There is some continuing interdependence, which leads to a sense of membership, and of being (temporarily) distinct from outsiders.

Activity 17.3 Teams or not?

Consider a Davis Cup tennis or Ryder Cup golf team, in which most of the action takes place between individual participants from either side. No significant coordination occurs between the members during each of the matches.

- In what ways would such teams meet the above definition?
- Can you think of other examples of people who work largely on their own but are commonly referred to as a team?

In normal conversation people typically use the words 'group' and 'team' interchangeably – they mean the same thing. This book follows that common usage, but it is essential to be aware that the words can mean different things. Some work effectively and others do not. Becoming an effective group or team costs time and effort. That cost is not necessary if the task could be done by well-motivated and cooperative individuals. It is worth taking a few sentences to clarify the meaning behind the terms.

Katzenbach and Smith (1993) define a team as: 'A small number of people with complementary skills who are committed to a common purpose, performance goals, and working approach for which they hold themselves mutually accountable' (p. 45). A group of people that works together is not necessarily a team on this definition. The essential point is that groups (or teams) differ in what they produce.

Katzenbach and Smith use the 'team performance curve' shown in Figure 17.3 to make the point clear. While many groups call themselves teams, most do not clarify their shared purpose or common approach, and so do not achieve as much as they could. They rely on the contributions and expertise of the individual members. Members engage in normal social courtesies and interactions, and perhaps exchange some task advice and information. But they are accountable for their work as individuals. In many situations such '**working groups**' (see Table 17.1) are all that is needed, provided individuals do their job competently. **Teams** use collective discussion, debate and decision to deliver 'collective work products' – something more than the sum of individual effort. Figure 17.3 shows this difference, with working groups delivering individual work products, while teams produce collective work products. Table 17.1 describes the five points on the curve.

A **working group** is a collection of individuals who work mainly on their own but interact socially and share information and best practices.

A **team** is 'a small number of people with complementary skills who are committed to a common purpose, performance goals, and approach for which they hold themselves mutually accountable' (Katzenbach and Smith, 1993).

Having, for the purpose of their argument, distinguished between working groups and teams, Katzenbach and Smith emphasise that they do not advocate particular labels. They recommend (and this author agrees) that people should use the terms with which they are comfortable. It is what groups and teams *do* that matter, not what they are called.

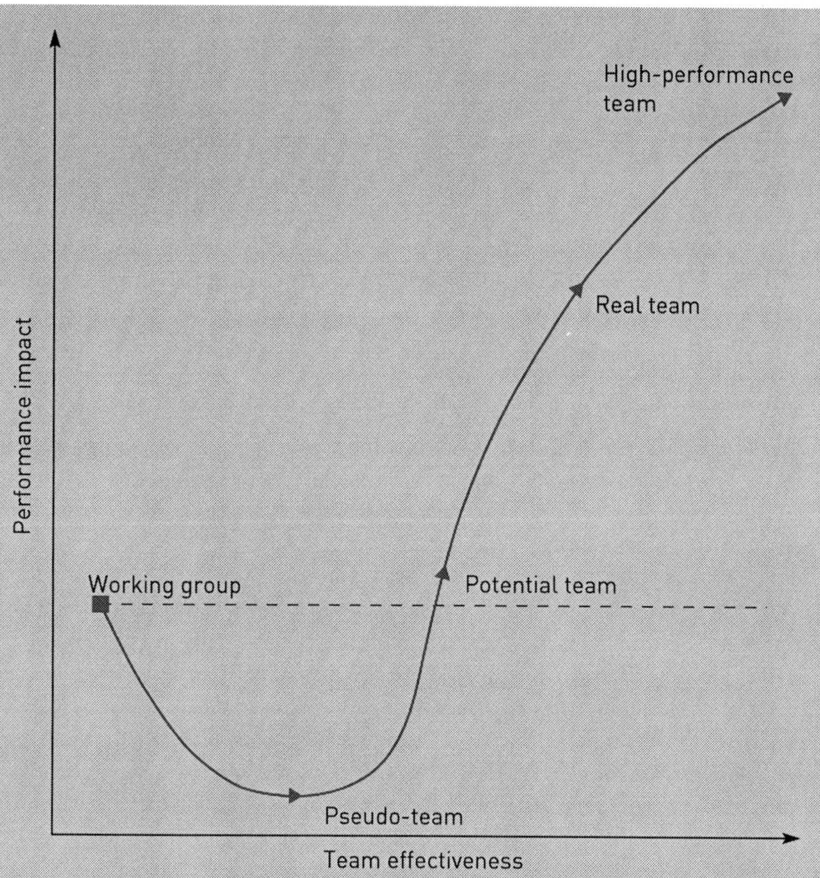

Source: Katzenbach and Smith (1993). Reprinted by permission of *Harvard Business Review*, copyright © 1993 Harvard Business School Publishing Corporation, all rights reserved.

Figure 17.3
The team performance curve

Table 17.1
Description of the points on the team performance curve

Point	Description
Working group	There is no significant need to become a team. The focus is on individual effort. Members interact mainly to share information and best practices. They help each other to perform within their area of responsibility. There is no strong common purpose or joint work product for which they are all accountable
Pseudo-team	There are opportunities for collective performance, but members have not focused on trying to achieve it. No interest in shaping a common purpose or set of performance goals, though it may call itself a team. Time in meetings detracts from individual performance, without any joint benefits. Whole is less than potential sum of parts
Potential team	There are opportunities for collective performance, and members are trying to achieve this. They still need to develop clarity over purpose, goals or joint work products. They may require more discipline in working out a common approach or to establish collective accountability
Real team	A small number of people with complementary skills who are equally committed to a common purpose, performance goals and working approach for which they hold themselves mutually accountable
High-performance team	Meets all the tests of a real team, and in addition members are deeply committed to one another's personal growth and success

Source: Katzenbach and Smith (1993), pp. 90–92. Reprinted by permission of *Harvard Business Review*, copyright © 1993 Harvard Business School Publishing Corporation, all rights reserved.

The definition of a team suggests the tools members can use to assess their progress towards becoming an effective team, in the sense of meeting others' expectations.

Small number

Groups of more than about 12 people have great difficulty operating as a coherent team. It becomes harder for them to agree on a common purpose and the logistical problems of finding a place and time to work together increase. Most teams have between two and ten people – with between four and eight probably being the most common range. Larger groups usually divide into subgroups.

Complementary skills

Teams benefit from having members with three types of skill between them. First, there are *technical, functional* or *professional skills*, relevant to the subject of the group's work. A group implementing a networked computer system will require at least some members with appropriate technical skills, while one developing a new strategy for a retailer will contain people with strategic or business development skills.

Second, a team needs to include people with *problem-solving* and *decision-making skills*. These enable the team to approach a task systematically, using appropriate techniques of analysis. These include SWOT analysis, project management methods, cost–benefit analysis, diagramming techniques and flowcharting.

Finally, a team needs people with adequate *interpersonal skills* to hold it together as a human institution. Members' attitudes and feelings towards each other and to the task change as work continues. The changing degree of commitment may generate irritation and conflict and someone needs to have the skill to manage these disagreements constructively.

Common purpose

Teams cannot work to a common purpose unless members spend time and effort clarifying that purpose. They need to express it in clear performance goals. These focus members' energy on activities that support their achievement. A common purpose helps communication between members, since they can interpret and understand their contributions more easily.

Common approach

Teams need to decide how they will work together to accomplish their common purpose. This includes deciding who does which jobs, what skills members need to develop, and how the group should make and modify decisions. The common approach includes supporting and integrating new or reticent members into the team. Working together on these tasks helps to promote the mutual trust and constructive conflict necessary to team success.

Mutual accountability

A team cannot work as one until its members willingly hold themselves to be collectively and mutually accountable for the results of the work. As members do real work together towards a common objective, commitment and trust usually follow. If one or more members are unwilling to accept this collective responsibility, the team will not become fully effective.

17.4 Types of team

Teams have to cope with different issues, depending on their function, formality, autonomy and location.

Function

Hackman (1990) distinguished seven types of team in terms of the functions they perform, and the risks and opportunities associated with each. Table 17.2 summarises these.

Table 17.2
Hackman's classification of team types and their associated risks and opportunities

Type	Risks	Opportunities
Top management teams – to set organisational directions	Underbounded; absence of organisational context	Self-designing; influence over key organisational conditions
Task forces – for a single unique project	Team and work both new	Clear purpose and deadline
Professional support groups – providing expert assistance	Dependency on others for work	Using and honing professional expertise
Performing groups – playing to audiences	Skimpy organisational supports	Play that is fuelled by competition and/or audiences
Human service teams – taking care of people	Emotional drain; struggle for control	Inherent significance of helping people
Customer service teams – selling products and services	Loss of involvement with parent organisation	Bridging between parent organisation and customers
Production teams – turning out the product	Retreat into technology; insulation from end users	Continuity of work; able to hone team design and product

Source: Hackman (1990), p. 489.

Case questions 17.3

- What kinds of team does Cisco use, in Hackman's typology?
- What other kinds of team from the list have you experienced?

Formality

Formal teams

Formal teams are created by the organisation as part of the business's basic structure. There are both vertical and horizontal teams, as shown in Figure 17.4.

A **formal team** is one that management has deliberately created to perform specific tasks to help meet organisational goals.

Vertical teams consist of a manager and his or her subordinates within a single department or function. The manager and staff in the treasury department of a bank, and the senior nurse, nursing staff and support staff in a unit of the Western General Hospital, are formally constituted vertical teams. So is a team leader and his or her staff in an ING Bank call centre in The Netherlands. In each case senior managers created them to support their goals.

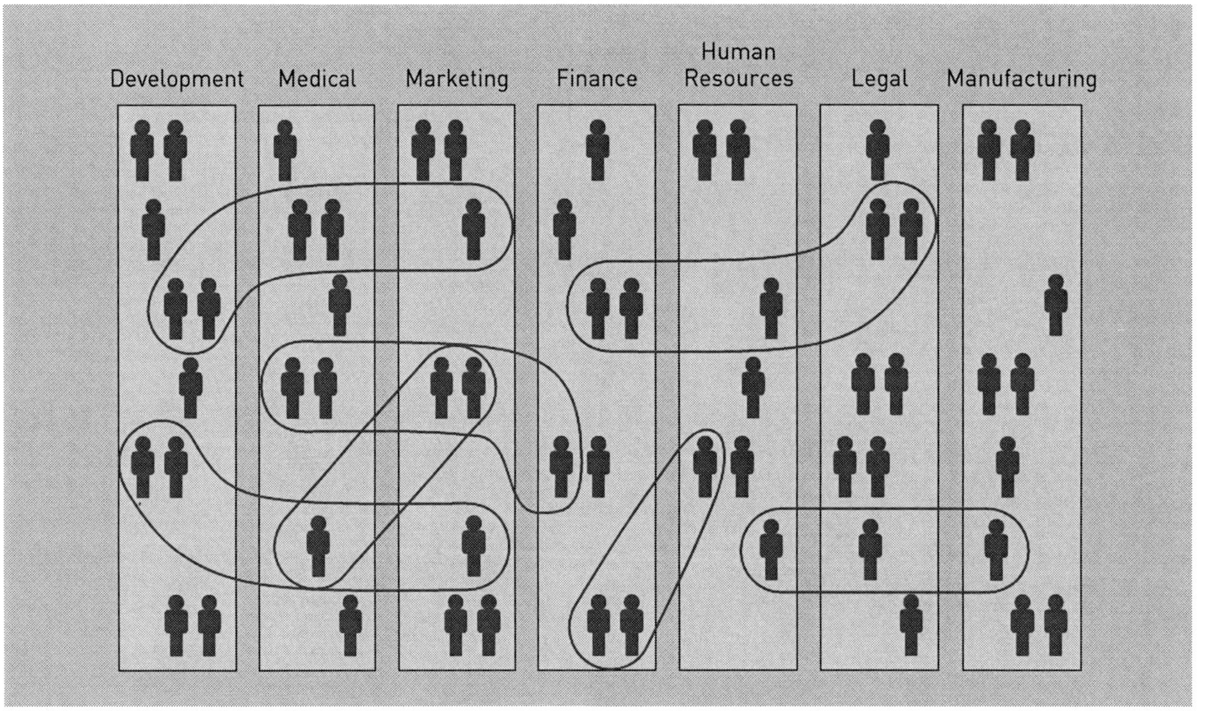

Figure 17.4 Horizontal and vertical teams within Eli Lilley (a pharmaceutical company)
Source: *Business Structures* (video), TV Choice Productions, Bromley, Kent, UK (2004).

Horizontal teams consist of staff from roughly the same level, but from different functions. The Cisco EMF team is an example, being brought together to release the new software. In Hackman's typology, task forces would be an example: often called cross-functional teams, these deal with non-routine problems that require several types of professional knowledge, such as how to develop a new product or process.

Informal groups

An **informal group** is one that emerges when people come together and interact regularly.

Although not created by management, **informal groups** are a powerful feature of organisational life. They develop as day-to-day activities bring people into contact with each other – who then discover common sporting or social interests. Work-related informal groups arise when people in different formal groups exchange information and ideas: staff using a software package may begin to pass around problems or tips. Staff in separate departments dealing with a customer may start passing information to each other to avoid misunderstandings, even though this is not part of the specified job. Informal groups may also develop in opposition to management – as when people believe they are being unfairly treated, and come together from across groups to express a common dissatisfaction with a management policy.

Autonomy

A **self-managing team** operates without an internal manager and is responsible for a complete area of work.

Another type of team that is commonly used is the **self-managing team**, a group of employees who operate without the close supervision of a manager and are responsible for a complete area of work. They reflect in part theories of motivation that advocate doing more to satisfy workers' higher-order needs. Members are responsible for getting

Informal networks: the company behind the chart

key ideas

According to Krackhardt and Hanson (1993):

> If the formal organization is the skeleton of the company, the informal is the central nervous system. This drives the collective thought processes, actions and reactions of the business units. Designed to facilitate standard modes of production, management create the formal organization to handle easily anticipated problems. When unexpected problems arise, the informal organization becomes active. Its complex web of social ties form every time colleagues communicate and solidifies over time into surprisingly stable networks. Highly adaptive, informal networks move diagonally and elliptically, skipping entire functions to get work done.

The authors argue that these informal networks can either foster or disrupt communication processes. They recommend that managers try to understand them in order to make use of their strengths, or even adjust aspects of the formal organisation to complement the informal.

Source: Krackhardt and Hanson (1993), p. 104.

the work done but have a high degree of autonomy in how they do it: they manage themselves, including planning and scheduling tasks, and assigning tasks amongst the members. They are also likely to establish the pace of work, make operating decisions, work out how to overcome problems and manage quality. They are also likely to have a considerable influence over selecting new employees.

Druskat and Wheeler (2004) examined the apparent paradox of the leadership of such teams – although referred to as self-managing, in practice they manage within constraints. A team that manages its work activities works within targets and expectations set by those in the wider organisation – receiving directions and reporting back to them. A manager external to the team will be responsible for its performance – and faces the dilemma of how best to carry out that role. From an empirical study of 300 self-managing teams in a single organisation they concluded that successful leaders of such teams had developed a distinctive set of skills, primarily those of managing the boundary between the team and the larger organisation.

Location

Modern communications technologies enable and encourage people to create teams in which the members are physically distant for most of the time, even though they are expected to deliver high-quality collective outcome. Many of the teams in Cisco are like this. The growing internationalisation of management means that people frequently work in **virtual teams** drawn from different nations and cultures, as well as working remotely, raising new teamwork challenges (Govindarajan and Gupta, 2001; Robey *et al.*, 2003).

Virtual teams are those in which the members are physically separated, using communications technologies to collaborate across space and time to accomplish their common task.

Virtual teams use computer technology to link members together, communicating via technologies such as e-mail, videoconferencing and online discussion through a website. They can perform all the functions of a team that is located in the same place, but lack the face-to-face interaction and discussion which helps to smooth working relationships. While virtual teams can sometimes use the fact that they are in different time zones to their advantage, Saunders *et al.* (2004) examine some of the challenges. At a superficial level differences of time zone create problems of managing different working hours, lunch breaks and holiday cycles. More fundamental difficulties arise from contrasting visions of time between cultures and nations – such as whether it is an objective or subjective notion, or differences in the meaning of words such as 'soon' or 'urgent'.

While virtual teams bring expertise together without the expense of travel, they require careful management to ensure the benefits of team working are retained. Practices include ensuring that some regular (or at least initial) face-to-face contact occurs, and that members resolve issues of roles, working methods and conflict management (Maruca, 1998).

17.5 Stages of group development

Putting people into a group does not mean they perform well immediately, as teams need to go through stages of growth. Some never perform well. Tuckman and Jensen (1977) developed a theory that groups can potentially pass through five fairly clearly defined stages of development. Figure 17.5 shows these.

Teams need to have the chance to grow up and to develop trust amongst the members. As the work makes progress people learn about each other, and how they can work well together. The closer they get, the easier it becomes to develop mutual trust.

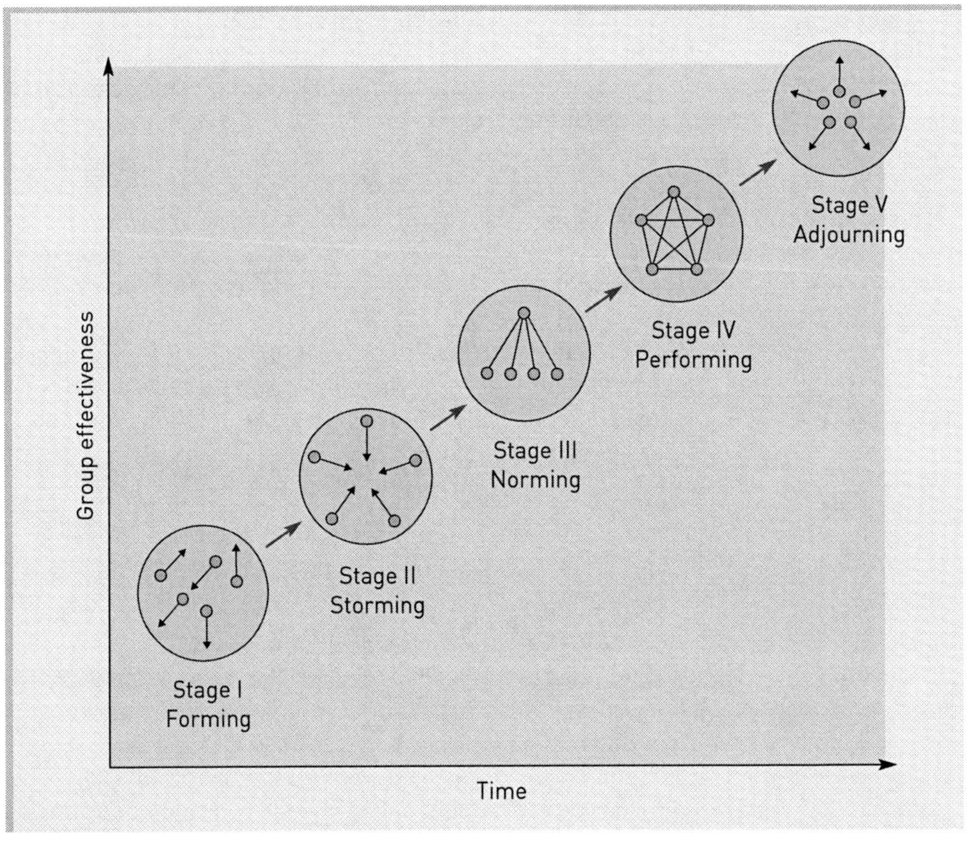

Figure 17.5
Stages of group development

Forming

Forming is the stage at which members choose, or are told, to join a team. Managers may select them for their functional and technical expertise or for some other skill. They come together and begin to find out who the other members are, exchanging fairly superficial information about themselves, and beginning to offer ideas about what the group should do. People are trying to make an impression on the group and to establish their identity with the other members.

Storming

Conflicts may occur at the storming stage, so it can be an uncomfortable time for the group. As the group begins the actual work members begin to express differences of interest that they withheld, or did not recognise, at the forming stage. People realise that others want different things from the group, have other priorities and, perhaps, have hidden agendas. Different personalities emerge, with contrasting attitudes towards the group and how it should work. Some experience conflicts between the time they are spending with the group and other duties. Differences in values and norms emerge.

Some groups never pass this stage. There may be little open conflict and members may believe the group is performing well – but may be deluding themselves. If the group does not confront disagreements it will remain at the forming or storming stage and will do no significant work. Performance depends on someone doing or saying something to move the group to the next stage.

Norming

Here the members are beginning to accommodate differences constructively and to establish adequate ways of working together. They develop a set of shared norms – expected ways of behaving – about how they should interact with each other, how they should approach the task, how they should deal with differences. People create or accept roles so that responsibilities are clear. The leader may set those roles formally or members may accept them implicitly during early meetings. Members may establish a common language to guide the group and allow members to work together effectively.

Performing

Here the group is working well, gets on with the job to the required standard and achieves its objectives. Not all groups get this far.

Adjourning

The group completes its task and disbands. Members may reflect on how the group performed and identify lessons for future tasks. Some groups disband because they are clearly not able to do the job, and agree to stop meeting.

A team that survives will go through these stages many times. As new members join, as others leave, as circumstances or the task change, new tensions arise that take the group back to an earlier stage. A new member implies that the team needs to revisit, however briefly, the forming and norming stages. This ensures the new member is brought psychologically into the team and understands how they are expected to behave. A change in task or a conflict over priorities can take a group back to the storming stage, from which it needs to work forward again. The process will be more like Figure 17.6 than the linear progression implied by the original theory.

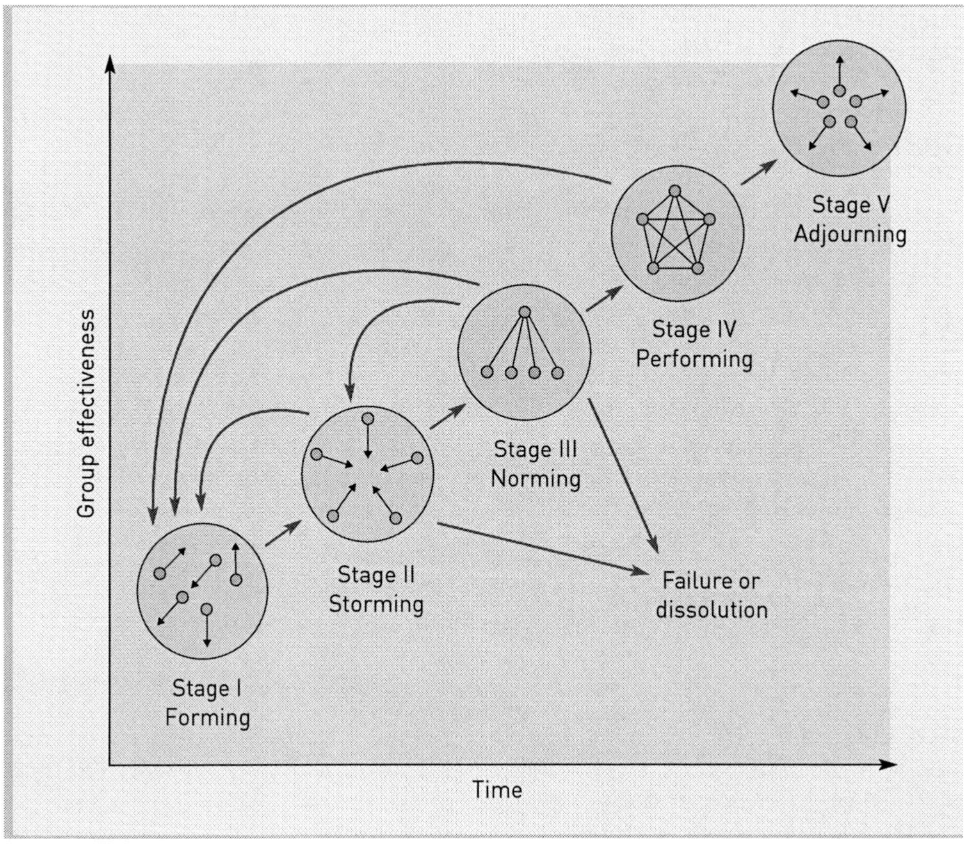

Figure 17.6
Modified model of the stages of group development

key ideas Managing the virtual team life cycle

Furst *et al.* (2004) noted the benefits of virtual teams in eliminating boundaries of time and space, but also found that they more often fail than succeed. To explain this they tracked the evolution of six virtual teams in a company, using the Tuckman and Jensen model. They found that virtual teams faced additional problems at each stage of the model, compared to those working in the same place.

Forming is more difficult, and takes longer, as there is less frequent communication, especially the informal chat between workers who meet regularly. This reduces the speed at which people make friendships and increases the risk of forming false impressions or stereotypes about other team members.

Storming can also be more fraught, as the absence of frequent non-verbal clues increases the risks of misunderstanding. Disagreements can be exacerbated or prolonged if people do not respond quickly to electronic communication – even if caused by differences in working times or poor technology.

Norming in virtual teams needs to clarify how to coordinate work, how to communicate, and how quickly to respond to requests. The process of norming itself is made more complex with electronic communication, as it is harder to try out ideas tentatively and to gauge reactions.

Performing depends on sharing information, integrating ideas and seeking creative solutions. The challenges of virtual working at this stage include competing pressure from local assignments, losing focus, and the fear of a failure that would damage a career.

Furst *et al.* use their analysis to suggest what those managing a virtual team could do at each stage to increase the chances of virtual teams reliably adding value.

Source: Furst *et al.* (2004).

Cisco – the case continues www.cisco.com CASE STUDY

Members of the team commented on the way the team developed. A common issue was the problem of scheduling meetings:

I've always found in virtual teams that when the team is first formed it isn't really getting any serious work done (unless we're under severe time pressure), it's about getting everyone together so they at least have some knowledge of the others in the team. (Steve)

Another said:

It was strange when we first started working together, because we didn't push on and get any testing or fixing done straight away. Steve was really pushing for us all to spend a few hours in conference calls getting to know each other and how we were all going to work together. We took our time to get into the actual work that was required. (Graham)

Other reflections included:

I had a few discussions with Steve . . . he wanted us to spend most of our time in conference meetings with the rest of the team, while my engineers already had a good understanding of the work that was needed and just wanted to get on with it. But Steve is the team lead so we had to go along with his approach. (Richard)

It's weird having to form such a close relationship with someone [when] you don't even know what they look like. But as we're using IM [Instant Messenger] just about every day you get used to it. I think you sometimes have to make an extra effort to talk directly to people, just to keep the relationship going. Sometimes it'd be easier for me to e-mail Rai, but I phone him, just so we can have a bit of a chat. (Eddie)

It means you have to be a bit more careful when it comes to communication. Most of the time you have to use e-mail and IM to discuss issues, which means there can be misunderstandings if you're not careful. When you interact in person you use things like facial expression and hand gestures – none of these are available when e-mailing so you have to state your arguments more clearly. (Jim)

Source: Communication from members of the project team.

Case questions 17.4

- Relate these accounts to the stages of team development.
- What examples of forming, storming and norming does it contain?

Evaluating team effectiveness

Hackman (1990) suggested three ways of evaluating team effectiveness, summarised in Table 17.3. These are subjective, and a team may succeed on some and fail on others. Judgement must also reflect the conditions in which the team is working.

Table 17.3 Criteria for evaluating team effectiveness

Criteria	Description
Has it met performance expectations?	Is the group completing the task managers gave to it – not only the project performance criteria, but also measures of cost and timeliness?
Have members experienced an effective team?	Is it enhancing their ability to work together as a group? Have they created such a winning team that it represents a valuable resource for future projects?
Have members developed transferable teamwork skills?	Are members developing teamwork skills that they will take to future projects? This indicates a team meeting the needs of the business and the team members

Source: Based on Hackman (1990).

Research with 27 teams of different types led Hackman to propose that to perform well a group must surmount three hurdles. Members must:

- be willing to exert sufficient effort to accomplish the task to an acceptable level;
- bring adequate knowledge and skill to the task;
- use group processes that are appropriate to the work and the setting.

These hurdles (see Figure 17.7) show how well a group is doing and where difficulties are arising.

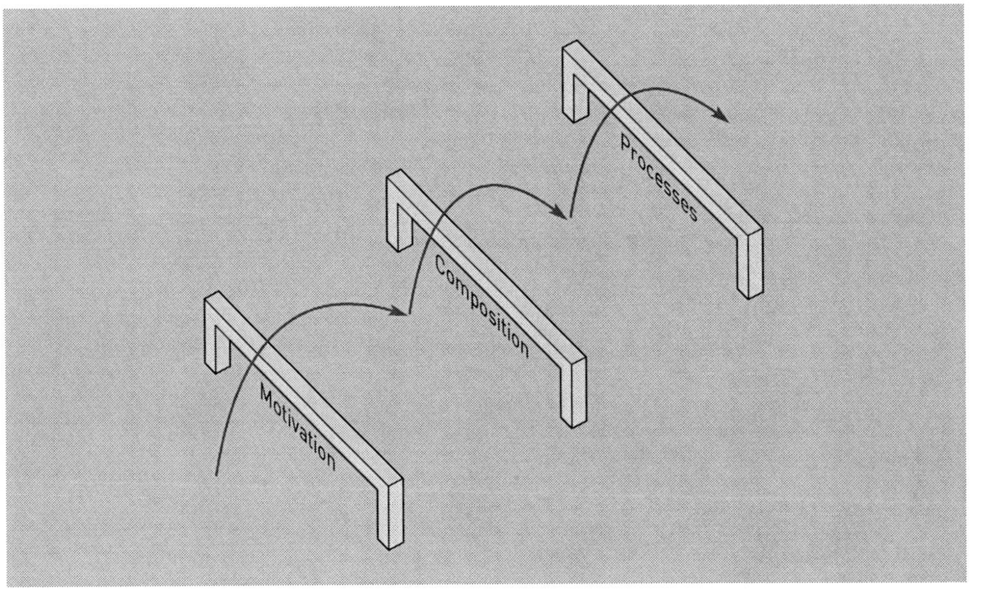

Figure 17.7 Hurdles in the way of team effectiveness

Team-based rewards are payments or non-financial incentives provided to members of a formally established team and linked to the performance of the group.

To overcome them, Hackman suggested that a team needs both internal and external support, as the manager cannot rely only on internal team practices or personal enthusiasm. He or she should also attend to wider organisational conditions such as the availability of **team-based rewards**. If both are in place it is more likely that the group will put in the effort, have the skill and use good team processes. Table 17.4 summarises these points.

Table 17.4 Points of leverage for enhancing group performance

Requirements for effectiveness	Internal conditions	Organisational context
Effort (see Chapter 15)	Motivational structure of task	Remedying coordination problems and rewarding team commitment
Knowledge and skill	Team composition	Available education and training, including coaching and guidance
Performance strategies	Working processes that foster review and learning	Information system to support task and provide feedback on progress

Source: Based on Hackman (1990), p. 13.

Securing adequate effort is essentially a matter of motivation and so draws on the ideas in Chapter 15 – such as the intrinsic nature of the task and whether adequate extrinsic rewards are available. The present chapter deals with the other two hurdles – team composition and team processes.

17.6 Team composition

In a mechanical sense, team composition includes questions of size and membership. Is there an acceptable balance of part-time and full-time members? Are the relevant functions represented? Equally important is whether members have the right skills and ways of working to form an effective team – Uhl-Bien and Graen (1998) warn:

> Although cross-functional teams may be highly effective if implemented correctly (for instance, staffed with strong team players), if implemented incorrectly (staffed with independently focused self-managing professionals) they may ... harm organizational functioning. (p. 348)

As people work in a team they behave in ways that reflect diverse perspectives, skills and interests, which lead them to take on distinctive roles. A group needs a balance of these, so a task for the team leader is to do what they can to shape its composition. Two useful ideas are the distinction between task and maintenance roles, and Belbin's research on team roles.

Task and maintenance roles

Some people focus on the task, on getting the job done, on meeting deadlines. Others put their energy into keeping the peace and holding the group together. Table 17.5 summarises the two.

Table 17.5 Summary of task and maintenance roles

Emphasis on task	Emphasis on maintenance
initiator	encourager
information seeker	compromiser
diagnoser	peacekeeper
opinion seeker	clarifier
evaluator	summariser
decision manager	standard setter

Teams need both roles, and skilful project managers try to ensure this happens.

Meredith Belbin – team roles

Meredith Belbin and his colleagues systematically observed several hundred small groups while they performed a task, and concluded that each person in a group tends to behave in a way that corresponds to one of nine distinct roles. The balance of these roles in a group affects how well or badly it performs.

key ideas Belbin's research method

Henley School of Management based much of their training on inviting managers to work in teams of up to ten on exercises or business simulations. The organisers had long observed that some teams achieved better financial results than others – irrespective of the abilities of the individual members as measured by standard personality and mental tests. The reasons for this were unclear. Why did some teams of individually able people perform less well than teams that appeared to contain less able people?

Belbin conducted a study in which observers, drawn from course members, used a standard procedure to record the types of contribution that members made. Team members voluntarily took psychometric tests, and team performance led to a quantifiable result. The researchers formed teams of members with above-average mental abilities, and compared their performance with the other teams. The 'intelligent' teams usually performed less well. Of 25 such teams only 3 were winners, and the most common position was sixth in a league of eight. The explanation lay in the way they behaved, typically spending time in debate, arguing for their point of view to the exclusion of others'. These highly intelligent people were good at spotting flaws in others' arguments, and became so engrossed in these that they neglected other tasks. Failure led to recrimination. The lesson was that behaviour (rather than measured intelligence) affected group performance.

Source: Belbin (1981).

The researchers identified different preferred team roles. Some people were creative, full of ideas and suggestions. Others were concerned with detail, ensuring that the team dealt with all aspects and that quality was right. Others spent their time keeping the group together. Table 17.6 lists the nine roles identified in Belbin (1993). Belbin observed that winning teams had members who fulfilled a balance of roles that was different from the less successful ones.

Table 17.6
Belbin's team roles

Role	Typical features
Implementer	Disciplined, reliable, conservative and efficient. Turns ideas into practical actions
Coordinator	Mature, confident, a good chairperson. Clarifies goals, promotes decision making, delegates well
Shaper	Challenging, dynamic, thrives on pressure. Has the drive and courage to overcome obstacles – likes to win
Plant	Creative, imaginative, unorthodox – the 'ideas' person who solves difficult problems
Resource investigator	Extrovert, enthusiastic, communicative – explores opportunities, develops contacts, a natural networker
Monitor–evaluator	Sober, strategic and discerning. Sees all options, judges accurately – the inspector
Teamworker	Cooperative, mild, perceptive and diplomatic. Listens, builds, averts friction, calms things – sensitive to people and situations
Completer	Painstaking, conscientious, anxious. Searches out errors and omissions. Delivers on time
Specialist	Single-minded, self-starting, dedicated. Provides scarce knowledge and skill

Source: Based on Belbin (1993).

Winning teams had an appropriate balance, such as:

- a capable coordinator
- a strong plant – a creative and clever source of ideas
- at least one other clever person to act as a stimulus to the plant
- a monitor–evaluator – someone to find flaws in proposals before it was too late.

Ineffective teams usually had a severe imbalance, such as:

- a coordinator with two dominant shapers – since the coordinator will almost certainly not be allowed to take that role;
- two resource investigators and two plants – since no one listens or turns ideas into action;
- a completer with monitor–evaluators and implementers – probably slow to progress, and stuck in detail.

Belbin did *not* suggest that all teams should have nine people, each with a different **preferred team role**. His point was that team composition should reflect the task:

> The useful people to have in a team are those who possess strengths or characteristics that serve a need without duplicating those that are already there. Teams are a question of balance; what is needed is not well-balanced individuals but individuals who balance well with one another. In that way human frailties can be underpinned and strengths used to full advantage. (Belbin, 1981, p. 77)

Preferred team roles are the types of behaviour that people display relatively frequently when they are part of a team.

Trainers use the model widely to enable members to evaluate their preferred roles. They also consider how the balance of roles within a team affects performance. Some managers use it when filling vacancies. A personnel director joined a new organisation and concluded that it employed few 'completer–finishers'. Management started initiatives and programmes but left them unfinished as they switched to something else. She resolved that in recruiting new staff she would try to bring at least one more 'completer–finisher' to the senior team.

Using Belbin's roles in film-making teams

management in practice

Hollywood had experienced a shift from long-term jobs to short-term project teams. With their highly skilled freelance staff who come together for a brief period to carry out specific tasks and then disband, film making offers a model for the future of work in the wider world. Angus Strachan has been using Belbin's model to help film directors manage expensive production teams more effectively:

> **Managing film teams requires a mature coordinator who can handle creative people with delicate egos and strong opinions ... A good unit production manager is a strong monitor–evaluator, someone who can carefully analyse the overall situation and make the big calls. The second assistant director needs to be a strong completer–finisher, passing on accurate information that enables the unit production manager to keep abreast of the situation ... A successful assistant director also needs to be a good communicator and organizer who has the flexibility to adjust schedules – in Belbin's terms to take on the resource investigator role.**

Source: Angus Strachan, 'Lights, camera, action', *Personnel Management*, 16 September 2004, pp. 44–46.

However, there is little evidence that companies deliberately use the model when forming teams from existing staff. Managers typically form teams on criteria of technical expertise, departmental representation, or who is available. How the team processes will work is a secondary consideration. This is understandable, but in doing so managers make the implicit assumption that people will be able and willing to cover roles if one seems to be lacking.

Whether the theory is widely used or not, it implies that a manager responsible for a team may find the work goes better if they put effort into securing the most suitable mix of members.

Cisco – the case continues www.cisco.com CASE STUDY

Recalling the roles within the team, Steve said:

My job was mainly to ensure that everything in the virtual team runs smoothly – often just a matter of arranging and coordinating meetings, but also encouraging some kind of creative spark that'll help discussion along. Gunzal takes his time to make decisions, but when he does, he's usually correct. Eddie is very systematic in his work, and very hard working.

Another commented:

I'd say Graham is often the one who comes up with original ideas, while Jim has an incredible range of contacts within the company, and can usually find the right person to go to. Rai is very precise in everything he does and it's very important that he receives the correct information from the engineers. If they don't explain something properly he's good at going back to ask for more information.

Source: Communication from members of the project team.

Case questions 17.5

- Which of the Belbin roles can you identify amongst the members of the team?
- Are any of the roles missing, and how may that have affected team performance?

Activity 17.4 Critical reflection on team composition

Evaluate a team you have worked with using Belbin's team roles.

- Which roles are well represented, and which are missing?
- Has that affected the way the team has worked?
- Which of the roles most closely matches your own preferred role?
- What are the strengths and weaknesses of Belbin's model to the manager?
- Have you any evidence of managers using it to help them manage teams? If so, in what way was it used, and with what effect?

17.7 Team processes

Effective teams, often with the help of skilled team coaches (Hackman and Wageman, 2005), develop processes that help them work together to accomplish their common purpose. These include developing a common approach, attending to the dominant type of communication, and observing team practices.

Common approach

A primary outcome of an effective 'norming' stage is that members agree both the administrative and social aspects of working together. This includes deciding who does which jobs, what skills members need to develop, and how the group should make and modify decisions. In other words the group needs to agree the work required and how it will fit together. It needs to decide how to integrate the skills of the group and use them cooperatively to advance performance.

The common approach includes supporting and integrating new members into the team. It also includes practices of remembering and summarising agreements. Working together on these tasks helps to promote the mutual trust and constructive conflict necessary to team success. Groups need to spend as much time on developing a common approach as they do on developing a shared purpose.

Team members need to control their meetings effectively – whether face to face or at a distance. That involves ensuring they are conducted in a way that suits the purpose of the task, without participants feeling they are being manipulated. Table 17.7 is an example of the advice widely available to managers about effective and ineffective meetings.

Table 17.7
Five tips for effective meetings

Meetings are likely to succeed if:	Meetings are likely to fail if:
• they are scheduled well in advance	• they are fixed at short notice (absentees)
• they have an agenda, with relevant papers distributed in advance and invite additions at the start	• they have no agenda or papers (no preparation, lack of focus, discussion longer)
• they have a starting and finishing time and follow prearranged time limits on each item	• they are of indefinite length (discussion drifts), time is lost and important items are not dealt with (delay, and require a further meeting)
• decisions and responsibilities for action are recorded and circulated within 24 hours	• decisions lack clarity (misunderstanding what was agreed, delay, reopening issues)
• they keep subgroups or members of related teams informed of progress	• the team is not aware of work going on in other teams that is relevant to its work

Categories of communication

Group members depend on information and ideas from others to help them perform the group task; a useful skill is to be able to identify the kind of contribution that people make (Chapter 16 illustrated patterns of group communication), and whether this helps the group to manage the task. To study and learn how people behave in groups we need a precise and reliable way to describe events. There are many such models, each suited to a purpose: Table 17.8 illustrates one such list of behaviours. The significance of this is the evidence that how a group uses its time between these categories of communication will affect performance. A group that devotes most of its time to proposing ideas and disagreeing with them will not progress far. A more effective group will spend more time proposing and building, which of course implies developing better listening skills.

Table 17.8
Categories of communication within a group

Category	Explanation
Proposing	Putting forward a suggestion, idea or course of action
Supporting	Declaring agreement or support for an individual or their idea
Building	Developing or extending an idea or suggestion from someone else
Disagreeing	Criticising another person's statement
Giving information	Giving or clarifying facts, ideas or opinions
Seeking information	Seeking facts, ideas or opinions from others

Observing the team

Observation is the activity of concentrating on how a team works rather than taking part in the activity itself.

Content is the specific substantive task that the group is undertaking.

Members can develop the skill of assessing how well a team is performing a task. There are many guides to help them do this, and anyone can develop their ability to **observe** groups by concentrating on this aspect rather than on the **content** of the immediate task. They work slightly apart from the team for a short time and keep a careful record of what members say or do. They also note how other members react, and how that affects the performance of the team. At the very least, members can reflect on these questions at the end of a task:

- What did people do or say that helped or hindered the group's performance?
- What went well during that task, which we should try to repeat?
- What did not go well, which we could improve?

With practice skilled members of a team are able to observe what is happening at the same time as they work on the task itself. They can do this more easily and powerfully if they focus their observations on certain behaviour categories, such as those shown in Table 17.8 – but suited to the purpose of the observation.

17.8 The disadvantages of teams

For all the undoubted benefits of teams, they have disadvantages and costs.

Take on their own purpose

Some groups take on a life of their own, and become too independent of the organisation that created them. As members learn to work together they generate enthusiasm and commitment – and become harder to control. The team may divert the project to meet goals that they value, rather than those of the sponsor. As experts in the particular issue they can exert great influence over management, by controlling or filtering the flow of information to the organisation as a whole, so that their goals become increasingly hard to challenge. Their work becomes relatively isolated from other parts of the organisation, and they focus on what they see to be key issues.

Use too much time

The benefit of wider perspectives comes from discussion. This inevitably takes longer than if an individual made the decision. Time spent in discussion may encourage participation and acceptance – but only if the group manages this well. If discussion strays over unrelated issues, or goes over matters that they have already dealt with, the team loses time. This can also be an opportunity for members opposed to the project to prolong group discussion and to use the search for agreement as a blocking tactic. Some members will complain about the time spent. In fast-moving situations they may simply not be able to afford the time and so withdraw their support.

Allow an individual to dominate

Some teams allow one member to dominate. This may be the formal leader of the group in a hierarchical organisation, where people do not challenge those in a position of authority. It may be a technical expert who takes over, when others hesitate to show their lack of knowledge or to ask for explanations. In either case the group will not draw on the experience available, and it will probably be a dissatisfying and unproductive experience. It may produce a worse result, and be more costly, than if one person had dealt with the issue.

Succumb to groupthink

Chapter 7 (Section 7.7) examined the concept of groupthink, which occurs when members become so attached to a group that they suppress dissenting views so as not to jeopardise their acceptance by the other members. This can lead the group to reach dangerously wrong decisions. Groupthink is an important aspect of team working, so you should check that section now.

Activity 17.5 Critical reflection on teams

Recall some teams of which you have been a member.

- Which of the advantages and disadvantages have you observed?
- When teams have performed well, or badly, can you relate that to ideas in this chapter, such as the stages of group development, or to Belbin's team roles?

17.9 Current themes and issues

Performance

While in many circumstances a well-designed and skilled team can produce exceptional performance, they are not always necessary. Individuals can handle many tasks as well as a group – and perhaps better. An example is where a task requires people to use their expertise on a narrowly defined technical issue with no wider implications. For such purposes an effective working group (in terms of Table 17.1) can meet the performance required and there is no need to invest the extra effort needed for team performance –

which could indeed be counter-productive. Off-site team development activities can be exciting and motivating. If members then find that the task to be done involves little real interaction beyond normal interpersonal cooperation they will feel let down by the effort to build a real, or high-performance, team.

If the task clearly does require people to work together to create joint work products besides individual contributions, then the risk and cost of creating a real, or high-performance, team will be worthwhile.

Responsibility

Many organisations use self-managed teams to secure business benefits and also to bring benefits associated with a greater degree of autonomy and self-control to staff. These are valuable benefits, but Barker (1993) raises the possibility that self-managing teams may in some cases exert a much tighter control over the actions of members than traditional bureaucratic structures. He showed how three teams in an electronics company developed a system of rules about how members should behave that controlled their actions more powerfully and completely than the former system. This system of **concertive control** arose as workers negotiated a consensus amongst themselves.

Concertive control is when workers reach a negotiated consensus on how to shape their behaviour according to a set of core values.

The components company that Barker studied was struggling to survive in an newly competitive market. One of the founders decided to organise the 90 manufacturing staff (two-thirds of whom were women) into self-managing teams. The factory was rearranged to form three distinct and self-sufficient work areas, with each team being responsible for part of the product range. The teams themselves had considerable responsibility, and had to work out for themselves how they would work together.

An example of how concertive control developed occurred when the late delivery of components meant that a team would miss a customer deadline. They were committed to meeting targets, so agreed to work late and also to accommodate the external commitments some members had. This agreement set a strong precedent for the way the team would behave in future. A member later described the continuing power of the team's internally agreed consensus about personal responsibility:

> I work my best at trying to help our team to get stuff out the door. If it requires overtime, coming in at five o'clock and spending your weekend here, that's what I do. (Barker, 1993 p. 422)

New team members began to obey the norms agreed by the original members, as the team's concertive control began to penetrate their attitudes and actions. A temporary employee at the time explained how she tried to conform to the norms: 'When I first started I really didn't start off on the right foot, so I've been having to re-prove myself as a team player' (p. 425).

Members rewarded those who conformed by making them feel part of the team and a participant in their success. They punished those who had 'bad' attitudes.

The norms gradually evolved from a loose system that the workers 'knew' to a tighter system of objective rules. This transformation most often occurred when new members were not acting according to the team's work norms, such as coming to work on time. One explained:

> Well we had some disciplinary thing. We had a few certain people who didn't show up on time and made a habit of coming in late. So the team got together and kind a set some guidelines and we told them, you know, 'If you come in late the third time and you don't wanna do anything to correct it, you're gone.' That was a team decision that this was a guideline that we were gonna follow. (p. 426)

Barker concludes that creating autonomous or self-managed teams does not free workers from the obligation to follow rules. Instead:

> The iron cage becomes stronger. The powerful combination of peer pressure and rational rules in the concertive system creates a new iron cage whose bars are almost invisible to the workers it incarcerates. They must invest a part of themselves in the team: they must identify strongly with their team's values and goals, its norms and rules. If they want to resist their team's control, they must be willing to risk their human dignity, being made to feel unworthy as a 'teammate'. Entrapment in the iron cage is the cost of concertive control. (pp. 435–436)

This research shows that for all the benefits of teams, especially self-managing teams, they are not without their negative sides. Peer-enforced concertive control can create constraining and even oppressive systems.

Internationalisation

A common feature of internationalisation is that companies create multinational or global teams to work on projects or regular activities. Such teams are often 'virtual', in the sense that although they are working on a common task they are physically separated and span different time zones. Their dominant means of communication is usually through computer-based systems such as e-mails and videoconferencing.

Virtual teams face all the challenges of team performance which face teams that are located in the same place, and in addition they need to overcome the difficulties of working with those from different cultures. Their transitory nature means that members may be part of several such teams simultaneously, limiting their ability to build close relationships with members of any particular one. Finally, virtual meetings lack the physical cues present in face-to-face meetings, which makes it more difficult for members to give and respond to the non-verbal cues that prevent misunderstanding.

Govindarajan and Gupta (2001) surveyed executives from European and US multinationals with experience of virtual teams, and concluding that they face unique challenges:

- **Cultivating trust amongst team members** Trust between members encourages cooperation and avoids conflict, and is highest when members share similarities, communicate frequently and operate in a common context of norms and values. By their nature, global teams suffer on all these dimensions.
- **Hindrances to communication** Distance hinders face-to-face communication, which technology can still only partially resolve. Language barriers are a further block to communication: even if people are speaking the same language, differences in meaning and usage can obstruct work. Cultural differences (Chapter 3) mean that members bring profound differences in values to the discussions. Those from collectivist cultures place a high value on achieving consensus, and are willing to prolong a meeting to achieve it: this can seem wasteful to those from individualist cultures who place less value on consensus.

Summary

1 Explain why organisations use teams for a wide range of tasks

- As management faces new expectations about cost and quality many see teams as a way of using the talents and experience of the organisation more fully to meet these tougher objectives.
- Teams also meet important motivational needs – for social contact and to be part of a collective achievement.

2 Distinguish the stages of development through which groups pass

- Forming, storming, norming, performing and adjourning. Note also that these stages occur iteratively as new members join or circumstances change.

3 Explain Belbin's theory of team roles

- Belbin identified nine distinct roles within a team and found that the balance of these roles within a team affected performance. The roles are: implementer, coordinator, shaper, plant, resource investigator, monitor–evaluator, teamworker, completer, specialist.

4 Evaluate the effectiveness of a team and identify possible reasons for variations in performance

- Criteria include meeting performance expectations, members having experienced an effective team, and members developing transferable teamwork skills.
- Team performance depends on effort, knowledge/skill and performance strategies – each of which can be affected by the team itself *and* by wider organisational factors.

5 Outline the organisational factors that influence team performance

- Effort can be encouraged by removing coordination problems and rewarding teamwork.
- Knowledge/skill can be fostered by education, training and coaching.
- Performance strategies can be encouraged by relevant technologies being available and by providing feedback.

6 Describe the meaning of 'groupthink', and give some examples of its symptoms

- When members become so committed to maintaining group cohesiveness, they may no longer look critically at alternatives. Symptoms include illusion of invulnerability, belief in the inherent morality of the group, rationalisation, stereotyping out-groups, self-censorship, direct pressure, mindguards, and an illusion of unanimity.

Review questions

1. What are the potential benefits of teamwork to people and performance?
2. Katzenbach and Smith (1993) distinguish between working groups and real teams. Describe the differences, and suggest when each form is appropriate to a task.
3. W.L. Gore and Associates (see Part Case) is beginning to form more distant teams. What management issues are likely to arise in this form of team?
4. How many stages of development do teams go through? Use this model to compare two teams.
5. List the main categories of behaviour that can be identified in observing a group.
6. Compare the meaning of the terms 'task' and 'maintenance' roles.
7. Evaluate Belbin's model of team roles. Which three or four roles are of most importance in an effective team? What is your preferred role?
8. Give examples of the external factors that affect group performance. Compare the model with your experience as a group member.
9. What are the potential disadvantages of teams?

Concluding critical reflection

Think about your experience of teams, and about the ways in which your organisation uses teams. Review the material in the chapter, and then make notes on these questions:

- Which of the issues discussed in this chapter struck you as being relevant to practice in your organisation?
- Thinking of the teams in which you have worked, which are effective and which ineffective? What happens in the effective teams that does not happen in the less effective ones? What team-building skills do people use, and to what extent are they supported or hindered by wider organisational factors? Are teams supported by specific coaching or guidance? What **assumptions** have people made when creating teams?
- What factors such as the history of the company or your personal experience have shaped the way you use teams? Does your current use of teams appear to be right for your present **context** position and company – or would you use a different approach in other circumstances?
- Have people put forward **alternative** working methods (such as introducing more self-managing teams), based on practice in other companies? If you could find such evidence, how may it affect company practice?
- What **limitations** can you identify in any of these team theories, or in your organisation's approach to using teams. Do people create too many teams, or too few?

Further reading

Belbin, R.M. (1993), *Team Roles at Work*, Butterworth/Heinemann, Oxford.

An account of the experiments that led Belbin to develop his model of team roles.

Hayes, N. (1997), *Successful Team Development*, International Thomson Business Press, London.

A lively and well-referenced account of many of the issues covered here.

Hackman, J.R. (1990), *Groups that Work (and Those that Don't)*, Jossey-Bass, San Francisco, CA.

Katzenbach, J.R. and Smith, D.K. (1993), *The Wisdom of Teams*, Harvard Business School Press, Boston, MA.

Both books contain many good examples of the use of teamwork.

Sandberg, A. (ed.) (1995), *Enriching Production*, Avebury, Aldershot.

A very wide range of perspectives on the use of teams at Volvo, and of the wider forces that affected the fate of the Volvo experiments.

Druskat, V.U. and Wheeler, J.V. (2004), 'How to lead a self-managing team', *MIT Sloan Management Review*, vol. 45, no. 4, pp. 65–71.

Govindarajan, V. and Gupta, A.K. (2001), 'Building an effective global business team', *MIT Sloan Management Review*, vol. 42, no. 4, pp. 63–72.

Two contemporary articles based on empirical research in a manufacturing plant and a series of global businesses respectively.

Hackman, J. R. and Wageman, R. (2005), 'A theory of team coaching', *Academy of Management Review*, vol. 30, no. 2, pp. 269–287.

Valuable overview of the development of interest in team processes, and of research into the skills of team development.

Weblinks

These websites have appeared in this and other chapters:

www.cisco.com
www.vuitton.com
www.microsoft.com
www.oticon.com
www.bmw.com
www.gore.com

Each has tried to develop new approaches to using teams – encouraging staff to share ideas and experience, as well as gaining personal satisfaction from them. Try to gain an impression from the site (perhaps under the careers/working for us section) of what it would be like to work in an organisation in which teams are a prominent feature of working.

Annotated weblinks, multiple choice questions and other useful resources can be found on www.pearsoned.co.uk/boddy

Week 10

The Practical Difficulties of Managing and Leading

CHAPTER 6

Managing to manage: power, decision making, ethics and the struggle to cope

Objectives

Having read this chapter and completed its associated activities, readers should be able to:

- Recognise that managers not only have to manage tasks but manage power relationships in which they are inevitably involved, noting the various ways in which the power of specific individuals or groups can vary, albeit within a basic pattern of power relations.
- Appreciate how the relative amount of power or influence exercised by an individual or group within an organisation relates to their involvement in the handling of *uncertainties* or perceived threats to the organisation's future continuation.
- Understand how managing participation in decision-making processes involves handling a great deal more than the rational analysis of situations and the choice of optimum solutions to given problems.
- Analyse decision-making processes as 'garbage cans' in which a multiplicity of issues and differences of power and perception are thrown together and help shape outcomes.
- Appreciate that managerial work itself has significant emotional dimensions to it and that managers can both be helped with and hindered by some of the *discursive resources* which are offered to them in, for example, managerial writing.
- Understand how managerial work involves people in a *double control problem*, whereby managers experience the pressure of both trying to control the activities – and even sentiments and values – of others while having to manage their own lives and identities.
- Be sensitive to the ways in which managerial work often leads those engaged in it to adopt forms of language use which differ from normal or straightforward language.

- Form a judgement about the extent to which the peculiarities of language among some managers, and others involved in work organisation matters, might reflect attempts of individuals to accommodate that dimension of managerial work which requires people to try to 'control the uncontrollable'.
- Come to terms with the fact that matters of value, ethics and morality run through every aspect of managerial work and that ethical issues are more usefully understood as one of the ways in which human beings cope with their world rather than as objective absolutes with which people do or do not comply.
- Understand that managers themselves have a degree of choice of being either relatively *ethically active* or relatively *ethically assertive* in their everyday work.

Power and the inevitability of organisational politics

It was seen in the final part of Chapter 5 that managerial work has a very significant social status element to it. It involves a lot more than just organising tasks in a neutral and apolitical manner. To be involved in managerial work is inevitably to be involved in power and politics. To manage a managerial role involves managing 'power' both in the sense of having to exercise it and in the sense of being subject to it. Managers often find this to be one of the most challenging aspects of their job; one of the hardest aspects of managing to manage. But before we develop our analysis of this aspect of organisational and managerial life we need to identify the various levels at which power operates and then decide how we can most usefully conceptualise 'power'.

Power operates at three levels:

- the level of societies, where some people have a much greater capacity to influence others and gain a greater share of the 'good things' of that society;
- the level of organisational structures and cultures, where certain people are put into positions where they can shape what others do and take a greater share of the 'rewards' made available by the organisation;
- the interpersonal level, where some people get other people to do things they otherwise would not do and, as a result of this, typically, 'do better' than these people in terms of the material and symbolic rewards available to people in the organisation.

What runs through these three aspects of power in social life is the capacity of individuals or groups to affect *outcomes* of situations to their advantage. These outcomes typically relate to the distribution of whatever 'goods' or resources are scarce and are valued in the society. Without 'scarcity' there would be no need for anyone to exert power.

Power *Concept*

The capacity of an individual or group to affect the outcome of any situation so that access is achieved to whatever resources are scarce and desired within a society or a part of that society.

If everyone could obtain anything they wanted without reference to other people (from a large country estate to a clean office floor, say) they would never need to act towards others in power terms at all. This is unimaginable of course. Not only are many desirable things inevitably in short supply but sometimes what one person wants necessarily precludes another person from having it. I might want music playing in the office, for example. But you do not. Negotiation is called for. But whichever of us is generally the more 'powerful' in the office is the one who is likely to get their way over this matter.

Even where a piece of 'power behaviour' occurs in private between just two people it cannot be understood as something separate from the culture, structure and patterns of advantage and disadvantage prevailing in the society and culture to which these individuals belong. A concept (or 'working definition') of power must therefore recognise the societal or structural–cultural dimension of power as well as the fact that it is often manifested at the level of individuals and groups.

Activity 6.1

Read Case 8.3, pp. 342–3, concentrating not so much on the issue of 'business process re-engineering' which is a concern of Chapter 8, but on the 'power factors which are operating in this managerial situation in Dovecote Components. What power factors can you see operating at

- the interpersonal level
- the level of organisational structure and culture
- the level of society?

The boardroom events which Roberto Auldearn reports involved interpersonal power rivalries between Roberto and two other senior managers. There seemed in this to be elements of both material interests ('territoriality') and emotions (personal dislikes are mentioned). Also at this level, we see Jerry Penick very clearly wielding power over all the other managers. He is exerting his authority as the managing director of the company – not just to 'put the boot in' to Roberto's ideas or to say who will and will not be involved in the 'action group'. He actually sacks the manufacturing and the finance directors. Jerry's use of his chief executive's authority to act towards these individuals in this way is connected to the interpersonal dimension and to the organisational structural and cultural dimension of the power that is operating here. And that dimension would not exist unless it, in turn, was embedded in a set of cultural institutions and wealth-ownership patterns at the societal level that gives chief executives the right to act in this way. But Jerry's power behaviour with regard to the re-engineering of the business also has to be understood in the light of the global changes in the way wealth and power is being restructured in an increasingly international market place. The power relationships between major corporations are shifting. And formal governmental politics are also involved in the power plays occurring in Dovecot Components, as Roberto's mention of government industrial relations policies suggests. However, the outcome of all of this goes way beyond the boardroom. The access to scarce and valued resources of all of those who lose their jobs as a result of the restructuring of Dovecote will be seriously affected. Power and politics in the boardrooms of work organisations create winners and losers both within those boardrooms and in the communities within which the organisations are located. What we shall shortly be conceptualising as 'micropolitics' must always be understood in the context of 'macropolitics' (see Further Reading on power and organisational politics, pp. 248–9).

It has repeatedly been stressed in *Organising and Managing Work* that people in organisations tend to have goals, priorities and ambitions of their own. All employees, managers no less than any others, are there to use the organisation just as much as the organisation is there to use them. This is fundamental to the employment exchange that all employees make with their employer. Inevitably, managers will at times see that attending to functional or departmental priorities rather than corporate ones can more readily further their personal interests. Most managers below the level of chief executive are located within one of the many 'sub-units' of the organisation – a function like finance, marketing or human resourcing, perhaps, or a department like a university's history, physics or education department. This inevitably risks managers prioritising the interests of their own sub-unit or their own personal interests, as people whose reputations are attached to that department. This tendency is made even greater if their sub-unit location is related to their occupational or 'professional' identity as an accountant, a HR manager, a historian or a physicist. Whatever their commitment to the larger entity of the organisation might be, the members of any sub-unit – the manager included – are likely to find themselves coming into competition with members of other sub-units. They will typically find themselves competing with other sections of the organisation for the scarce resources that they might want, sometimes to carry out their sub-unit function successfully and sometimes to satisfy other personal or group wants.

Micropolitics/organisational politics *Concept*

Processes occurring within work organisations as individuals, groups and organisational 'sub-units' compete for access to scarce and valued material and symbolic resources.

The *micropolitics* that go on in organisations are not all to be understood in terms of sub-unit commitments, however. Neither are they only indulged in by managers. It is possible that coalitions of women might form within part of an organisation to compete with groupings of men who have been trying to exclude them from certain rewards, for example. Or younger employees might get together to challenge certain older individuals who have tried to maintain a monopoly over particular resources. Equally, we are likely to see competition between individuals for scarce and valued resources varying from car parking spaces or sunny offices to salary increases and career promotions.

Micropolitical conflicts often occur over obviously material resources like budgets, floor space or salary increments, but almost every material resource also has a symbolic value. To have the biggest office in a building means more than simply having the most office floor space, for example. For a person or a group to be given better material resources than others is typically associated with their being afforded higher prestige or respect. It is not unknown for an individual to feel that their whole working life and standing in the organisation has improved simply because they have been allocated a reserved parking spot, for example.

Micropolitics, or the competition between organisational members for scarce resources, is far from a trivial matter. It is much more than a 'side-show' to the main organisational performance of producing goods or services. One frequently hears people complain that the organisation in which they work is 'very political' and implying that this might not be the case in another organisation. Although it might well be the case that the 'politics' in some organisations are more vicious and potentially destructive than in others, there is no possibility whatsoever of discovering, this side of utopia, an organisation in which politicking was not a significant fact of life. Managing to manage inevitably requires an ability to cope with politics. But are micropolitics necessarily counterproductive to organisational effectiveness? Competitive behaviour between members of organisations may indeed undermine productive cooperation between organisational members. Yet it can also contribute to successful organisational performance (for reasons we shall see shortly). Either way, micropolitics are an inevitable and intrinsic part of organisational life and activity. This is so for a number of reasons.

First, micropolitics are inevitable because human beings, by virtue of being human, are 'strategic animals'. They continually strive to establish who they are and they seek to meet the material requirements of themselves and their families. To do this they will inevitably have to cooperate with others, both at work and outside it. But they will just as inevitably come into competition with others – given the scarcity of many of the things that human beings tend to want, as we recognised earlier. We could say, then, that a degree of competition and rivalry between people is a normal part of the human condition and is as likely to manifest itself in work relationships as anywhere else in people's lives.

Micropolitics are inevitable, second, because of the way organisations themselves are set up. This relates to the point made above that the division of labour in an organisation and its allocation of people to organisational 'sub-units' tends to encourage people to act in the interests of that grouping rather than in the interests of something much more difficult to identify with – the 'organisation as a whole'. And if a group does not have this 'bigger interest' or 'wider loyalty' to discourage them from acting sectionally then they are likely to find themselves competing with other sub-units, given the scarcity of many of the resources that each sub-unit will be seeking. These are resources varying from budgets to premises and from able new organisational recruits to prestige within the corporate status hierarchy. At the level of the sub-unit managers, such tendencies are exacerbated by the fact that managers across any particular level of an organisation's sub-units are often in competition with each other for posts at the next higher level on the organisation's narrowing managerial career ladder. Figure 6.1 illustrates this. In a classic analysis of micropolitics, Burns (1961) pointed out that organisational members 'are at one and the same time co-operators in a common enterprise and rivals for the material and intangible rewards of successful competition with each other'. This is a key feature of the institution of bureaucracy – a defining characteristic of every organisation (Chapter 2, pp. 37–40). The bureaucratic structure works both as a control mechanism and a reward ladder. These two aspects of the structuring of all organisations are bound to come into tension with each other.

FIGURE 6.1 Organisation hierarchies are both control structures and – narrowing – career ladders

In the case of a school, for example, this dual control/reward aspect of organisational structure might mean that all the teachers of science would be required to cooperate with each other to gain a good assessment of science teaching in that school by the visiting quality inspectors. One of the 'motivators' to positive and cooperative behaviour for each of these teachers is the possibility of future promotion to the better-paid and more prestigious post of head of science. But only one of these teachers can become the head of department. Thus cooperators are simultaneously competitors. This is competition *within* a sub-unit or department. What about *across* sub-units? If we look at the next level of hierarchy in this school, we see the post of deputy head teacher, and the potential competitors for this are all the heads of department across the school. So here we see departmental managers being required to cooperate with each other to make the whole school successful at the same time as those sub-unit leaders are put into competition with each other. Career pressures are thus added to pressures of which department is to get the better classrooms, the better book budget, and so on.

The third set of factors making micropolitics inevitable relates to what we saw in Chapter 5 (pp. 174–5) to be the high degree of ambiguity and uncertainty that runs through all organisational situations. It is impossible for anyone to have the 'full facts' of any situation, for them to understand fully what is going on at any given time or for them to be able to predict the outcome of any action taken. This characteristic of organisational life helps explain how managers come to depend on other people in their work situations and why they need to make trading, negotiating and influencing others so central to their work. Political processes play a significant part in the handling of all of this, but the concern here is with how ambiguity both makes possible and encourages competitive behaviour between organisational members. Such micropolitical behaviour is something that managers are liable to engage in on their own account – promoting their own careers, for example. They will also get involved in micropolitics as they find themselves having to handle the political activities of other employees – ensuring that the career competition between members of their own department is channelled in such a way that it does not prevent productively cooperative work being done by those individuals, for example.

Ambiguity exists, we said, when the meaning of a situation is unclear or confused and is therefore open to a variety of interpretations (p. 174). Given the considerable scope for people to offer different interpretations of what is going on, it is not surprising to find individuals and groups exploiting such situations to their own advantage. There might be ambiguity, for example, about whether a new and influential job would be best done by one of my friends and allies or by one of your friends and allies. In such a situation it is quite likely that you and I will compete in arguing for giving the job to our own respective friend and political ally. In doing so, we would be acting micropolitically. In doing so, we might be acting to further personal and private interests (helping a personal friend along in their careers). Equally, we might be acting to further the interests of our respective departments (ensuring someone is appointed who will favour my department rather than yours in future contests between your departmental interests and mine). What is most likely, though, is that we will be acting to further or defend *both* our personal situation *and* that of our departments. We might even be politicking to get an outcome that we believe will benefit the organisation as a whole as well as serving our sectional interests. Alternatively, though, we might be acting to bring about something that will favour our sectional interests at the price of corporate ones. Which of these is the case in any particular circumstance will always tend to be ambiguous, of course!

Uncertainty is closely related to ambiguity and was conceptualised in Chapter 5 by treating it as an aspect of ambiguity that is related to the future. Uncertainty exists when the *understanding of a future situation or an event* is unclear or confused and is therefore open to a variety of interpretations (p. 175). This brings strategic matters into the picture – strategy being essentially about how the organisation is to develop into the long-term future. One of the key tasks of organisational strategists is to know, at any point in time, which of the constituencies with which it trades or 'exchanges' are most 'strategic' at that time – in terms of the degree of uncertainty they are creating for the organisation's long-term future. If a group of workers in an organisation without which the organisation cannot survive are threatening to leave, for example, it might become a strategic priority to find an inducement to keep them 'on board'. At another time perhaps, the managers of that organisation might discover that they are desperately short of funds to invest in a new product that is vital to long-term survival. Faced with this uncertainty, the search for investment funds is likely to become a strategic priority.

Strategic contingency theory of power

Concept

A sub-unit of an organisation will have greater relative power or influence within the organisation the more it (a) is central to the organisation's workflow, (b) cannot be substituted by another unit, (c) reduces uncertainties perceived to be of strategic significance to the organisation.

The fact that strategic priorities change over time in the light of changing organisational uncertainties has considerable implications for micropolitics. One of the main sources of relative power enjoyed by any person or sub-unit – in the sense of having relatively good access to scarce and desired resources – is the role it plays in handling uncertainties thought to be facing the organisation with regard to its future. Thus, the person who persuades the vital group of workers to stay with the organisation will be well placed the next time a promotion comes up or a smart new office becomes available. Also, they are likely to find themselves being listened to by managers at senior levels on subsequent matters. Their influence and the likelihood of their further succeeding in micropolitical activity has thus been enhanced by dealing with a strategic uncertainty. They are well placed to repeat such successes and generally advance their power and gain further rewards in the future. Similarly, if a particular department were seen to be solving the problem (overcoming the uncertainty) that had arisen with regard to new product investment, that department or function would be likely to rise up the departmental 'pecking order' of the organisation. The relative power of the sub-unit is enhanced and, again, its members are better placed to succeed in subsequent micropolitical manoeuvrings. This would only be the case, however, if that sub-unit was regarded as substitutable by another sub-unit, as is pointed out by Hickson *et al.* (1971) in their analysis of what they call 'strategic contingencies' (strategically important uncertainties) as key sources of sub-unit power. Power would not go to either the individual keeping the key workers in the organisation or to the department obtaining the investment funding if, in either case, it was seen that another party could just as readily solve such problems. Neither would this happen if that individual or sub-unit were not, in the first place, seen as relatively 'central to the workflow of the organisation'. One is not likely suddenly to acquire power and influence by dealing with an uncertainty if one is generally regarded as peripheral to the key operations of the organisation.

As we shall see in Chapter 7, it is important to treat all these contingencies as matters of interpretations (or 'enactments') made by members of the organisation and not as objectively existing circumstances. Thus, an important element of the political behaviour of an individual or a sub-unit within an organisation wishing to increase their relative power would be the *persuading* of people with the greatest relative power that a certain contingency, such as a shortage of investment funds or the likely loss of a key customer, should be regarded as a serious strategic threat. If they wish to persuade the 'powers that be' that they are the people to solve the problem they will have to work on the way they are themselves perceived. Their being 'central to workflow' or as 'unsubstitutable' is always a *perceived* centrality or an *understood* irreplaceability. To 'politick' successfully one has to persuade the people in charge that one is both central to operations and that one's role cannot be played by anyone else. Bearing this in mind we can turn to the example of a person who sees himself as an especially successful organisational politician.

Activity 6.2

Look at the account Derek Duffus gives in Case 6.1 of his 'rise and rise' in the newspaper industry and identify:

- the 'rewards' of micropolitical activity that come to Derek or to any other of the people in the story (i.e. what 'scarce and desired resources' we see anyone obtaining as a result of politicking);
- the micropolitical moves or 'tactics' that are mentioned by Derek;
- situations where the handling of strategic uncertainties perceived to be facing the newspaper were relevant to the obtaining of 'power' (i.e. the winning of access to scarce and desirable resources) either by individuals or by organisational sub-units.

The rise and rise of Derek Duffus

Case 6.1

I've heard you say a couple of times that you are a particularly 'political animal'. You've also said that every newspaper editor has to be 'a consummate politician'. How do you relate these two things?

In the obvious way, I suppose. I think it is true that to do a job like that of an editor of a big paper you have got to have a lot of cunning and a great deal of skill at getting what you want from people. And I have both of these things. That's why I have got to the top here much younger than I would if I'd been a less political animal. And I have beaten others to get where I am. There's no denying that. I wasn't the only candidate for the editorial chair.

OK, then. Can we first just look at you and your career and then come back to the editor's job? Take me back as far as you can with your life as a 'political animal'.

Gosh, I suppose I should try to remember some playground stories to tell you. I can't remember much beyond the fact that I once did a deal with a teacher. I gave her some strong hints about where the smokers were going at break time for their illegal fags. In return, she helped me become a school prefect. That had some quite nice perks which made my last year at school more comfortable than it might have been – nothing special, just things like having a chair to sit on at assembly instead of having to sit on the floor with all the rest.

And when you were at college?

Yes, I suppose I developed that sort of knack further. Making friends with a couple of the journalism lecturers certainly helped me – you know, allowing me more generous deadlines for assignments and all that. In fact, yes it's coming back to me now, there was this tutor who'd once had a glorious career on a national Sunday before being ruined by the drink. I used to go down the pub with him. And on several occasions he gave me an assignment mark for telling him, over several pints, what I would have written if I had got around to putting things down on paper. That was a good deal. We both saved time – I didn't have to write the essays and he didn't have to read them.

Did you feel you were cheating?

Only occasionally. I mean I did actually learn a lot in my chats with him. I am sure I would have got good marks if I had put in proper assignments.

And were you in this on your own?

Oh gosh yes. I wouldn't have trusted more than a couple of my best mates with that secret. I probably did tell them about it, but they did the assignments like everybody else. I do remember, though, conspiring with these two friends to make sure that, every year, two out of the three of us got elected as year representatives. We always made a point of praising the quality of the teaching, even when it was crap. I'm sure that helped us get better marks than we might have got, especially from one of the really bad lecturers. He particularly had to – how shall I put it? – look after me and my mate so that complaints about his incoherent lectures didn't get to the course committee.

It sounds like you were training yourself in more than journalism at college then?

I'd never thought of it like that before. But I suppose you are right. I certainly looked around pretty quickly to work out which of my fellow reporters I could team up with when I got my first proper job. I had just one mate there and he and I decided to take up golf, just to get in with the news editor, who was obsessed with the little rubber ball. I think it worked for a while. We both got allocated to more interesting stories than the other younger reporters, I think. But it nearly backfired on us. The others recognised what we were up to. They didn't like our little alliance. They sarcastically called us the 'super cubs' and they made life so difficult for us that I decided to drop the golf thing. But I made up the ground I'd lost by taking on a sort of informal leadership of the younger reporters. Most of us disliked the older clique, who looked down on us with contempt. We called them the 'old farts'. And sometimes, when we met as a group down the pub we would devise tricks that would get one or more of the old farts out chasing non-stories.

How did you do that?

The best example is where we got one of the girls to ring up one of these blokes and pretend she was a councillor who was worried about corruption on the local authority. We had a couple of the old journos chasing their tails for weeks on that one.

And did they realise they had been tricked.

Oh yes. They caught us out eventually. After that it was real war.

Who won?

They did. Generally speaking. It turned out that they were much better at that sort of thing than we were. They wiped the floor with several of us 'pathetic cub reporters', as they called us. But I turned things round to my personal advantage, I must admit.

How?

In the end, this battle between the 'old farts' and the 'young ones' was doing real harm to the paper. The editor called us all in and put it to us that if things didn't change the paper might be sold and merged with another one. 'You had all better get your eyes back on the ball, or your jobs are at risk,' he said. I decided to go and see the editor a couple of days later. I told him that I wanted some personal advice from him on my long-term career and whether it was a good idea to try to become an editor. I didn't really want such advice from him. But I did want to find out whether the paper was under real threat. It turned out that it really was. The news operation had to be sharpened up or else. At the end of the meeting he asked me if there was anything I thought I could do to mend fences between the factions on the paper. 'Of course', I said 'I will do my utmost.' And indeed I did – using all the charm I could muster to persuade people to work together rather than work against each other. And in the process of this I became a sort of protégé of the editor. A bit of patronage here and there never does any harm, I always say. I used to see him regularly for what he called 'our mentoring chats'. And, in the process of discussing his advice I used to drop in little bits of information that might be useful to him and the management of the paper. And, guess what? My salary went up rather nicely. My expenses got queried much less than anybody else's. And when the news editor retired, guess who replaced him?

You did.

How did you guess? Yes, the rise and rise of Derek Duffus was really under way. I was heading for the editor's chair.

But you were just news editor at this stage?

That's right. But I saw that as just a step to the top job.

And was it?

Not as directly as I had calculated. It turned out that, of all people, it was the sports editor who was the most powerful baron at court. He was even more influential than the financial and the marketing people. I saw straight away that he was someone I had to sort out.

Why was he so influential?

It all turned on one particular sports writer. Francis Khyber was immensely popular with readers and everybody knew that several nationals were courting him. He was a natural networker. He had a network of contacts across the sporting world, and indeed well beyond it. He basically named his own salary here. But the sports editor argued that it was his relationship with Francis that kept him on the paper. The editor himself, the finance and the marketing people therefore tended to allow the sports editor first say on all sorts of things. Through his relationship with just one of the newspaper's best assets, Francis Khyber, he made himself indispensable. Whether it was true or not, the whole editorial and management team assumed that the loss of this one writer would do real damage to circulation. With the editor just a few years away from retirement, I had a serious rival for his job. Sport, in effect, counted for more than news.

I can't wait to hear how you dealt with this.

Think about it. It's dead simple really.

Well, assassination comes to mind, but I'm sure . . .

Well I did consider a bit of character assassination when I discovered that the sports editor had a minor criminal record – years back. Only I had this killer information. But no, I calculated that if I played things that dirty I would risk my own integrity. I didn't want to risk being seen as that ruthless. Papers do want their editor to be seen as a person of integrity.

So you . . .

Yes, I worked out that if one asset, one writer, was the source of a rival's power, then perhaps I should try to acquire that asset for my own department. It turned out that this was much easier than it might sound. I made a point of getting to know Francis Khyber and soon discovered that he was quite keen to 'develop out of sport'. He had done one or two feature articles with only tenuous sporting links and was quite close to the features editor. He'd been thinking of moving in that direction but was having doubts. The affair he was having with the features editor was becoming a problem to him. So you can see where I saw my chance. I started discussions with him about joining my team. I persuaded him that his networking abilities could be exploited in news journalism much better than anywhere else, which was absolutely genuine. I discovered that he already knew several key politicians very well and that a couple of very senior police officers were amongst his family friends. He'd met all these people schmoozing at sports events apparently.

And that's what you did?

Yes, after an almighty fight I was allowed to recruit Francis to my team. There was blood on the carpet, I can tell you. The sports editor bitterly fought me over my claim that Francis would be an even bigger asset to the paper if he featured more on the front pages. And he nearly went berserk when I said that moving him to my area would be the only thing that would keep him on the paper. In the end, as you can guess, Francis said what he wanted to do. And nobody could argue. Consequently, I moved to the top of the pecking order, below the editor. And when Jack retired? Well here I am.

Editor and 'managing editor' I notice.

Yep, king of the castle – a power in the land.

We must be careful not to take this example of a self-proclaimed 'consummate politician' as typical of managers and others who engage in the everyday micropolitics of the average work organisation. However, this man's exceptionally frank and colourful story is full of insights into the way power and conflict can manifest themselves in organisations. The language used here is very much the language of power, power clashes, ambition and political intrigue. Scanning the account gives us terms like 'cunning', 'beating others', 'alliances', 'conspiring', 'war', 'battle', 'barons at court', 'influencing', 'networking', 'sorting someone out', 'killer information', 'sources of power', 'blood on the carpet', 'pecking order' and, of course, 'king of the castle' and 'a power in the land'. But such language is far from unusual in the discussions of relationships and activities that occur every day in corporate offices and the 'corridors of power' of organisations ranging from banks to breweries, government departments to opera houses, schools to newspapers. The micropolitics that occur in all these settings are part and parcel of how bureaucratic enterprises operate and the ways in which individuals, groups, 'sub-units' pursue power – in the sense of seeking or maintaining access to whatever resources are scarce and desired.

We hear of various types of 'resource' being pursued in the school and the newspaper that feature in Derek Duffus's story. Promotions and good salaries were resources we are not surprised to hear mentioned and these were clearly central to much of the politicking in the newspaper organisation. Derek's career advancement is the central theme of this slice of autobiography but, on the way, he makes sure to mention that his salary was 'going up nicely'. We also hear that Francis Khyber had got himself into a position whereby he could 'name his own salary'. Political advantage can also mean that one's expenses are queried less than those of others, it would seem. And the rewards of power or influence can include 'perks' as modest as having a chair to sit on at school assemblies. They can also include having a greater amount of 'free' time, as we saw in the case of the alternative to a written assignment that Derek negotiated with the college lecturer. Later, one of the rewards that Derek receives as a result of his cultivating the news editor is his allocation to news stories that were 'more interesting' than the ones given to other young reporters.

An impression that we tend to get, not just from this story but from other accounts of organisational politics, is that power and influence *themselves* are rewards that power and influence can bring. At a simple level, this can be understood as a matter of the sense of achievement that accompanies the possession of power and influence. The very tone of Derek's story-telling suggests that this might be the case with him. But there is another level at which the 'power as a reward of power' phenomenon operates. People pursue power not just to obtain the immediate resources that come from having power – money, status and general 'comforts of life'. They also pursue it to put themselves in a position whereby they will be able to obtain whatever they might turn out to want in the future. To have power is to have the potential to 'do better' in the future. We do not know what Derek might want in the future – wealth, lovers, opportunities to travel, career advancement for his children or even entry into national politics and government. But his current position as 'king of the castle' at his newspaper puts him in a better position to obtain these things than he would be in if he were just one of the underlings at court.

The outcomes of micropolitical success are clearly many and varied. But the methods or tactics used to achieve micropolitical success are equally numerous and varied. We hear of numerous tactics and stratagems in Derek's story.

- *Doing deals and making exchanges.* Derek actually refers to the 'good deal' that he made with the college tutor. It was a trade from which both benefited. One party to the trade had less assignment writing to do. The other party had less marking to do. All the exchanges that Derek makes across the range of his politicking activities can be understood as *strategic* exchanges. They are trades, sometimes minor and sometimes major, that play a part in advancing his career or life strategy.

- *Seeking patrons.* Derek learned of the advantages to be gained by establishing relationships with more powerful people when he was still at school. We see him doing something similar at college. Early on at work, we see him seeking the patronage of the news editor to help advance his situation. Later, he manages to get the editor himself to be his patron. He initially flatters the editor by pretending to be seeking career advice. He then builds up the relationship, and creates a degree of dependence by trading 'little bits of information' that might be useful to the editor and to 'the management'. He does this for both immediate material reward and for a crown prince role – the position of heir to the throne.
- *Making alliances.* Derek sought to 'team up with' selected colleagues as soon as he got his first job. He soon found a 'mate' to join him in gaining advantage over the other reporters.
- *Conspiring.* Derek uses this term to describe the earlier alliance at college when he and two friends exploited their position on a course committee to get higher marks than other students.
- *Mobilising groups and assuming informal leadership roles.* This type of alliance making is seen in Derek's mobilising of younger reporters into what might be called a 'cabal' to oppose the older 'clique' he labelled the 'old farts'.
- *Lying and cheating.* This is seen both in the 'praising' of bad teaching at college and the effective blackmailing of certain lecturers. It also comes into the 'tricking' of the older journalists into pursuing non-existent news stories.
- *Making strategic retreats.* Derek is willing to take a step backwards if he perceives an immediate advantage potentially compromising longer-term success. He 'dropped the golf thing' when he found other reporters getting hostile about his cultivation of the news editor. He recognised the disadvantages of fellow reporters 'making life difficult' for him and his fellow 'super cub'. He made a further strategic retreat when he sought to end the war with the 'old farts' who were proving too clever for Derek and his gang.
- *Using charm and skills of persuasion.* It appears that Derek uses such skills regularly. He explicitly mentions them when telling us about his efforts to repair relationships between the factions in the news office.
- *Networking.* We can assume that Derek himself will have built up a network of contacts that he can 'trade with', especially as a means of obtaining news and information. However, it is Francis Khyber's networks that he tells us about, and he paints a picture of Francis 'schmoozing' with influential people at sports events. Derek sees this aspect of Francis's skills as a key resource he can draw on to assist in his own personal advancement.
- *Talent spotting, selective recruitment and adopting protégés.* A key method many managers use to advance their own or their department's interests is to look out for talented people outside their own sub-unit that they can bring into their fold. This often leads to competition between unit heads, as we see when Derek 'poaches' Francis from the sports department. Francis may be too established a figure to be a protégé of Derek, but we can expect Derek to be as

adept at adopting able junior people as protégés as he was earlier in his career when he sought to become the protégé of more established people himself. The patron–protégé relationship is a form of strategic exchange in which the more junior person gains a 'push up the ladder' in return for loyalty given and favours done for the patron.

- *Gathering information that may actually or potentially be used against a rival or otherwise to advance one's interests.* At some stage Derek has clearly researched the sports editor's background and found potentially damaging information that, as it happens on this occasion, he does not use. He also seems keen to let us know that he has 'dirt' on the features editor in the form of knowledge of her affair with Francis Khyber. To what extent he used this to advance his interests when negotiating with Francis we do not know. What we can infer, however, is that he regarded this piece of knowledge as politically advantageous. We also see Derek gathering information that he can trade with others to gain advantage in other ways. This happened early on at school with the information about where other boys smoked on the school premises being traded for help in 'promotion' to a prefect's position. The information he supplies to the editor and the management of the newspaper in the period prior to his inheriting the editor's throne is clearly an important key that helped him unlock the throne room.

Throughout his career, Derek Duffus strategically exchanges in a variety of ways with people around him. He gives something here, he takes something there – all to help with the shaping of his life and his work career. But he most significantly advances his interests (increasing his relative organisational 'power') when he links his *personal strategic exchanges* directly to issues of the newspaper's *organisational strategic exchanges*. This is where the strategic contingency insight is helpful to our understanding of what is happening on the newspaper. We hear of the newspaper facing perceived strategic uncertainty on two occasions. The first is when the in-fighting between news reporters is beginning to threaten the quality of the paper and, hence, its circulation figures and long-term survival. And what does Derek do? He is already regarded as central to the workflow of the paper when he puts himself forward to the editor as the person who can reduce this uncertainty. Given the shrewd political operator that he is, we can assume that he will have put himself forward as the only person who can do this. He will have ensured that he is perceived as unsubstitutable.

The second time Derek reveals his understanding of the strategic contingency principle is over the uncertainty created for the paper's future by the possible loss of Francis Khyber. It would appear that Francis himself has some grasp of this principle. He has made himself central to the paper's journalistic work. He has made himself a unique and therefore unsubstitutable 'star' reporter. He has control over the strategic uncertainty he himself creates: he can choose to go or stay. Derek sees in Francis's position an opportunity to increase his own power and influence and to make the news department a more powerful subunit than the sports section. By taking Francis into his own department and making it more likely that Francis will stay with the paper, he – and his sub-unit – is handling a strategic uncertainty for the paper. Both he and his department thus move up the micropolitical pecking order. The paper is better placed to exchange strategically with its readers, advertisers and all the other constituencies with which it deals if Francis stays on board. Francis, Derek and the news department are thus rewarded for their contribution towards this strengthened strategic position of the paper.

Activity 6.3

Look back over all your own organisational experiences, whether in school or college or arising from managerial activities (or possibly in books, films or TV programmes with an organisational setting that you have seen), and:

- note down examples of some of the micropolitical tactics reported by Derek Duffus that you have personally observed;
- if possible, note down any further types of politicking activity that you might have come across;
- consider whether you are able to point to any examples of the 'perceived strategic contingency' factor playing a part in the organisational politicking you have observed.

Organised anarchy and decision making in the garbage can

Within the micropolitics that occurs in all organisations we see numerous goals and purposes being pursued by individuals, organisational sub-units and the coalitions or alliances that are always forming and re-forming. There are inevitably winners and losers in every political engagement and, sometimes, the outcomes of these engagements will strengthen the strategic position of the organisation and sometimes they will compromise the organisation's long-term survival. The resulting *negotiated order* (Chapter 2, pp. 66–72) that, in effect, constitutes 'the organisation' at any point in time is not just an outcome of random human efforts to advance or defend their sectional interests, however. The official structure and culture of the organisation – the formal blueprint or 'organisational design' – contributes to the negotiated order of the organisation as much as do the calculations and actions of organisational actors.

The way the hierarchical structure of organisations functions as both a control system and a narrowing career ladder is an important illustration of this. The outcome is that whenever we look at an organisation we see, at one moment, a pattern of order in which things seem 'very organised' and, at another moment, something that is much more 'disorganised' – anarchic even. The term *organised anarchy* was used in a study of several universities to capture this quality of organisational life (Cohen, March and Olsen, 1972). The term usefully brings out the rather paradoxical quality of all organisational processes:

their tendency, at the same time, to be both very organised and very disorganised. Similarly, the *garbage can model of organisational choice* developed by these same researchers can usefully help us see how this 'disorganised-organisation' quality of organised life manifests itself in decision-making situations in organisations generally. (See Further Reading on decision processes for the wider background of this style of thinking, p. 249.)

Garbage can model of organisational choice *Concept*

Organisational decisions are influenced by the various problems that exist at the time of the decision; the various available solutions which might be attached to these problems; the people who are around at the time; the amount of time these people have available.

The 'garbage can' concept can help us understand further the way that the general *negotiated order* of an organisation comes about by focusing on the specific processes that occur in particular decision-making or organisational choice events. The model is invaluable in sensitising us to the complexity of 'what is going on' in the typical decision-making meeting that occurs daily in work organisations.

Our consideration of micropolitical processes has already made us aware of the variety of different goals and interests that are brought into play when managers make organisational choices. But the garbage can model makes us aware that there are plenty of other factors 'at play' when managers meet to make decisions. It is the idea that a complex mixture of items is thrown together in the big vessel of the decision-making event that leads to the use of the metaphor of the garbage can. The model could just as easily be called the 'big suitcase' or 'loaded shopping trolley' model. Figure 6.2 represents the garbage can of the decision-making event.

We can immediately see in Figure 6.2 a departure from conventional conceptions of decision-making situations and processes. We normally assume that a decision-making process is a linear one (pp. 87–90). It starts off with the identification of a problem that requires solving. People with relevant interests and knowledge are then brought together to discuss all the relevant information they can gather. Out of this emerges the solution to the problem – one that is best for the organisation. Such an approach is eminently sensible, and most of us who work in organisations regularly try to follow such a sequence to help us make 'good decisions'. However, if we are shrewd, we will be aware that there is a great deal more going on in the typical decision-making event. The garbage can model points out how complex the mix of factors is.

- There is typically more than one problem 'floating around' at the time. A meeting may have been called to tackle a specific problem, but people will tend to bring along further problems that might be dealt with at the same

FIGURE 6.2 The variety of factors at play in the decision-making garbage can

time. A meeting is called, for example, to tackle the problem of the ineffective heating system in a building, but the problem of the shortage of car parking spaces is 'brought along' by several of the meeting's members.

- Solutions are rarely 'created' in the decision-making process. People will bring along various already existing solutions to a problem-solving event. Sometimes these are solutions to problems that are quite different from the focal one on the official agenda. There is nevertheless the possibility that pre-existing solutions might be attached to the problem the meeting is tackling. A decision-making event might be organised to decide where to place a contract for the replacement of a heating system, for instance. Several participants come along to the meeting, however, with the 'solution' that the building itself should be demolished and replaced (perhaps by a building with a large underground car park!).
- The people who turn up to contribute to the decision-making process, and those who fail to turn up, will affect outcomes. The outcome of a decision-making event about the heating of a building might be very different if the individuals with some knowledge of heating engineering fail to turn up.

- The amount of time the people who are involved have available – or, indeed, the extent to which they are willing to concentrate on what is going on – will make a difference to the decision that is reached. If the heating engineer present at a meeting has just arrived back from holiday, is sick and jet-lagged and has to leave early for a doctor's appointment, a different decision might be made about how to improve the heating system from the one that might have emerged if this individual had been fully alert and present to the end.

Our awareness of the importance of micropolitical processes encourages us to pay close attention to the 'variables' of who is present and what amount of time or concentration each of them is going to devote to the event. But it is not just the personal or sub-unit interests that each person brings with them that are important. People will certainly act to defend or further their personal or departmental interests. They may also act to support a 'friend' (or someone to whom they owe a favour), or they might act to undermine somebody they dislike. Alternatively, they might support someone to whom they are physically or emotionally attracted. Sometimes people will speak up simply in order to impress others or make a lot of interventions because they enjoy taking centre stage wherever they go. We should not underestimate the 'play' element that comes into organisational decision-making events. It is far from unknown for people to pursue a certain line in a meeting to amuse themselves, to reduce boredom or simply to create a 'good story' to take home to tell their husband or wife over supper. This might merely waste a certain amount of time without affecting the decision that is eventually made. On the other hand, such activity might make a material difference to the organisational choices that are made. All these matters are ones that any individual who tries to lead a decision-making process or manage a choice-making meeting has seriously to take into account. Godfrey Nairn is well aware of this.

Activity 6.4

Read Godfrey Nairn's account in Case 6.2 of the meeting that he called to make organisational choices about surveillance systems for the Links Leisure Centre, of which he is the General Manager. Then identify:

- what problems are floating about in the garbage can, in addition to the one that the meeting was intended to focus upon;
- what solutions are available in the bin to be attached to any of these problems;
- how the meeting is affected by the particular mix of who is there (and who is absent) and by the variable levels of time and attention that people are willing to pay to the main issues;
- what conflicts and key alliances come into play;
- how anyone's interest in 'play' influences events.

Managing in the garbage can

Case 6.2

I think that chairing meetings is one of the most difficult aspects of a manager's job. This is especially the case if you're trying to get to a decision that is important for the business. It should be straightforward. But it isn't. Everybody always seems to have their own idea of what is best. You have to cope with all the different characters who each want to have their say. And you have to work out where every one of them is coming from. That's not easy. Everyone has their own agenda, whatever the topic is meant to be. I've never yet run a management meeting where everybody was willing to follow my agenda – let alone sing from the same company song sheet.

Yes, I can give you an example of what I am talking about here. I organised a meeting last week that went on from lunchtime into the middle of the evening. And it got me nowhere. The basic problem that I had in mind, as the General Manager of the Links Leisure Centre, was that of how we are going to cope with security problems in next year's busy season. I am conscious that the new motorway into the town and the improved rail service are going to bring us a lot more customers. And I think that the customers will be much more socially and generationally mixed. We are going to be catering for older people, for families with children and for youths who tend to come along in gangs, all at the same time. We have got to think hard about how we are going to maintain order so that one type of customer doesn't spoil things for another. Des Cromarty, the Chief Executive of the company that owns the Links Leisure Centre is keen on our security measures being 'tight but low profile'. That's company policy he says, and he suggested that I call a management meeting to consider introducing an electronic surveillance system – visible and hidden cameras, secret microphones and all that. So that's what I did. I got together Todd, our Head of Marketing and Publicity; Potter, the Security Manager; Wadley, our Accountant; Dixon, the Human Resources Manager and Cooper, the Technical Services Manager. I also invited a police crime prevention officer along and arranged for a security consultant to join us.

The first thing that went wrong for me was that neither the police officer nor the security consultant actually turned up on the day. The absence of people like these, with specialist knowledge and with some independence from all the political crap that goes on within our management team, was a blow. I also thought that my colleagues might be more polite to each other than usual if we had guests at the meeting. But there was no sign of either of these. And, on top of this, Todd was late. We really needed his marketing and publicity input and I wanted his personal support, as the most senior person in my management team.

The second disaster was an extremely rude intervention from Desmond Cromarty, the Chief Executive. I knew he was calling into the Centre that day to show around an important investment analyst. But just as I was halfway through outlining the key issues to the meeting, in pops Des. He walks over to the plate of Danish pastries I had sent out for in case people got hungry later in the afternoon. He picks up two of these, says 'Good afternoon ladies and gentlemen' and walks out again. My colleagues laughed half-heartedly about this and someone said, 'Oh we all know about Desmond and his ability to sniff out food wherever he goes.' Nice as my colleagues were trying to be, I felt humiliated. I am sure Desmond did it to show off to his guest, at my expense.

I was just getting back into my stride and was ready to open up the debate when in marches Todd, munching a Danish pastry. 'I just bumped into Des and look what he gave me,' he announced, grinning broadly. I was furious. In retrospect I am sure he deliberately came into the meeting late. I also wondered, in retrospect, whether one of this group was responsible for deterring the police officer and the security consultant from joining us. Todd had turned up late like this several times before. It was a ploy, I think, to show that he was too important to turn up on time like the others. He just has to show that he is 'different'. I wonder too if he hadn't been deliberately hanging around in the hope of 'bumping into' Des Cromarty.

I think my one-time close friend, Todd, is getting rather jealous of my success in this job. We go back a long way. We worked together at the same level in another company – 'God and Todd' they called us. He increasingly seems to like the sound of his own voice at meetings and at this one he seemed quite indifferent to the issues being discussed. I think he was intent on spending the afternoon getting in as many of his little jokes as he could and taking pleasure in needling Cooper, whom I think he hates. Without Todd, we would have got on much better, I regret to say. And he left, too, well before the end of the meeting, claiming that he had to make an important phone call. I had been hoping that, at the end of the meeting, he might make up for all his nonsense and use his considerable skills to help me push people toward some kind of clear conclusion. He has done that before and showed that he and I can still be a good team. But he didn't this time.

Potter, I think would have been willing to stay all night. His priority was clear. He didn't want the surveillance system at all. He wanted the money to be spent on increasing the number of his security staff. He also wanted their rate of pay to go up so that he could 'recruit a better quality of person' which, in turn, would enable him to put a proportion of his security people on plain-clothes patrol. Nothing could more perfectly fit company policy than to have 'tight but discreet security', he argued. This sounded reasonable and was discussed at length. Dixon, our HR manager, was utterly opposed to this however. She argued that her 'labour market research' showed that such a policy was doomed to failure. Potter got very angry with Dixon and very nastily accused her of taking the line she was simply because she had been instructed by the company Human Resources Director to get the 'indirect headcount' down 'at all costs'. Surprisingly Dixon didn't argue with this. She just coldly suggested that she knew that Potter had boasted to his staff that he could get them all a wage increase and that he would 'do anything to bring this about'. She also said he had problems about his status, believing that he could 'only feel important if he had a large workforce'. 'But size is not what counts,' she said with a sly grin on her face.

Wadley then came in and tried to calm things down a little by saying that he was 'neither for nor against the proposal'. If a system could be bought which would be covered by the budget that he was putting forward, he was happy. But if the price were anything more than a 'gnat's whisker above my figures', it was 'not on'. Dixon said that she fully supported everything that Wadley was saying. This led Todd to make some unpleasant insinuations about accountants and HR people always wanting to 'get into bed together'. He saw me glare at him when he'd said this and he explained that he had noticed a general tendency for these 'so-called expert types of manager in HR and accounting always to stick together'. I had, in fact, noticed something like this myself. But I had put it down to the fact that both Dixon and Wadley were university graduates and knew that this made the other managers, none of whom had degrees, rather wary of them.

At this point, Cooper spoke for the first time. I was surprised that he had stayed quiet for so long. We all knew that he loved anything 'high tech'. It was central to his personal image in the leisure centre world that he be associated with a 'state of the art' centre. Sophisticated surveillance systems were nowadays 'state of the art' he said. Although he 'respected the need to be cost conscious' he felt that a 'top notch' system would be an excellent investment that would release us from the pressures of having to 'recruit clapped out retired police officers and train them as security officers'. In response to this, Potter went into a long and boring account of the virtues of every security officer he had ever recruited or trained. I should have stopped him but I knew I had to keep him on board. Passions were running much higher than I had ever imagined they would and I had to keep things going if I was ever to reach a conclusion.

In fact I never reached a conclusion that night. Well, there was some conclusion to the meeting. But it was what I have always felt is a coward's conclusion to such an event: I set up a working party to look into the advantages and disadvantages (with special reference to costs) of all the surveillance systems on the market. This, I knew, was just buying me time. But before calling any other meetings of this group, I was going to spend time with each of these individuals and try to get a fuller understanding of exactly what agenda each of them was working towards. If I could reach a decision on the security and surveillance issues without having to get all the protagonists into the gladiatorial arena at the same time I might end up deserving the title of General Manager. In the meantime, I had better drop my little joke of introducing myself to people as 'Godfrey Nairn – just call me God'.

Godfrey Nairn's story is an excellent illustration of how 'messy' managerial relations and decision-making processes can get. Perhaps it justifies the 'garbage' element in the title of the garbage can model, though no model is going to resolve the messiness of this situation and it is not a simple matter to apply the categories of the model to these events. We can attempt to do this, however, by first looking at what *problems* are floating about in the bin. There is the initiating problem, of course, of how order is going to be maintained in the leisure centre when both the number and the variety of customers increases in the new season. The slightly more specific problem identified by Des Cromarty is one of developing security measures that are 'tight but low profile'. However, contributors to the problem-solving process inevitably bring along their own problems to the party. Not surprisingly the person from the accounting function, Wadley, brings along the ever-present organisational problem of keeping costs under control. Dixon, from HR, keeps on the table the related problem of keeping the organisational 'headcount' under control. Problems with a more departmental (as opposed to functional) focus are brought into play by Potter, who has a problem of his staff's pay, as he sees it, being too low. It also seems possible that he has a personal problem, one involving the relationship he is alleged to see between his status in the organisation and the number of people he employs. Cooper's interventions also seem to be influenced by a personal problem of self-identity, the problem of maintaining his image and reputation as someone involved with 'state of the art' initiatives.

When we turn to the *solutions* that are floating about in the bin, a corresponding variety of positions is visible. It was Des Cromarty, from outside the meeting, who first threw in the solution of buying an electronic surveillance system. Cooper's version of this solution is to buy the most sophisticated one of these available, but Potter's solution, of course, is completely contrary to this. He argues that a bigger and better paid security force would perfectly fit the bill of 'tight but discreet' security. Dixon presumably favours the technological solution and, given the tendency of Dixon and Wadley to support each other, we can assume that they would both support the purchase of an electronic surveillance system that did not exceed Wadley's budget limit.

When we come to consider who was present at the meeting, we inevitably recognise that the particular mixture of Nairn, Todd, Potter, Wadley, Dixon and Cooper – without the calming influence of any external or more neutral characters – was a volatile one. It seems reasonable to assume that things might have gone differently if the police and the consultant experts had been present (and note how Godfrey speculates that one of his managers might have discouraged them from attending). It is also possible that Des Cromarty, who initiated the whole process, might have been present. His seniority would possibly have led to a more positive debate. But perhaps not. His very brief presence on the occasion undermined Godfrey Nairn and his rudeness left its mark on the proceedings, as Todd's late arrival and early departure may have done too. Nairn is clearly of the view that Todd could have helped him significantly if he had been willing to devote more time and attention to the business in hand. There is clearly a degree of conflict between Nairn and Todd, in spite of their long friendship, and we are told that Todd 'hates' Cooper for some reason. The tensions between Cooper and Potter are clearly based on certain diametrically opposed interests (the former seeming to prefer 'high tech' solutions and the latter labour intensive ones) and the reference by Cooper to 'clapped out' retired police officers suggests that a degree of passion to the conflict exists here. Something similar is suggested by Dixon's barbed reference to Potter's interest in 'size'. In fact, given all these cross-cutting conflicts, it is almost warming to see one case of people supporting each other, but the others do not necessarily see the alliance between Dixon from HR and Wadley the accountant as benign.

Todd's suggestive remark about Dixon and Wadley 'getting into bed together' certainly implies that their alliance is not generally approved of. It is hard to say, however, just when a remark like Todd's is a straightforward piece of work-related or political behaviour and when it is just a matter of someone having fun – making a joke to pass the time or to impress other people. The serious and the playful frequently overlap in organisational behaviour and it is often difficult to judge precisely what is 'meant to' happen in certain circumstances and what is 'not meant to happen', as we saw in our analysis of organisational mischief in Chapter 4.

Managing and not managing

What has been identified in earlier chapters as a systems-control frame of reference manifests itself among many managerial practitioners in a form that can be characterised as *managism* (Watson, 2001b). The new word 'managism' has been devised to characterise this everyday discourse of the managerial world from 'managerialism', a term that is most often used these days to refer to a belief that most social and political problems can be solved through managerial interventions, as opposed to social or political action.

Managism *Concept*

An everyday discourse at the heart of which is the belief that there is a distinctive managerial expertise based on a body of objective management knowledge which managers should apply to enable them rationally to design, maintain and drive organisational systems in the same way that expert engineers design, maintain and drive machines

Managism is, in effect, an 'operating faith' because, like religious faiths, it takes a set of beliefs about how the world is and, on the basis of this, advocates what people should do. But faiths also have a psychological role in the lives of those who adopt them. They give comfort to people and reassure them in the face of the doubts, confusions, ambiguities and threats that they meet in their daily lives. And ambiguities, threats and confusions, we might say, are an everyday feature of the work organisations in which managers 'have to manage'. Their authority is regularly open to challenge, they are frequently faced with getting people to do things they do not wish to do and they frequently have to act on the basis of partial knowledge or inadequate understanding. It is therefore comforting to adopt a faith that teaches that managers actually can 'engineer' work organisations. Commitment to that faith is demonstrated every day in the mechanistic language so popular with many managers. This is the managist talk of 'putting in place' new structures or systems, 'delivering' strategies and 'driving through' changes. Such language is increasingly heard in the world of the modern corporate manager, as we shall see later in the present chapter.

Managism, then, has a possible psychological function for people in managerial jobs. It can function as a comfort in the face of the doubts, ambiguities and threats that managers face in their work. It can give some security in the face of finding that one's authority is regularly challenged, that one has to get people to do things they do not wish to do and that one frequently has to act on the basis of partial knowledge or inadequate understanding. In many ways, one might say, such pressures exist in a range of occupations other than that of management. This is undoubtedly the case, but the dominance of the systems-control view of work organisations and the foundations of this in the modernist faith that human beings can rationally control their world and their destiny has created expectations of what managers should be able to do which are wholly unrealistic. Much of the management literature, in book and magazine form, on offer to the aspiring manager is based on tales of management heroes – of supermen and superwomen who make and break the big corporations that make the world go round. The rising manager is encouraged to aspire to *mastery* of their domains, whether or not they choose to certify this with that badge of advanced competence, the *master* of business administration (MBA) degree.

There is no reason to see anything *inherently* stressful in managerial work. But it is possible to argue that there is a particular danger of managers becoming stressed if they find that they are not in a position to behave or 'perform' in the ways expected of them as *managers*. This is especially likely to become a problem if they are influenced by a dominant discourse that portrays managers as strong, cool, reflective planners who see further ahead than everyone else and are able to exert control over all those around them to ensure that their visionary strategies and plans are implemented. This is where the 'managism', which we have recognised as being a potential *comfort* to managers faced with all the ambiguities, anxieties and unpredictabilities of their work, can also become a *threat* to them. It can create unrealisable expectations of managers as supermen and superwomen. It demands that they should constantly be demonstrating their high-level technical (engineering-like) skills. It demands that they regularly demonstrate their possession of near-mystical personal virtues like 'vision' and 'leadership qualities'. And, of course, it demands that they prove themselves all the time by achieving the ever more demanding 'results' that the increasingly pressured and competitive political–economic context encourages their employers to require of them.

Much of the discursive material that is available to managers to enable them to frame their work and the occupational pressures they face incorporates elements of 'managist' thinking. And it incorporates the 'double-edged blade' of that discourse. It can help managers cut through the vines and creepers that impede them as they make their way through the jungle of corporate life. But it can come back on the wielder of the blade and do them an injury. In stress terms, it can help in handling the sources of managerial stress but it can also make this more difficult. It is worthwhile looking at some of the material written for managers to see how this works.

Activity 6.5

'Popular', as opposed to academic, management literature can be seen as both trying to reassure or assist managers and also as something which puts heavy pressures on them by creating unrealisable expectations or ambitions. Look for evidence of each of these tendencies (*potentially reassuring* and *potentially disturbing*) in:

- books in shops, including high street bookshops and those in railway stations or airports;
- articles and advertisements in management magazines and the business pages of newspapers;
- recruitment advertisements for management jobs.

In performing this exercise, it might be noticed that much of this documentary material contains the potential to reassure and to frighten, at the same time. Process-relational thinking would encourage us to recognise that there is no unambiguous meaning or message in any piece of text, however. The reader actively makes sense of what the text was intended to imply – they 'make their own reading' in the light of their own past experiences, current concerns and future aspirations. Thus one can note the potential for the reader of the book club brochure quoted in Table 6.1 to be given confidence, or to be frightened off – or a combination of these two possibilities – by the array of books offered.

This advertising material can be understood as functioning like many stories do (pp. 99–100). It builds up anxieties in the reader and then implies that these anxieties will be overcome by the purchase of the product. The writers of the book club brochure have worked hard to remind the reader how frightening the managerial (or 'business') world is. We are told that a very uncertain future is facing us and there are many skills that we must acquire if we are to be successful. We are reminded that we have to solve problems and make decisions, deal with markets and manage our time and the stress that our work takes us into. We are not allowed to forget any anxieties we might have about how assertive we are, how capable we are at communicating generally and, especially, how confident we will be when we have to get up on a platform to give

Table 6.1 Books to help you manage: excerpts from a book club brochure

Books get you Skilled

- Financial Engineering: tools and techniques to manage financial risk
- The Handbook of Skilful Management
- The Shorter MBA: a practical approach to business skills . . .

Books get you Ahead

- Corporate Strategies of the Top 100 Companies of the Future
- Focus: the future of our company depends on it
- Profitable Purchasing Strategies: a manager's guide for improving organisational competitiveness through the skills of purchasing
- The New Dynamics of Goals Setting: flextactics for a fast-changing future
- How to be a Better Problems Solver
- How to be a Better Decision-maker . . .

Books get you Success

- Management Masterclass: a practical guide to the new realities of business
- Re-inventing Leadership: strategies to achieve a new style of leadership . . .
- The Master Marketeer . . .
- Imagination Engineering: the toolkit for business creativity . . .

Books get you Noticed

- Emotional Intelligence: why it can matter more than IQ
- 10-Minute Time and Stress Management . . .
- Super-learning 2000: new, triple-fast ways you can learn, earn and succeed in the twenty-first century
- Great Answers to tough Interview Questions
- The Perfect CV . . .

Books get you Heard

- Assertiveness at Work: what to say when you are dying on the platform
- Dealing with Difficult People: proven strategies for handling stressful situations . . .
- How to Write Proposals and Reports that get Results
- The Handbook of Communication Skills . . .

Books get you Results

- NLP for Trainers: communicating for excellence
- Managing Change Through Training and Development
- The Success Culture: how to build an organisation with vision and purpose . . .

a speech. We are presented with the horrific prospect of 'dying' in front of an audience. And we are confronted with the spectre of the 'difficult people' we have to handle and nudged to remember that we are likely to face tough questions in the interviews we will be put through. Not only that, but we are also prompted to believe that these interviewers will expect a 'perfect' curriculum vitae to accompany any application we make for the jobs we want to get. We have a lot to cope with if we are going to travel upwards and onwards into the sunny uplands of the 'success culture'.

To reassure us that all of this can be handled, the copywriters make use of a whole range of 'managist' discursive resources in presenting their wares. Work organisations can be *engineered*, if we acquire the right *skills*. Not that we should worry too much about acquiring these skills: they are available in a 'handbook' or a single-volume MBA. Not only can the potentially terrifying world of finance be 'engineered', so can our very imaginations. We need not worry therefore about whether we are creative or not – we simply have to buy the 'tool kit'. What we can achieve is *mastery* (available in the 'Masterclass' if not in the shorter MBA). That means that we will not be ordinary marketing managers. We will become master marketers. And, we will not just be ordinary management learners. We will become 'superlearners'. But if we do not want to be 'masters', then we can become generals or field marshals, devising strategies left, right and centre: corporate strategies, purchasing strategies, strategies for becoming leaders and strategies for handling stressful situations. And, if the role of strategist does not appeal, then we might resort to what the author of one of these books calls, 'flextactics'. For some, this might be a 'neologism too far' (to borrow a phrase applied by a friendly critic to the present author's invention of the word 'managism', Watson, 2001b). But maybe the term has something to offer as a new discursive resource for managers who want to be highly adaptable, dynamic and fast on their feet – managers who are more excited by the prospect of being the guerrilla fighters of the fast-moving twenty-first century rather than the crusty old generals of the slow-moving past.

Kurt Delnies, whom we shall meet shortly in Case 6.3, tries to summarise the problems that these materials are attempting to address when he observes that 'managers are expected, in principle, to control that which, in practice, cannot be controlled'. The search for control, whether explicitly spoken of or not, is the *leitmotif*, the slogan, the war cry of all these management books – and of many more, academic ones included. Control was something Ken Steary spoke of directly when he was referring to his difficulties in the hotel company (Case 4.3, pp. 127–9). He was 'meant to be in control' he said, and he felt that he could not afford to be seen to drop what he referred to as the 'façade of control'. Even when he felt out of control of the situation (and, hence, laughed and cried at the same time), he kept the manifestations of this collapse private. The hotel manager was not in a position to reveal too much of his humanity. On top of that, he had no one to turn to for help, he said. This, of course, is not to say that he might not have friends, advisers or family to help him in this respect, as Tim Dyke did in Case 4.5. But Ken was suggesting something particularly 'lonely' about the position of the manager, someone who has to be an exemplar to the rest of the staff in many ways. Again, it is something of a pressure to be more than human – taking on the role of the manager as the hero, superman or superwoman of the popular management literature. And these pressures are added to, not just by the monitoring of the managers by more senior managers, but by the career-competitive environment that many managers work in.

Jackall (1988) provides an especially disturbing research account of the pressures faced by managers in certain American corporations. He observes managers continually expressing excitement and enthusiasm for what they are doing while covering up the profound anxieties they are experiencing. They display cheerfulness and 'iron self control' in the face of recurring fears of losing their jobs or losing the chance of career advancement. They see constant threats from the capriciousness of the corporation and from the contingencies of the corporation's circumstances. This means they must constantly be on the watch for reorganisation or recession. They feel as if they are all the time 'on probation' and are in constant danger of being caught out making mistakes or of being blamed for the mistakes of others. They worry about being evaluated against performance criteria to which they cannot make a difference and they get anxious about simply finding themselves in the wrong place at the wrong time.

How generalisable Jackall's rather extreme account is to other corporations or to organisations in other societies might be debated. There has certainly been evidence to suggest that many people in 'middle management' have been made increasingly insecure and pressured by trends to remove layers of management from organisations and from general pressures for increased performance. One study suggested that a high proportion of British managers could be characterised as 'reluctant managers' (Scase and Goffee, 1989). Other studies, however, have suggested that the same restructuring of organisations can lead to an increase in the sense of autonomy and job satisfaction for *some* managers in such organisations (Dopson and Stewart, 1990, Thomas and Dunkerley, 1999; see also Further Reading on managerial insecurities and the pressures on middle managers, pp. 250–1). The *extent* of the pressures to show control in the face of the uncontrollable which were put upon the managers studied by Jackall may be especially high and may be particular to the corporate settings concerned. But the general nature of those pressures and anxieties is something that we can expect to see, to a greater or lesser extent, in many other organisational and managerial situations. The closer the researcher gets to managerial activity, by adopting an ethnographic or participant observation style of investigation, the more apparent this kind of thing becomes. What also becomes apparent are the various ways in which these underlying worries manifest themselves in managers' behaviour, as the following observations made in a British research situation suggest:

> The more I saw of the managers at Ryland, the more I became aware of the extent of human angst, insecurity, doubt and frailty among them. I observed managers being rude to their staff, refusing to listen to advice given to them within their departments, curtly announcing unexplained decisions, losing their tempers with people from other departments, creating rows with fellow managers. I came across numerous examples of

> managers offending others by failing to reply to telephone calls or by writing curt memoranda or electronic mail messages rather than explaining decisions face-to-face to people, of managers spreading malicious gossip about others, of managers failing to turn up to meetings where their presence was important. On a number of occasions I found myself mediating between managers who had fallen out with each other and were unwilling to meet to sort out difficulties. And on three occasions, I actually found myself having to persuade a manager that it would not be advisable to go and exert physical violence against another.
>
> (Watson, 2001a, p. 178)

It was suggested in the study at the Ryland plant that a number of the managers were tending to fall in with the assumptions of classical management thinking which required managers to be the rational planners and the analytical designers of corporate systems. They were thus setting themselves above and apart from many of the daily organisational actions and 'shopfloor problems' in which more junior people in the company felt these managers should have involved themselves. Managers were tending to spend more and more hours in management meetings, as business difficulties became increasingly apparent. They were risking knowing less and less about what was going on in the factory and amongst the sales force – at the same time as they had to continue to give an impression of knowing everything. Not only did the anxieties that this created lead to various emotional outbursts and illogical and over-personalised clashes between managers, it seemed to encourage them to work even harder at devising new 'systems', new organisational structures and an endless stream of fashionable 'new initiatives'.

Managers' attitudes to new management fashions, fads and consultant-led initiatives were not straightforward, this research suggested (see also Chapter 5, pp. 186–7 and Further Reading on management thinking: fashions, fads and trends, p. 251). The managers tended to be ambivalent about them – loving and hating them at the same time (Watson, 1994b). The same managers who would complain one day about 'the launch of yet another new management idea' (usually something given an acronym or abbreviation like PDP, TQM or BPR) would, another day, be heard talking enthusiastically about some equivalent manifestation of 'new management thinking' which they felt was relevant to the problems faced in their own area of management. The initiatives undertaken and the consultants' reports commissioned were sometimes recognised as managerially effective, but often they were not. They all, however, functioned in part as a means of managers handling the pressures and anxieties of the type of work they were in. They gave some kind of emotional reassurance. They were all ways of helping with the *double control problem* that all managers have to handle. This is the challenge that every manager faces of having to handle the requirement to control the activities of others (and increasingly the sentiments and values of others) at the same time as they have to control their personal identities and manage their own lives.

Double control problem

Concept

That pressure that is put on managers to manage the activities and thinking of others at the same time as they have to manage and shape their own identities, lives and personal projects.

A further manifestation of the behaviours that arise when all of this becomes difficult is resorting to tortuous language.

Manager pseudo-jargon and controlling the uncontrollable

It is often observed how the management world increasingly requires its inhabitants to talk in an unnecessarily jargon-ridden way. There is nothing wrong with jargon in itself, of course. Every specialist activity, from engineering to psychology and cattle breeding has its own technical language. However, the question arises as to why people in managerial work often speak in ways that depart from normal language when, in practice, they are talking about matters where normal language would be more than adequate.

Managerial pseudo-jargon

Concept

A form of language widely used in corporate settings which is neither a jargon in the sense of the specialised language of a group of experts nor a jargon in the sense of meaningless verbal noise making but which uses metaphors and expressions which tend to make organisational abstractions sound more solid than they really are and make managerial work sound like a more 'special' activity than it actually is.

This 'corporate gobbledegook', 'management babble' or 'business bollock-speak' is used in part to impress people, inside and outside of management, but a more likely explanation of the phenomenon is that it can give emotional reassurance to managers in the light of the anxieties and pressures that they are having to handle. The manager feels that little bit better revealing a worry about coping with a new job by telling an interview panel, 'I am cognisant of the steep learning curve I shall confront' instead of perhaps saying, 'I know I am going to have to learn a lot rather quickly'. This kind of talk might be dismissed by a cruel commentator as a matter of 'whistling in the dark'. But we should remember that when we are out on a very dark night and feeling unsure, whistling a bold melody can make us feel a lot better and a lot more confident about the possibility of reaching our destination. The sound produced might not mean much to anyone who hears it but the whistler copes better with the darkness and feels less afraid of the unknown world through which they are travelling. But, should they be fooling themselves in this way? Kurt Delnies thinks not.

Activity 6.6

Read Kurt Delnies' story in Case 6.3 of how he changed his approach to his job and avoided 'falling over the edge of the cliff', paying particular attention to the role that 'managerial language' played in this. If you are in a position to listen to, or read, some of the 'pseudo-jargon' (or 'bollock-speak', as Delnies calls it) that is used in work organisations:

- note down as many words or phrases as possible that you only hear in a managerial or organisational context – ones you would not expect to hear outside the workplace;
- think about why such language is used in this context;
- consider how much validity there is in Jill Gollanfield's theory – her idea that the use of such language might be a sign that someone is 'losing it'?

Kurt crawls back from the edge

Case 6.3

How long have you been in charge of the company, Kurt?

I have been Chief Executive here for nearly a year now. It's good, yeah.

You seem very pleased with everything.

I am. The business is going great. The Chairman puts that down to me. And if you're implying that I sound pleased with myself, then I confess to that. But this is not a confession of smugness or complacency, let me reassure you.

What is it then?

I am pleased with myself precisely because I know all about becoming smug and self-satisfied. I therefore consciously avoid – avoid like the plague – getting complacent.

I notice that you say you 'consciously' avoid this. You've thought hard about these things?

If your career goes really well, like mine did in my first ten years, you get the idea that you know it all. Then you don't see the dangers creeping up on you. You become blind to the cliff edge that you are getting close to. Or perhaps it would be truer in my own case to say that I half sensed that I was getting near to the edge of a precipice. But all I did, in practice, was to run faster towards the edge. I just held my head up in the air, looked over the heads of all the people round me and, I suppose, talked over the people who might have warned me.

What was this precipice?

It was the appearance of a competitive product that could easily have smashed our market share. But let me tell you first how I got into this position. I got a first class degree in electronic engineering and joined the company's design department where they treated me as a bit of a star. They sent me to the States to get an MBA. I thought I was popular with the other design engineers but, I now recognise, this was only because they could come to me for help with difficult problems, ones that I always seemed able to solve faster than most of them. I was promoted very fast and, before I knew where I was, I was Director of Business Development. The RAE 3000 was my baby and with the sales force working their socks off and the engineers making regular upgrades on the software side, we got the bulk of the European market. My personal knowledge of Germany was a big factor in that. Anyway, I was tasked to grow the US market. So I developed a marketing plan and I invented a way we could build up the functionality of the unit in the future. Following this?

Yes, I think so.

Well, never mind the technical details. I can't be sure about all this but, looking back, I think I was half aware that the sales people were looking less confident when I addressed them at our monthly meetings. And I was sort of conscious of the engineers being edgy with me at the team briefings. They seemed to have nothing to say and I found I was more and more talking at people. But being the determined chap I was, I brushed this off. However, I am told that my 'speeches', as my talks and briefings were referred to, were becoming increasingly – what was the word? – yes, 'convoluted'. That's what I was told. What this apparently meant was that I was not just rambling but that I was using more and more pseudo-business jargon, you know, management bollock-speak. Looking back, it appears that as I got more and more anxious (inwardly or subconsciously, I suppose), the more I gabbled out this stuff. Anyway, I realised what I was doing. I stopped thinking that I could mastermind all the engineering and all the marketing and I started to listen to my colleagues. I related much better to people generally and I crept back from the edge of the cliff. After a brilliant team effort, we managed to get out an RAE 5000, and beat the competition. So now I am in the top job. That's the story. We re-engineered our best product and I re-engineered myself. That sounds good, doesn't it?

Very good. But it does sound a bit, a bit unconvincing. I don't mean the outcomes but how you came to have this epiphany. You can't tell me that you saw a blinding light on the road to Damascus sitting here in this corporate office block? How did it happen?

I'm not sure I want to talk about that. It's, er, sensitive.

It's completely in confidence. I won't write anything that anyone will pin down to you.

I am not sure. It was all to do with my having an affair with my secretary, you see. Well, you know Jill. It wasn't a sordid affair, let me tell you.

But will you tell me?

OK then. Yes, I feel I have to, having said what I have. I was happily married, and I still am. So is Jill. But I was obviously getting in something of an emotional state at work. Jill Gollanfield is a wonderful person as well as a great secretary and she understood far better than I did what was happening. Anyway, I noticed that she was increasingly altering the letters I was dictating to her. I mentioned it on one occasion. Apparently, like a lot of the other managers in the company, I kept using the world 'substantive' when I should have used 'substantial'. She thought this was pompous as well as ignorant. But she said nothing. It was only when the topic came up again at breakfast in a German hotel, after the first night we spent together would you believe, that she really put me in the picture about myself. It was amazing. You couldn't make it up.

What couldn't you make up?

She even had shorthand notes in her handbag of some of the things I had been saying at briefings. That's when she used the word 'convoluted'. And she had this idea that the more people in organisations, and in management especially, start to 'lose it', the more they descend into affected language. I call it bollock speak, but she wouldn't use such a term. Anyway she realised that I was 'losing it' and, bloody hell, she was monitoring my progress to the cliff edge by the extent to which I was burbling.

So you've reverted to plain English?

Oh yes, I call a cock up a cock up and not a 'contingent operating difficulty', if that's what you mean. But it's not getting rid of the old bad language – the pompous bollock-speak I mean, not the good old Anglo-Saxon – that is important. Jill helped me see that. For all the stuff I did in the past, and the Wharton MBA I took, Jill has been the best management teacher I have had. What I now realise is that the manager, and the more senior you are the more this is the case, is dependent on other people. Business circumstances, organisational and engineering matters as well, are too complex for any manager to control. It seems that managers are expected, in principle, to control that which, in practice, cannot be controlled. However clever you are, you've got to learn the importance of using the people around you, using their eyes and ears and using their knowledge.

And you and Jill, are you . . . ?

Er, only now and then. But Jill, I think, is cleverer than me. She has weaned me off depending on her emotionally. But she and I are a great team.

This story is relevant to many of the issues we are considering in this chapter, but let us concentrate for the moment on the issue of managerial pseudo-jargon. Kurt Delnies tells us that Jill Gollanfield has a personal theory about the connection between how managers talk and their confidence in their jobs. Indeed, the less confident Kurt became, the more he resorted to what Jill calls 'convoluted language'. There is probably a valuable insight here, something that Kurt seems to appreciate when looking back to when he was beginning to 'lose it', and was using such expressions as 'contingent operational difficulties', rather than plain English. A similar insight is offered by Hoggart, as he chronicles in his parliamentary sketches the ways in which government ministers borrow from 'modern management-speak' and 'have a special love for buzzy words such as "delivery", "best practice" and "excellence", as illustrated in a minister's statement that "we are putting in place the job search programmes which have already had considerable success at the pilot stage, offering practical help, and are delivering people into the jobs which are there"' (Hoggart, 2000a). Hoggart suggests that no minister could bear to say 'we're doing three things to tackle this'. Instead they announce a 'three-pronged integrated strategy'. He calls this 'Lego language' because it works like the children's building blocks: 'start fixing it together and you soon have something sturdily built but quite impossible to recognise'. In a sense, government ministers are facing some of the biggest managerial challenges of modern societies and Hoggart gets close to the Gollanfield theory that people involved in managerial work are showing signs of panic (or 'losing it') when they resort to convoluted pseudo-jargon. 'You know when things are bad', he says, 'when ministers start to hammer on about "rolling out new cross-cutting initiatives at local level"' (Hoggart, 2000b).

But how relevant is this type of explanation to the language examples that you have collected or to the expressions included in Table 6.2? There appear to be two variants of managerial pseudo-jargon, both of which one would be unlikely to hear outside the work organisation context. One of these we can categorise as weakly discursive. Here, the main function of the language is the fairly straightforward one of using metaphors to 'concretise' the relatively abstract elements of organisational life. It has a discursive dimension, however, in that it draws to some extent on the discourse of managism that we identified above. The 'making solid' of what are really rather intangible aspects of organisational life implies that these things can readily be managed by the relevant expert – by the manager as organisational engineer, cook, football player or whatever. We thus get all the talk of rubber stamps, feelers, ballparks, windows, drivers, levers, movers, cores and deliverables. The abstract is made concrete, the vague is made solid, the ungraspable is made graspable, and the uncontrollable is made controllable. Examples of such expressions are shown in the left-hand column of Table 6.2.

In the right-hand column of Table 6.2 we see language which is much more 'strongly discursive', in the sense that it is much more closely tied to the managist discourse. In addition to reassuring managers that they are dealing with something concrete and thus manageable, the language seems concerned to give a degree of legitimacy to their power as managers. By giving a jargonistic

Table 6.2 Organisational expressions heard being used by managers

Weakly discursive expressions	Strongly discursive expressions
• We'll run it up the flagpole and see how it flies • Shall we put that on the back burner? • I would appreciate more input and a lot more feedback • Run it past me again – are we really talking telephone numbers? • Would you rubber stamp that scenario? • Put some feelers out while I see if there's a window in my diary • Let's touch base • Shall we take that on board and offer them a ballpark figure? • We can suck it and see, and perhaps float the idea elsewhere if it works • If we do lunch I can share my thoughts with you • Let's see if we can get them to buy into the mission • We'll ditch the offer if we find it's dead in the water • It's a matter of deliverables and walking the talk – so get real • They tell me that the management information system will be rolled out in August – and the human resources information system will be off the ground by Christmas	• We are becoming much more client-centred and less finance driven • The executive away-day envisioned a bolder strategic emphasis for the division • Downsizing is not our preferred option, we must smartsize • We have the strategy in place to deliver our vision • Our premier market position has been achieved through the unflaggingly professional delivery of quality services • Having bottomed it out and made the appropriate and timely interventions domestically, we made several strategic withdrawals on the global side • Resource deployment will be highly leveraged in this instance • You will be the prime mover on the development of a platform of sustainable and robust strategies for the delivery of the core business activities of the portfolio • What we can offer is an integrated management development experience and the benefits of buying into the achievements of an internationally recognised centre of excellence • The business has the right architecture in place to ensure the delivery of sustainable competitive advantage

and thus technicist 'spin' to the managers' talk, it is implied that what they are trying to achieve is a matter of applying neutral technical expertise to circumstances rather than a matter of exerting power over people. They are neutral authoritative experts whose specialised knowledge and skill allows them to 'deliver visions', 'put strategies in place' and 'drive forward missions'.

A variety of factors might encourage people to speak and write in the rather artificial, unspontaneous or 'convoluted' ways we often come across in organisational contexts. For example, it is obvious that much of the language reported in Table 6.2 is the result of people simply mimicking others. The tendency of managers across Kurt's organisation to misuse the word 'substantive', for example, can be taken as a simple matter of people imitating whoever it was that first committed this error, consciously or otherwise. It might be that the first person to speak in this way was simply being pompous for the sake of being pompous, as Jill implies, as opposed to being pompous in order to handle any managerial angst. The question arises, however, of why rather unnatural language forms seem to arise in the context of the management of work in the first place. Even if much of the transmission is a matter of imitation, how did such strange language come to be there to imitate?

How effective any of this bizarre language actually is when it comes to successful communication is surely questionable. Perhaps we can see some point in Jill Gollanfield's suspicion that managers and others who resort to this kind of talk are losing touch with reality rather than grasping it. There could, however, be a rational motive behind a manager's choice to talk in this way. They might, for example, have calculated that it would help them in their work by impressing the people they are dealing with. Or the language might be part of a deliberate attempt to avoid communicating – to avoid being challenged perhaps. Hoggart suggests that such an effect comes about in parliament when, for example, government ministers refer to 'new job retention pilots', 'better regulation taskforces' and endless 'rollouts'. People, he suggests, do not challenge this kind of thing because nobody 'knows exactly what it means' (Hoggart, 2000a). One suspects, however, that there is a much greater emotional significance to the choice of such language. Again, it is to do with the emotional pressure of being in a job where one has to try to control that which is not readily amenable to control. There is a degree of 'whistling in the dark' about all this peculiar talk, but the emotional and the rational should not be separated too much. As was implied earlier, there is a degree of rationality in choosing to whistle or sing in the dark. If we know it will make us feel better and less afraid of the dark, then we might be wise to handle the emotions of fear or insecurity by holding our heads high and singing in the loudest voice we can manage about 'sustainable competitive advantage', 'robust platforms' and 'timely interventions' – or whatever other catchy numbers we hear belted out by other singers who are also making their way through the murk of the organisational, political, managerial or ethical jungle. And to talk of the ethical jungle takes us into the issue of the ethical dilemmas that the manager may face and have to come to terms with as part of their 'managing to manage'.

Managing right and wrong: ethical dilemmas in managerial work

In Chapter 3 we identified the basic logic of managerial work as one in which managers work towards securing long-term corporate survival. To look at their work in this way might appear, at first sight, to be a way of avoiding questions of the moral rightness or wrongness of managerial and corporate actions. Indeed, such a view of their role could be used by managers to argue that their work is morally neutral. They could use it to suggest that it is not part of their job to consider the ethical aspects of organisational activities. They might argue that they are employed simply to do what is best for the long-term future of the organisation that pays them. But even if we accept that managers tend not to be employed primarily to 'do good works' in the world, it is a total nonsense to suggest either that their work is morally neutral or that they can do the job without at least taking into account the ways in which their acts and decisions are likely to be judged in moral terms by others. Even if we avoid the morally dubious language of 'managing people' and are careful not to talk of *people* as 'human resources' (see Chapter 10, pp. 403–4) we have to recognise that the treatment of people as means towards ends rather than as ends in themselves is an intrinsic element of managerial work, and questions about the rights and wrongs of *using people* in different ways are at the centre of many ethical debates. Part of Kant's famous *categorical imperative*, an idea that has long been at the centre of the western tradition of philosophical debate, is the injunction to treat people as 'ends in themselves' and not primarily as the means of meeting the needs of others.

No managerial act can be morally neutral. This is because every such act occurs in the context of relationships in which there is, at the very least, a potential for exploitation. By the same token, no manager is likely to succeed in their work, at least over any significant period of time, if they fail to take into account how others might morally judge their actions. A manager who gave no attention to whether their actions or decisions were likely to be judged as fair or unfair, just or unjust, honest or dishonest by people both inside and outside their organisation would be a fool. They would be unlikely to survive in their job for long. And any manager who assumed that they had sufficient authority for no one to question and potentially challenge their actions would equally be a fool. Glenn Ferness is anything but a fool – but she still talks of the insoluble moral dilemmas that face her in her work.

Activity 6.7

Read what Glenn Ferness, the general manager of a large city branch of Logies department stores, says about the ethical dimension of her work in Case 6.4 and:

- note the ways in which moral or ethical criteria come into her managerial work and how these criteria relate to her personal concept of 'self' and her overall life career;
- consider how far you agree with her argument that the only way for a manager to change things they are morally unhappy with in an organisation is to argue 'the business case' rather than the moral case as such.

My company right or wrong? — Case 6.4

Your colleagues tell me that you are a particularly ethically aware manager.

Oh dear.

You don't take that as a compliment?

I suppose I should. But I am rather sensitive to being viewed in that way. Although it is true that I am a very ethically conscious person, I am terribly aware that it can be used by certain people, certain men in the business especially, to suggest that one is less than fully focused on the 'interests of the business'. It doesn't help your career to be seen that way – especially if it can be used by the male dinosaurs who still dominate this company to argue against putting other women into senior positions. I know there has been talk like this about me.

But I hear that you feel it is very important to increase women's opportunities in the business.

Yes, but don't say that too loudly. I am slowly increasing the proportion of women managers in my own store. But my stated justification for it is that it is 'best for the business' to use all the talents available to us. I argue the same way for the equal opportunities and diversity policies that we apply generally. I have a profound personal moral belief that we should treat everybody with equal regard and that it is desperately wrong to judge people on the basis of their sex, ethnicity, or their age for that matter. But arguing the moral case, in those terms, gets one nowhere. So I argue the case for using all the talents we have got or I argue that it would be 'bad for business' to be known as an employer who unfairly discriminated against various groups.

Bad for business?

Perhaps in terms of recruitment – all sorts of people might avoid joining a company known to be an unfair employer. But we also have to think about the public – our customers especially. We are well aware that a lot of the more 'discriminating' public (in the nicest sense of that word; you know, 'nice people') in this city use our store. A lot of them – quite rightly in my view – would stay away from a shop that did not treat its entire staff with the highest regard. Do you see what I mean?

Yes, are you saying that there are personal 'causes' and moral purposes informing your work but to fight for those causes you have to play down your role as a 'moral crusader' and argue every moral case as a business case.

That's it. I've always thought of myself as something of a crusader, as you've inferred. But I soon realised that being seen in this way would not only ruin my career. It would also make me a rather useless crusader.

But why would a 'crusader' come into retailing at all? What brought you into this business?

I sometimes wonder that myself. For years I expected to go into something like social work, hospital management or even politics. But shopkeeping is also in my blood. My parents ran a small shop for years. So, looking back, it seems as if I tried to resolve these two sides of my character by coming into this top chain store with a view to trying to 'make a difference' to what happens – 'from the inside', so to speak, rather than through going into politics. I think I am having some success with this. But I wouldn't exaggerate it.

So, do you believe that operating ethically as a business is the key to long-term business success?

I used to. But I am afraid it just isn't as simple as that. Let me give you an example. I am currently expanding the food side of our business here. Some old houses were demolished next to us. So we bought up the land and have extended our store. I know it is going to be very profitable to have more space for fresh food. It's more than just the extra sales, though. It's also because it will allow us to cover an even bigger proportion of people's shopping needs in our store. We will simply be a bigger retailing force in the city. That's an important element of our general business strategy. But one of the consequences of this is that we will put out of business several small shops that I know are already struggling in the city.

That troubles you?

With my background you can see why it might. I agonised over the development. It was a real moral dilemma for me. In fact, I talked to my parents about it and, in the end, they helped me reach a position that enabled me to go ahead and put my plan to head office. We concluded that although I had a moral duty to those small shopkeepers I also had a moral duty to my employer. I decided it would be wrong not to tell my employer that there was this opportunity to increase the long-term viability of the company. But I still feel bad about it. There's no 'my company right or wrong' for me.

But what if the company insisted on your doing something that you felt was ethically unacceptable to you personally?

I might have to leave. It might have happened last week for instance. I was taking part in an annual strategy review at head office and one of the issues discussed was our discovery, via the press, that one of the suppliers from whom we were buying a lot of health training equipment was not only using child labour abroad to produce some of their lines but was also, through a subsidiary, selling torture equipment to some very questionable foreign governments. My personal reaction to this was to get straight back to my store and remove every item of that company from our shelves. Although, at the end of the day, I would have felt it necessary to leave my job if the company had not decided to stop buying from that supplier, I was able to join what turned out to be the winning faction of senior managers who argued for ending our contract with the firm. And, guess what? We won the case on the grounds that it would be damaging to our business, in the long term, if we continued to use a supplier that was 'getting a bad press'. We needed to 'protect our reputation for fair dealing in the world' as the Chief Executive concluded at the end of the debate.

You must have been relieved at this outcome?

I was. But I didn't really expect the decision to go the other way. I actually have a lot of faith in our current Chief Executive. I know him well and he and I share a lot of personal values. We have only had one significant managerial disagreement since I have been working closely with him.

What was that about?

It was over his proposal to make a link between top managers' bonuses and the business's share price. He saw it as a virtue, as he put it, 'to align manager and shareholder interests'. I saw this as quite wrong. Firstly, it does not feel right to me to align managers' interests with any one stakeholder in the business rather than another. At least with a link between managers' pay and business performance you are rewarding them for contributing to something that might benefit employees and customers as much as shareholders. And, secondly, I pointed out the dangers of pandering to the short-termism of the financial markets. You can imagine managers doing all sorts of things to bump up the share price in the short term.

Such as?

Such as downsizing the workforce in the stores for example. That sort of thing is always popular with certain investment interests.

Go on.

That sort of thing would harm the business in the longer run – long-term share price included, of course. I managed to persuade Chris not to go ahead on that one, I am delighted to say. What pleases me is that, like me, he is acutely aware of the moral dilemmas that we face in management.

Can you give me other examples of managerial moral dilemmas?

One we have talked about several times, very much in private I must stress, is our shared disgust about trends in farming: the way all sorts of risks are taken with the public's health (in the case of the BSE crisis with beef, for example) and even with the very long-term viability of the countryside itself (seen with the effects of the dreadful foot and mouth disease outbreak, for example). As a retailer, Chris and I have reflected on whether Logies should go along with this constant pushing down of food prices with all the evils of industrial farming that follow from it. He experimented with getting a couple of stores just selling organic foods for a period. But our sales went down badly. Both Chris and I would like to see our stores selling mainly locally grown organic fresh foods in the long term. In that we are following our moral impulses. But we will only be able to move in that direction if and when a larger proportion of our customer base comes to share the same values.

You mean being willing to pay more for a more 'ethical' product.

Yes, but it is only 'ethical' at present in the eyes of some of us. For others there's no ethical issue. Life would be so much easier if there was a shared set of values in society, easier for everyone. But, even then, I am not sure how easy being a retailer or manager would be. Say, for instance, we put up the price of food in the interests of a more ethical approach to farming. What would happen to all those poor families that would not be able to afford those prices? How do you solve that one? And, managerially, what do I do about this dilemma: I am generally increasing the discretion that our ordinary shop workers have, you know 'empowering them'. This is to me an obviously morally right thing to do. It gives people a more fulfilling working day – and it seems to be working by making people both happier and more effective as sale persons. Yet it is causing distress to a number of our older supervisors and section managers. They tell me I am letting them down by reducing their authority and their status in the shop – something they earned by years of dedication to Logies. This is, they say, quite simply 'wrong'. And I can see their point of view.

So what you are doing is both morally right and morally wrong – in your own terms?

That's just how messy and ambiguous managing is. There's no way one can be ethically pure in managerial work – any more than I suppose you can in life generally. You have to come to terms with the fact you are going to face a lot of insoluble moral dilemmas. You just have to make the best of things – given the circumstances and given your own moral values.

So what are you doing about the empowerment issue?

What I have had to do is to balance things out in the way I just mentioned – making the best of things without either compromising my own values or my responsibilities to the company that pays me. In this case, like with so many managerial initiatives, there are going to be winners and losers. On this matter I have decided to accept that I have to hurt a section of our workforce (although I will do my best to minimise that hurt) on the grounds that my changes will help the long-term success of my store. But that's not the whole story. There is also a personal moral concern behind my wanting to empower staff. I think it is morally right to give people at work as much control over their situations as is compatible with effective performance. So it pleases me to think that I am improving some people's lives and, at the same time, improving the business that pays me. I've simply got to go away now and think of how I can do my best to help those whose working lives I have spoiled.

Glenn is very anxious to see herself as an ethical person, a generally 'good person' who does the 'right thing' in her life. To help both herself and her interviewer to make sense of how she relates her private moral views to her managerial work she gives us some insight into her own identity, biography, emotions and her broad *orientation to work*.

Glenn's parents and upbringing have clearly been an important influence on her and she still seeks their help when faced with moral dilemmas such as that which caused her to be torn between furthering the interests of the business she worked for and protecting the interests of the small shopkeepers – people with whom she clearly felt empathy. Being 'ethically aware' is important to the sort of person she believes herself to be. Although it is the interviewer who introduces the idea of Glenn as a 'crusader', it is a label that she seems happy to accept. It fits with her earlier career interest in politics and her talk of 'fighting the cause' of getting more women into management.

The sense-making work that Glenn engages in when talking to the researcher can be seen as part of her *managing to manage* – coping with all the pressures of what she calls the 'messy and ambiguous' nature of managerial work. All of this, together with her reference to learning from her experiences, gives us a picture not of a person with a given bundle of managerial 'competencies', but of an *emergent manager* who is constantly learning and developing herself as she faces the moral and practical dilemmas of changing managerial circumstances (Watson and Harris, 1999). It is also a picture of a *reflective practitioner* who can step back from immediate work pressures and critically examine what they are doing and why (Schön, 1983). Glenn, in her practical management thinking, shows the sort of sensitivity to human values, differences and conflicts of interest that *critical management and organisation study* attempts to highlight in the academic context. She has no doubts, for instance, there often have to be 'losers' as well as 'winners' as a result of managerial decisions and actions.

One way we can make sense of Glenn's policy of making a business case, rather than a directly moral or political case, for tackling issues of gender, ethnic and age discrimination or inequality might be that she is aware of the extent to which such matters relate to the broader social and cultural context in which her organisation exists. To try to take on major social change issues from the position of a manager in just one organisation would be highly unrealistic, but a small contribution might be made to such change if the manager seeks opportunities to make business decisions that fit with notions of a fairer society.

Ethical ambiguity and the inevitability of moral dilemmas

It is difficult to see a pattern in Glenn's personal morality that fits with any of the schemes of *normative ethics* that philosophers or religious thinkers have proposed over the centuries – schemes that give the basic grounds for deciding what one should and should not do in any particular situation (see Further Reading on ethics, management and organisations, pp. 251–2).

- Sometimes she seems to be using what philosophers call *deontological* grounds for deciding what is right and wrong. This is where one simply takes one's duty in the world as a given and makes moral decisions in the light of that duty. This might take the form of following Kant's categorical imperative about treating all human beings as ends in their own right, for example. Her dislike of exploiting employees and her belief in treating all people 'with equal regard' could be related to deontological thinking.
- At other times, however, she seems to be basing her position on what ethicists often call *consequentialist* (and sometimes 'teleological') grounds. Here, one starts with a notion of what is 'good' in the world (a state of general human happiness, or the pursuit of the virtuous life, say). One then treats as 'right' those acts that help achieve this state of affairs. A 'right action' is one that would bring about the best possible consequences. We see Glenn adopting this type of principle when she suggests that it is 'morally right' to give people at work as much control over their circumstances as is compatible with business interests.
- Glenn is coming close here to applying *utilitarian* principles. Utilitarianism is perhaps the best known version of consequentalist thinking and, in its classical form, it involves deciding what is right on the grounds of what will give the greatest amount of happiness to the greatest number of people.

- An one point Glenn appears to be taking what philosophers call an *emotivist* line when she speaks of something *not feeling right* for example.

It is perhaps unsurprising that Glenn does not consistently follow any single scheme of normative ethics. It is rare to find someone who does, at least in the world of 'practical affairs'. Also, there are fundamental difficulties with both deontological and consequentalist approaches to ethical choice making. In the case of deontology, it is far from clear where people might take a notion of duty from. The human world does not universally respect any single lawgiver, god or biblical text. So how can there be a shared notion of duty and hence a shared morality across a variety of different people? There is a serious flaw in consequentialist thinking too. As has often been pointed out, especially with regard to utilitarianism, it could justify executing an innocent person for a crime if, for example, the public is happy that an apparently guilty person had been punished. The utility of such an act, and its contribution to the sum of human happiness, might be even greater if it were seen to deter the commitment of further such crimes. To most of us it would still be far from 'right' to kill that person, however much general human happiness was brought about by such an act. We can imagine Glenn arguing, along lines similar to this classic criticism of consequentalist ethics, that it would still have been wrong, say, to have promoted a woman into a job in which she was likely to struggle, even if her appointment had led to happy outcomes for people in the company generally.

In the end it would appear to be impossible to establish a clear *foundationalist* moral framework that managers, or anyone else in the modern world, can follow. The problem can be solved no more easily by the application of *rational* methods (calculating the relative amounts of human happiness and unhappiness likely to be caused by a certain act, for instance) than it can by simply following the simple emotivist line of doing what 'feels right'.

In a modern world where so much emphasis is placed on rational thinking, one might expect that moral principles might be derived from rational analysis of the human predicament. Max Weber, the key theorist of the rationalisation of the modern world, pointed out why this is impossible (Weber, 1949) and one can see in Glenn Ferness's notion of the insolubility of ethical dilemmas echoes of Weber's important notion of the *ethical irrationality of the world.*

Ethical irrationality of the world

Concept

Judgements about what is right and wrong cannot be derived from rational or scientific analysis of the human condition given that no system of values can be established that will make every value consistent with every other or ensure that right actions always lead to right outcomes (or wrong actions necessarily lead to wrong outcomes).

There are two aspects to the idea of the world as ethically irrational.

- First there is an *axiological* dimension of this ethical irrationality. This recognises that the world is full of different *and often irreconcilable* human values, goals, purposes and interests. A very obvious illustration of this is the problem that arises for people who believe it is fundamentally wrong to kill another human being while nevertheless being able to envisage a situation in which acts they regard as equally evil are likely be committed if certain people are not killed. Glenn gives managerial examples of this aspect of ethical irrationality. She recognises, for example, the 'rightness' of charging higher food prices to make possible a more ethically acceptable agricultural system. At the same time she believes in the 'rightness' of providing food that can be afforded by the poorer members of society. But these two things are not compatible. She also points to the impossibility of doing the 'right thing' for the shop workers in Logies without doing the 'wrong thing' with regard to the supervisors and section managers.
- The second dimension of Weber's idea of ethical irrationality involves the *paradox of consequences*, something that has enormous implications for all managerial work. Doing what Glenn took to be a 'right thing' for the ordinary shop workers in Logies had the unintended consequence of doing what she felt was a 'bad thing' to the supervisory staff. Glenn's awareness of the likely counterproductive consequences of trying to encourage Logies' top managers to work more effectively by relating part of their pay to the business's share price might also be seen as fitting into the paradox of consequences aspect of the 'ethical irrationality'.

Glenn's warning to her chief executive colleague about relating managerial rewards to the share price echoes some powerful warnings that various writers have given about the negative effects on the long-term corporate performance resulting from the general managerial prioritising of the pursuit of shareholder value (Deal and Kennedy, 1999) or of the specific tying of managerial rewards to share values through the issuing of *stock options* to corporate managers (Kennedy, 1999). It is argued by these and other commentators that the long-term future of some previously very successful organisations has been significantly damaged as managers have boosted their own incomes by impressing stock markets through their downsizing, outsourcing, restructuring and merger activities. Such short-term activities, through their damage to security, commitment and trust within the organisation, can seriously damage long-term corporate performance. The paradox of consequences can clearly operate at the level of a whole political economy as well as at the organisational level.

Morality and managerial practices

In the light of the ethical irrationality of the world and the immense ambiguity that confronts anyone trying to act morally in the world, how can managers and others involved in the managing of work succeed in bringing any moral criteria whatsoever into their actions? Some research suggests that managers have little choice other than to 'bracket' or leave their private moralities 'at home' and to pursue corporate interests ruthlessly and amorally (Jackall, 1988). Other research suggests that managers continuously draw upon, and mix together, criteria of *expedience* (what will 'work') and moral *principle* (what is 'right') in their day-to-day work (Watson, 1996b, 2003c). Thus managers, in explaining their personal 'theories of management' to the researcher, said things like:

- managers *ought* to listen to their workers and, if they do, they will *get better work from them*;
- it is a *good thing* to encourage employees to develop their skills and responsibilities at work and this will mean that people will *do a much better job* if you treat them in this way;
- it is good and *moral* to establish relationships of trust with the people around you and this *pays off* corporately;
- bullying people, being overly secretive and lying is *wrong*, it also tends to be *unhelpful* to managers, in the longer run, in getting them what they want from people.

Arguments like these encourage us to abandon the type of 'either–or thinking' which would suggest that people have to be *either* 'pragmatic' *or* 'principled' or have to be *either* 'expedient' *or* 'ethical'. In practice people tend to be 'pragmatically principled' or 'ethically expedient'. This appears to be the case with Glenn Ferness's 'making the best of things' in the light of both her own moral values and the organisational or business circumstances. Such an approach also seems to be behind the position that is taken by all of those arguing for high commitment and high trust work organisations. The implication is that it is a 'good thing' for managers to trust and value people within the organisation and that this 'good treatment' is likely to be reciprocated by 'good behaviour' by everyone in the organisation – 'good behaviour' that will make the organisation an effective and successful one, to the benefit of all its members.

Writers influenced by MacIntyre's (1981) critique of 'bureaucratic managerialism' have put forward a set of grounds for developing morally responsible managerial practices. Anthony (1986) and Roberts (1984, 1996), for example, take up MacIntyre's understanding of the relevance of Aristotle's ideas to management practice. It is argued that managers can find a moral base for their authority and their actions by treating their organisations as *moral communities* in which the interdependence of all members of that community is recognised. Managerial power is morally justified by its dedication to achieving the good life that it makes possible for members of that community. There is a serious catch in this kind of approach, however, if it keeps its focus at the level of the organisation as a moral community. A manager talking about high trust organisations in an ethnographic account of a managerial discussion about management and morality graphically illustrates this catch (Watson, 1998a). He says he can envisage an organisation that has high trust relations, caring welfare policies, serious empowerment practices and a strong culture with tight values that all members operate within and benefit from. He then shocks his colleagues by pointing out that such a strongly morally focused organisation could exist, and yet be in the business of contract murder. Would that really be a moral organisation he asks? Of course not, his colleagues inevitably but reluctantly admit.

Morality is something that clearly cannot be localised to the practices within a work organisation. In so far as managers are going to bring moral criteria into their work, they will have to look to the wider cultural world within which their organisation operates. To do this they can be expected to act in the light of two sets of criteria. First, they will look to the personal values that they bring to the workplace from their own upbringings, cultural roots and sense of 'the sort of person I am'. We saw this very clearly with Glenn Ferness and noted how she recognised that moral circumstances could occur at work that might cause her to leave the company. Second, managers inevitably have to look to the values and moralities of the various constituencies with which the organisation strategically exchanges to enable it to continue into the future. Glenn gives us the example of the dangers to the survival of Logies that could arise if the sort of people who use their shops were to learn that the company unfairly discriminated against people on grounds of their race, gender or age or if potentially valuable workers were deterred by such a reputation from seeking employment with the business.

Given the ethical irrationality of the world, managers are not going to find a single clear and unified set of ethical principles that all their organisational decisions can be based upon. However, this does not mean there is not a *variety* of ethical schemes or sets of moral principles to which managers will make reference. It is precisely because the world is ethically irrational that human beings have had to *create* cultures and ethical and religious systems, as Weber pointed out.

There is in the world a complex plurality of cultural and ethical systems and this is a plurality to which managers have to be sensitive. Even if there were a single set of moral rules that were acceptable within and across cultures, it would not avoid people having to face moral dilemmas. Nor would it straightforwardly help them resolve dilemmas. The existence of shared cultures – at an organisational, a societal or even an international level – would simply make the ultimately ambiguous moral aspects of human existence more manageable by providing languages and criteria that human beings can use to debate and contest the rights and wrong of their actions. Glenn Ferness in Case 6.4, we have shown, made use of more than one type of ethical criterion in developing her personal ethical orientation. She also, when looking at the corporate aspects of decision making, looked to the plurality of values that impinged on things that the organisation might do: the value that customers would put on the employment reputation of Logies, for example, or the public's current view of the ethics of industrialised agriculture. While most of Logie's customers did not object to current food industry practices, it would not be in the interests of the organisation to move to the more expensive organic and locally grown foods which Glenn and Chris would prefer, on personal ethical grounds, to sell. Should these values change, Logies could then realistically change its practices to fit better with the personal preferences of these two senior managers.

All of this analysis suggests that managers clearly cannot operate in an ethically neutral way. They are bound to attend to the ethical and cultural expectations of the various parties with which they 'trade'. But does this mean that managers simply *follow* the 'ethical flow' of the world in which their organisations operate? In large part, they do, given the logic of their work as helping the organisation survive into the future through processes of exchange with resource dependent constituencies, all of which bring a vast range of goals, interests and values into the exchange relationship. But to speak of managers 'going with the ethical flow' is to tell only part of the story. There are two basic possibilities for the individual manager.

First there is the possibility of taking a relatively *ethically reactive* stance. This does mean 'going with the flow' of what is sought from their organisation by some of the constituencies with which they deal and which is supported or allowed by other constituencies. Thus if a nation state says it is legal for a company to sell tobacco products within their territory and sufficient customers are willing to pay for those products then the managers in that company may well decide that there is no ethical difficulty in producing and marketing products that are likely to harm the health of many of those who choose to buy them.

Second, there is the possibility of a relatively *ethically assertive* stance. We see this at its simplest in the case of managers choosing not to work for an organisation that, say, makes tobacco products, sells armaments or buys material from what they regard as ethically suspect organisations. We see a stronger version of such a stance with the manager who decides to leave an organisation because of moral qualms about some of its activities (as when Glenn Ferness contemplated leaving Logies if the company did not cease to use the supplier of fitness equipment). However, the strongest case of the ethically assertive managerial stance is that which we see exemplified in Glenn's general approach to her managerial work. We are left in no doubt about her strong moral concerns and we are also firmly made aware of her understanding of the role of expedience in managerial work. She brings these two things together with her concept of 'making a business case' for things which, privately, she wishes to bring about for moral reasons. She accepts this compromise, recognising that there is no 'shared set of values to which everyone can be expected to subscribe'. Things that she sees in a moral light might, she recognises, only be seen as 'ethical in the eyes of some of us'. She therefore only presses moral causes for which she believes she can make a 'business case'. 'Arguing the moral case', she has learned, 'gets you nowhere.' For a manager to talk too much in ethical terms is to suggest that the manager is 'less than fully focused on interests of the business'. Hence, Glenn works to further her 'cause' of increasing the proportion of women managers in Logies by arguing that the business is better served by using all the 'talents' available to it. This is much more likely to succeed than directly putting a moral case (in terms such as those of 'women's rights' or of 'equality' presumably). Similar arguments, together with warnings about a poor employer reputation potentially alienating customers, are used to persuade people to go along with other fair treatment policies in the shop.

Glenn Ferness is probably an unusually ethically aware and morally assertive manager and, in the 'competence' terms looked at earlier in this chapter, she appears to be an exceptionally able and, indeed, effective manager. Even in her case, though, the scope for making the world a better, fairer or happier place is exceedingly limited. It is inevitably a great deal less for the average manager. Yet managerial decisions and actions, especially as they add up to form larger corporate and inter-corporate patterns, make a significant difference to people's lives, as one organisational example after another in *Organising and Managing Work* has shown. In making decisions, however, managers have nothing like a complete freedom of choice. In Chapter 7 we will see the interplay of managerial choices and organisational circumstances in the shaping of work organisations.

Summary

In this chapter the following key points have been made:

- Power is most usefully understood as a capacity that is possessed by an individual or group to influence outcomes of situations so that they gain access to whatever resources are scarce and desired in their organisational setting or in society more generally.
- Power operates at various interrelated levels: the level of the relationships between individuals, the level of the structure and culture of work organisations and at the level of the wider society and political economy. One cannot understand the way in which one organisational employee is able to get another to do something they would not otherwise do, for example, without locating that act within the broader organisational power structure. That power structure, in turn, cannot be understood without looking at the pattern of power and advantage across the society of which the organisation is a part.
- The very way in which work organisations are structured into hierarchies and into sub-units makes it inevitable that organisational members will compete *micropolitically* for access to scarce and desired organisational resources. Especially important is the fact that organisational hierarchies function not only as organisational control devices but are also competitive career ladders for managerial employees. Managers thus tend both to cooperate with each other and to compete with each other for advancement. This competition occurs in the context of considerable ambiguity and uncertainty, all of which creates opportunities for competitive power behaviours.
- There are numerous tactics that can be adopted by parties wanting to improve their organisational power position. However, a perceived ability on the part of a party to

deal with strategic uncertainties facing an organisation is especially helpful in advancing that party's interests – as long as they are relatively central to the organisation's operations and are unsubstitutable.

- Micropolitical interests and activities inevitably influence the outcome of any organisational decision-making event. But there are other factors present in the 'garbage can' of the choice situation. There will always be a variety of problems and a variety of solutions 'floating about' in any decision-making situation and the outcome will also be influenced by precisely who is present at the time and how much attention they pay to what is going on.
- Stress is not inherent in managerial work any more than it is in any other kind of occupation. However, there are particular emotional pressures upon people in this kind of work which can be understood as deriving, in part, from the expectations which are attached to particular managerial appointments and, in part, from *managist* discourses which tend to frame managerial activity in modern societies. Paradoxically the *discursive resources* of 'managism' can function both to reassure managers faced with the challenge of 'controlling the uncontrollable' and to increase their sense of insecurity in the face of the *double control problem* which characterises managerial work. This results from the fact that managers are required to shape and control the activities and even the feelings and values of others at the same time as they have to cope with controlling their own lives and identities.
- Managerial and organisational work often involves people adopting a pseudo-jargonistic style of convoluted language that can be understood in part as reflecting a struggle to handle the anxieties and unpredictabilities of organisational work. The often bizarre expressions to be heard in managerial and organisational situations may have other functions too and any particular organisational practitioner would need carefully to consider both the advantages and disadvantages of talking in a way which departs from normal language use. They would be wise to bear in mind the possibility that resorting to 'managerial bollock-speak' is not just an indication of possible communication breakdown but a sign that a manager is beginning to lose their grip on what they are doing.
- A manager's reflection on such matters as the type of language they use would entail their reviewing their basic orientation to managerial work, as well as judging how well they are performing the tasks allocated to them. It would also relate to how they were managing their own emotions, their identity and the general strategic exchange processes in which they are engaged.
- Managerial work can never be carried out in an ethically or politically neutral way – it always and inevitably has value implications and ethical consequences. Managers who do not take the value implications of their actions into account are not only open to moral judgement by commentators on management or by critics of management, they are also unlikely to be successful in their work.

- There is no clear set of uncontested ethical principles to which managers can look to help them in handling the ethical dilemmas that inevitably arise in their work. What is right and wrong in any given situation is not only open to different interpretations by different people operating with different interests and values, it is also complicated by the fact that 'good' acts do not necessarily lead to 'good' outcomes – and vice versa.
- Moral criteria relevant to managerial practice are, in practice, drawn from the cultural (and, often, multi-cultural) contexts in which managers shape their lives and identities and do their jobs. *Ethical* considerations are mixed together in various different ways with considerations of *expedience*.
- The most significant way in which ethical or moral considerations come into managerial work is as a result of managers needing to take into account the values and priorities of all the groups with which their organisation deals. Managers have little option but to take notice of the value preferences and priorities of, for example, customers, clients, employees, potential employees, shareholders and, on the behalf of members of society generally, the nation state. Within all of this, however, some managers will be more ethically assertive than others but, if they do attempt to further a personal ethical agenda, they will generally find it necessary to justify what they propose in terms of the interests of the organisation rather than by giving a direct moral argument for what they wish to bring about.

Recommended reading

The extent to which politics permeate organisations and managerial behaviour is powerfully brought out by David Buchanan and Richard Badham in *Power, Politics, and Organizational Change: Winning the turf game* (London: Sage, 1999) whilst James March brings together some of the influential writing done by himself and colleagues on decision processes in *A Primer on Decision-making: How does it happen?* (New York: Free Press, 1994). The original 'garbage can' study is included in the collection. Robyn Thomas and Alison Linstead bring us back to matters of managerial identities and show the part these play in the difficulties that middle managers often experience in 'Losing the plot? Middle Managers and Identity' (*Organization*, 9(1): 71–93, 2002). And Brad Jackson provide valuable insights (and perhaps some antidotes) on the fashionable ideas that managers might be tempted to turn to in his *Management Gurus and Management Fashions* (London: Routledge, 2001). And returning once again to fieldwork-based studies, Tony Watson shows how, in practice, managers can find themselves confronting and reflecting upon major ethical dilemmas in 'Ethical codes and moral communities: the Gunlaw temptation, the Simon solution and the David dilemma' in Parker, M. (ed.) *The Ethics of Organisation* (London: Sage, 1998).

Further reading

Further reading Power and organisational politics

Armstrong, P. (1989) 'Management, labour process and agency', *Work, Employment and Society*, 3(3): 307–322

Brown, A.D. (1998) 'Narrative, politics and legitimacy in an IT implementation', *Journal of Management Studies*, 35(1): 35–59

Buchanan, D. and Badham, R. (1999) *Power, Politics, and Organizational Change: Winning the turf game*, London: Sage

Burns, T. (1955) 'The reference of conduct in small groups: cliques and cabals in occupational milieux', *Human Relations*, 8: 467–486

Burns, T. (1961) 'Micropolitics: mechanisms of institutional change', *Administrative Science Quarterly*, 6: 257–281

Clegg, S.R. (1989) *Frameworks of Power*, London: Sage

Daudi, P. (1986) *Power in the Organisation: The discourse of power in managerial praxis*, Oxford: Blackwell

Fincham, R. (1992) 'Perspectives on power: processual, institutional and "internal" forms of organizational power', *Journal of Management Studies*, 26(9): 741–759

Guth, W.D. and Macmillan, L.C. (1986) 'Strategy implementation versus middle management self interest', *Strategic Management Journal*, 7: 313–327

Hardy, C. (ed.) (1995) *Power and Politics in Organizations*, Aldershot: Dartmouth

Hardy, C. (1996) 'Understanding power: bringing about strategic change', *British Journal of Management*, 7(special issue): 3–16

Hickson, D.J., Hinings, C.R., Lee, C.A., Schneck, R.E. and Pennings, J.M. (1971) 'A strategic contingecies theory of intra-organizational power', *Administrative Science Quarterly*, 16: 216–229

Huczynski, A.A. (1996) *Influencing Within Organizations: Getting in, rising up and moving on*, Hemel Hempstead: Prentice Hall

Jay, A. (1970) *Management and Machiavelli*, Harmondsworth: Penguin Books

Kakabadse, A. (1983) *The Politics of Management*, Aldershot: Gower

Knights, D. and Murray, F. (1994) *Managers Divided*, Aldershot: Gower

Lukes, S. (2005) *Power: A radical view, 2nd edition*, London: Palgrave

Maccoby, M. (1976) *The Gamesmen*, New York: Simon and Schuster

Mangham, I. (1979) *The Politics of Organizational Change*, Westport, CT: Greenwood Press

McKinlay, A. and Taylor, P. (1998) 'Through the looking glass: Foucault and the politics of production' in A. McKinlay and K. Starkey (eds) *Foucault, Management and Organizational Theory*, London: Sage

Mintzberg, H. (1983) *Power In and Around Organizations*, Englewood Cliffs, NJ: Prentice-Hall

Pettigrew, A.M. (1973) *The Politics of Organisational Decision Making*, London: Tavistock

Pettigrew, A.M. and McNulty, T. (1995) 'Power and influence in and around the boardroom', *Human Relations*, 48(8): 845–873

Pfeffer, J. (1992) *Managing With Power: Politics and influence in organizations*, Cambridge, MA: Harvard Business School Press

Watson, D.H. (1992) 'Power, conflict and control at work' in J. Allen, P. Braham and P. Lewis (eds) *Political and Economic Forms of Modernity*, Cambridge: Polity
Watson, T.J. (1982) 'Group ideologies and organisational change', *Journal of Management Studies*, 19(3): 259–275
Wildavsky, A. (1979) *The Politics of the Budgeting Process*, Boston, MA: Little Brown
Zugbach, von R. (1995) *The Winning Manager: Coming out on top in the organization game*, London: Souvenir Press

Further reading Decision processes

Agor, W. (1986) 'The logic of intuition: how top executives make important decisions', *Organizational Dynamics*, Winter: 5–15
Agor, W. (1989) *Intuition in Organizations*, Newbury Park, CA: Sage
Behling, O. and Eckel, N. (1991) 'Making sense out of intuition', *Academy of Management Executive*, February: 46–54
Brunsson, N. (1982) 'The irrationality of action and action rationality: decisions, ideologies and organizational actions', *Journal of Management Studies*, 19(1): 29–44
Brunsson, N. (1985) *The Irrational Organization: Irrationality as a basis for organisational action and change*, Chichester: Wiley
Chia, R. (1994) 'The concept of decision: a deconstructive analysis', *Journal of Management Studies*, 31(6): 781–806
Cleverley, G. (1971) *Managers and Magic*, London: Longman
Cohen, M.D., March, J.G. and Olsen, J.P. (1972) 'A garbage can model of organizational choice', *Administrative Science Quarterly*, 17(1): 1–25
Cyert, R.M. and March, J.G. (1963) *A Behavioural Theory of the Firm*, Englewood Cliffs, NJ: Prentice-Hall
Feldman, M. (1991) 'The meanings of ambiguity: learning from stories and metaphors' in P. Frost, L. Moore, M. Louis, C. Lundberg and J. Martin (eds) *Reframing Organization Culture*, Newbury Park, CA: Sage, 145–156
March, J.G. (1998) *The Pursuit of Organizational Intelligence*, Oxford: Blackwell
March, J.G. and Olsen, J.P. (1976) *Ambiguity and Choice in Organisations*, Oslo: Universitetsforlagtt
Miller, S.L., Hickson, D.J. and Wilson, D.C. (1996) 'Decision-making in organizations' in S.R. Clegg, C. Hardy and W. Nord (eds) *Handbook of Organization Studies*, London: Sage, 293–312
Mumby, D.K. and Putnam, L.L. (1992) 'The politics of emotion: a feminist reading of bounded rationality', *Academy of Management Review*, 17(3): 465–486
Simon, H.A. (1957) 'A behavioural model of rational choice' in his *Models of Man*, New York: Wiley
Srivasta, S. and Associates (eds) (1983) *The Executive Mind*, San Francisco: Jossey-Bass
Streeck, W. (1987) 'The uncertainties of management in the management of uncertainty', *Work, Employment and Society*, 1: 281–308
Weick, K.E. (1979) *The Social Psychology of Organizing*, Reading, MA: Addison-Wesley
Weick, K.E. (1983) 'Managerial thought in the context of action' in S. Srivasta and Associates (eds) *The Executive Mind*, San Francisco, CA: Jossey-Bass
Weick, K.E. (1995) *Sensemaking in Organisations*, Thousand Oaks, CA: Sage
Weick, K.E. (2000) *Making Sense of Organization*, Oxford: Blackwell

Further reading Managerial insecurities and the pressures on middle managers

Dopson, S. and Neumann, J.E. (1995) 'Uncertainty, contrariness and the double-bind: middle managers' reactions to changing contracts', *British Journal of Management*, 9(special issue): 53–71

Dopson, S. and Stewart, R. (1990) 'What is happening to middle management', *British Journal of Management*, 1(1): 3–16

Dopson, S. and Stewart, R. (1993) 'Information technology, organizational restructuring and the future of middle management', *New Technology, Work and Employment* 8(1): 10–20

Hallier, J. and James, P. (1997) 'Middle managers and the employee psychological contract: agency, protection and advancement', *Journal of Management Studies*, 34(5): 703–728

Hallier, J. and Lyon, P. (1996) 'Job insecurity and employee commitment: managers' reactions to the threat of outcomes of redundancy selection', *British Journal of Management*, 7: 107–123

Mant, A. (1979) *The Rise and Fall of the British Manager*, London: Pan

McGovern, P., Hope-Hailey, V. and Stiles, P. (1998) 'The managerial career after down-sizing: case studies from the "leading edge" ', *Work, Employment and Society*, 12(3): 457–477

Mulholland, K. (1998) ' "Survivors" versus "Movers and Shakers": the reconstitution of management and careers in the privatised utilities' in P. Thompson and C. Warhurst (eds) *Workplaces of the Future*, Basingstoke: Macmillan

Newell, H. and Dopson, S. (1996) 'Muddle in the middle: organizational restructuring and middle management careers', *Personnel Review*, 25(4): 4–20

Redman, T., Wilkinson, A. and Snape, E. (1997) 'Stuck in the middle? Managers in building societies', *Work, Employment and Society*, 11(1): 101–114

Scarborough, H. (1998) 'The unmaking of management? Change and continuity in British management in the 1990s', *Human Relations*, 51(6): 691–716

Scase, R. and Goffee, R. (1989) *Reluctant Managers: Their work and lifestyles*, London: Unwin Hyman

Thomas, R. and Dunkerley, D. (1999) 'Careering downwards? Middle managers' experiences in the downsized organization', *British Journal of Management*, 10(2): 95–184

Thomas, R. and Linstead, A. (2002) 'Losing the plot? Middle managers and identity', *Organization*, 9(1): 71–93

Thornhill, A. and Saunders, M.N.K. (1998) 'The meanings, consequences and implications of downsizing and redundancy: a review', *Personnel Review*, 27(4): 271–295

Wacjman, J. and Martin, B. (2001) 'My company or my career: managerial achievement and loyalty', *British Journal of Sociology*, 52(4): 559–578

Westley, F.R. (1990) 'Middle managers and strategy: microdynamics of inclusion', *Strategic Management Journal*, 11: 337–351

Worrall, L. and Cooper, C.L. (1999) *The Quality of Working Life: The 1999 survey of managers' experiences*, Institute of Management Research Report, London: Institute of Management

Worrall, L., Cooper, C. and Campbell, F. (2000) 'The new reality for UK managers: perpetual change and employment instability', *Work, Employment and Society*, 14(4): 647–668

Further reading Management thinking: fashions, fads and trends

Abrahamson, E. (1996) 'Management fashion, academic fashion, and enduring truths', *Academy of Management Review*, 21(3): 616–618
Barley, S. and Kunda, G. (1992) 'Design and devotion: surges of rational and normative ideologies of control in managerial discourse', *Administrative Science Quarterly*, 37: 363–399
Clark, T. and Salaman, G. (1996) 'The managerial guru as organizational witchdoctor', *Organization*, 3(1): 85–107
Collins, D. (2000) *Management Fads and Buzzwords*, London: Routledge
Furestan, S. (1999) *Popular Management Books – How they are made and what they mean for organisations*, London: Routledge
Huczynski, A.A. (1993a) *Management Gurus: What makes them and how to become one*, London: Routledge
Huczynski, A.A. (1993b) 'Explaining the succession of management fads', *International Journal of Human Resource Management*, 4(2): 443–463
Jackson, B. (1996) 'Re-engineering the sense of self: the manager and the management guru', *Journal of Management Studies*, 33(5): 571–590
Jackson, B. (2001) *Management Gurus and Management Fashions*, London: Routledge
Jackson, N. and Carter, P. (1998) 'Management gurus: what are we to make of them?' in J. Hassard and R. Holliday (eds) *Organization-Representations: Work and Organization in Popular Culture*, London: Sage
Kieser, A. (1997) 'Rhetoric and myth in management fashion', *Organization*, 4: 49–74
Shapiro, E.C. (1996) *Fad Surfing in the Boardroom*, Oxford: Capstone
Sturdy, A. and Fleming, P. (2003) 'Talk as technique – a critique of the works and deeds distinction in the diffusion of customer service cultures in call centres', *Journal of Management Studies*, 40(4): 753–773
Thomas, P. (1999) *Fashions in Management Research: An empirical analysis*, Aldershot: Ashgate
Watson, T.J. (1994) 'Management "flavours of the month": their role in managers' lives', *International Journal of Human Resource Management*, 5(4): 889–905

Further reading Ethics, management and organisations

Ackers, P. (2001) 'Ethics' in T. Redman and A. Wilkinson (eds) *Contemporary Human Resource Management*, Harlow: FT Prentice Hall
Barrett, E. (1999) 'Justice in the workplace: normative ethics and the critique of human resource management', *Personnel Review*, 28(4): 307–318
Fisher, C. and Lovell, A. (2004) *Business Ethics and Values*, Harlow: FT Prentice Hall
Legge, K. (1998) 'The morality of HRM' in C. Mabey, D. Skinner and T. Clark (eds) *Experiencing Human Resource Management*, London: Sage
Maclagan, P. (1998) *Management and Morality*, London: Sage

Mangham, I. (1995) 'MacIntyre and the manager', *Organization*, 2(2): 181–204
Mitroff, I.I. (1998) 'On the fundamental importance of ethical management: why management is the most important of all human activities', *Journal of Management Inquiry*, 7(1): 68–79
Parker, M. (ed.) (1998) *Ethics and Organization*, London: Sage
Roberts, J. (1984) 'The moral character of management practice', *Journal of Management Studies*, 21(3): 287–302
Royal Society of Arts (1996) *Tomorrow's Company*, Aldershot: Crouler
Sorell, T. and Hendry, J. (1994) *Business Ethics*, Oxford: Butterworth-Heinemann
Watson, T.J. (1996) 'How do managers think? – morality and pragmatism in theory and practice', *Management Learning*, 27(3): 323–341
Watson, T.J. (1998) 'Ethical codes and moral communities: the Gunlaw temptation, the Simon solution and the David dilemma' in M. Parker (ed.) *The Ethics of Organisation*, London: Sage
Watson, T.J. (2003) 'Ethical choice in managerial work: the scope for managerial choices in an ethically irrational world', *Human Relations*, 56(2): 167–185
Wray-Bliss, E. (2002) 'Abstract ethics, embodied ethics: the strange marriage of Foucault and positivism in labour process theory', *Organization*, 9: 5–39

Week 11

People and Organisation

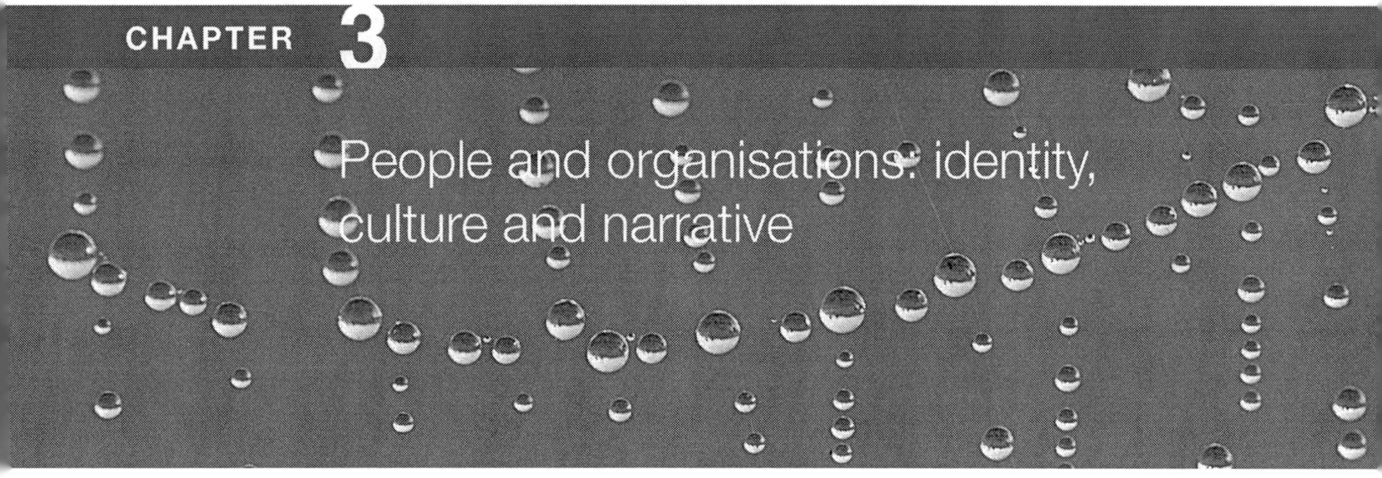

CHAPTER 3

People and organisations: identity, culture and narrative

Objectives

Having read this chapter and completed its associated activities, readers should be able to:

- Recognise how people's 'humanness' is best understood by relating it to basic issues of how human beings manage their existence and shape their *social institutions* as well as how, as a species, they have developed *cultures* to help deal with these existential challenges.
- Understand how industrial capitalist forms of economy and society fit into this broader social patterning and how, in turn, modern work organisations and the occupation of management fit into it.
- Recognise that to understand organisational and managerial processes we have to come to terms with the complex relationship between human individuals and their social and cultural context.
- Appreciate that orthodox organisational behaviour and management thinking tends to apply a systems-control frame of reference to understanding human individuals, one which partly parallels that which is applied to organisations.
- Identify the ways in which we have to go beyond the systems-control way of looking at human beings in societies and organisations.
- Understand the advantages of viewing human 'individuality' in a process-relational way: as both *relational* (only existing in relation to others) and *emergent* (always in a process of 'becoming').
- Appreciate the importance of narratives and discourses in the patterning and functioning of human cultures and individual identities.

Individuals, societies and the role of culture in the managing of human existence

Whilst the management of work is the focus of the present book it has to be realised that managing work is itself part of something even more fundamental: the managing of human existence. The processes by which we manage work tasks in human societies cannot be understood separately from the processes by which we manage our human existence. When we are at work we are doing much more than simply completing work tasks. We are also 'working at' or 'managing' our basic humanity, our relationships with others and our identities. Managing life and managing work are inextricably connected. We cannot properly understand one without understanding the other, and we cannot understand either without an appreciation of where humans differ from other animals. Here, culture, discourse and narrative have a vital importance.

What separated the species *Homo sapiens* from other animals, as its uniquely large brain evolved, was its capacity for language. Accompanying this, as an eminent anthropologist put it, was the 'possibility of making value judgements and exercising moral choices' (Leach, 1982, p. 104). Humans now had the capacity rationally to analyse the situations they found themselves in and to choose how to act in those situations. But humans did not lose their instincts. Whereas other animals continued to be more-or-less completely driven by their instincts (patterns of behaviour being 'wired into their brains', so to speak) humans found themselves facing choices about how those instincts would be channelled, directed or suppressed. As humans evolved they found themselves confronting the fact that what they should eat, for example, how and when they should eat, with whom they should eat, and so on, was a matter of choice. Once this possibility of discrimination and choice was recognised, it became inescapable. What also became inescapable was the potentially high level of *angst* that arose from the terrifying recognition that everyone is going to die. Such a realisation was only possible once there was language and the capacity to conceptualise such matters. Thinkers at various times in human history have marked the start of human culture (or religion, or art, or philosophy) as the point at which humans first confronted the ultimate existential angst: anxiety about their own mortality. This, together with the challenge of the potentially vast range of value choices confronting the human individual, had to be handled socially. The choice-making dilemma and the fear of mortality had arisen in the first place along with the essentially social phenomenon of language.

Human beings' capacity for language and their highly social nature were intimately tied up with each other from the start. For reasons varying from the way they acquired and processed food to the fact of the immense and long-lasting vulnerability of their babies and small children, human beings were dependent on each other and had to develop patterns of exchange between them. These exchanges might be simple ones of task responsibility: 'You make a bonfire, I'll cook dinner'. They might be straightforward barters: 'You give me an axe head, I'll give you a necklace'. Or they might be matters of complex commitments:

'You join our community and we'll protect you from marauders' or 'You live and sleep only with me and I'll live and sleep only with you' or 'You be an obedient child and I'll be a gentle parent'.

To manage these patterns of *reciprocity* – of give and take exchanges – which brought human societies into existence, there had to be shared understandings of what should and should not happen, what was right and what was wrong. Rules and moralities are at the heart of the sets of shared understandings and meanings that we conceptualise as human *culture*.

Culture *Concept*

The set of meanings shared by members of a human grouping which defines what is good and bad, right and wrong and consequently defines the appropriate ways for members of that group to think and behave.

Without culture, each human being would be left without guidance on how to handle the choices that occur at every moment of their waking existence (when to get up, what to wear, what to say to one's lover . . .). Without culture, we would simply go mad. Without guidance on choices ranging from when we should get out of bed to whom we might marry or how we should bury our dead, we would spin into a state of ontological chaos – a very breakdown of 'being'. Without help in making sense of what the obligations are between man and woman or parent and child, without help in making sense of our bodies and our sexuality, without help in making sense of sickness, pain and death, we would become psychologically overwhelmed and collapse. We cannot handle such matters on our own. Our species therefore worked, and continues to work, to construct cultural resources to assist us. Culture provides a degree of order (*nomos*) instead of *chaos*, predictability instead of crippling ambiguity, sanity instead of madness. It guides us on how to balance instinct and social commitment, how to balance rationality and emotion and how to balance our sense of a unique self and our sense of membership of society (Berger, 1973).

Activity 3.1

Make a list of the instincts that human beings have – drives that come from the animal aspects of our existence.

For each of these instincts, think of the ways in which 'culture' plays a part in their expression, satisfaction or suppression.

As humans, we do not swoop on the first piece of edible material we see when we feel pangs of hunger. Neither do we leap upon the first body we see when we feel a desire to mate. Culture has to be 'referred to' in every case. Even when human beings find themselves facing a wild beast or a human enemy threatening to kill them, they are likely to think – however fleetingly – of cultural notions like courage or cowardice, before fighting or fleeing. (Note how this observation is pertinent to Chapter 1's critique of the 'hierarchy of needs' thinking.)

If human evolution and the invention of culture by human beings had straightforwardly developed along the lines we have suggested here, human social existence would be a warm and comforting experience with a high level of social reciprocity giving a life of mutual and universal love and care. It has not worked out like that, however. The cruelties and unhappiness we see occurring every day in our homes, streets, workplaces and across the globe testify to this. But might it have turned out differently? We do not know. But it seems likely that if complete mutuality and reciprocity had been achieved at any stage in human evolution, then social and economic development would have ceased at that point. It is hard to imagine a society with any dynamic aspect whatsoever that did not contain human rivalries, conflicts and a determination for some to have more than an equal share of whatever goods were currently scarce and socially desired. It is likely that, from the start, human cultures were developed both to encourage human assertiveness and competitive acquisition and to keep it under a degree of control to prevent what the philosopher Thomas Hobbes called 'a war of all against all'. Yet from as far back as we can know from the historical and the archaeological record, humans have mobilised themselves into coalitions of interest and engaged in *social closure* practices.

Social closure

Concept

The process whereby a group seeks to gain or defend its advantage over other groups by closing its ranks to those it defines as outsiders.

All societies have their own patterns of inequality and divisions into groups, factions, elites, tribes, classes, races and the like. And conflict and competition has occurred in every social order, both between and within these groupings, for scarce and desired resources.

Much of what we have established so far is represented in Figure 3.1 (p. 84), this being a rather audacious attempt to pull together a lot of social science thinking in a single diagram. It is not an attempt at grand social theory however. It is, rather, a conceptual scheme using the rather crude devices of overlapping circles (or 'ellipses', to be accurate) and double-ended arrows to emphasise that the *individual* aspects of human existence must be seen as intimately related to the *structural* aspects. It takes as its starting point the fundamental human problem of having to manage existential dilemmas. The structural aspects of how these are handled are identified in the 'societal' and the 'organisational' ellipses in the figure and these are seen as mediated by the *industrial capitalist* patterning of contemporary societies and the institution of employment (p. 54). The more individual aspects of the 'individual–structural duality' are covered in the ellipses labelled 'the individual' and 'managers'. The issue of managers' identities and self-shaping identified in the 'managers' ellipse are to be discussed in Chapter 6 and the organisational exchange processes identified in the 'organisations' ellipse will be central to the concerns of Chapter 9.

The top two ellipses in Figure 3.1 relate to 'the societal' aspect of human existence and 'the individual' aspect, respectively. But this separating of the societal and individual is simply an analytical distinction that is made with a degree of tentativeness. It is necessary to be tentative. It is seen as very important that when we are thinking about people and their social context we should not go too far in treating individual and social factors in human existence as anything but extremely closely intertwined. It is increasingly recognised across the human sciences that few aspects of our existence can be treated as social factors *or* individual factors in an 'either–or' fashion.

Individuals and organisations: beyond 'either–or' thinking

The social factors/individual factors dualism is related to another basic dualism. This is the one that has occupied the minds of thinkers throughout history. It is the dualism which philosophers, theologians and various other thinkers have typically conceived in terms of individual free will, on the one hand, and determinism on the other.

The ancient free will/determinism debate was carried over into the modern social sciences as they tackled questions such as whether human actions and behaviours derive from our individual characteristics and inclinations or are determined by 'society' or 'culture'. This is no abstract and esoteric debate of limited relevance to the study of work organisation and management. One of its crudest manifestations, for example, has been the discussion that one still hears about whether leaders are 'born or made'. Is it our individual characteristics, inherent in us as unique beings, that leads us to be good leaders, or is it something that can be developed in people through social processes like training and personal development? At a more sophisticated level, we might consider the extent to which how we behave in organisations, as individuals, is a matter of what each of us 'is like' as an individual and the extent to which our behaviour is determined by the rules or the 'culture' of that organisation.

To some extent, social scientists have moved away from a simple dichotomising of 'the individual and society' or 'nature and nurture'. Inevitably, there has been a trend towards seeing the two as influencing each other. It might be said, for example, that it is a particular mixture of individual characteristics and social experience that makes some people more effective leaders than others. Similarly, we might argue that the way people behave in a particular workplace is the outcome of interplay between what they are 'like' as individuals and what the organisational structure, culture or managerial authority pushes them towards. To argue this way might seem like a simple solution to the problem. But it is only a start.

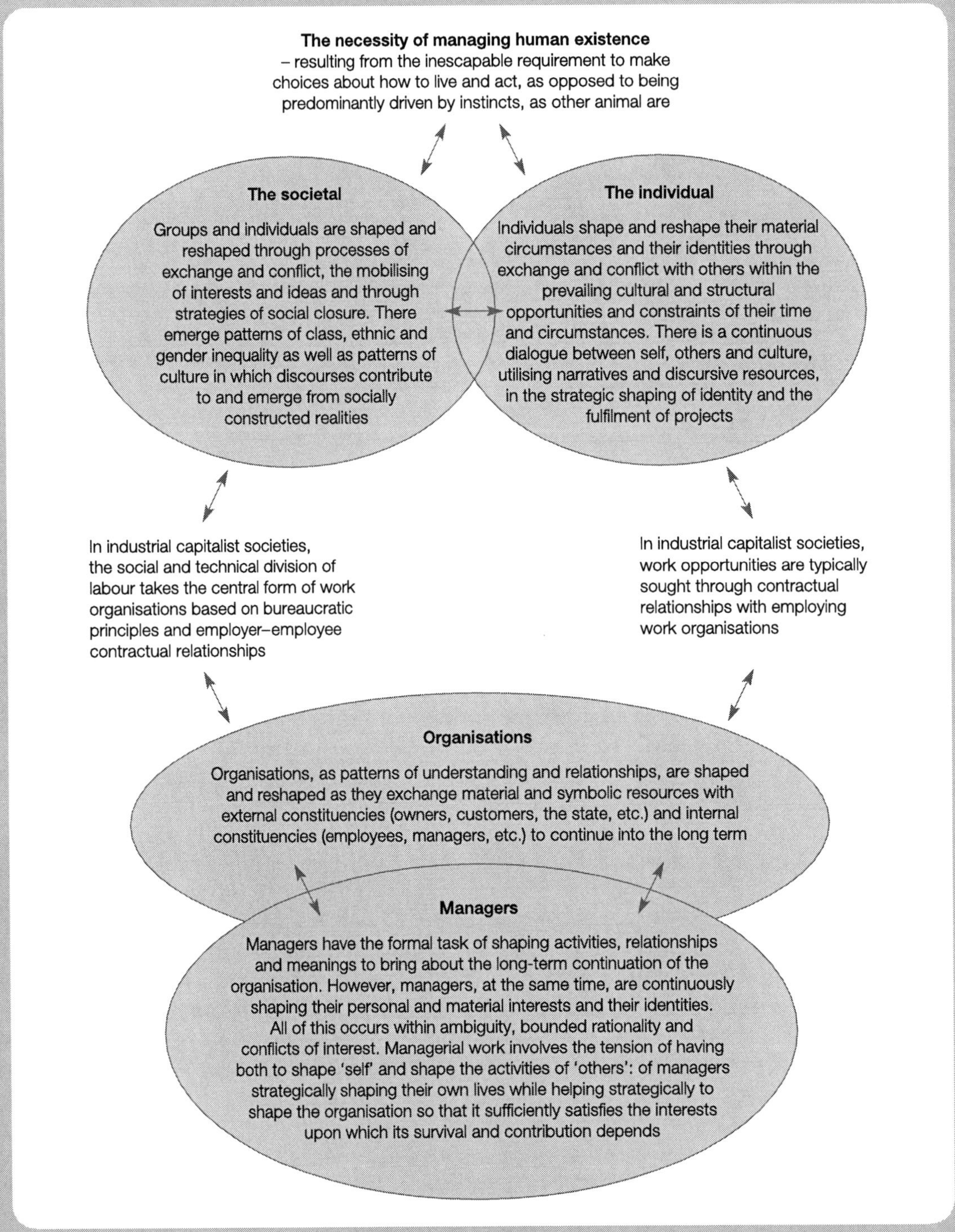

FIGURE 3.1 Organisations and managers in their societal and human-existential context

What we need to understand better, in any given organisational or social setting, is just how the interaction between the 'individual' and the 'social' operates – if indeed it is realistic even to separate the two. Some theorists see the interrelationship between human individuality and structural context as so intimately related that we should abandon even trying to separate them. The position taken here is clearly that there is an immensely strong relationship between our individual natures and our social involvements. In organisations, for example, the behaviours of organisational members cannot be understood separately from the organisational circumstances in which they are acting. But – by the same token – these 'organisational circumstances' (rules, structures, cultures and so on) cannot be understood in isolation from the human actors that make them and are otherwise caught up in them. Neither the 'organisational member' nor the 'organisation' itself, in the final analysis, exists separately from the other. Without an organisation there cannot be an organisational member (or employee) any more than there can be an organisation without any employees or other organisational members.

While it is accepted here, however, that human individuality and social or structural circumstances are so intimately related that, in practice, they each shade over into the other, it is felt worthwhile *analytically* to separate the two. This is equivalent to analysing a so-called 'black and white' photograph. In practice, few such photographs actually have any black or white in them (technically, they are 'grey-scale' images). However, it is *analytically useful* to have in our minds the concepts of 'black' and 'white' when we are studying how the image is made up – or 'works'. So it is when we study the organising and managing of work. No human act exists separately from the organisational context in which it occurs and no organisational circumstance exists separately from the human actions that occur with regard to it. But it is helpful to analyse organisational processes by treating human agency and organisational influences *as if*, for the moment of analysis, they were separate. The precise way in which they *come together as a singularity* can only be appreciated if we treat them analytically as a *duality* (a 'duality' being a pair of essentially inseparable things – 'two sides of the same coin' perhaps, whereas a 'dualism' implies the existence of two separable things – two coins).

These matters take us back to the important influence on western modernist thinking of René Descartes. We briefly encountered Descartes when we were considering Enlightenment thinking (p. 35) and again when we looked at organisations and social construction (p. 57). In this latter discussion we introduced the idea of *Cartesian dualism*, where the thinking mind, which to Descartes was the essence of the human individual ('I think therefore I am'), is seen as something separate from both the human body and the rest of the world 'outside' that mind (Damasio, 2000). The essential being of each of us, in this view, is the *deus ex machina*, the ghost or spirit inside the machine of our physical frame (Figure 3.2).

The influence of Descartes' way of thinking about human beings has been enormous and has been at the heart of the orthodox psychology that has been widely applied to the study of people in work organisations. However, Cartesian

FIGURE 3.2 Descartes and the 'thinking self' as the ghost in the machine

dualism not only encourages us to go too far in separating the organisation as an entity which is relatively autonomous with regard to its constituent members and from the world in which it exists; it also splits human individuals from their social world and their culture. It sees humans as relatively free-standing entities (forgetting John Donne's poetic reminder that 'no man is an island entire of itself'). This contrasts with the process-relational framing, which sees a human's 'being' as in large part defined by *relations* with others in the social world and as always in a *process* of 'becoming'. Before we develop this framework, however, we need to note the ways in which the systems-control frame of reference is applied to human individuals in ways that parallel its applications to organisations. It is based on the either–or dualisms of modernist thinking.

The systems-control framing of people – dualisms in action

The systems-control way of 'framing' of the individual in orthodox thinking about work and organisation was introduced in Chapter 1 in the scheme represented in Figure 1.4. This way of framing human individuals sees them, in effect, as a little machine-like system in which goals or 'motives' operate as a motor 'powering' the human entity so that it behaves in a particular way. Like the systems-control notion of the organisation, the individual is an entity with 'goals', which converts inputs into outputs. Every human individual has built into it a set of needs, to which these goals or motives are related, and if opportunities are offered that might satisfy these needs, the individual is 'motivated' by the prospect of need satisfaction. Thus, need-satisfying inputs of food, water, or pleasure, say (or cash with which to purchase these), are converted into outputs of need satisfaction for the individual and task completion for the employer. The employer, in effect, fuels the employee to get work done. To put it like this, of course, is to caricature the perspective, but such a caricature can be justified as a means of getting us critically to reflect on the assumptions which are so easily taken for granted in managerial thinking about people and work.

The notions of 'motive' and *motivation* are clearly central to this way of thinking about working human individuals and the concept of motivation is an immensely popular one in management thinking, as we noted in Chapter 1. However, it is not the only psychological concept used in conventional organisation behaviour thinking. *Personality* is the key concept used to recognise differences between human individuals, and other concepts like *perception*, *communication*, *attitudes* and *learning* are used to look at the way the individual-as-entity relates to the world around them. As was noted earlier (pp. 27–8) different concepts can relate to the same word – 'communication', 'personality', 'learning' and so on are conceptualised in different ways at different times. Generally speaking, however, orthodox thinking about human individuals and work has conceptualised these facets of human existence in ways which stay close to the systems-control assumptions outlined so far. It also stays faithful to the Cartesian dualism that emphasises the separation between the individual, as an entity, and the individual's social existence.

The dualism inherent in orthodox modernist psychology – and in the systems-control framing – works in two ways:

- It divides up human experience and splits human beings from their worlds by applying various dualisms. Most importantly, it splits the individual from society and thinking from behaving. It also makes strong divisions between speaking and acting and between reason and emotion.
- Having split these facets of human experience (treating useful analytical 'dualities' as 'dualisms', as we put it earlier) it typically treats the relationship between them in a *linear* manner. Hence, the individual first exists and then becomes social (or is 'socialised', as the jargon has it). And the individual first thinks (or 'plans' or 'makes a decision') and then acts (or implements the plan or decision).

Linearity and dualism in analysing human behaviour

At first sight, the notion of distinguishing between such processes as thinking and acting, and then looking at how one precedes the other seems wholly reasonable. Indeed, it might be argued that an intention or a plan precedes an action or a motive comes before an action, by definition. We start with a *reason* to behave. And we then behave. However, if we think more deeply about this, and apply *critical* common sense to it (Chapter 1, p. 11), we can see that things are not as simple as this in practice. Assumptions of *linearity* of this kind can be very misleading if we wish to understand human behaviour in a way that is actually helpful to us when confronting the 'realities' of human practice. Although it is true that we sometimes think carefully and make plans about what we are going to do before we act on a particular matter, it is equally often the case that we operate in a much more complex way. Regularly, in our everyday lives we 'find ourselves doing something' without actually identifying a motive or a reason for doing it.

Activity 3.2

Read the story of Grant Park leaving his desk to buy a cup of coffee in Case 3.1. Then

- try to remember something like this that you have done recently at home or at work (or something you *might* do, if you prefer). It needs to be a case of where you could be said simply to have 'found yourself' acting in a certain way;
- think about the relationship between your thoughts and your actions, and consider whether either one came before another or whether they were completely mixed up with each other;
- think about the rational aspects of your actions (where means are clearly chosen to meet specified ends) and the emotional dimension to the behaviour (where feelings came into the matter), and consider whether either was dominant or whether the two were jointly involved;
- consider in what ways your actions can be seen in 'individual' terms and in what ways they had a 'social' dimension – in the sense that either the behaviour itself or the thinking associated with it took into account your relationship, or possible relationship, with other people.

Grant Park gets thirsty, or does he? — Case 3.1

Grant Park was sitting at his desk in the publishing company where he worked. He had been trying all day to finish a rather difficult management report that he had to do for Marjorie, the editorial executive. The report was already two days late. Grant had only been back from his lunch break for thirty minutes when he found himself wandering away from his desk in the middle of compiling a table of figures on book sales. He then found himself putting money in the vending machine down the corridor and pressing the button for a cup of his usual brew of white coffee with extra sugar. As he turned away from the coffee machine and looked down at the cup of muddy liquid which was burning his hand, he paused and asked himself, 'Just what am I doing here with yet another cup of this awful stuff?'. For a moment, he thought he heard Marjorie coming out of her office. He wondered just what he would say to her if she questioned his being away from his urgent task. Marjorie did not appear. But Grant found himself wondering what he would say to her. What indeed was he doing visiting the coffee machine at this time? He asked himself,

> 'Now, did I do this because I was thirsty?
> No, I've been drinking coffee all morning.
> It might just be a habit I've got into.

Or, then again, it might be because I was hoping to come across that bloke from management accounts I need to speak to.
But perhaps it was to reward myself for having written two whole pages.
On the other hand, it could have been to cheer myself up for having written so little in four hours.'

What Grant Park is doing, in envisaging being asked to explain his actions, is trying to *attach a motive* to his behaviour *post hoc* – after the event. The action has preceded the motive, goal or purpose, we might say. This is not to claim, however, there were absolutely no reasons or motives behind his actions, even if he cannot remember them subsequently. In practice, then, thinking and acting are often muddled up, and not only does this lead us to question the thinking/acting Cartesian dualism, it also makes us aware of the inadequacy of the rationality/emotion dualism. In the processes, whatever they were, that involved a walk from the desk to the coffee machine, there were clearly emotions at work just as much as analytical reasoning (implicit in the notion of reward and, even more so, in the notion of cheering oneself up). But a further dualism also has to be abandoned if we are to understand what is going on here – that of the 'individual' and the 'social'. The issue of why the desk was left only arose because Grant contemplated how he might explain himself to someone else. Thus *motives* in human behaviour – things that at first would seem to be very individual matters – are actually *social* or *relational*. Their logic is as much one of making an act seem sensible to another person (real or imagined) as it is a logic of behavioural causality.

To make this point about the social aspects of individual motives even more forcefully, we might say that the 'motive' in a murder case is as much, or more, a social matter (something to be established by police and in a court of law) as it is a cause or a straightforward 'reason for' the murder having occurred. Although we all take for granted that crimes have 'motives', just think for a moment about any murder that you might have read about in detail at some time. Then ask yourself if it was really likely in that case that there was a 'motive' acting as a single 'mainspring of action'. Although our society and culture would tend to demand that such a 'cause' be identified for such a horrid event and put in the public records, it is difficult to believe that things could normally be that simple or that 'mono-causal'.

We are therefore better placed to come to terms with the complexities of how thinking and planning (cognitive aspects of human functioning), on the one hand, and acting or doing on the other relate to each other if we move away from anything resembling simple cause–effect sequences. There is a multiplicity of motives and goals relating to any given human act, whether it be going to buy some coffee at work or murdering someone. Also, the cognitive and action aspects of behaviour tend to work in a process where we think, act, think, act, think, act in a complex and iterative way – with the process potentially starting with *either* a thought *or* an act. This *processual* way of looking at thoughts and behaviours is contrasted with the typically modernist *linear* way in Figure 3.3.

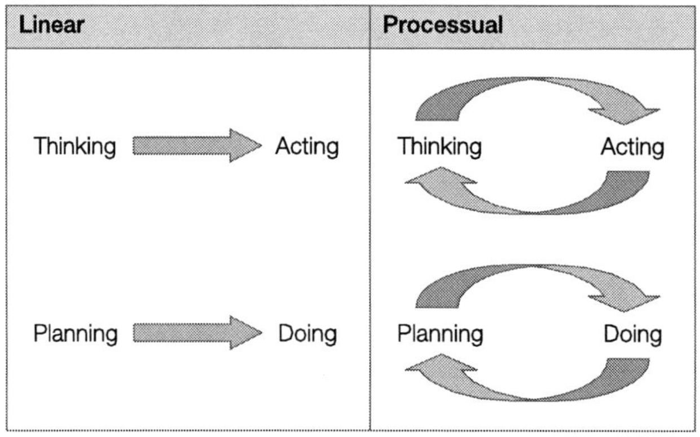

FIGURE 3.3 Linear and processual relationships between cognition and action

At its simplest, this means that human beings are typically thinking about or planning their activities as part of the same process of actively dealing with the world. We think as we act, we act as we think. Sometimes managers give emphasis to the thinking side of things before they act ('shall I go to visit customers today or shall I stay in the office?'). And sometimes they prioritise actions ('I just had to deal with the letters, e-mails, phone calls, knocks on the office door that *came at me* through the working day'), reflecting or 'thinking' after these events just what might have been achieved ('have I wasted my time today or have I helped move the business forward?'). These latter thoughts, which might pass through a manager's mind while driving home at night, could be thought of as the manager identifying the 'goals' or 'objectives' which can be attached to what they did that day – to make sense of that day.

We have illustrated these rather basic matters about human behaviour and social activity with fairly simple and relatively individualistic behaviours. But the insights that we are trying to crystallise with Figure 3.3 are ones that are relevant at other levels of analysing work and its organisation. It is highly relevant to assumptions we tend to make about many areas of our personal lives and about how decision making and strategy making occur in organisations. And we shall see that it is especially relevant to how we understand matters of organisational decision making (Chapter 6, p. 215) and organisational strategies (Chapter 9, p. 359).

There is one more very important dualism that we have to consider before we move towards setting out a frame of reference that is less 'either–or' than typical modernist ways of thinking about human beings and their social existence. This is the separation that is made between what we think and what we say (or write) – the separating of *language* and *action*.

Language and action

A different view of *language* and how we use it is fundamental to the way in which many philosophers and social scientists are encouraging us to move beyond the limitations of modernist assumptions about human behaviour. In what is often called the *linguistic turn* in philosophy (a 'turn' which, later, came to influence organisation theory) thinkers like Austin and Wittgenstein questioned the idea that what we say is something that can be separated either from what we think or what we do (see Further Reading on language and discourse, p. 109). It is normal, within everyday common-sense thinking (Chapter 1, p. 10), to assume that when we say or write something we are reporting what is 'in our heads'. We have a thought, in the privacy of our individual mind, so to speak, and then we express or 'externalise' it. The only exception to this normal way of communicating that we recognise is the lie – a deliberate attempt to deceive people. However, if we apply critical common-sense thinking to the common assumption that speech simply externalises what is 'in the head', we will recognise two things. First, we recognise that thinking cannot happen separately from language-use (speaking or writing) and, second, we realise that thinking should not be separated off as something which either precedes or follows speaking. Speech (or writing) is action in itself. Let us look at each of these points in turn.

First, let us deal with the argument that thoughts cannot precede language. We need words as concepts to form our thoughts in the first place. We cannot think, 'I shall go and serve that customer' without the concepts or linguistic devices of 'go', 'serve' and 'customer'. In a sense, then, we are already talking when we are thinking – talking to ourselves in a sense. This means that no thought is totally personal, private or 'individualistic' – it has to use concepts taken from the culture or 'language community' to which the thinker belongs. Not only this, but we must also recognise that one is not only 'talking to oneself' when this thinking occurs. In a sense, all thinking is *relational* – one is rehearsing what one might say, or has said previously, to another person. Sometimes this happens more clearly than at other times and the thinking process in which Grant Park engaged is a clear example of how one can, in effect, enter a dialogue with oneself *in one's head*. In this case Grant is prompted by the prospect of a particular person, Marjorie, arriving on the scene. But he might have considered other people, too, and imagined having dialogues with them. Grant might well move on from thinking what he might say to Marjorie to imagine himself mentally 'debating' with the writer of the article in a magazine he read about how too much coffee can be harmful. We might also imagine him 'arguing' with a colleague who recently accused him of being incapable of concentrating for long on a work task. We might even picture him 'disputing' in his mind with his mother about her suspicion that Grant is becoming addicted to coffee. Thought, then, is very much a social, relational and indeed *rhetorical* matter (Billig, 1987). Arguments are set one against another as we engage with the world mentally; the decisions that emerge from any thinking process have to be understood as having this social or *relational* nature.

Activity 3.3

Reread the story of Grant Park and his coffee-drinking activities (Case 3.1). Envisage him continuing to ponder upon why he has left his desk yet again to visit the coffee machine, and try to imagine other people he might 'bring to mind' and what they might 'say' to him and what he might 'say' to them in his thoughts.

Second, we have to abandon the Cartesian dualism between *speech* and *action*. At the heart of the *linguistic turn* in philosophy was the recognition that *speech is action*. When we speak to someone we are *acting with regard* to that other person, not simply reporting our thoughts to them. This was always understood with respect to some speech acts like attempts to persuade or command someone to do something. What we need to recognise is that all communication has this dimension to it, even where it is not immediately obvious. No speech act is a simple 'reporting' of what is in the speaker's mind or a simple 'description' of what they have seen or done. We can turn to philosophers like Austin (1962) to tell us that language is action or to social scientists like Goffman (1959) to point out that all communication involves a 'presentation of self' dimension ('how will I be regarded if I speak this way rather than that?'). But the application of critical common sense will remind us that we learned this kind of thing for ourselves when we were children. In fact, we all learn early in life that when people speak they are not straightforwardly describing what the case is, or straightforwardly reporting the world. When a parent tells us something so seemingly straightforward as, 'It is warm outside – the sun is shining', we put these words in context and think to ourselves 'Aha, I wonder if it is really warm enough for me? Could it be that my father is trying to get me to get out of the house?'. We all operate in this way when we listen to people. 'She would say that, wouldn't she?', we think to ourselves when someone tells us that they are the best qualified person in the office to undertake a certain job. In ordinary life we put into context whatever we hear, endlessly applying the proverbial 'pinch of salt' to what people say.

In spite of our all having this very commonsensical understanding that when people speak to us they are 'acting towards us', it is often suspended when we do social science research, engage in market research surveys or try to interpret employee questionnaires. Typically, when we carry out surveys or get people to complete psychological questionnaires, we take what they say as if were 'the case'. We take it that if 70 per cent of people tick a box to indicate that they enjoy their work, then it is the case that this proportion of people take pleasure in what they do at work. Little thought is given to the possibility that, for some reason, some of these people might have decided that this would be a 'good' or an impressive thing to say, or that they might be attempting to persuade the sponsor of the investigation that this is so (or persuade themselves, for that matter). Why do so many of us become dopes in this way once we move into an allegedly 'scientific' type of activity? Why do we suspend our critical faculties?

A possible answer to this question is that people tend to hope, against their better judgement, that these seemingly scientific procedures can produce a degree of certainty about other human beings that, in normal everyday life, we know to be impossible. This parallels the hope for certainty, predictability and control that probably lies behind the faith that many managers have in organisational or managerial 'systems' – a faith connected with the systems-control orthodoxy. They aspire to management becoming a science or, at least, becoming a systematic activity similar to engineering. In our ordinary lives we are well aware, in the famous cliché, that trying to manage or control people is like trying to herd cats (see Chapter 1, p. 3). But such are the pressures on many people in managerial work to achieve the near impossible, that it is comforting to take up a faith in the various sorts of quasi-scientific devices that involve asking people questions and then assuming that their answers 'reveal' the attitudes or beliefs that exist 'inside their heads'. It becomes too easy to forget that what people say in any situation is an act taking place within a social and cultural process. We need to remember that what people say or write cannot be interpreted without regard to those processes and the relationships between the people involved in that situation. Statements must never be 'taken out of context', we might say. This pushes us towards adopting a process-relational frame of reference for looking at people and organisations.

A process-relational framing of individuals in their human and cultural context

It is now possible to outline a broad process-relational framework for applying to the more individual side of the individual/structural duality (duality not dualism!). Table 3.1 sets out its main features, alongside the systems-control orthodoxy that it tries to go beyond. This table can be looked at in conjunction with Table 1.4.

It could be argued that what are outlined in Table 3.1 are simply two ways of talking about human psychology. This is true in part. There are words in the process-relational column like 'making sense', 'enactment', 'orientation' and 'narrative' that do not play a part in systems-control language. And some of the terms that are widely used in orthodox psychological language, especially 'personality', 'attitude' and 'motivation', do not play a part in the process-relational way of speaking about human beings and their behaviour. In other cases, similar words are used, but they have undergone a conceptual shift – with 'memory' or 'reason and emotion' being spoken of in different ways across the two 'languages'. While it is reasonable to talk of these two frames of reference as two languages, it would nevertheless be profoundly wrong to suggest that they are *merely* two languages in the sense of their being simply two ways of talking about the same thing. To take such a line would be to ignore the fundamental point that language – how we talk and write about the world – cannot be separated from what we *do* in the world in this way.

Table 3.1 Systems-control and process-relational views of the human individual

The systems-control view of individuals	The process-relational view of individuals
The individual is a more or less fixed entity with a given *personality*	The individual is always in a process of becoming with an *identity* which is always 'emergent', never finalised
People *perceive* the world which is external to them and cognitively process the *data* which this perception 'inputs' to the brain to enable a *decision* to be made about how to behave	People *enact* the world. In the light of the *language* and understandings of their *culture*, the individual actively *makes sense* of the *ambiguous* world of which they are a part, and then acts in the light of these *interpretations*
Behaviour occurs, in the light of data gathered, as the individual is *motivated* to fulfil *needs and wants*	Actions take place, in the light of interpretations made about the world, to *enact* whatever *projects* individuals are undertaking *strategically* to *shape their lives* and to manage *existential challenges*
Knowledge and information which people hold as data about the world can be acquired from others or communicated to others	Knowledge and understandings about the world are negotiated as people work together at making sense about the world – with some people being more influential than others in establishing 'how things are'
Learning involves acquiring knowledge or skills through experience and acquisition of knowledge from others	Learning is a process of changing – through experience, dialogues and 'negotiation of realities' with others – understandings of how the world 'works' and how one can skilfully operate within that world
Individuals acquire *attitudes* towards various aspects of the world as they are influenced by other people in society to be predisposed to act in certain ways with regard to those aspects of the world	Individuals have continuously *emergent orientations* towards various aspects of the world, which shift as individuals come to terms with changing situations and make sense of them in the light of their life-shaping and situational projects and in light of the *discourses* and *linguistic resources* available to them in the culture
Remembering involves *recalling* information from the memory – where it was recorded when the individual acquired it from direct experience or communication by others	Remembering involves *reconstructing* experiences or knowledge in the light of current circumstances and the *narratives* about the world which are available in the culture with which the individual engages
Individuals have both *emotions* and a capacity to reason; they are capable of putting emotions to one side to enable rational analysis and decision making to occur unaffected by feelings and values	Rationality and *emotion* are simultaneously involved in all thought and action; rational analysis and decision making cannot occur unaffected by feelings and values – but *reflective reasoning* is possible which takes into account that feelings and values are part of it

To conceptualise the world in different ways is to *frame it* in different ways – to position ourselves differently with regard to it. For example, work supervisors who adopt a systems-control frame of reference and think about their staff as people who are motivated by certain needs which they bring to the workplace are likely to develop a particular understanding of those people when considering how to influence their behaviours. However, supervisors who work with a process-relational view of their staff are likely to take into account the more subtle aspects of their staff and hence be better placed to influence employee behaviour. Their greater awareness of how each individual has their own identity, emotions and personal projects inside and outside of work makes them better placed when it comes to influencing staff behaviour. Also, they are more likely to recognise the extent to which people change as their life circumstances change. And they will be more aware of the extent to which understandings and behaviours are things to be negotiated within the employment relationship, as opposed to matters imposed by a system or by managerial command.

The process-relational view of human individuals suggests that the most helpful way for us to understand our fellow human beings is as:

- *emergent*: people's identity is always in the process of becoming; the person is not a fixed entity with an 'essence' and a given 'personality'; they are continually adjusting to the world and learning;
- *social*: a person's distinct individuality is only possible through their relating to others ('I am only me and you are only you because you see me as me and I see you as you', we might say);
- *strategic* and *situationally sensitive*: people always act with regard to their specific context, given their broader projects in life and what they currently regard their identity to be;
- *exchanging*: people's physical and their psychological survival both depend upon give-and-take exchanges with others; they exchange meaning-giving and emotional resources as well as material goods or necessities;
- *rational and emotional*: people's reasoning capacities and their feelings mutually influence each other in everything they do; to relate to others and to influence others they must take into account the feelings of others as well as their rationality;
- *culturally, linguistically and discursively located*: people are both enabled and constrained by the cultural and discursive resources available to them; they can only deal with what they can speak of as they struggle to come to terms with the potentially disabling ambiguities of existence; cultures (which individuals both take from and contribute to) contain discourses and narratives which provide resources to be used in making sense about both self and the world;
- *story users*: they tell and listen to narratives about people and the world as a primary way of coming to terms with the world.

Identity and change

The view of the human being that is emerging from all of this is one of someone who has to 'work at' their identity (see Further Reading on identity, p. 107).

Identity *Concept*

Identity is a notion of who a particular person is – in relation to others. It defines in what ways the individual is like other people and in what ways they differ from other people. It has various *self-identities* components (the individual's own notions of self) and *social identities* components (the notions others have of who the person is).

People also have to work at securing their material survival. A person has continually to make adjustments in their thinking and their actions as they come to terms with the changing circumstances of their existence. They can be seen as *strategic* because they must actively shape their lives, their identities and their biographies. Survival depends on this. Without making arrangements to take care of their physical needs they would die. And without developing a sense of self-identity – some consistent notion of who they are, where they have come from and where they might be going – they would lose their sanity. And this would displace them from 'society'. A sane person is someone who has sufficient consistency of 'self' to enable them to relate to other people and for other people to relate to them. Identity is simultaneously individual and social. The person has their own notion of who they are – their *self-identity* – and they are identified by others through the attribution of various *social identities*. However, these are really two parts of the same thing (a 'duality' as opposed to a 'dualism', as we put it earlier). You can only hold a concept of 'who you are' in the light of how other people act towards you. And who others 'take you to be' will be influenced by how you present yourself to them.

Orthodox psychology deals with the issue of each human being having certain consistencies or an 'existential integrity' with the concept of *personality*. This is something which is typically treated as a 'given', as fairly fixed and even as measurable. Process-relational thinking also gives recognition to the notion of a consistency and an integrity to each individual's 'being' (as they see themselves and others see them). However, it treats this as something that is 'worked at' or 'achieved' rather than given, and as something liable to change over time as the person shapes and reshapes themselves in changing circumstances of age and situation. And this does not deny a role to genetic make-up or the nature of one's 'given' body. One may inherit a range of characteristics, from a tendency to depression, say, to a very tall stature, or a black skin. But these will not *determine* who one is. A self-identity and a social identity will still have to be negotiated with the others to whom one relates in life and to the material and emotional exchanges one makes with others in both one's private and working lives. Those processes of negotiation and exchange will take into account an individual's propensity to be depressively ill from time to time, say, or they will deal with the fact that someone is much taller than everyone else in the office where they work, or they will assist with handling the pressures of being one of the few black managers in an organisation.

Activity 3.4

Read what Colin Darnaway says in Case 3.2 about his 'fragility' and some of his life experiences:

- Consider how this relates to the notion of one's identity being something which is not fixed.
- Consider the relationship between Colin's two aspects: his *self-identity* and his *social identity*.
- Try to think of situations in your own life when you found your sense of 'who you are' threatened by something which happened to you.
- Try to think of situations in your own life when you found your sense of 'who you are' being enhanced by something which happened to you.

Colin's shifting self-identity

Case 3.2

When I was told out of the blue just before Christmas that the company I had been with for ten years was going to make me redundant I took the experience very badly. To come to terms with what was happening to me I found myself looking back to some experiences I had when I was quite young.

When I was about 12 my parents moved house and I had to go to a school which was completely different from the one I had previously attended. In the first school I was top of the class and the teachers used to point to me as an example to other kids. I liked this. It made me feel good. It was almost too good to be true, with the teachers, the other pupils and my parents all reinforcing my idea of myself as somebody a bit special. I came to earth with a crash when I arrived at the other school. There were other kids cleverer than me and I was rather looked down upon. This bothered me a lot. I began to feel like a stupid person. This got so bad that one day when we were doing mental arithmetic in class I found that I couldn't even answer the simple questions. I was laughed at by the class and by the teacher. I went home that night humiliated. And for months after that I was simply a different person from what I had been before we moved. The bright and lively kid was now the dull and stupid kid. But my parents were very good about this and they kept pointing out that, to them, I was the same person I had always been. They persuaded me that I should think of myself the way they did, and the way my grandparents did. I suppose that they persuaded me to 'believe in myself', whatever others tried to make out about me.

So this was something that went through my mind a lot when I lost my job. My company, who had always rated me very highly, had now decided that I was surplus to requirements. I took this to mean that I was useless. It certainly reminded me of those experiences at school. 'Pride before a fall', perhaps. But I also realised that I had to come to terms with this personal 'fragility' which seemed to be part of my life. I had thought about this a lot when I was in my final year at school and I was beginning to go out with girls. I remember so clearly an occasion when I made a date with a girl who I thought was the most magical creature I had ever seen. For a whole week before the Saturday night I was to go out with her I was on top of the world. I felt tall, handsome – the epitome of male desirability. But when Saturday night came I not only tripped over and spilled beer down my new shirt within minutes of meeting the girl, I later got my face slapped by her when I tried to kiss her as we were queuing to get into a club. I tell you, I never felt so small and useless in my life. The next day I couldn't even get out of bed. For months I was, as my friends kept saying, 'a different person'.

I know all this sounds a bit pathetic, but I don't think I am desperately more fragile than other people I know. I got over the late teens uselessness like I had got over the early school experience. At that time I got support from my family and a couple of good mates at school. And with this redundancy thing I realised that I had to reinvent myself yet again. At first my wife was very strange with me and, let me tell you, if this had continued I would have been finished. If she had followed through the threat to leave me, which she made at one point, I would definitely have become a pisshead – a useless unemployed drunk. But I persuaded myself that I was really still the person I had thought myself to be. I made sure that I presented myself to potential employers as a really good worker whose previous employer had been foolish enough to let go. This wasn't easy. But here I am now. I have got an even better job. They've given me a company car, after only six months with them. I am a successful man. I have a great marriage. That's who I am now.

In looking at how there are 'ups and downs' in Colin's self-identity, we can see situations in which the identity he is 'given' by others influences his self-identity (his teachers at one school 'building him up', the teachers at another 'taking him down' for example). At other times, we see his self-identity influencing the social identity he persuades others to attach to him (the way he negatively presents himself to the girlfriend, for instance, or the positive way he 'presents himself' to later employers). But, in spite of the fact that Colin is implying that he is one person at certain times of his life and another person at another, we should not treat this as denying any consistency of 'self' over his biography. While it is wise to move away from the orthodox psychological notion of a fixed personality, we still need to recognise that there is something of the 'same Colin' running through his biography. This partly comes from matters external to him – the body he is born with and the parents he is born to for example. But it is also something that he achieves by the way he *strategically* shapes his own life and his sense of self. The very act of speaking about his post-redundancy reflections is part of this shaping. He is both telling us and *telling himself* 'who he is'.

Coming to terms with the shifting or *emergent* nature of identity is vital to the understanding of work and managerial behaviour. However, some of the key features of the process-relational framing of human beings and their behaviour still need more explanation.

Narratives and stories in culture and identity work

The challenges that face us as human beings as we develop our identities and come to terms with what we ought or ought not do in our lives are almost infinite. But if we tried to reflect deeply on everything we do and to agonise over every choice facing us – from how to cut our hair and what clothes to wear, to how to treat our families or other people at work – we would go crazy. To give too much thought to the risks we take every time we cross the road or to dwell too long on how we will eventually die could drive us to distraction. How do we cope with all of this then? In part, we cope through our direct relationships with people around us. As children, for example, a lot of help and guidance comes directly from our parents and teachers. But this is not enough.

The resources of meaning that are needed for each of us to work out who we are, where we are going and how we are to handle the normal fears of human existence are far too great for them to be supplied by our families or close associates. The guidance comes, instead, from a vast range of 'others' who exist in the culture of the society in which we live – albeit guidance that is mediated by those to whom we directly relate. We tend to know about these cultural 'others' from the stories we hear, see and read about. We constantly make reference, throughout our lives to 'cultural others' – people who may be living or dead, 'real' or fictional. We exchange with the culture we live in by listening to and telling stories.

Narratives and stories *Concept*

Narratives are accounts of the world which follow a basic form of 'this, then that, then that' and which, when applied to human affairs, typically take on a more developed *story*-like form involving characters with interests, motives, emotions and moralities.

How the world 'is' is not a given. We have to 'make up' our understanding of it. Hence, we learn about it, and teach others about it, to a large extent through narratives (see Further Reading on narratives and organisational story-telling, pp. 108–9). From the stories our parents tell us about their past or what they have been doing at work to the fairy tales they tell us and the stories we read in comics or see on television, we find resources to use in working out who we are and how we might live our lives. This goes on throughout our lives as we engage with gossip at work, read murder stories in novels and newspapers, watch soap operas on television or read case studies and tales of business heroes in management books.

This process of working out our identities and how we are going to act in the world through engagement with the 'cast of thousands' who inhabit the cultures we relate to is only partly a conscious one. We 'use' stories as an alternative to engaging in the sort of continual and exhausting rational decision making which would undermine our sanity. To be a cultural being is to be a user of stories – someone who comes to terms with the world by listening to and telling stories. The clearest example of the non-conscious functioning of stories in our lives is the role they play in dealing with our fear of death. Most of us, most of the time, do not consciously worry about death. But this has not been handled by the evolving human species managing to 'forget' about mortality – quite the opposite in fact. In modern societies, most of us confront death several times a day, albeit through stories. Our engagement with 'the news' is typically an engagement with death and agony, as is much of our novel reading and film watching. Stories give us a way of confronting horrors (the horror of marital infidelity, the horror of our house burning down, the horror of being murdered or the horror of losing our job) by taking us into the experiences of 'others' (real or fictional) and then reassuring us by giving the comfort of leaving the cinema, switching off the television or closing the newspaper. The archetype of all of these stories is, of course, the child's fairy tale. This is typically structured so that it frightens the child with its cast of giants, monsters, ghosts, devils and goblins before seeking a resolution in the victory of good over evil and an assurance that everyone 'lived happily ever after'. It would seem that countless cultures have recognised that the use of the story to frighten and then reassure the child enables the child to sleep better at night than it would if the horrors of the world were denied. The same explanation can be offered of why most of us, as adults, read news stories, watch films, pass on 'urban myths', tell jokes – and all the rest – that deal with the worries of adult life. There are, of course, narratives of joy, fulfilment and delight in all cultures. But typically stories make sense of these by setting them against their possible or actual loss.

In the process of the narrative-based engagement with culture, human beings are helped to negotiate a social order and work out a morality. And they are offered sense-making resources that help them work out an identity for themselves and help them make choices about the sort of work they want to do. Jane Cawdor gives us some insight into this when she talks about how she came into managerial work.

Activity 3.5

Read Jane Cawdor's account in Case 3.3 of some of the stories which helped her shape a notion of who she is and influenced her career interests. Ask yourself whether:

- you can think of any stories which you heard or read in childhood, or since, which have played a part in the shaping of your identity or your career interests;
- the stories you tend to hear about managers and managerial life would tend to encourage or discourage somebody contemplating becoming a manager themselves.

Jane Cawdor's stories of heroines and engineers

Case 3.3

Most of my friends from school went into the health service or into teaching and they thought that I was strange becoming an engineer. I don't know what they would think of me now being the chief executive of an engineering company. But I must admit that when I was at school I got tired of hearing all those stories about how girls had gone on to university and then came back to the town to teach in one of the local schools. And I definitely took offence at the stories that some of my friends' parents used to tell about girls who had gone into nursing and then ended up as doctors' wives. Yuk! Come to think of it, though, there was a time when I thought I might like to be a doctor. I think that was something to do with a story my own parents told me – to counter these other tales of soppy nurses I think – where a friend of theirs had got really good exam results and, instead of going to be a nurse like her friends, went to medical school and became a doctor herself. I wonder if they made that up to persuade me to do more homework?

I suspect my parents had noticed that I always liked stories and books about women who were outstandingly successful in some way. However, that was only part of what got me on the track of becoming an engineering manager. I think the stories that influenced me here were my father's stories of when he was in the army; a lot of stuff about building bridges and mending tanks under enemy fire. This appealed to me and sometimes when I feel that I am 'under fire' in this present job, I think back to those stories and try to see myself as the heroic figure who is going to win through. I'll be the woman that leads the company through its battles, beats the competition and defends people's jobs.

Managers, then, can be seen as 'users' of stories in their personal identity management or 'self-shaping'. However, stories have a further significance for many people involved in managerial work. In all societies there are people who make a bigger input into the shaping of cultures than others. The politicians, priests, generals and business leaders – whoever the most powerful happen to be in any society – will play a major role in shaping a culture so that the culture's norms and values are supportive of their power and advantage. The powerful within any culture will prefer the stories that are told to be ones which go with the grain of their interests. Story-telling, we might say, is neither politically nor economically innocent. Managers are inevitably caught up in structures and processes of power, with many of them being required to shape the meanings that employees attach to their involvement in an organisation or that customers attach to the products or services that they buy from the organisation. Thus story-telling skills are likely to be relevant to the work tasks of many managers – not least when they are trying to shape the cultures of the organisations in which they work (as we shall see in Chapter 7, pp. 283–9).

When culture was defined earlier, it was said to involve a *system* of meanings. This was meant to recognise that the cultural aspects of societies are in some ways patterned, with the various elements of that patterning being related to each other. We should not go too far with this, however. We must remember, for example, that certain stories told within any culture will contradict other stories in what they encourage people to believe. Cultures provide a multiplicity of sense-making resources on which we draw as we choose our own preferred identity or way of life (to be a social worker, say, rather than the manager of a massage parlour). Nevertheless, the sense-making resources upon which we draw when we 'exchange' with our cultures are patterned in significant ways. We have already alluded to this in noting certain patterns that can be found across seemingly different forms of story-telling. Narratives as diverse as nursery tales and television advertisements, for example, 'play upon' existential anxieties – with monsters threatening to devour children in one case, perhaps, and germs threatening to take over our happy homes in the other – before giving reassurance through the closure of the story or advertisement and the child falling asleep or the viewer contemplating buying the cleaning product. Another form of patterning can be seen in the range of *discourses* which exist in any given society at any particular time in its history.

Discourse, language and human practices

The concept of *discourse*, as it is increasingly used in the social sciences, is one that bridges the concepts of culture and language.

Discourse *Concept*

A set of connected concepts, expressions and statements that constitutes a way of talking or writing about an aspect of the world, thus framing and influencing the way people understand and act with regard to that aspect of the world.

Discursive framing *Concept*

The process whereby human beings draw on sets of discursive resources (concepts, expressions, statements, etc.) made available in their culture to make sense of a particular aspect of their lives and are thereby influenced in the way they conduct themselves in that part of their life.

At this stage we are formalising the notion of 'framing' that we have been using so far in *Organising and Managing Work*. The notion of 'discursive framing' relates to the concept of *discourse*, understood as the set of linguistic resources – concepts, terms, statements, expressions, sayings and so on – that are used to provide a frame of reference for applied sense making in the world (see Further Reading on language and discourse, pp. 109–10). The concept, as it is used here, has some similarities to that developed by Michel Foucault in his influential and controversial historical and social writing (Foucault, 1979, 1980). However, the notion is used here within a conceptual scheme which differs in some significant ways from Foucault's. A powerful illustration of the concept's value is nevertheless seen in Foucault's account of how, over a particular period of western history, the notion of 'being mad' was reframed (as we might say) to one of 'being mentally ill'. Foucault goes further than simply pointing out how various aspects of social life become redefined or re-labelled at different times. A whole set of ideas, terms and practices – a system of talk belief and action, we might say – *sometimes* comes to replace another. Where, at one time, people spoke of someone being 'possessed' by demons which needed to be 'cast out', they later framed the problem as one of that person being 'ill' and needing 'treatment'. It is clear that we have both a shift in language and a shift in practice. There is a shift in *discursive practices*, as it is sometimes put. Deranged people are not only spoken of differently, they are treated differently. Not only this, but they are given a different 'subjectivity' – a different identity.

The danger in this type of thinking is that we can come to treat discourses as determining our practices or dictating to us what our identities are. But this is the same danger – that of *cultural determinism* – which threatens all forms of cultural analysis and encourages us to see human beings as *cultural dopes*. To avoid this, we need to recognise that people are *active* sense makers whose identities and understandings of the world are not *determined* by culture. People are nevertheless powerfully constrained in terms of what they can 'be' and what they can do by the discursive patterns of their culture. There is a mixture of choice and constraint. Because there are varieties and variations in the discourses which are current in any given social order at any particular time, people can, to some extent, draw on different *discursive resources* when shaping themselves, their lives and their practices. If, today, one found oneself regularly going berserk and out of control one could choose to define oneself as mad and either seek a priest to drive out one's demons or try to channel that madness into some creative artistic activity. Alternatively, one could define oneself as mentally ill and go to seek medical treatment. However, if one was living in an earlier age, when the discursive resources of mental illness, psychiatry and so on had not yet been devised, one would not face the option of defining oneself as a mentally sick person, let alone going to seek treatment.

Activity 3.6

Look closely at what Mike Kilrock has to say in Case 3.4 about himself to support his application to be promoted in his organisation and

- identify as many as you can of the discursive resources which Mike draws upon to make his case to the interviewing panel;
- try to identify any of the discourses that Mike draws these ideas from.

Mike Kilrock promotes himself

Case 3.4

'I am sure that you have all carefully read my CV and that you can see how I have developed myself over the past few years to make myself worthy of promotion to this important post. The first thing I want to draw your attention to are my leadership qualities. You can see how I have built up successful teams who really have delivered and have increased business in their areas. I think that if you speak to any of the people who have worked for me, they will tell you that I am someone with vision and someone who really can make a difference.

I am not just someone who gets things done, though. I am very much an entrepreneur. I know that this organisation has got to find new opportunities and find new markets. The world does not owe us a living and you will be aware that I was responsible for several of the new initiatives that have occurred in my region. And I hope that my professionalism is also apparent in everything that I do. I have all the technical qualifications that are important in our area of activity and I know that all my clients feel that they benefit from the discretion and confidentiality I apply in all my dealings with them.

I will now be pleased to answer any questions you wish to put to me. Do tell me if anything is unclear in my application or if there is anything further that you want to know about the contributions that I have already made to developing this firm into one of the most successful in the country. My vision and ambition is to see us being recognised as the country's leading funeral directing business.'

Almost every concept that Mike uses is, inevitably, a discursive resource that is related to one or another of the discourses that make up the culture in which both he and his interviewers live. But three discourses, or clusters of discursive resources, are drawn upon in particular in this piece of self-advancement occurring in a promotion interview: discourses of leadership, enterprise and professionalism.

- The discursive resource of 'leadership qualities' is clearly part of a set of concepts and terms that constitutes a particular discourse about *leadership* which exists in modern cultures. In fact Mike uses several other discursive resources from that cluster of concepts: 'building a team', 'vision' and 'making a difference'.
- He then moves on, with his claim to be an entrepreneur, to a discourse of *enterprise*. He uses from that particular 'language game' (as the philosopher Wittgenstein might label it) concepts of opportunity, initiative, market and the notion of the world 'not owing one a living'.
- He then, ingeniously, moves from this discursive realm to one that is often seen as a rival to the entrepreneurial one – that of *professionalism*. Here he draws on that set of cultural ideas which recognises certain occupations as being special, by virtue of their control of specialist knowledge and their rules of treating *clients* with confidentiality and with discretion.

We should note with reference to this third discursive area that the discursive resource of 'client', which is a key concept within the discourse of professionalism, is used rather than the concept of 'customer' – a discursive resource which plays a correspondingly key role within the discourse of enterprise. Mike Kilrock, in fact, is showing great skill and cunning in carefully selecting elements from different, and partly rival, discourses to help construct a case for his own promotion. Such a skill has been identified elsewhere as one of *discursive ingenuity* (Watson, 2001d). And we should assume that everyone is as discursively ingenious or, we might say, rhetorically skilled. Much of the time we all accept as taken for granted the discursively located subjectivities offered within our cultures.

Mike Kilrock is working to construct an occupational identity to sell to his employer a notion of himself as a businessperson, a leader and a 'professional', all at the same time. It is interesting to note that he does not use the discursive resource of 'manager'. The concept of 'manager' is very much a product of a particular historical period – as were Foucault's 'mad person' and his 'mentally ill person'. In modern times one can choose to 'become a manager' only because there is a discourse current which makes such a self-conception or occupational identity possible. But if one were living in fifteenth century France or seventeenth century Britain this would not have been possible. There were undoubtedly people in those times and places who earned a living of some kind through 'organising work activities', as we might put it in twenty-first century terms. But to try to understand what somebody was doing in that period when they were directing the efforts of others in a field or farm by applying the concepts of a modern management discourse would not give us much insight into either the practices or the thinking of those people. We would have to consider what discursive practices and resources were used in that setting: concepts of *master* and *servant* being an obvious starting point.

It is convenient to demonstrate the value of the concept of discourse by looking at fairly clear historical examples of how thought, language and practices change over time in a closely associated way. But this concept is equally valuable for looking at contemporary situations. In the first place, it can help us understand how power and authority is being exerted in both societal and organisational settings. The politician or manager who can influence how others frame the realities they experience is going to be well placed to exert authority over them. In the second place, the concept of discourse is helpful because it gives us a tool for understanding patterns of contemporary change. We might point here, at one level of analysis, to discourses of workplace *empowerment* appearing in some organisations (see Chapter 7) and, at another level, to a discourse of *globalisation* being used to come to terms with, and shape behaviours within, changing international patterns. In the third place, we are sensitised to the contested nature of the social and organisational arrangements that we make. We are, for example, prompted to be aware of the existence of alternative or rival discourses which might be current at the same time – even within the same organisation. We might see, for example, a contest within a single organisational management over whether a 'worker empowerment' discourse should be developed or a discourse of 'management's responsibility to manage' should continue to prevail. Similarly, we might see the senior managers of a police organisation taking different views of whether the discourse of a 'police force' should be replaced with a discourse of a 'police service'. The managers in these cases do not themselves use the concepts of *discourse, discursive framing, discursive practices* or *discursive resources*. These are nevertheless invaluable conceptual tools that we can use to analyse in a process-relational manner the issues that are arising and the events that are occurring in these organisations. And, were it the case that these managers themselves had this conceptual equipment to hand, it can be argued, they too would be better placed to make sense of the challenges with which they are dealing.

In the next chapter we shall be using some of the concepts that have been introduced in recent pages to look at a variety of individuals and their organisational and managerial involvements. Focus will be given to the application of concepts we have developed here – ones like emergent identity, narrative and discourse – with the use of the key concepts of *work orientation, implicit contract* and *strategic exchange*. There will then be a return to the issues of *emotion* and *stress* and the roles these play in work experience generally and managerial work specifically before moving to analysing the whole range of activities that can be characterised as 'organisational mischief' – with some reflection on the deeper significance in human life of humour and joking.

Summary

In this chapter the following key points have been made:

- The behaviour of human beings in contemporary situations can only be fully understood if it is seen in the context of how human beings, as a species, have developed *cultures* and *cultural resources* to help them handle fundamental problems which are unique to the species.
- Within the variety of cultures and institutional arrangements which human beings have devised over their history as a species, the specific institutions and cultural priorities of *industrial capitalism* have come to dominate recent human history. Modern work organisations and the occupation of 'management' are to be understood as elements of this modern form of economy and society.
- It is very common to talk and write about human individuals as entities that can be understood separately from the society or the culture of which they are a part. It is also common to analyse societies or cultures as if they had an existence in some way independent of the people who live within them. By the same token there has been a tendency to speak of individual organisational employees as if their actions could be separated from the organisational processes in which they participate – and vice versa. This kind of either–or thinking needs to be avoided and, although it is useful to distinguish between 'individual' and 'structural' *aspects* of any feature of social life, neither of these should ever be looked at in isolation from the other. To understand any human activity or organisational event we have to look at the interplay between factors of human individuality, choice and sense making on the one hand and the structural and cultural setting in which it occurs on the other.
- Orthodox thinking about work and organisational behaviour has tended to treat the human individual in systems-control terms – as a miniature machine-like system which is 'powered' or 'motivated' by need-satisfying 'fuels' to behave in a certain way. This maintains either–or thinking and encourages an unhelpful separation between the individual and their social/organisational context, between thinking and acting, between reason and emotion and between language and action. It is assumed, for example, that people reason before they act – whereas it is just as possible that a person will act, and then attach a reason, or a motive to that action. Human thinking processes and human behaviours can be better understood by abandoning both this kind of *linearity* in our thinking and the 'either–or' *dualisms* with which it is associated.
- A process-relational frame of reference has considerable advantages over conventional systems-control thinking when trying to understand human behaviour. It recognises that human individuality is always *relational* (only existing in relation to others) and *emergent* (never becoming fixed – always in a process of 'becoming').

- Within a process-relational frame of reference, common psychological concepts such as personality, perception, motivation, needs, attitudes, tend to be avoided. Instead, key concepts are identity, enactment, culture, dialogue, negotiation and sense making. Even where terms are used which sound similar to those used in systems-control language – learning and emotion, for example – they are used in a rather different way in process-relational analysis.
- The cultural resources which people draw upon (and, to a certain extent, themselves create) to help with both everyday sense making and the handling of existential anxieties are patterned in various ways. First, there is the key part played in all cultures of *narratives* and *stories*. Second, there are *discourses* – ways of framing particular aspects of human reality that involve both specific ways of using language and associated patterns of action. Realities are not handled as 'givens' but are framed by people using the discursive resources which are available to them in their culture or which they themselves develop. The fact that some people in societies and organisations are more active than others as 'story-tellers' and some are more *discursively ingenious* when it comes to processes of *discursive framing* than others has important implications for power relationships in general and managerial authority in particular.

Recommended reading

The value of the idea of 'identity' as a means of understanding how managers operate in their organisational contexts is effectively demonstrated by Stefan Sveningsson and Mats Alvesson, 'Managing managerial identities: organizational fragmentation, discourse and identity struggle' (*Human Relations*, 56(10): 1163–1194, 2003). And the advantages of applying the notion of 'narrative' to such matters are set out by Barbara Czarniawska in *A Narrative Approach to Organization Studies* (London: Sage, 1998). To get a good understanding of the much broader issue of deploying the idea of 'discourse' to organisations it is useful to browse through and read selectively from *The Sage Handbook of Organizational Discourse* edited by David Grant, Cynthia Hardy, Cliff Oswick and Linda Putnam (London: Sage, 2004). A closely focused study of managers using just one aspect of discourse, that of 'rhetoric', is to be found in Tony Watson's 'Rhetoric, discourse and argument in organisational sense-making: a reflexive tale' (*Organisation Studies*, 16(5): 805–821, 1995).

Further reading

Further reading Identities

Alvesson, M. and Willmott, H. (2002) 'Identity regulation as organizational control: producing the appropriate individual', *Journal of Management Studies*, 39(5): 619–644

Baumeister, R.F. (1986) *Identity: Cultural change and the struggle for self*, New York: Oxford University Press
Brown, A.D. (2001) 'Organization studies and identity: towards a research agenda', *Human Relations*, 54(1): 113–121
Collinson, D.L. (2003) 'Identities and insecurities: selves at work', *Organization* 10(3): 527–547
Czarniawska-Joerges, B. (1996) 'Autobiographical acts and organizational identities' in S. Linstead, R. Grafton Small and P. Jeffcutt (eds) *Understanding Management*, London: Sage
du Gay, P. (1995) *Consumption and Identity at Work*, London: Sage
Foucault, M. (1980) *Power/Knowledge: Selected interviews and other writings*, Brighton: Harvester
Giddens, A. (1991) *Modernity and Self-identity: Self and society in the modern age*, Cambridge: Polity
Goffman, E. (1959) *The Presentation of Self in Everyday Life*, Harmondsworth: Penguin
Hassard, J., Holliday, R. and Willmott, H. (eds) (2000) *Body and Organization*, London: Sage
Kondo, D.K. (1990) *Crafting Selves: Power, gender and discourse of identity in a Japanese workplace*, Chicago: University of Chicago Press
McKinlay A. and Starkey K. (eds) (1997) *Foucault, Management and Organization Theory: From panopticon to technologies of self*, London: Sage
Mead, G.H. (1962) *Mind, Self and Society*, Chicago: University of Chicago Press
Miller, P. and O'Leary, T. (1987) 'Accounting and the deconstruction of the governable person', *Accounting, Organizations and Society*, 12(3): 235–265
Sveningsson S. and Alvesson, M. (2003) 'Managing managerial identities: organizational fragmentation, discourse and identity struggle', *Human Relations*, 56(10): 1163–1194
Taylor, C. (1989) *Sources of the Self: The making of the modern identity*, Cambridge, MA: Harvard University Press
Watson, D.H. (1996) 'Individuals and institutions: the case of work and employment' in M. Wetherell (ed.) *Identities, Groups and Social Issues*, London: Sage

Further reading Narratives and organisational story-telling

Betelheim, B. (1976) *On the Uses of Enchantment: The meaning and importance of fairy tales*, New York: Knopf
Boje, D.M. (1991) 'The storytelling organisation: a study of storytelling performance in an office-supply firm', *Administrative Science Quarterly*, 38(4): 106–126
Boje, D.M. (2001) *Narrative Methods for Organizational and Communication Research*, London: Sage
Boje, D.M., Alvarez, R.C. and Schooling, B. (2001) 'Reclaiming story in organization: narratologies and action sciences' in R. Westwood and S. Linstead (eds) *The Language of Organization*, London: Sage, 132–175
Brown, A.D. and Humphreys, M. (2003) 'Epic and tragic tales: making sense of change', *Journal of Applied Behavioral Science*, 39(2): 121–144
Bruner, J. (1987) 'Life as narrative', *Social Research*, 5(1): 11–32
Bruner, J. (2002) *Making Stories: Law, literature, life*, New York: Farrar, Straus and Giroux

Currie, G. and Brown, A.D. (2003) 'A narratological approach to understanding processes of organizing in a UK hospital', *Human Relations*, 56(5): 563–586
Czarniawska, B. (1998) *A Narrative Approach to Organization Studies*, London: Sage
Czarniawska, B. (1999) *Writing Management: Organization theory as a literary game*, Oxford: Oxford University Press
Gabriel, Y. (1998) 'Same old story or changing stories? Folkloric, modern and postmodern mutations' in D. Grant, T. Keenoy and C. Oswick (eds) *Discourse and Organisation*, London: Sage
Gabriel, Y. (2004) 'The narrative veil' in Y. Gabriel (ed.) *Myths, Stories and Organizations: Premodern narratives for our time*, Oxford: Oxford University Press
Hatch, M.J. (1996) 'The role of the researcher: an analysis of narrative position in organisation theory', *Journal of Management Enquiry*, 5(4): 359–374
Humphreys, M. and Brown, A.D. (2002) 'Narratives of organizational identity and identification: a case study of hegemony and resistance', *Organization Studies*, 23(3): 421–447
Polkinghorne, D.E. (1988) *Narrative Knowing and the Human Sciences*, Albany, NY: State University of New York Press
Richardson, L. (1995) 'Narrative and sociology' in J. Van Maanen (ed.) *Representations in Ethnography*, Thousand Oaks, CA: Sage
Sims, D. (2003) 'Between the millstones: a narrative account of the vulnerability of middle managers' storying', *Human Relations*, 56(10): 1195–1212
Sims, D. and Galpin, S. (1999) 'Narratives and identity in flexible working and teleworking organizations' in P. Jackson (ed.) *Virtual Working: Social and organizational dynamics*, London: Routledge, 76–94

Further reading Language and discourse

Alvesson, M. and Karreman, D. (2000) 'Taking the linguistic turn in organizational research: challenges, responses, consequences', *Journal of Applied Behavioral Science*, 36: 136–158
Austin, J.L. (1962) *How to do Things with Words*, Oxford: Oxford University Press
Bahktin, M.M. (1981) *The Dialogic Imagination*, Austin, TX: University of Texas Press
Billig, M. (1987) *Arguing and Thinking: A rhetorical approach to social psychology*, Cambridge: Cambridge University Press
Boden, D. (1994) *The Business of Talk*, Cambridge: Polity
Edwards, D. and Potter, J. (1992) *Discursive Psychology*, London: Sage
Gergen, K. (1991) *The Saturated Self. Dilemmas of identity in contemporary life*, New York: Basic Books
Grant, D., Keenoy, T. and Oswick, C. (eds) (1998) *Discourse and Organisation*, London: Sage
Grant, D., Hardy, C., Oswick, C. and Putnam, L. (2004) *The Sage Handbook of Organizational Discourse*, London: Sage
Harré, R. and Gillet, G. (1994) *The Discursive Mind*, London: Sage
Harré, R. and Stearns, P. (eds) (1995) *Discursive Psychology in Practice*, London: Sage
Jackson, N. and Carter, P. (2000) *Rethinking Organisational Behaviour*, Harlow: FT Prentice Hall
Mumby, D.K. (1988) *Communication and Power in Organizations: Discourse, ideology and domination*, Norwood, NJ: Ablex

Nelson, J.S., Megill, A. and McCloskey, D.N. (1987) *The Rhetoric of the Human Sciences: Language and argument in scholarship and human affairs*, Madison, WI: University of Wisconsin Press

Potter, J. and Wetherall, M. (1987) *Discourse and Social Psychology: Beyond attitudes and behaviour*, London: Sage

Watson, T.J. (1995) 'Rhetoric, discourse and argument in organisational sense-making: a reflexive tale', *Organisation Studies*, 16(5): 805–821

Watson, T.J. (1997) 'Languages within languages: a social constructionist perspective on multiple managerial discourses' in F. Bargiela-Chiappini and S. Harris (eds) *The Language of Business*, Edinburgh: Edinburgh University Press

Watson, T.J. (2000) 'Discourse and organisation' (review article), *Human Relations*, 53(4): 559–597

Westwood, R. and Linstead, S. (eds) (2001) *The Language of Organization*, London: Sage

CHAPTER 4

Organisations and people: orientations, emotions and mischief

Objectives

Having read this chapter and completed its associated activities, readers should be able to:

- See how a *strategic exchange* perspective can be developed within a process-relational frame of reference to help us understand particular aspects of the relationship between people and organisations.
- Recognise the importance of the *implicit contract*, which is made between the employee and the employing organisation, to an understanding of work behaviour and organisational relationships.
- Apply the concept of *work orientation* to people's involvement in work organisations, appreciating that organisational employees are better understood not as 'motivated' to work in particular ways but as 'oriented' to their work circumstances by the meanings they both bring to the organisation in the first place and by the way these meanings change as they move on through their life and work careers.
- Understand the importance of matters of *emotion* and *feelings* in the work context and come to terms with the fact that these permeate every aspect of organisational activity.
- Recognise that an emotional dimension is sometimes deliberately built into the design of certain kinds of work and that people in various kinds of work, including management, find themselves engaging in *emotional labour*.
- Appreciate how emotional matters are involved in situations of individual stress and how the experience of stress, or work-related distress, can best be understood in terms of an interplay of factors in the organisational circumstances and factors in the individual's own life – especially their 'personal resources'.
- See how practices that can be characterised as *organisational mischief* – from fiddles and sabotage to sexual, joking and 'play' activities – all relate to matters of power, identity and negotiated order in the workplace.
- Recognise the particular significance of sexuality and humour in both challenges and adjustments to organisational controls.

Shaping lives and shaping organisations: a strategic exchange perspective

Within the process-relational way of framing human and organisational activities that has been unfolded over the previous chapters we can now develop a more tightly focused perspective to help us deal with specific aspects of the relationships between organisations and people who work in them. This is the *strategic exchange* perspective. It is intended to draw our attention to two things. First, attention is drawn to the *parallel* that exists between human beings and organisations: the fact that both people and organisations, albeit in different ways, have to make exchanges of various kinds with the world in order to survive in that world into the future. And, second, attention is drawn to a key *link* that exists between people and organisations: the exchanges that occur between organisations and people as part of their survival processes. The idea of organisations existing without some kind of giving to and taking from 'people' is clearly ridiculous. It is possible, however, to envisage people surviving without trading with organisations. But that would only be possible in a very simple society where there were no bureaucratised state bodies or commercial enterprises with which people have to deal in order to participate in society. In modern societies it is out of the question for anyone to contemplate living without some kind of give-and-take relationship with enterprises, institutions, firms and corporations.

The importance of exchange in human existence generally was stressed in Chapter 3 where it was pointed out that people's physical and psychological survival depends upon give-and-take exchanges with others. People exchange meaning-giving and emotional resources as well as material goods or necessities (p. 95). And a proportion of these exchanges is inevitably with organisations – in activities ranging from the buying goods and services from an organisation to the entering of an employment relationship with one of them. It was also recognised that human beings are 'strategic' in the sense of actively shaping their lives, identities and their biographies. People are 'strategic and situationally sensitive' (pp. 94–5): people always act with regard to their specific context, given their broader projects in life and what they currently regard their identity to be.

Although the lives of all of us are influenced and constrained by the social-structural, cultural and other circumstances in which we find ourselves, none of us can simply lie back and adopt a totally passive stance towards the world. It is true, of course, that people vary considerably in how purposefully active ('proactive') they are in shaping their lives. But human survival, in both the physical and psychological senses of the term, requires of everyone a degree of strategic initiative-taking, a degree of life shaping and the pursuit of survival projects. In Table 1.4 (p. 30), where process-relational thinking is contrasted with systems-control ideas about human beings, it was pointed out that people are not best understood as 'need-led'. Rather, they are sense-making and project-oriented creatures who, in the light of how they interpret their situation, make exchanges with others to deal with their material, psychological and emotional circumstances.

People can be seen, then, always to be striving to come to terms with the circumstances in which they find themselves and to shape their existence. Their 'biography' does not just write itself. People, in part, have to be the authors of their identities and biographies. They therefore pursue their projects in life and manage their continuously emerging identities through exchanging meanings and resources with others and, as we argued in Chapter 3, through a 'dialogue' with their cultures. And, here, there is a parallel with organisations.

Organisations are most certainly not people. But their future existence, just like the future existence of the human individual, depends on their making exchanges with others – in this case with customers, suppliers, employees and so on. Both organisations (as sets of understandings and arrangements), and the people involved in them (as individuals with identities and biographies) are shaped and shape themselves to continue their existence into the future. This shaping may be relatively deliberate ('planned') or it might be very reactive, haphazard even.

Strategic exchange

Concept

As both individuals and organisations shape themselves and are shaped to continue their existence into the future, the exchange of material and symbolic resources occurs (a) between individuals and others in their social worlds (including employing organisations) and (b) between organisations and their internal and external constituencies upon which they are resource dependent (including employees).

The concept of strategic exchange draws attention to the interplay that occurs between how people involved with work organisations shape and make sense of their lives and the way organisations themselves are strategically shaped. People make many exchanges, materially and symbolically, with the whole range of people whom they encounter in their lives. The exchange they make with the work organisations in which they become involved, typically in an employment relationship, is an important one for many people. And organisations themselves would be nothing without exchanges made with all of those who become attached to the organisation as owners, workers, managers and so on. The exchange between such individuals and the organisation is represented in Figure 4.1. This exchange is a contractual one – a point we will develop shortly.

This 'interplay' between individual and organisational exchange processes, at the heart of which is a specific contractual exchange, will be seen in many of the cases that we shall encounter in coming chapters. The interplay can be seen in an especially clear way in the story of Peter Brodie in Chapter 5 (Case 5.2, p. 177). We will see there how this chief executive of a charity was simultaneously working to shape his own life and that of the Youth Links organisation which employs him. We will see how the organisation was being shaped, and

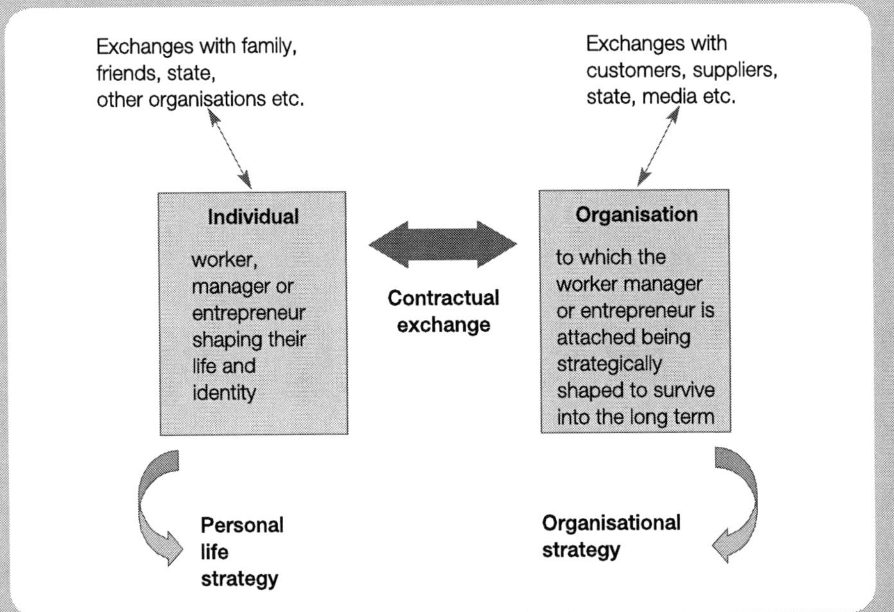

FIGURE 4.1 Individual–organisation exchange in the context of personal life shaping and organisation strategy making

taken forward into the future, through processes of economic, political and social exchange. These exchanges were managed by Peter to ensure that the resources of effort, support, accommodation and so on, needed by the organisation to survive and continue into the long term, were obtained from employees, politicians, police officers, landlords and the rest. He did all this in a way that shaped and expressed his own life and identity at the same time as it shaped the enterprise he was running. And we will see similarly striking evidence of this type of interaction between individual's life-shaping efforts and the strategic managing of a guitar-making firm in Case 9.4 (p. 388) where the entrepreneurial individuals who created a business confront, at the same time, questions about where they are going with their personal lives and questions about the future of the Strath Guitars. In this case the two are very tightly interrelated indeed.

The focus of the present chapter is not so much on the organisational shaping side of the picture presented in Figure 4.1 but on the exchange that occurs between workers and organisations generally. Although we are focusing on one side of the picture, it is vital to recognise that this exchange would not come into being were it not playing a part in the other side of the picture. Organisations, in principle at least, do not pay and otherwise reward people for involvement that has no significance for the strategic shaping of the enterprise as a whole.

Implicit contracts and orientations to work

Our main concern for the present is with the exchange that occurs between organisations and the people working in organisations. This exchange is identified in Figure 4.1 as one of contractual exchange. There is a trade, a 'deal' at the heart of the exchange relationship. And much of this contract is implicit. The normal way for people in a modern society to join a work organisation is to enter into an exchange with that organisation whereby they trade their application of skills and capabilities for a bundle of 'rewards' including cash, security, status, work satisfaction, opportunity for advancement and so on. Certain elements of this exchange are formally agreed and a very limited proportion of it is written in a formal contract of employment or perhaps a more short-term formal contract of engagement. However, the bulk of the 'understanding' that comes about between the employer and the worker is unwritten and is, in large part, unstated. The concept of implicit contract first started to be used (Levinson *et al.*, 1966) at about the same time as the work orientation concept, to which we shall shortly connect it, and is related to the concepts of *effort bargain* (Behrend, 1957, Baldamus, 1961) and *psychological contract* (Schein, 1978). (See also Further Reading on work orientations, implicit and psychological contracts, p. 160.)

Implicit contract

Concept

The tacit agreement between an employing organisation and the employed individual about what the employee will 'put in' to the job and the rewards and benefits for which this will be exchanged.

The implicit contract is clearly a relational matter. It is an exchange between an individual who is seeking employment as part of the way they are strategically shaping their lives to take them into the future and an employer who requires their services to shape its activities to take it into the future. It takes the form of a set of understandings negotiated between the employee and the employer, much of which is unlikely to have been explicitly stated, let alone written into a formal contract. There will be unstated understandings about such matters as how long the job is likely to last, what sort of career advancement might be available or how much overtime can be earned. Inferences will be made about how willing the employee will be to take orders from managers and how adaptable the employee will be if organisational circumstances change. What all of this means is that the employment relationship is a highly ambiguous one. It is also a potentially fragile one, given the very different power positions of the employee, on the one hand, and the employer on the other (an observation central to Marx's classic critique of class relations in capitalist societies).

As the individual approaches the organisation to seek work, they take into the potential relationship more than just the skills and working capacities that they possess. As the strategic exchange perspective highlights, the individual also takes with them an identity and a biography as well as various values and feelings or emotions about the world. The human being approaching engagement with the organisation is a whole human being, not just a human resource. But, as they approach an organisation, many of these aspects of their lives and identities will, in the light of their particular life circumstances at the time, inform a particular meaning which they attach to the work and the job they are going into: a *work orientation* (or 'orientation to work').

Work orientation

Concept

The meaning individuals attach to their work which predisposes them both to think and act in particular ways with regard to that work. There is an *initial orientation* at the point of entry to work and this is liable to change as circumstances and interests change within the continuing employment relationship.

At the stage of approaching engagement with the organisation we can refer to an initial orientation to work, in recognition of the fact that it is liable to develop and change once they have joined the organisation. The concept of orientation to work has its origins in sociological studies that were carried out in the 1960s in Britain. Goldthorpe, Lockwood and their colleagues (1968) developed the concept as they recognised the inadequacy of need-based motivational analyses for understanding the groups of employees that they studied. The concept of work orientation was seen as a more realistic tool for analysing what employees were seeking when they took certain jobs. The researchers argued that to understand the way different groups of workers behaved one should examine what those workers' jobs meant to them and what calculated choices they were making when entering that particular employment. Some people had an orientation to work that caused them to seek jobs which offered promotional opportunities or the opportunities to apply manual skills, for example, while others sought simply to maximise the money they could earn and *discounted* opportunities, say, for job interest or career advancement. Clearly these choices were made in the light of the abilities and aptitudes which people possessed as well as their value preferences. Most famously the study showed that many of the people working in the car assembly factory had chosen this work to maximise the income they could then spend on their families. And this meant forgoing the potentially more satisfying, but lower paid, work that they could have taken, should they have so chosen.

A way of linking the concepts of work orientation and implicit contract, as well as identifying some of the elements of the employment bargain is suggested in Figure 4.2. This recognises that the individual's 'understood deal' or *perceived implicit contract* is at the centre of their work orientation. It does not exist 'in the head' of the worker in isolation from their relationship with the employer but it does play a key part in how they *enact* their work roles and their

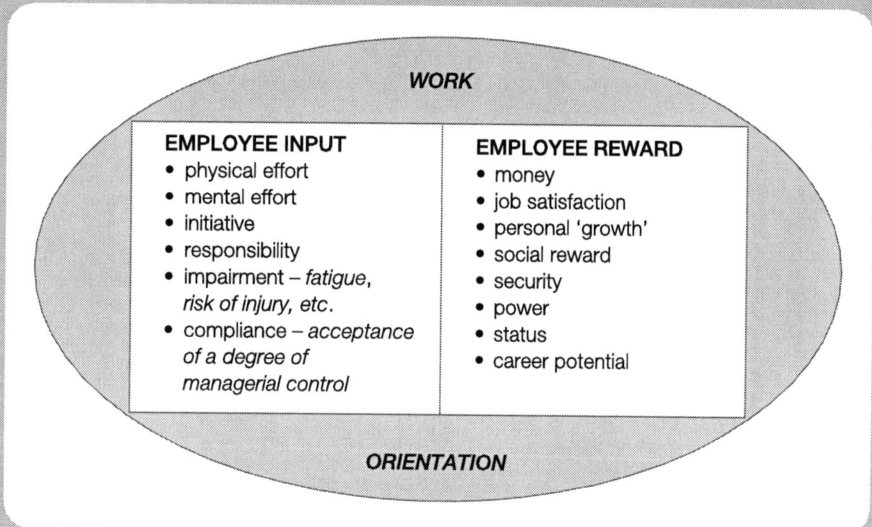

FIGURE 4.2 **The individual worker's perception of their implicit contract with the organisation**

relationships with the managers in the employing organisation. Every employed individual, in the light of their current circumstances, their self-identities, life projects and the rest, has a notion of what they are exchanging with the employer: what mix of *inputs* of physical and mental efforts, the taking of responsibility, willingness to take risks of accident, stress and acceptance of managerial control is being traded with the employer for a particular mix of money, job satisfaction, social reward (satisfaction of serving the community, say), employment security, status, and opportunity to wield power, develop skills and advance a career.

This way of looking at people's work meanings and behaviours takes us a long way from the old-fashioned debates about whether people generally 'go to work mainly for the money' or seek employment for some other reason. Such 'either–or' thinking is simple-minded and of little value in understanding either work behaviour generally or the behaviour of particular groups of worker. In practice, every one of us has our own bundle of expectations and wants that we take into the strategic exchange we make with an employing organisation. There may be times in the life of each of us when we prioritise, say, money over job interest or security over high pay. But such a situation is recognised in this process-relational focus on orientations and implicit contracts as something which is particular to a particular person at a particular time and in particular circumstances. This is not to say that the concept cannot, to a certain extent, also be applied to groups, however.

A pattern of similar orientations may be seen across groups of employees who are similarly placed in the organisation or have come to the organisation from similar situations. It would tend to be the case that highly qualified senior staff would have different orientations, as a group, from unskilled and temporary manual workers, say. And it is possible that a different pattern of orientation might be found amongst people coming from one ethnic grouping, age or gender group rather than another, within the same organisational area of activity. Clearly, the cultural or age-group expectations of different groups of employees will vary, as will the bargaining strength which different types of prospective employee will take into their negotiation of an implicit contract – these varying with the skills, competencies or experiences they have to 'trade'. And, in circumstances where there is a formal trade union or other group representation, the bargaining over some aspects of the contract of employment will actually take place collectively. Nevertheless, even where there are clear patterns of orientation across groups of organisational members, it is necessary to recognise the variations that occur between individuals, albeit within these group patterns.

To understand any individual's or group's work behaviour we have to look at how they are predisposed to act in certain ways in the light of their orientation at that time and their perception of the deal they are making with the employer. We have to consider how they *enact* their role within the organisation, in other words. This, however, has to be set in the context of the employees' lives before they enter the organisation. We can see the importance of this in the case of Ravi Barr and how he came to be in the management job that he now does, by looking at the *initial orientation* which he brought to his present employing organisation. To look at processes of work entry and 'occupational choice', as it has traditionally been called, in the process-relational way, which a focus on work orientation involves, means once again turning away from the kind of *serial thinking* which was criticised in the previous chapter. Orthodox thinking tends to see the process of work entry as one in which we develop our interests, values and aptitudes as we grow up and go through education and then make a *choice* of occupation or career to fit this. Thus 'choice' precedes entry into a job or occupation. But, in practice, it does not work as simply as this, as Ravi Barr's story illustrates. What is the outcome of choice and what is adventitious, or a matter of circumstance and chance, is far from straightforward when we look at how people come into the sort of work we find them in at any point in their lives, in practice.

Activity 4.1

Read the conversation with Ravi Barr in Case 4.1 and consider the following questions:

- To what extent did Ravi 'choose' his career? Did he 'make a choice' of career and then enter it. Or did he 'find himself' in a job and then give this the rationale of a choice? Or was it a combination of these two?
- How has Ravi's work orientation changed over time, from the work he did in the family business, to the part-time jobs he took as a student, to the jobs he has done in the organisation he joined when he left school?
- How has Ravi 'managed' his identity? Because he has lived 'between two cultures', as he puts it, he is especially conscious of how identity is not a 'given' or fixed thing.

Ravi Barr gets oriented

Case 4.1

Tell me how you came to be a human resources manager, Ravi?

It was pure accident really. I was working as a supervisor in one of our shops, a job which I took when I got chucked out of university in my second year. I had always liked playing with computers, would you believe, and when a job came up in the home electrics department, as it was then called, I jumped at the chance. They said they wanted someone to build up that side of the department's business and I thought this would suit me. In fact it built up quite fast and I was soon spending a lot of my time recruiting new staff and training people on the computing side of things. I was training myself as I went along but I persuaded the general store manager that I was much more expert than I really was. The consequence of this was that he promoted me to a store-wide training job, getting managers and supervisors across the departments up to speed with computing. This went so well that when a personnel officer's job came up, I got it and then when the top human resources job become vacant I chose to go for that. I found I enjoyed the status I was building up and I liked the power that went with it. So here I am.

But you said, a moment ago, that it is 'pure accident' that you are in this job. And a few breaths later, you are telling me how you 'chose' to apply for the job. Can you explain this seeming contradiction to me?

Sorry about that. I suppose what was in my mind is that I originally wanted a career in marketing. This is what I hoped to specialise in on my degree course. So it's a sort of accident that I am now firmly in an HR career. I suppose that, on the other hand, there is consistency in that I am in a managerial sort of career. I wanted something that would give me seniority in an organisation – although I never thought of retailing as the industry I would end up in. And it is true that I enjoyed the human resources module I did in the second year at university – even if I failed it like all the others because I was enjoying myself too much pubbing and clubbing to do any academic work.

So why did you take the risk of not getting into a managerial career by not working at university?

Believe me, that is something I thought hard about at the time. In part, it was me sorting out who I was. You see my parents are in retailing and I was brought up to be a 'good hard-working Indian boy' who would eventually run the family business. And through my school years I accepted this. Well I more or less did. I worked enthusiastically in the family business whenever I had got my homework out of the way. I simply fitted into the business, like my older brothers, and did whatever my father asked me, whether it was delivering orders or sorting out the invoices. I didn't think of myself as cheap family labour. At home I was their dutiful Indian boy. At school I played that down and was just 'one of the lads' who were particularly interested in computers and computer games. Some of that group were Asian, others weren't. And it didn't matter. Asian identity was something for home. I was just another of the 'computer boys' at school. I sort of shifted my identity about across the two cultures I lived in. But I didn't really think about it at the time. I only started to think about all of this when I was at university. It was when I came home on the first vacation and found that I was expected to carry on the same as before. I started to see myself then as cheap family labour. I began to resent this and I got more and more awkward with my father and brothers – doing the minimum amount of work and refusing to take any kind of initiative at all. This all ended up in a big row and for the next few vacations I got work near the university, refusing to go home. I resolved never to have anything to do with retailing again. Apart from that, I did any work I could get, my main concern being to earn as much money as I could as fast as possible. I did labouring, worked in bars. I even did some horrible work in a chicken factory.

You just worked for money?

Exactly. The work was a means to an end.

And the end was?

Having a good time. And the money I made enabled me to carry on partying in term time too. I was sort of shaking off all those years of being the quiet conscientious boy. And I was also refusing the plan my parents had for me, as the first one in our family to go to university and, hence, the one who would eventually run the business (something I knew my elder brothers really resented).

But now you are a senior manager in a retailing business.

Funny isn't it? I am very career oriented now. I am making sure that I am learning about every aspect of this business so that I can eventually be a chief executive of a large retailing outfit. My parents have now accepted that I do not want to work in the family business. I think they are proud of what I have achieved and I suppose I want them to be even more proud of me when I really get to the top. My wife, who comes from a similar background, thinks similarly about her career as an accountant. I think my marriage, in fact, has been an important factor in my approach to career. Her family wanted to arrange a marriage for her and she had to fight them to marry me. So we have both had to make our way, and establish who we are, by sort of escaping from our families. So we are both making careers away from the Asian community. But, as we have both realised, we are still very much the products of the community and families that, in part, we turned away from. Yes, funny, isn't it. There are so many reasons for what you do, aren't there?

Ravi Barr's closing words rather neatly summarise the story he has told. But what is really interesting about his story is not just the large number, or even the variety, of the factors that have shaped his life and career. It is also the fascinating way that they interact with each other – home factors with work factors, family pressures with school priorities, ethnic influences with individual assertiveness, and so on. So complex is this interplay, in fact, that Ravi finds himself, rather paradoxically, talking of his career 'choices' since leaving university in terms of 'accident' one minute and 'choice' the next. This is not unusual when one interviews people about their work histories. The work biographies of most of us involve a complex interplay of choice and chance factors and when we report them to others we find ourselves, at certain points, drawing on all those stories in our culture which have the theme, 'Isn't it strange what things happen to people in life?'. And at other points in the narratives or biographies we present to people interviewing us, we draw on the discursive resource of the 'rational man or woman' who carefully plans a career to make the best use of their talents in the labour market. The 'either–or' dualism of choice *or* chance is not in fact helpful to understanding people's biographies. The two aspects of the duality do, however, interact with each other in different ways in different people's biographies. As we shall see in Chapter 10 (p. 442), the way we present that biography to employers or potential employers can have important consequences for recruitment and promotional decisions made by employers.

Ravi Barr's orientation to work is clearly tied up with his family and his ethnic background and with the process of managing his identity. He is making choices about his own life but those choices are very much made in the context of the structural situations in which he has found himself – whether these be the family and community structures into which he was born, or the structure of opportunities he later found himself in within the company for which he is now working. In different work situations in which he has found himself he has made different *implicit contracts* with the people employing him. When he first worked in the family firm he exchanged hard work and a willingness to be flexible for personal security and the social reward of belonging to a family and a community. Once he had left home and he felt that this reward was not what he was seeking, he was less willing to 'put in' so much effort or, as he points out, show so much initiative. The orientation to work and the implicit contract had changed, albeit with the same person and the same work situation. Ravi's changing concept of who he was and what he wanted from life led to a change in his work orientation. And when he sought employment while at university he thought of it in terms of a very simple trade – he wanted to maximise the money he could earn.

After the shock of having to leave university, Ravi approached his employment in the department store with a different kind of orientation. He was clearly willing to put more into that job than he had into the temporary jobs. And one of the rewards which was important in his understanding of the implicit contract with the company was the opportunity to work with computers. We can see then his orientation shifting further as he discovered his abilities in recruiting and training people. The ambition which then developed meant that the 'career potential' element of the reward side of Figure 4.2 was becoming more salient. Undoubtedly it was not replacing an interest in monetary reward, because we can presume that this was increasing at the same time, as were the rewards of status and power. We can see him trading a particular bundle of work inputs for a particular bundle of rewards. And this exchange is not just influenced by his relationship with the employing organisation. His current family life plays an important part in his emergent identity and his shifting work orientations. And this current family situation is itself related to his own and his wife's biographies. They are still working out their pasts as they work on the present and on their futures. Their exchanges with their present employers and with all the other people in their lives are indeed *strategic exchanges*. We each make strategic exchanges in our lives in our own ways.

Activity 4.2

Moving your attention away from Ravi Barr's story to your own, ask yourself the following questions.

- In what ways have both choice and chance played a part in your own unfolding work career or career ambitions?
- What different implicit contracts have you made in different work situations at various stages of your life? Use the employee input/employee reward boxes in Figure 4.2 to chart the perceived 'trades' you made in different jobs you have done.
- To what extent have you ever changed your orientation to work (and, of course, the way you perceived your implicit contract) within the same job? If you wish to be prompted on this question, you may choose to give a quick initial glance at what Sacha Boath has to say about how 'people change at work' in Case 4.2.

Varying and changing work orientations in a corporate affairs department

Case 4.2

Yes, you will hear several of the managers here refer to me and my department as Sacha and the Seven Dwarves. As Director of Corporate Affairs, I am the only woman in the company's top team and they like to tease me about being tall and fair-haired. That's OK, I can handle the banter and I suppose being compared to the fairy-tale Snow White is not really uncomplimentary. I do get bothered sometimes, though, that they are rather diminishing my team by referring to them as dwarves. Only one of them is really a small person, even if they are all shorter than me. In fact some of them have actually 'grown' in the job you might say. I think it's really interesting how people can change at work. Let me tell you about them; 'Smithy' Smith, 'Biffy' Currie, 'Sniffy' Gerardo, 'Snippy' Spedale, 'Chippy' Bliss, 'Iffy' Humphries and 'Sparky' Learmonth, as the managers call them.

Smithy, Biffy and Sniffy are my three public relations officers. Biffy and Sniffy are amazing cases of people who have changed. When I came here I was told they were simply miserable types. It was also said that they both had 'chips on their shoulders' because they had lost their jobs when the second of the town's papers closed down. They felt they were demeaning themselves by working in public relations. Both were well on the way to becoming alcoholics and they ruined their marriages, largely because of the drink. However, about a year ago there was this amazing change. In part, it was down to my giving them the most almighty shouting at – 'Shape up or ship out' is what I basically said. But it was also to do with some kind of conversion experience they had, as our Managing Director put it. They had both joined Alcoholics Anonymous and, at the same time, they discovered the delights of line dancing. Somehow the smartening up that went on with getting off the booze and their meeting women at the dancing sessions translated into their work. It was amazing. Almost overnight they changed from lazy and uninspired individuals who were in danger of letting the company down to smart and reliable characters who I can happily allow to speak for the company. Smithy, on the other hand, is somebody I increasingly can't trust. In her case, the change seems to have come about after moving in with a new partner, as opposed to losing a partner. She is my languages person and used to be brilliant at dealing with almost any issue where we needed to deal with Europe. It seems that her bloke has been getting resentful about her travelling abroad for us and this has led to her taking it out on all of us in the office. She's managed not to go abroad for six months now and the other day she rushed out of the office screaming, 'Oh, sod the

French'. One of my best people has become a complete liability for reasons which, it seems, have nothing to do with the company.

Changes at work do seem to be the source of the changes we've seen with Snippy, however. Her job is to monitor press coverage. She used to be the life and soul of the office. She would sit over there, snipping away at her press cuttings and joking with everybody who came into the office. But since we've rearranged the office and her desk is less central to what is going on, she seems to have completely dropped her role as the office wit. I shall have to rethink the office layout, I think. But, for some reason, she's recently taken up smoking and keeps disappearing to the smoking room across the road to have a cigarette. In the past, I could have spoken to her about that, but the way she is just now would make that difficult.

In some ways Snippy's social role in the office has been taken on by Iffy. She is my secretary, sorry PA – personal assistant. She used to be a total misery. She was a graduate trainee with the company. She said she didn't mind taking on a 'graduate secretary' role but she resented the fact that it was only female graduates who did that. They called her Iffy because she was always saying things like, 'If a man were asked to do that, he'd refuse.' So what's made the difference? I don't really know. The job title change might be a factor, but I don't think it was that important. And it might be that she became aware that I was never going to ask her to make me coffee or go out to buy flowers for me to give to my mother on Mother's Day (something she says happened to her before I came). Actually, I think it is simply that she and I have become good friends. We do meet socially but, at work, we really enjoy working together. There's no doubt that I am 'the boss', as anyone will tell you ('the blonde Tsarina', Iffy called me the other day, when I stormed into the office generally threatening murder all round). The simple truth is that Iffy enjoys working with someone she gets on with, and that has led her to take on more and more tasks which she then finds she really enjoys.

I wish I could bring about a similar change in Sparky. He runs the computing and IT side of the department – our web site and all that. When he was here first I think he felt that he was a pioneer and that he understood things none of us had a clue about. He was a cheerful chap to have around – a really sparky character in fact. It seems now that everything has settled down and his work is more routine, he is a bit bored. Consequently he is not helping people as much as he should be. He's well paid though and I think that he has got himself locked in here by the salary. He has taken on a mortgage on a new house recently and doesn't want to risk a job change. He's pretty secure too, given the relevance of his skills to our work. I can't see what promotional opportunities we can offer to 'turn him back on'. I'll have to look for some exciting new project.

Chippy is someone for whom everything is a new project. I have rarely seen anyone so positive about his job. He came to us from the maintenance department who 'redeployed' him when that operation was downsized. His resentment of moving into here was palpable. He thought he was simply going to be some sort of odd job man who would only occasionally use his carpentry skills when we needed a display preparing. However, once he realised that he could make the job an important one, by seeking opportunities to make exhibition stands and by being the key person at out-of-company presentations, he really changed. He regularly travels abroad now – which he had never done before, and I often think he has developed better public relations skills than some of the professionals. The job is very much what he has chosen to make it. After that first miserable couple of weeks here he just seemed to decide, 'Right, let's make something of this'. The MD – ever the joker himself – actually asked me the other day, 'Is that Chippy of yours still a chirpy chappy?'. Indeed he is.

These brief portraits painted by one manager of the staff in her department very effectively illustrate the foolishness of looking at the demeanour or the behaviour of any given person at work and concluding, 'Aha, that is the sort of person they are'. Although there will be certain consistencies which could be perceived over time in the lives and identities of each of these individuals, the orthodox psychology categories of 'personality type' hardly seem relevant to the complexities of what is going on in these seven lives and to the work orientations of 'Smithy' Smith, 'Biffy' Currie, 'Sniffy' Gerardo, 'Snippy' Spedale, 'Chippy' Bliss,' Iffy' Humphries and 'Sparky' Learmonth. The concepts of emergent identity, work orientation and implicit contract are far more helpful than any concept of personality type.

Activity 4.3

Carefully examine each of the individuals that Sacha Boath talks about and, using the model in Figure 4.2:

- note what factors appear to have led to their changed orientations;
- given that Sacha has only a partial picture of what has happened in each case, speculate about what other kinds of factor might also have come into play (i.e. things you might 'look into' if you were trying to do a research project on the orientations of people in this Corporate Affairs – or 'public relations' – department);
- try to think of any examples of people, other than yourself, whose work orientations appear to have changed during their employment within a particular job.

A complex multiplicity of factors seems to be relevant to the workplace identities and the work orientations of each of these people. Numerous factors influence how they see the implicit contract they have with their employer. Sacha Boath has clearly tried hard to understand each of these people and, indeed, she gets close to analysing how they might perceive the implicit contracts they have with her and the company. Notice, for example, the way in which she analyses how Sparky might be thinking about the rewards he is getting from the company: he has got security and good pay but he is not getting any intrinsic rewards or fulfilment from the job itself. He is bored. This might be compensated for by promotional opportunities, but that is not really a possibility. Sacha is therefore considering what she might do to give him more excitement in the job. She is not getting the work 'inputs' she wants, given what rewards she is offering. She therefore needs to act to get a better trade. And this takes us into that area of management often called 'motivation' and which, in Chapter 8 (pp. 315–24), we will be reconceptualising as a process in which managers manipulate the perceived implicit contracts of workers.

For the present, however, we simply want to give full recognition to the extent to which a person's identity is always *emergent*, their work orientation is always liable to change and their involvement at work has to be seen in the context of the strategic exchanges which are going on in their lives and biographies as a whole. And if we are going to look at people in this holistic way, then we have to recognise that they do not simply go to work to act as task-completing biological machines. The 'whole person' goes to work, as we recognised earlier.

And that means that they approach the organisation with feelings, preferences, beliefs and the whole range of human vulnerabilities, as well as the skills, aptitudes and willingness to follow instructions that the employing organisation is buying from them.

Feelings, emotions and the experience of stress

Work organisations are parts of an institutional pattern which has developed at a very recent stage in the overall evolution and history of the human species. This pattern is associated with *modernism* which, as we saw in Chapter 2 (p. 36), involves a concerted attempt to apply rational thinking to human activities and institutions in order to increase humans' control over their circumstances. The principles of *reason* and of *control* are thus central to the work of trying to shape modern organisations and, as we established earlier, the form which this reason takes is that of 'instrumental rationality', whereby calculated choices are made to find the best means for achieving given ends. People in modern organisations are not meant to perform work tasks in the way that they *feel* like doing at a particular moment. They are not meant to carry out tasks in a particular way because they *guess* that this is how to do it. And they are not meant to do a job in a particular way because that is the *traditional* way in which it has always been done. To act in these ways is to go against the principles of carefully, or scientifically, calculating the most efficient way of carrying out work tasks.

Max Weber, the key theorist of these matters, pointed out that this would mean that if modern organisations or 'bureaucracies' were to exist in a pure form, they would have no place for 'love, hatred and all purely personal, irrational and emotional elements which escape calculation' (Weber, 1978, p. 975). The key phrase here is 'which escape calculation'. Weber was identifying here the aspirations of those building and leading the large organisations of the modernising world and, as Albrow (1997) points out (in contradicting a common misreading of Weber), Weber was well aware that they were not seeking to *exclude* an emotional or affective dimension from organisational life. We might say that what they were seeking were ways of *harnessing* the 'humanness' and the emotional involvement of human labour. This was indeed the logic of the attention given to 'informal' aspects of organisational functioning in those classic 1930s studies by Roethlisberger and Dickson and by Barnard, which we looked at in Chapter 2 (pp. 61–2). Managers should pay heed to the 'sentiments' of workers in shaping factory activities, argued the former, while the latter put the management of 'informal activities' at the centre of the executive's job.

In effect, Barnard was recognising the need of organisational managers to appeal to employees' hearts and sentiments as well as to their minds. His social science influenced analysis of all of this, and the advocacy which follows from it, can itself be seen as part of what Weber recognised as a trend not to allow 'emotional elements' to 'escape calculation'. Emotions are all very well in the modern work organisation, in this view, but they must be kept under control and, wherever possible, harnessed to the ends being pursued by the organisation's controllers. Hatred for an enemy would probably be a managerially desirable emotion to be felt by soldiers in a modern army during a war. And passion for the product being sold by a commercial enterprise could be very welcome to those in charge of that enterprise. However, if either of these got 'out of hand' – beyond calculation and control – the soldiers might disastrously run amok and the over-passionate sales person might frighten away some of their customers.

It has been recognised in recent years that the bulk of management and organisational texts attend too little to the emotional side of organisational life and work involvement (see Further Reading on emotions and work, pp. 160–1). Where it is given recognition in standard texts, it is dealt with in an indirect, and often rather 'bloodless' way. Sometimes it is seen as a dimension of gaining employee compliance – rewarding people with *self-actualisation* or overcoming their *resistance to change* for example. At other times it becomes pertinent because of an interest in overcoming tendencies of individuals to break down through *stress* or the inclination of certain groups overenthusiastically to pursue *grievances*.

We can usefully reflect on why there has been little direct attention to the emotional aspects of working lives. The subjective states of the individuals whose feelings and emotions make up the 'emotional side of organisational life' are not easy to understand and, partly as a result of the ambiguity and unpredictability that such matters involve, people can readily become quite uncomfortable when trying to address them. It might also be the case that when we are working as researchers, or as thoughtful managers, in specific organisational situations, we feel uncomfortable about invading the privacy of the people we come across. We might ask whether we have the right to enquire too deeply into the emotional states and the private feelings of the people we meet in work situations. This would be a proper ethical question to ask. Yet if we want to understand the full complexities of organising and managing work, we need to attend to matters of feeling and emotion in the workplace. The ethnographic style of research, in which the researcher gets closely involved with the people living or working in the particular setting being studied, enables such factors to be looked at. An ethnographic episode which demonstrates the type of insight that can be gained in this way is that of Ken Steary's collision with his office desk (Case 4.3). At this stage we have not formally conceptualised the issues that arise in this broad area of the 'emotions and feelings'. This is deliberate. We will look at some events occurring in Ken Steary's hotel and then consider how we might bring some conceptual rigour to bear on them.

Activity 4.4

Read the researcher's conversation with Ken Steary in Case 4.3. Then:

- list all of the ways in which issues of emotion and feeling come into these events;
- identify any way in which those running this hotel organisation – represented in this story by the regional manager – appear to have taken account of the emotional dimension of what goes on in hotels.

Ken Steary laughs, cries and falls over

Case 4.3

You don't look good, Ken.

I don't feel good, mate.

You look altogether stressed.

Stress is supposed to be a mental thing, isn't it? Well, you see this black eye. That's stress for you. It's physical and it hurts. And I know what you think. You think that I am going to tell you that I got so stressed last night trying to manage this bloody hotel that I got into a fight with a customer. Well that isn't what happened.

Did a member of staff thump you, then?

No. I didn't get into a fight with a member of staff. It was my office desk what did it.

I see.

No you don't. I was at the end of my tether last night, stressed up, tired out and on the point of laughing and crying at the same time. But I am the manager and I am meant to be in control. I can neither afford to let the staff see me crack up nor let the hotel guests see me fall apart. So I went up to my office and drank myself stupid. And then I fell over, catching my eye on the corner of the desk. I thought I was doing really well, keeping up the façade of the man who is always in control – dealing with my pathetic grief in private. And now I've got to explain to everybody how I got the black eye. I've already told three different stories to explain it away. I am really losing the plot.

OK, tell me the plot then. What is the real story?

The problems started yesterday with the visit from the Regional Manager. She comes round every month to look at 'the figures' with me and generally to keep me on my toes. I really hate her, the officious cow. She has a go at me for things that she couldn't do. She really likes to wind me up.

How do you mean?

Well, yesterday, I started off in a good mood. I was feeling good because I knew the figures were OK. Our occupancy figures have been really excellent, the bar and restaurant turnovers are on the up and up and the staff turnover figures are slightly down. I've even got the wages tightly under control. But guess what? Did they thank me? Did they congratulate me? Did they hell. No, what I got from madam was, 'Region are perturbed about some complaints they have received.' They had got a couple of complaints about the sullen behaviour of my reception staff. I'd like to see her try to deal with a problem like that.

You recognise that this is a problem, then. I must admit that I was put off earlier by the rather surly manner of one of your barmen. I felt most unwelcome and would have walked out if I hadn't been meeting you.

Don't you start. I thought you were my friend. But, yes, you are right. This is an issue that has been bothering me. I just didn't like the idea of my bosses sitting around their boardroom table tut tutting about poor old Ken Steary not being able to make his staff smile at the punters. And that cow of a regional manager wouldn't be able to make a drunk on his honeymoon smile. So who is she to lecture me?

But you accept that there is a problem?

Oh yes. And I could do with some help handling it. But who do I turn to? I am the boss here. And you can get very lonely, even in a big hotel full of people like this one was last night. I've got to show a smiling face to the world and my staff know damn well that they need to do the same. Even on my way up to my office last night I smiled at a grumpy guest who refused help with his suitcase and then complained that the steps on the stairs were too steep. 'What's wrong with using the lift, you stupid bastard?', I said under my breath as I felt my skin burning and my colour rising. But my expression was a picture of genuine sympathy. And since I've had this black eye, I have smiled a hundred times at one member of staff and one hotel guest after another.

But you can't get all of your staff to act in this way?

Most will, they know their jobs depend on the hotel doing well and that it won't do well if the guests are not treated hospitably. That doesn't seem unreasonable. And they have chosen to work in the hospitality industry, for God's sake. They are paid to be hospitable.

But are they paid to be actors?

Would you like a black eye too?

Matters of feeling and emotion come into this story from the beginning. One of the first things Ken says is that he does not *feel* good. He talks about how his black eye 'hurts' – suggesting that the abstract phenomenon he calls 'stress', itself 'hurts'. His reference to his hotel as 'this bloody hotel' is clearly emotionally loaded, as is his worry that one might infer that he had fought with a customer. He loads his account of his feelings the previous evening with terms like 'the end of my tether', 'tired out', 'crack up', 'fall apart', 'drank myself stupid', 'pathetic grief' and 'losing the plot'. The description of his 'laughing and crying at the same time' involves the use of a discursive resource commonly used in the wider culture to give a picture of somebody who is so out of control that they have gone beyond the cultural norm of crying to express sadness and laughing to express happiness. He talks of hating the Regional Manager and, twice, uses another common discursive resource which is applied to express strong antipathy to a woman, as does his ironic use of the term 'madam'. Positive feelings are expressed when Ken looks back to earlier the previous day when he 'felt good' and was, it seems, feeling that he deserved thanks and congratulations. These are aspects of the sort of reciprocity we referred to in Chapter 3 when discussing culture and social exchange (p. 81). His looking for these endorsements and the manager failing to provide them reveal significant *relational* aspects of the emotional temperature which built up for Ken. Also, the Regional Manager's use of language in saying that the 'region is perturbed' is interesting. She is mystifying exactly who is worried by *personifying* 'Region' (see above p. 50), something which, if Ken is reporting her verbatim, we might take to be slightly provocative. It implies that some power greater than any nameable human individual is looking down upon the insignificant figure of Mr Steary. The formality of the word 'perturbed' rather than the more obvious 'worried' has been taken by Ken, we can infer, as a further attempt to 'wind him up'.

The alleged 'sullenness' of the reception staff, and the researcher's mention of the 'surly manner' of a bar worker, are clearly matters of emotional interpretation made by customers of the apparent emotional state of these hotel employees. The researcher speaks of *feeling* unwelcome and Ken goes on in the conversation to paint a picture of a very emotional state he was in the previous night and the equally emotional state he is in at present with the use of one emotionally loaded expression after the other. He also makes a bitter joke about the Regional Manager's demeanour, one that has all sorts of sexual and sexist undertones (couldn't 'make a drunk on his honeymoon smile') and he even threatens the researcher with violence, even though (as it happened) he says it with a smile on his face, echoing back to the pathos of the earlier 'I thought you were my friend'.

This episode is packed with emotionality and it could be argued that an exaggerated picture of the role that feelings play in organisational life is being painted by the selection of an episode in which there has been a crisis in the life of one particular individual. There is some truth in this. But it can be argued that critical events like this simply reveal factors and issues that are present all the time but only come fully to the surface when circumstances arise in which the normal controls of social life are weakened and conventional courtesies are strained. For example, if the Regional Manager had been polite to Ken and thanked him for his good work before diplomatically raising the question of the customer complaints, there would still be emotional factors in play. The Regional Manager would have been taking Ken's feelings into account and he might have 'felt good' about being thanked and he might have appreciated the senior person's 'sharing' a managerial problem with him. This kind of social exchange process and the maintenance of reciprocity is so common or 'normal' in social and organisational life that we tend not to be consciously aware of it. It is when there is some breakdown in it that the presence of feelings and emotions in the work context become starkly apparent. They are, however, never absent.

The emotional issues raised by Ken Steary's tale go beyond ones of staff relationships. The issue that triggered Ken's distressing experience was one of how the organisation, as a business, relates to its customers. It does not apparently stay in business simply by selling food and renting beds to customers. It provides *hospitality* to its *guests*. The very tasks which are done 'in the organisation's name' (above p. 58) are ones with a strong emotional dimension. Ken is fully aware of this. And one can reasonably infer from his outburst, 'they have chosen to work in the hospitality industry, for God's sake', that a key source of frustration to him is the difficulty he is having in getting some of the staff to *engage emotionally* with their work, by acting in a friendly and smiling way towards 'guests'. We notice that he stresses how the Regional Manager would be unable do this. And we note that he emphasises how he is willing to 'make his face a picture of genuine sympathy', even when he is in a bad mood and is provoked by a 'stupid bastard' and 'grumpy guest'. A concept which we will use to look at the issues that arise here is that of *emotional labour*. But, before we can properly deploy that concept, we need to conceptualise the more general phenomena of emotion and feeling.

It has been possible in the above analysis to refer in a broad way to 'feelings and emotions' as if they were more or less the same thing. This is what we tend to do in everyday life. We talk about 'feeling happy' on one occasion, for example, and refer to the 'emotion' of happiness on another. It has been normal, in the history of human reflection, to link feelings and emotions. So why should we consider splitting them – distinguishing between the two? The only justification for doing this would be the pragmatist's one of developing our conceptual tools to enable us to analyse something more effectively than we would otherwise do, with a view to better informing our subsequent practices. On these grounds, it is useful to conceptualise feelings and emotions as separate, but closely linked, phenomena.

Emotions and feelings

Concept

Feelings are sensations felt bodily which relate to a psychological state. *Emotions* are the way these sensations are made sense of with reference to culture, either privately or socially.

It is helpful to follow Fineman in separating *feelings* – the 'subjective experience' in which 'we are aware "in" ourselves of some bodily state, peturbation, or more diffuse psychological change' (Fineman, 1999, p. 546) from the more culturally mediated *emotions* with which they are associated. Fineman, however, treats emotions as *displays* of these feelings. He does this to enable him to distinguish between, say, the way someone might express the *emotion* of anger in a situation, by shouting and raging, while actually *feeling* pleasure in what they are doing. There is clearly an important distinction to be made here (to understand situations like the one Ken Steary was in when he *felt* angry with the grumpy customer while he *displayed* sympathy). However, it is felt more analytically useful here to say that the *feeling* was the physical sensation Ken describes when he says 'I felt my skin burning and my colour beginning to rise'. And the *emotion* is the cultural label of 'anger' that might be attached to this feeling when we try to make sense of it. The two are closely linked but the 'animal' sensation that Ken experienced does not automatically read across to the cultural interpretation of 'anger'. Ken himself, or somebody else hearing about his experience, might choose to interpret or 'construct' that experience as one of 'going mad', 'being disgusted', 'getting furious' or 'being appalled'.

The distinction between feeling and emotion, then, is a way of taking account of both the 'animal' and the 'cultural' aspects of our natures – our humanity. As we said earlier, with regard to instincts (pp. 81–2), everything in the human being, is culturally mediated. Animal 'things' are 'there in us', as indeed our body is ontologically 'there'. But they are always subject to processes of social construction, to cultural interpretation, to enactment. The situation is not as simple as, say, good *feelings* first being 'there', or being 'experienced', and then being *enacted* in a particular way as happiness, joy, contentment or whatever. To assume this is again to fall into the trap of the 'linear' type of psychology we rejected in the previous chapter (pp. 87–8). It might be possible, for example, for one to start off sad and then, with the cultural notion of happiness in mind, to lie back on a pile of comfortable cushions, smile to oneself and actually experience the sensation we label 'happiness'. It has been widely observed, in fact, that choosing to smile can make one 'feel happier' than one was before the smile appeared on our face.

We are getting ourselves involved here in matters which philosophers and psychologists have agonised over for centuries. Why should we trouble to engage with such matters? It is to sharpen our conceptual tool kit in order to come to terms with the issues that were raised in Ken Steary's story. If we are going to require people like Ken and his staff to perform in ways which involve emotional labour, then we need to understand the relationship between the feelings these people might have and the emotional face they are required to present to the world. What are we asking of people who we require to smile at – and 'make feel good' – hotel guests, airline passengers, hospital patients, shop customers and a multitude of other consumers of services in modern societies?

Emotional labour

Emotions and the way these are presented play a key part in all the exchanges we make with other human beings. We smile at a child to show our approval of its behaviour or we frown at a friend who fails to notice the new clothes we are wearing. This is an exchange, in the sense that we are suggesting certain emotions on our own part in order to elicit certain emotions in the other person, ones that will take the relationship forward in the way we wish it to go. This kind of emotional management, which characterises much of our private lives, is called *emotion work* by Hochschild (1985) and she contrasts it with *emotional labour*.

Emotional labour — *Concept*

An element of work activity in which the worker is required to display certain emotions in order to complete work tasks in the way required by an employer.

Here, emotional work on the part of an organisational employee is carried out to further the interests of the employer who is buying their services. There is a close relationship between the emotion work which is a normal part of everybody's lives and emotional labour. In the workplace, one does 'emotion work' all the time, simply in order to relate to the other human beings with whom we come into contact. But this overlaps with those efforts that we feel obliged to make as part of our implicit contract with the employer. In dealing with other people at work we would generally be unaware of any tension between our 'natural' inclination to interact, say, in a warm and friendly way with colleagues or customers and what our employment entails. However, once our 'private self' (our self-identity as we are experiencing it at that moment) finds itself in some tension with our self as an 'organisational representative' (a manifestation of our social identity, as required of us by our employment) we are likely to experience discomfort. We tend, then, to become aware of that which we conceptualise as emotional labour. Such an awareness is reported by Ken Steary when he describes the friendly and sympathetic demeanour he presented to the grumpy guest. He felt obliged to behave in this way because of his understanding of his contract with the hotel company. As a hotel manager and a representative of the organisation he had to behave in this way. His private self, however, was silently addressing the customer as a 'stupid bastard'. He could not show this to the guest because to do so would be to break his implicit contract with the employer. And he believes some of his staff are doing precisely this. The reception staff who were complained of were forgetting, or ignoring, what Ken takes to be implicit in the agreement made between employees and employers in the *hospitality* industry: that employees should act hospitably.

A useful distinction that Hochschild makes when examining emotional labour is that between *surface acting* and *deep acting*. Ken Steary's behaviour was an example of surface acting, because he was aware that he was 'putting on a show'. He might be deceiving the guest, but he was not deceiving himself. With deep acting, the employee either 'works up' a feeling in themselves which fits with the emotion they are expressing in doing their job or, as Hochschild puts it, they train their imaginations to achieve the same effect. We see an example in some of the experiences of Cindy Sutor, a sex worker who is reflecting on her work and what it requires of her 'self'.

Activity 4.5

Cindy Sutor's work (Case 4.4) takes her towards the more extreme end of the 'emotional labour market'. Consider:

- how the concepts of *deep acting* and *surface acting* can be applied to Cindy's experiences;
- how the implicit contract she used to make with the clients or with the employer she now works for contains limits on what can be expected emotionally;
- having looked at this relatively extreme case of emotional labour, how many relatively 'normal' jobs can you think of which involve *emotional labour*;
- what elements of *emotional labour* there have been in any jobs you have done and to what extent (a) this involved deep and surface acting, (b) there were limits built into the implicit contract, as you perceived it, which helped in the managing of the emotional demands of the job.

Cindy sets the limits for emotional engagement in her work

Case 4.4

I have recently stopped working as a prostitute on my own account and I now do just five shifts a week for the sex phone line company. It pays less but it's safer. It's also different because I now just *talk* about what I actually used to have to *do*. But there are lots of similarities. In both kinds of work, you have got to protect your own idea of who you are. You must not sell your whole self. When I was working on the street I knew that I had to show a certain level of interest in the punter – but not too much. I'd say something like 'Come on, big boy', without really implying that I thought that he was a big boy. You train your clients to know what they are paying for. You show a certain amount of interest in the man, especially if you are hoping for repeat business, but what you don't do is show any kind of excitement and, certainly, absolutely no hint of passion. I'd demean myself if I let that happen. And if I felt myself getting interested I'd damn quickly shut that off. The only exception to this was when I got into the posh call girl game for a while. You get paid a lot more then. So you play it just a little more positively.

Working on the telephone line is really an acting job. You sometimes put on a sexy voice and tell the punter that you are dressed in a skimpy nightie. But, as you tell them this, you make sure you keep a blank face and you look down at the dirty old jeans you are wearing.

Sometimes, though, I get bored with this. If I then find myself talking to someone who sounds really nice I let myself imagine that he is someone that I would actually like to go out with. Then I close my eyes and let myself stop pretending. Sometimes I quite enjoy this, get genuinely excited even. It helps the shift go a bit faster. It's only daydreaming, though. But perhaps those punters do get a better deal – something more genuine. I doubt it though – a proportion of our calls are monitored by the management and I would not want that creep in the 'control room' to think I was giving more than I am being paid for.

As Cindy Sutor is engaged in activities which potentially have deep emotional significance yet which occur within a framework of instrumental economic transaction, she has to work hard to manage boundaries and to 'set limits'. The public or temporary social identity she is paid to adopt must not be allowed to take over her private self-identity. Such issues arise for workers in an increasing number and variety of occupations, ranging from the airline workers, to whose work Hochschild first applied the *emotional labour* concept, to sales staff, call centre workers, entertainers, medical workers, and the 'greeters' who welcome customers as they walk through the entrances of some supermarkets. The more work organisations attempt to develop internal cultures which follow the 'quality management' principles of treating fellow workers as 'internal customers', the more we will see a requirement for most employees to go beyond the 'emotion work' which is a normal and spontaneous part of all human exchange and to be monitored for the quality of the *emotional labour* they put in.

It might be argued that issues of this general kind have to be handled by all workers: protecting themselves from what has often been called the *alienation* of self or, in a more recent formulation, the 'corrosion of self' (Sennett, 1998). The notion of alienation is more a philosophical than a social scientific one and it adopts an *essentialist* view of the human individual, instead seeing 'humanness' *processually* as something which people 'work at' and 'achieve'. But the notion has played a major part in critiques of modern work institutions and the effects they have on the integrity of the human individual. It is consistent, however, with the process-relational recognition of the need of each human being to manage their identities. Identity has to be managed and a logic found or created which links people's self-identities and their social identities to keep them sane and capable of competently playing a part in social life.

Alienation *Concept*

The destruction of the integrity of the human self – a splitting of one part of a person's 'being' from another.

Cindy Sutor's management of identity involves a high degree of 'distancing' of her 'self' from her work and this means that much of her 'acting' is of a surface kind. However, she does talk of occasionally moving over into some 'deep acting' when she decides to use her imagination and let herself 'daydream'. But even that is circumscribed by the contractual setting in which she is operating – and by the constant reminder of this in the form of the monitoring manager in the 'control room'. Just as she did not want her prostitution clients to get more than they were paying for, she was not willing to exceed the 'inputs' she was making in her implicit contract with the phone line company. We can well imagine Ken Steary's unsmiling hotel workers in Case 4.3, in the same spirit, arguing that for the money they are paid they cannot be expected to put 'heart and soul' into their jobs. They cannot be expected to treat hotel guests in the way that they would treat guests in their own houses, any more than Cindy would treat her 'punters' as if they were lovers. We might not expect Ken, as a manager, to go along with such an argument. But if Ken were to point out that he always treats customers as if they were his personal guests, we can imagine his reception staff pointing out that Ken is much better rewarded than they are for continuously presenting a positive 'face' to customers. Implicit contracts are not only perceived differently by different parties to them. They are also frequently contested.

Stress, strain and distress

The stressed executive, falling apart under the strains of heavy responsibility, has been one of the clichés of modern life for some time. But this image is coming to be replaced by the one of employees of every kind afflicted with the pathology of *stress* in every corner of the pressured and increasingly competitive organisational world. We hear of people being 'off work with stress', in the same way that they might be off work with mumps or measles. But stress is not something that one 'has' in this way. The notion simply implies that someone is suffering in some way under the strains of their work situation to the extent that they are becoming unable to perform satisfactorily in that work. Stress is a reaction to circumstances and it can arise in situations other than work. A poor single parent with several energetic and demanding children could well find themselves approaching an emotional state where they no longer felt able to act as a parent is expected to act. A husband or wife, oppressed by the nature of their relationship with their spouse, could well find themselves emotionally unable to continue to act as a husband or wife is expected to behave. Similarly a teacher, office cleaner, social worker, factory worker or manager might reach a stage of emotional agitation within their work experiences in which they become incapable of fulfilling the tasks required of them.

Stress *Concept*

A sense of distress arising because of pressures experienced in certain social or economic circumstances that render the sufferer emotionally, and sometimes physically, incapable of continuing to behave in the ways expected of them in those circumstances.

What characterises the state of being 'stressed', in work or elsewhere, is clearly being in a position where the person *feels* they cannot continue to perform as they are expected (see Further Reading on work and stress, p. 161). It is a subjective state – it is not just a matter of being incapable. Someone who found that they simply did not have the patience to look after children, that they were no longer attracted to their spouse or that they were no longer physically strong enough to continue in their current job could *rationally decide* to abandon their children, leave their spouse or resign from their job. Stress – as the etymology of the word suggests – implies something oppressing, pressurising or 'drawing tight' around one. This leads to a feeling, a subjective state, in which one cannot tolerate these pressures. And that subjective state may be accompanied by one or more physical afflictions in which there is a breakdown of some part of the body. No sense can be made of the many experiences of stress if one persists with the Cartesian dualism which separates body and mind and tries to suggest that suffering has to be *either* in the body *or* 'just in the mind'.

While there is no denying the 'reality' of stress, as something which people experience and which can be manifested in physical symptoms, it is important to recognise that this reality is nevertheless one which involves processes of social construction (see above, pp. 56–8). People are making sense of their situation through the use of discursive resources which are available in their culture (pp. 102–5). In another place and time, a worker suffering from what we would nowadays label stress might simply be dismissed as a 'weak character' and a soldier who would, today, be recognised as undergoing stress might be shot at dawn as a coward. But to recognise the importance of processes of construction, interpretation or enactment in how stress is experienced and handled is not just a matter of how we are socially labelled. The sufferer from 'stress' will make sense of their situation in their own way, albeit in the context of the discursive resources which are available to them. Each individual will also be better or worse placed with regard to personal resources such as experience, physical strength, intelligence, intellectual ingenuity and a self-identity which entails their defining themselves, say, as a relatively robust or vulnerable person. They will also be better or worse placed with regard to friends, relatives or advisers to whom they can turn for advice and emotional support. All of these resources, cultural and personal (not that in the final analysis these can be separated – to decide that one is a 'fighter' rather than a 'quitter' is clearly both a personal and a discursive matter), are drawn upon to deal with whatever pressures, strains or 'stresses' are being experienced. Thus, in any workplace or occupational stress situation we choose to look at, we have to consider the interplay of two sets of factors: the *pressures of the work circumstances* and the psychological, emotional and *social resources of the worker* facing those circumstances.

Activity 4.6

Look at the experiences of Tim Dyke and Con Tessock in Case 4.5 and:

- note the ways in which the personal resources of the two individuals made a difference to the ways they experienced and dealt with the stress of handling the pressures of the work circumstances they faced;
- identify any work or organisational situation you have witnessed, experienced or can envisage in which different individuals react differently to the same potentially stressful situations, noting which factors you think were the most important in leading to these different reactions.

A tale of two deputies

Case 4.5

We were seen as a team over the several years we worked together as classroom teachers – Tim Dyke and Con Tessock, the dedicated teacher twins. Then, when the school got into trouble and they put the new Head Teacher in to sort it all out, it wasn't seen as strange that we were both appointed as deputy heads. I was to look after the lower school and Con the upper school. In some ways mine was the more difficult job because I had a higher proportion of disruptive pupils. By the time you reached the senior classes, which were Con's, the worst troublemakers had left. But we had both been pretty good at classroom control and we both had managed to get reasonable examination results with the sort of pupils which we had to handle. What I am saying is that we both started off the managerial stages of our careers similarly placed, similarly matched – not that there was any competitiveness between us, as far as I could see at the time anyway. So it's really interesting to try to work out why I am now about to become a head teacher and Con is a retired teacher at 48, 'put out to grass' on ill health retirement because he couldn't take the stress.

Because the school had been inspected and deemed by the inspectors to be an officially 'failing school', the local authority got rid of our old head teacher and put in Winnie Knowe with a brief to act as a 'superhead' and 'turn the school around'. So, from Winnie's arrival and the appointment of Con and myself as deputies, we were being constantly watched and monitored. We knew that everything we did was in order to get a clean bill of health when the Ofsted inspectors came back in. Every little success had therefore to be recorded, every little failure had to be explained and we had to write policy documents for every single aspect of school life – from a careers advice policy to a buildings maintenance policy. The workload was enormous, with all these tasks being piled on top of what was thrown at us by daily events in the school. Con and I seemed to cope well with this, not least because, as mates, we were able to work together. We had each other's shoulders to cry on, if we needed it. So far, so good. But, after a while Con started to get bad tempered with me and he increasingly failed to meet the deadlines we agreed to set each other. I first realised that things were really going wrong one day after he'd had a meeting with Winnie. He came into the staff room absolutely fuming. Winnie Knowe had failed to support a decision that Con had made about disciplining a girl who had been found with a pocket full of illegal pills. Not only had she not backed him, but Winnie had apologised to the girl's parents for the school not being 'sympathetic enough' to a girl 'going through a difficult time'. I couldn't blame Con for getting angry. What sort of time did Winnie think we were all having? I had got angry with the Head on a couple of occasions, for exactly the same reasons. She was clearly unwilling to back Con and me in any risks we took. When we were successful she used to take the credit, and when something went wrong, she blamed us.

Having a boss who does not back you when you are doing an already difficult job is a real strain, believe me. And not only was this made worse by her not giving us any kind of reward or thanks for good work done, she was always sneaking around asking the other staff about us. So, all of the time you felt you were being watched and that you would get slapped if you fell short. The stress of all this was made worse by the press, who seemed to be very keen to see us fail again. Anything negative they could get hold of, they would make a fuss about. You began to feel the whole world was against you. The kids in our school always were difficult. Con and I both knew that before we went there. But somehow the parents were now getting even more of a problem than they had been before. They had never been wonderfully supportive but, now, they seemed to take the attitude that we should sort out their kids all on our own. Disciplining these obstreperous teenagers was our job, they seemed to think. When we asked for their help they tended to look at us and say, 'Just because you are useless – a teacher in a failing school – don't expect us to do your job', and all that.

At times I thought the job was too much. At one point I came out in this rash. The doctor just laughed this off and told me that she knew it was just a stress symptom that I should 'shake off' – because she got exactly the same problem when she found her workload beginning to get too much for her. After that visit to the doctor, I decided that there wasn't much else I could do but will the rash to go away. That didn't work exactly, but once I got into the habit of a glass of good malt whisky every night, it slowly disappeared. Poor old Con, on the other hand, was down at the doctor's all the time. He developed an ulcer, which tended to make him even more evil tempered than he had already become. And he started to talk about a blood pressure problem too. With all of this he became more and more unpredictable, failing to turn up to meetings and one day he actually hit a pupil who, he said, had come out of a French lesson and called him 'Con the con'. It was his final downfall. So they got him out: a 'victim of the government, the Head Teacher and of stress' he said at the embarrassing leaving party we held for him.

Why, I ask myself, did I cope and my pal didn't? We were both able and confident teachers. We both had exactly the same stress problems at work. In a sense, I probably just made up my mind I was going to cope and realised that both of us couldn't go under. I sort of took responsibility for him as he started to break down. I needed to do that because I knew he was getting no support from his wife. She's a successful fashion designer who could not see how he couldn't deal with what she saw as the simple problems that face teachers. My wife, on the other hand, was once a teacher and she used to 'talk me down' some nights when I got home. And the kids used to take my mind off things. Con doesn't have kids, just a temperamental dog which is more unpredictable than our worst pupils. I thought at the time that Con had support from his parents, who are both ex-teachers, whereas my parents show no interest in my work. But I rather think, in retrospect, that his parents were just another source of pressure, always telling him what he might do in his job, without realising just how different a school like ours was from the old grammar schools they had taught in.

I also think that Con was starting to be troubled by his association with a notorious and rough school. 'Doesn't it damage your self esteem, having people know you work in such an awful place?', Con asked me one day. 'Self esteem, what's that?', I thought. On reflection I have come to the conclusion that I had no problems in this area. I had convinced myself that the world was a rough old place and that perhaps I was a bit of a hero taking on the challenge of working at the rougher end of the educational service. Con, on the other hand, convinced himself that things shouldn't be the way they are and that the world was somehow against him personally. 'The whole effing world, and this ulcer, is against me' he sobbed one day into his empty coffee mug, the one with the slogan 'A good teacher can make a world of difference' painted on it.

These two individuals involved in managing a large problem school were faced with considerable sources of stress. Not only did they have an enormous amount of work to do, at both the operational and the policy levels, but they also received very little support in the job. Even worse, they tended to get criticised from every quarter – by the head teacher, by journalists and by parents of pupils. Stress, as an emotional and physical reaction to these circumstances was something that Tim and Con both experienced. But Tim was better placed in terms of personal resources to manage the symptoms. Just at the physical level, it would seem that Tim was fortunate in that his body did not react as negatively as Con's did. But, we must be careful not to de-couple the physical and the emotional or mental aspects of human functioning in a Cartesian manner. We cannot assume that there was an initial physical difference between the two men. The mental state of each could itself have been a factor in the physical state that each found himself in, just as the physical state of each of them could have been a factor in their respective emergent mental and emotional states. However, it would seem that Tim was better placed than Con in terms of social and family resources, and the support and opportunity to relax that he could find at home.

On top of all of this, we can see Tim actively adopting a certain orientation towards his work which helped him manage his situation. He opted to define himself by applying a particular culturally available discursive resource to himself: the notion of a 'hero' who takes on a challenge. He also takes his relationship with Con into account in trying to explain his emergent orientation to events – suggesting that taking some responsibility for his friend was a factor in his adopting a positive stance towards the difficulties of their shared circumstances. Notice also that he adopts a positive characterisation of the school, as 'rough' as it was, as part of an educational *service*. And where Tim takes a stoic philosophical view of the world, seeing it as a generally 'rough place' that one has got to make the best of, Con adopts a different view of the world as one which 'ought' to be better than it is. Whereas Tim is willing to try to take control over circumstances, Con seems to be adopting an orientation in which he resigns himself to losing control, because the world is against him.

In looking at this case study in occupational stress and how individuals manage it, we must remember that we cannot read it as if we were actually seeing into the minds of these two individuals. Tim is creating an account of what happened, rather than neutrally 'reporting' it. He is constructing a plausible tale which helps make sense of things both for himself and for the researcher that he is speaking to. The only account we have of Con's experience is that which his old friend gives us, on the basis of what he remembers seeing and hearing. We might also note that Tim Dyke is taking part in the ongoing social construction process, whereby work researchers, and others, analyse the sort of events that happened here in terms of 'stress' factors and personal resources for 'managing stress'. Nevertheless, in pragmatist terms, there is value in using an analysis of this kind. It is invaluable in helping us to understand and, potentially, to manage stressful situations.

We are making use here of a process-relational style of analysis in which exchanges and reciprocities – positive ones and negative ones – are seen to play a part in the way two individuals manage their identities, their work and their lives. We have a framework that we can apply to situations of stress and stress management generally. It suggests that we should not regard stress as something that necessarily results from having either heavy responsibilities in our jobs or being faced with a heavy workload. The emotional and physical difficulties which we label 'stress' arise when the individual does not have the personal and social 'resources' to enable them to define the pressures of this responsibility or workload as *manageable*. Occupational stress, or *distress*, is avoided when the occupational or organisational circumstances are ones over which the individual feels they can assert control, rather than ones which will swamp them or lead to their 'breaking down'.

One of the ways in which stress at work can be handled is by having a home or family life that enables one to balance the stresses of work with the pleasures and recreation of home life. However, the growing problem of a 'long hours culture' in work organisations has made this increasingly unlikely for many professional and managerial employees – even if it were true in the first place that home life is the haven of peace and relaxation that we often would like it to be. In spite of employers claiming to be concerned with helping employees to find a 'work–life balance', organisational restructuring and the associated insecurities have increased the pressures on managers to spend long hours at work (Worrall and Cooper, 1999). For many people the stresses of family life and the stresses of work have come to be mutually reinforcing, leading to a situation when, as Hochschild (1997a and 1997b) has put it, 'work becomes home and home becomes work'.

One of the ways that people handle, or avoid, stress at work is to indulge in practices that we can characterise as acts of workplace mischief.

Workplace mischief and the organisational underlife

There are both 'official' and 'unofficial' aspects to the negotiated order of every organisation. It was shown in Chapter 2 (pp. 61–3) that, in different circumstances, unofficial or 'informal' practices can contribute either positively or negatively to the long-term survival of the organisation – towards officially approved ends, we might say. This applies to what we can call 'organisational mischief'.

Organisational mischief *Concept*

Activities occurring within the workplace that (a) according to the official structure, culture, rules and procedures of the organisation 'should not happen' and (b) contain an element of challenge to dominant modes of operating or to dominant interests in the organisation.

Although we are now focusing our attention on something explicitly called *mischief*, the same ambiguity arises with regard to its likely corporate effects. *Organisational mischief* is a category of unofficial workplace activity that involves some kind of challenge by organisational members to the dominant order of the enterprise (see Further Reading on deviance and misbehaviour in organisations, pp. 161–2). It clearly has the potential to undermine a dominant order or to thwart dominant interests. However, there are *unintended consequences* of mischievous actions just as there are unintended consequences of formal and official corporate initiatives (Chapter 2, pp. 63–73). This is illustrated by the story of the man who set fire to the premises where he worked as an extreme expression of the contempt he and his workmates felt for the company that employed them. After initial resentment at this act of sabotage, the senior management came to see it as an immense piece of good fortune. The building completely burned down, but it was old, inefficient and awkwardly located. New premises that were much better suited to strategic managerial priorities were built with the insurance money that the company received and a new, much more compliant, workforce was recruited to work on the new site. The challenge had misfired. An act of gross organisational mischief had the unintended consequence of reinforcing the order and the interests that it had been intended to undermine.

Much of the mischief that routinely occurs in the unofficial or informal *underlife* of an organisation challenges the dominant order much less directly, and often less deliberately, than was the case with the aggrieved arsonist. An employee might, for example, falsely claim that they were taking a day off work because they were ill when, in fact, they simply wanted to avoid the pressures of a typical Monday morning in their office. Such behaviour, especially if it becomes widespread or persistent, will have the effect of challenging organisational interests. The worker has prioritised their own interests over those of the employing organisation – in spite of the commitment they have made to the employer through their employment contract.

The *implicit contract* that employees make with employing organisations is the most useful starting point for any attempt to understand what is going on when people go absent from work, engage in sabotage, steal from the workplace, or 'misbehave' at work in any of the variety of other ways we will shortly be considering. A key element of the implicit contract between the employee and the employer is the employee 'input' of *compliance*, the acceptance of a degree of managerial control over the worker. This means that whenever someone joins an organisation as an employee they *surrender a degree of personal autonomy* but, as we have frequently observed, human beings do not readily give up control of their circumstances or their 'selves'. This is especially the case in modern democratic societies, where the concepts of human rights and the autonomy of the 'free citizen' are culturally significant and people are only willing to submit to the control of others to a very limited and closely circumscribed extent. When one takes a job, for a certain level of pay, job security, opportunity for fulfilment, and all the rest, one accepts that certain people, to a certain extent, may tell one what to do. Such an acceptance is typically loaded with reservation, reluctance and caution. Resistance to any attempted control that falls short of total legitimacy in the employee's eyes is to be expected in every workplace circumstance. And where that resistance cannot take the direct form of a straightforward refusal to comply – which often it cannot – we can expect the employee to seek one means or another to maintain their pride or otherwise protect their identity.

To defend their sense of 'self' and, in effect, to restore some balance to a threatened implicit contract, people engage in activities ranging from burning down their workplace to stealing a pencil from their desk; from circulating rude cartoons round an office to playing practical jokes on people. To point to this 'defence of self' aspect of such activity is not, however, to deny that people at work often joke with each other simply for the sake of enjoying a joke or take a pencil home simply because there is no one looking and the pencil from the telephone pad at home has worn out. However, this should not stop us recognising that there is often a further and a deeper significance to many of these acts – a significance that we must always take into account when trying to understand behaviour in organisations.

Many of the studies of workplace resistance to organisational control have focused on manual workers in industrial situations, and deep insights into the importance of acts of defiance and anti-authority cultural gestures have been gained by close studies of the experience of working class employment. It is unfortunate, however, when managerial workers are excluded from analyses of organisational mischief, as is done in the review of what they call 'organisational misbehaviour' by Ackroyd and Thompson (1999). Managers are themselves employees of organisations and the majority of them are subject to controls over their behaviour by more senior managers – controls that may be experienced by a manager as a 'threat to self' no less significant than the threat felt by a non-manager. Indeed the controls to which managers are subject can be far more sophisticated or even insidious than those experienced by more junior employees. Managers frequently invest more of their 'selves' in their work than do ordinary employees. Consequently, 'defence of self' gestures and acts of 'resistance' through mischief are to be seen from the top to the bottom of the organisational hierarchy. This is apparent in the case we will look at in Chapter 6 (Case 6.2, p. 219) where the later arrival and early departure of the senior manager Todd is not essentially different from that of an ordinary worker cutting short their working day. And the suspected discouraging of the visit by the police officer and the security consultant by the security manager is not essentially different from, say, a gym assistant in that organisation persuading a maintenance engineer not to repair an exercise machine that she does not like.

Mischief at any level of the organisation is likely to involve a mixture of the more 'psychological' *defence of self* and the more material pursuit of *self-interest.* A day 'illegally' taken off work may, for example, benefit a worker by giving them the satisfaction of upsetting a supervisor who has been overloading them with work. The worker's pride and sense of autonomy is thus defended and if they use that day to paint a room in their house, they also save the money they might otherwise have had to pay someone else. Their material self-interest has thus been served at the same time as they were protecting their sense of self-integrity and personal autonomy.

Some forms of mischief are relatively individualistic and involve just one person defending their sense of self, engaging in an act of personal resistance or otherwise furthering their personal interests. We might include here:

- *Spontaneous individual acts of absenteeism.* The shop worker staying away from work on the day that it is rumoured the company's 'mystery shopper' will be visiting the store to check up on the quality of service.
- *Inattentiveness through day-dreaming or chatting to work colleagues.* The counter staff in a council office failing to notice someone entering to pay their rent because they are too busy discussing rumours about their manager's private life; the police officer allocated to a particularly boring beat failing to notice a street crime because he is replaying in his mind the football match he watched the night before.
- *Minimal compliance with instructions.* The activities of the 'jobsworths' or 'bureaucratic personalities' we came across in Chapter 2 (p. 72); the warehouse labourer who was told to 'get those boxes moved out of the gangway before you go home' moving a pile of cardboard boxes containing fragile goods out into the yard so that heavy overnight rain destroys their contents.
- *Keeping information to oneself.* The maintaining of a strong sense of indispensability and 'being in control' by a bank's branch manager who gives staff only minimal information about the headquarters' guidelines to which the branch is meant to be working.
- *Bullying.* The regular tormenting of the weakest member of a work team by a supervisor who feels aggrieved at having to take orders from a manager who is 'half my age and barely out of college'.
- *Sexual harassment.* The repeated commenting on the sexual characteristics of women colleagues by a male employee who also pinned photographs of naked women to the wall above his desk and who only modified his behaviour when the women took to decorating another wall of the office with pictures of naked men.
- *Opportunistic pilfering or embezzlement.* The taking of a couple of new books from a library by a library assistant who feels that he is too poorly paid to

afford to buy books and who finds himself left alone to lock up a local library one evening; the regular siphoning-off of amounts of money by an accountant who finds that a particular very rich client rarely checks the figures with which they are provided.

- *The sabotaging or breaking of goods or equipment in a moment of individual frustration.* The throwing of a crate of bottled beer down the cellar stairs by a bar manager whose staff had failed to turn up for work, leaving him to cope with a rush of customers.
- *Using work premises or equipment for private purposes, both within and sometimes out of working hours.* The use of a production machine to make a toy for one's children; the photocopying at work of invitations to an employee's birthday party; the sending of flirtatious or aggressive personal e-mails to other employees.
- *The punishing of an awkward customer who has offended the worker.* The waiter who spits in the third plate of soup to be taken to a customer who has sent back a first plate of soup because it was too cold and a second plate of soup because it was too hot.
- *Leaving the organisation at an especially inconvenient time.* The university professor falling out with the faculty dean and resigning from their post so that their departure coincides with the beginning of the vital and difficult report-writing stage of a major research project which they have led and which only they fully understand.

All of these relatively individualistic pieces of mischief still have a social dimension. They all relate to problems in the employment 'trade' with the employing organisation. And it is likely that individual acts such as going absent from work will develop into a more general pattern of absenteeism, as more and more people see staying away from work as a defence against work overload. This possibility needs to be recognised when we identify some of the more social and group-oriented types of organisational mischief:

- *Acts of absenteeism or inconvenient resignation that accord with unofficial norms which have developed in an organisation or a sub-unit of an organisation.* The standard practice of people claiming to be ill when allocated to the shift in a restaurant when the most difficult customers tend to turn up.
- *The setting of group work-output norms that suit group members but are managerially defined as 'restrictions of output'.* The refusal of a group of machine operators in a garment factory to allow any of the group members to produce more than 15 garments per hour or fewer than 13 garments (because that is deemed a 'reasonable and fair' work rate by most of the group) in spite of the fact that the management want a higher output and indeed operate a bonus system that would give higher pay for higher output.
- *Organised fiddles.* The standard practice among staff in a public house of overcharging customers who are thought unlikely to check their change; shop staff giving extra change to customers to whom they are related.

- *'Dehumanising' or 'putting down' customers or clients – typically behind their backs but sometimes 'to their faces'.* The practice of referring to all customers as 'punters', 'marks' or 'Johns' rather than customers; the norm among motor mechanics in a garage of telling customers that the fault with their car is something different from what the customers say they believe it to be; the labelling by workers in a fish and chip shop of all customers into categories like FOBs (fat overeating slob), TLTCs (too lazy to cook) and SUBs (soaking up the beer).
- *Using work premises for group-sanctioned non-work purposes.* The use of a medical room by nightshift workers taking turns to snatch an illegal hour's sleep during the shift; the playing of competitive computer games involving several workers during office hours.
- *Workplace games.* The weekly competition between senior managers in a company to collect as many as possible management 'buzzwords' used by the managing director, both orally or in documents; the throwing of an item such as a chicken leg from worker to worker in a food factory whenever supervisors or managers are not looking.
- *Practical jokes, organised 'piss-takes' or 'wind-ups'.* The pinning of a large sheet of paper bearing the legend 'pompous bastard' to the back of a manager's jacket, unknown to him, before he shows a group of visitors around a new building; the nursing tutors in a hospital always ensuring that they send at least one member of each new intake of nurses to the medical stores to collect an item such as a 'bronchial tube' or a bottle of 'mild infarction'.
- *Organised bullying and harassment.* The persistent persecuting of black men and women workers in a textile factory, involving name-calling and the damaging of work in progress, by a group of white male maintenance workers whose supervisor not only encourages such behaviour but discriminates against men in his team who do not join in these practices by giving them fewer overtime opportunities and by allocating them to more than their fair share of unpleasant jobs.
- *The organised sabotaging of goods or equipment.* The regular damaging of an assembly line to give all the workers on it a break from machine-pacing; the deliberate overloading of an organisation's e-mail system by people widely and unnecessarily circulating copies of lengthy documents and large attachments.
- *The mobilising of groups to take sanctions against management as a means of resolving a grievance.* The decision of a group of design engineers, after taking a vote, to work on only one design at a time – this sanction to continue until the company brings the department up to its official full staff strength; the agreement by a group of van drivers that their union representative should tell management that no overtime will be worked until the pay is brought up to the level of a rival delivery service company; the refusal, after a brief lunchtime meeting, of all the departmental managers in a large retail store to attend meetings called by the general manager after the 6 p.m. closing time.

In each of these more group-oriented types of organisational mischief, we again see people protecting or advancing the material aspects of their implicit contract with the employer. The van drivers want more pay, for example, and are disrupting the overtime arrangements to achieve this. The cheating of drinkers in the public house is a means of maintaining a higher level of income than the employer provides in the pay packet. A certain level of pay – part legal, part illegal – has become part of the implicit contract associated with their employment, in effect. The machine operators who fix an output norm are also working to shape their implicit contract (as were the workers in the famous Bank Wiring Observation Room study at the Hawthorne plant reported by Roethlisberger and Dickson, 1939). There is, then, a degree of informal bargaining between employers and employees occurring in all of this misbehaviour. Does this mean we should reject the 'mischief' label, then? It does not. All of these behaviours are, to some degree, taken against the dominant order of the organisation. They constitute a refusal simply to accept the roles and rewards laid down for them by the employer. Just as with the more individualistic types of behaviour, these group-oriented actions have a 'defence of self' or protection of autonomy dimension for the members of the groups. This works in conjunction with the pursuit of shared material interests. Each member of the workgroup that has agreed its own definition of a 'fair day's work' can work with a sense that group membership protects them from managerial pressures. The food workers throwing food around the factory are ritually undermining the supervisors' control over their activities. The managers who mock their boss's pretentious language and the managers who refuse to attend their general managers' out-of-hours meetings, are expressing a degree of independence or distance from their senior managers. The strategies of independence that we see in all of these groups are not acts of rebellion or a fight for full autonomy. As part of their implicit contract with their employer, they submit to a certain amount of managerial control but what their collective misbehaviours are in effect saying to those in authority is 'This is who we are. So far and no further.'

Organisational employees who deal directly with customers or clients have an additional need to protect their personal identities and their sense of autonomy. It is not just the manager or supervisor who exerts pressures here on the worker to behave in a certain way. It is also the customer. In many aspects of service and retail work the worker is required to act like a servant. The emotional pressures that this can put on both the worker and the manager alike were looked at earlier and the problems of engaging in *emotional labour* were illustrated both by the hotel manager Ken Steary in Case 4.3 and the sex worker Cindy Sutor in Case 4.4. Some important psychic relief from the pressure to act subserviently is thus achieved by the rude labelling of clients in the chip shop and by the motor mechanics always claiming to know better than the motorists what is wrong with their vehicles. The notion of 'getting one's own back' on people who are put into the master or mistress role, vis-à-vis the service worker's role as servant, can take some very unpleasant forms. The ploy of the waiter who, behind the scenes, spits in the diner's food is a classic example of this, but repulsive as such behaviour may seem, it is far from uncommon in the food and drinks industry, at both the customer service end of the business and at the food processing stage. It is rare to find anybody who has worked in a food processing plant who cannot relate tales of people throwing rat droppings into food mixing machines, urinating into beer vats or tipping floor sweepings into hoppers of cereal. Outside the food industry, one hears similar reports of people chalking obscenities on the insides of the items of furniture they are making or leaving hidden parts of metal products insufficiently protected against rust. One hears of unspeakable things being done to dead bodies in hospitals or undertakers' workshops. All of these are human gestures of defiance and demonstrations of personal or group autonomy, however alienated or degraded a form of human expression we may deem them to be.

In the conversation about some of the examples of workplace mischief that they have come across as managers, Hazel Hopeman and Jenny Elgin recognise that there is 'something deeper' going on in what Jenny calls the 'underlife' of organisations.

Activity 4.7

Read the conversation in Case 4.6 between Hazel Hopeman, a manager in an airline, and Jenny Elgin, the manager of a supermarket, and:

- note down examples arising in this conversation of the various types of organisational mischief that we identified above (recognising that certain activities may straddle more than one category);
- think about any examples of organisational mischief that you have come across or heard about that you might have thrown into the conversation if you had joined Jenny and Hazel in their discussion;
- consider the extent to which Hazel and Jenny's attempts to make sense of (or 'theorise' about) these activities fit with the attempts to understand organisational mischief that have been made in this chapter so far.

Hazel and Jenny probe the organisational underworld

Case 4.6

What really started me thinking about these things was a strange experience I had one day when I was a victim of a practical joke organised by a couple of my departmental managers. I was walking around the shop doing my usual thing of smiling at everyone and having a friendly word with a customer here and a colleague there. One of the customers made a very strange comment. 'You don't look very sore to me', he said. I was puzzled, but carried on. Then one of the checkout operators said, 'You don't look sore to me Jenny.' Again, I said nothing. But when a customer who I'd helped with a query about Sunday opening hours asked me, with a rather enigmatic smile on her face, 'So what are you sore about, Miss Elgin?' I let my puzzlement show. 'Look at your badge, dear', the customer said. And when I looked at my 'Jenny Elgin, Store Manager' badge, I saw that it had been skilfully doctored to say 'Jenny Elgin, Sore Manager'.

I expect that did make you a 'sore manager'.

I was not pleased, I can tell you, Hazel. But I had been rather short tempered with my management team for more than a week. They knew I was having problems with my car and that I was getting tired of having to drive so far to work at this branch. 'Don't take it out on us', the grocery manager had said to me only the day before. He was very understanding. I don't think the others were. They were getting their message over to me another way.

And they were obviously having a good laugh too.

I am sure they were. But what occurred to me was that you always have to look for deeper meanings in these things. There are all sorts of things bubbling away, seething sometimes, beneath the surface – in the underlife of a business, if you like. I'm sure part of the context of 'the laugh' that my managers were having was the fact that I am the only woman manager in the store and that I am the only graduate manager they have ever had close contact with. They know I will be moving on in my career. But I doubt if any of them will. So they 'brought me down a bit'. I said nothing about what happened. But I've never forgotten about it.

I agree that you have to probe beneath the surface, as a manager, when you come across anything like this. One partly hilarious and partly very serious problem I had to deal with was the case of a cabin crew whose male and female members swapped clothes towards the end of a flight. When the passengers were disembarking, there were the cabin crew as usual, thanking passengers for flying with us and very politely wishing them well. But the women were in the men's trousers, and far more peculiarly, the two chaps were in dresses. As you can imagine, we got some complaints.

What was going on, Hazel?

In a way it didn't surprise me. As a management we are well aware of this issue of 'emotional labour' that researchers write about. The man who was behind the jape told me, 'Sometimes you've just got to burst out and be yourself.' 'Cross-dressing is being yourself?' I came back – incredulous. 'Well it is for me,' he said, winking at me in a very camp manner. I believed him. 'But what about the others?' I asked. 'Oh, they'd never done it before. But, you ask them, they all say that the laugh did them good.'

So who were they having a go at – the airline, the managers, the passengers?

Oh, I think all of these. And none of them at the same time. I don't think it is as direct or as specific as it was with the case of your managers 'having a go' about your irritability. I think it's all got to do with this 'underlife' that you talk about. All sorts of things are going on behind the scenes in every type of organisation, aren't they?

Yes, but I can't imagine that a lot can go on behind the scenes in an airliner. The cabin crew are on display most of the time, aren't they?

Absolutely right – and that's why I was very lenient with them.

And there must be little scope for them to engage in the sort of fiddles that we have to deal with in retailing.

Well, there is just one. The biggest fiddle in the past – one that used to give them a lot of satisfaction as well as being materially rewarding – was the fiddling of time.

Claiming more hours that they actually put in?

Exactly. But that's now gone with computerisation. The only scope they have to line their pockets and 'have one over the airline' at the same time is with regard to complementary alcohol. We can't know how many free drinks passengers have or have not accepted. So a good proportion of those drinks go home with the cabin crew. We are well aware of this. But, as I say, it's the only thing we are aware of. I'm sure it's much more complicated in your business?

It certainly is. We get everything from people hiding stock that they know is going to go down in price the next week to check-out staff keeping vouchers they should give to customers. I've caught staff eating food they have taken off the shelves and which will obviously never go past the till. You get people swapping the tickets on items so that they are scanned at a lower price than they should have been and colleagues giving discounts to friends who are not entitled to them. And a scam was recently discovered in which store managers in one region were getting builders retained by the business to build conservatories on their houses, and charge these to the company.

And do you get people deliberately causing damage?

How do you mean?

I was thinking about what goes on with the men who load and unload planes. They are largely young blokes who are young and very strong. You get the impression that they are very conscious of their masculinity. And I think that their very low status in the airport's pecking order is experienced as some kind of threat to this.

So what do they do?

Well, first, they are always fighting with each other. They have time on their hands when there's no plane to work on and, of course, they have quite a mixture of nationalities and ethnic backgrounds. It can be quite explosive. And when they are not knocking each other to pieces, they are prone to smashing up luggage or bits of freight.

Yes, I've only had a couple of fights to sort out in my career so far. But damage to goods is not uncommon. I had a disgruntled bloke regularly leaving stock out of refrigeration last year and we had a spate recently of staff damaging goods in order to get them reduced in price. There was also the time we caught one of the shelf stackers opening jars of peanut butter and scratching little smiley faces into the surface of the product. What amazed me was that we only received a handful of complaints from customers. Yet he must have contaminated scores of jars, from what we understand. It could have been very damaging for the business. But it didn't even get in the press.

You confined it to the store's 'underlife'?

Thank goodness, yes. The young man who did it apparently felt he was 'having a laugh' at the expense of shoppers who, he said, never bother to speak to him or even smile at him when he is filling shelves.

Oh this is something we are very aware of with our cabin crew. In their training we have to prepare them for ungrateful or rude passengers. They know the score and are generally very good.

Generally?

Well I suppose so. A story is told about one of our crews who got really sick of a man who was regularly rude to them. He was also very demanding. So, one day, they laced his coffee with a strong laxative. That really sorted the bloke out.

Do you think that really happened? I mean it sounds unlikely to me – given that the crew who did it would probably end up cleaning up any mess that got made.

True. But if the story is apocryphal, it is rather interesting, isn't it, that people still take pleasure in passing it on. It always gets a good laugh. It sort of helps keep the customer in their place, psychologically speaking.

Yes, that reminds me of a rather different story – a true one that happened here. But it also has that element of the employee putting a distance between themselves and customers. There was this very attractive young woman who used to shop in here. The male colleagues were always looking out for her coming into the store. Well it turned out that she did some modelling for one of those erotic magazines. When the blokes discovered this, they made sure they obtained plenty of copies of the pictures and passed them round all the staff – men and women alike. It meant that a lot of silly and unpleasant giggling went on whenever she came into the shop. It also led to a game among the lads of 'talent spotting', as they named it. I discovered that they were competing to identify likely models that they might contact a particular magazine about. Fortunately, the first woman who was approached, as far as I know, came straight to me. She was very good about it. But two of those young men no longer work for us!

If only we could get these young men – I'm thinking of our baggage handlers again – to leave their sexuality, and their problems with their masculinity, at home.

And women?

Yes, we ought to be fair here. But I think that the women cabin crew who work for us are all very discreet and sophisticated about how they relate to male passengers. There's no way they could – or, to be honest, we would want them to – leave their sexuality at home. But all sorts of trouble follows if sex does rear its beautiful head at work.

How do you mean?

I was thinking of the time that the airport security caught a couple of our employees having sexual intercourse on the altar of the airport chapel. It was after a party and the place was locked. But they had got a key and thought that no one would disturb them in that part of the building. They were both single and I don't think it even occurred to them that the tabletop they were using was meant to be an altar. But none of this stopped my boss from ordering me to sack both of them. I really had to fight him on this and, in the end, I refused to do it. What amazed me was how hot under the collar he got about the whole business. I mean it really upset him. I argued that there were no serious business or managerial implications whatsoever and that, at the most, it was a minor disciplinary matter. But he had a real problem with it.

I think it's the fear some managers feel about having the lid lifted on this 'underlife', as I call it. Some managers just don't want to acknowledge that people are a lot more than little robots. I think it's the idea that employees are flesh and blood that bothers them. I had a similar difficulty when I discovered that one of the office workers occasionally played this game of leaning out of her office window during her lunch break – the window is immediately above the shop entrance – and passing the time of day with customers. What they didn't know was that, while she was doing this, she was getting served from behind by her boyfriend.

What did you do about that?

Nothing. It was me who caught them. And I decided that their embarrassment at being caught 'at it' was punishment enough. I am utterly confident that they won't do it again. No damage was done. Nobody else knew about it. But when I related this story at a corporate training event, ages after the event, I found that several of the managers there were absolutely appalled. Several people regarded as an utter outrage what I thought was quite an amusing, and even touching, piece of mischief. 'It simply shouldn't have happened' one of them kept muttering. 'The workplace is no place for that sort of thing', another spluttered before walking out of the room.

What was their problem?

What indeed? But I always remember that phrase, 'The workplace is no place for that sort of thing'. If only it were that simple!

This conversation represents a good example of managers taking a step back from their everyday practice and reflecting on the significance of some of the activities that they come across, and indeed have to deal with at work. All of the activities about which they are comparing notes fit more or less with the categories of organisational mischief set out earlier. A series of *practical jokes* or 'wind-ups' make up perhaps the most significant category here. Such a joke is played on Jenny herself and Hazel reports jokes played on airline passengers both as a group (with the cross-dressing farewell) and on one particular passenger who was 'punished' with an unwanted laxative drink. These latter two pieces of mischief to some extent also fit into our category of *putting down customers* – something that would also apply to the 'talent-spotting' *workplace game* Jenny talks about. The same might apply to the office worker communicating to customers from her office window and enjoying the irony of the fact that she was taking certain pleasures they knew nothing of. However, this case, and that of the late night use of the airport chapel for lovemaking was an example of *the use of premises or equipment for private purposes* rather than for organisational ones. *Sabotage* occurs in the loading and unloading of aircraft at the airport and in the interfering with the peanut butter in the shop. We hear of *fiddles* occurring in the airline with regard to alcoholic drinks and both money and goods in the case of the shop.

Jenny and Hazel are doing more in their conversation than simply swapping stories about their respective work organisations. They appear to have a shared interest in making sense of the various examples of organisational mischief that they present to each other. They recognise a straightforward role that these activities play *at a surface level* in organisational members' lives. People enjoy the 'laugh' that follows from the practical joking. Service workers feel better for 'having a go' at or 'keeping in their place' both managers and customers. And employees 'line their pockets', as Hazel puts it, by engaging in fiddles at work. However, both women feel that there is something more significant about these activities, something going on *at a deeper level*. Jenny suggests that there are 'deeper meanings' to these activities and that there are all sorts of things 'bubbling away' or even 'seething' below the surface. Hazel seems to agree with this and takes on Jenny's notion of an organisational 'underlife'. And there is some interesting theoretical reflection that fits with this concept in her interpretation of the behaviour of the cross-dressing cabin crew members. She uses a notion of people 'bursting out and being themselves' to make sense of what was occurring here, thus seeing their gesture as a particularly positive form of the 'defence of self' aspect of much organisational mischief. She also connects the fighting and the sabotage that occurs among the young men who load and unload the aircraft with problems that she thinks they have with both their ethnic identities and their masculinity. In thinking about such 'deeper level' factors she is still aware that the behaviour also has a more 'surface level' function of relieving boredom between flights.

Sexuality, humour and the struggle for control

Jenny and Hazel both imply that the area of human sexuality may be one in which clues might be found about the deeper issues that organisational mischief relates to. They both speak of managers who 'had a problem' with the idea of sexual behaviour occurring at work. They were frightened, Jenny suggests, by the prospect of 'having the lid lifted' on the 'underlife' of the organisation. Both sexuality and humour appear to play a major part in the organisational underlife of the organisations that these two managers work in. Can we go more deeply into these matters to explore the full depths of the organisational underlife and what its significance might be in the lives of organisational managers and employees? This is quite a challenging question, and Activity 4.8 is an invitation to take it up.

Activity 4.8

Reread the conversation between Hazel and Jenny and:

- Consider why it might be that some of the managers that both Hazel and Jenny have come across seem to be especially troubled about sexual behaviour occurring in the workplace. Why do they consider the workplace to be 'no place for that sort of thing' do you think?
- Look back to the discussion of narratives and stories and how they can be seen as elements of human culture that help people to handle existential problems (pp. 99–102) and reflect on whether the 'laughs' that Hazel and Jenny talk about have a significance which fits with this kind of analysis. Does this workplace humour have a function that goes beyond simply providing 'fun at work' or the pleasure of 'getting one's own back' on certain people?

Jenny Elgin offers one explanation of why managers might be troubled by sexuality in the workplace. To lift the lid from the organisational underlife and contemplate its sexual dimension is to come to terms with 'the idea that employees are flesh and blood' (see Further Reading on sexuality in organisations, p. 163). This means accepting, Jenny thinks, the fact that 'people are a lot more than little robots'. Sexuality, this suggests, stands for the basic humanity – and the fundamental 'animality' we might say – of the people that managers might prefer to treat as cogs in the organisational machine. To be reminded that employees are living creatures with bodies, desires and libidinal drives might make some managers uncomfortable. It reminds them of how limited their capacity to control human beings is. For a manager to be reminded that employees are living animals with emotions and desires is to be reminded that one is being required to control the uncontrollable – to 'herd cats' (Chapter 1, p. 3). It is perhaps also discomforting because it reminds the manager of their own desires and the sexuality that they too are required to leave behind when they come to work. But sexuality, desire, and indeed the enjoyment of laughter, are not things that can be left behind when the human being goes to work, whether as a manager or as an ordinary employee. And they are behaviours that defy organisational control.

Work organisations are set up to be places where rational and instrumental behaviour occurs and where attention is to be focused on the completion of formal tasks. If there is to be love, it is to be love of work or love of the company. If there is to be passion, it is to be passion for the product or a passion for customer satisfaction. If there is to be desire, it is to be desire for the success of the organisation and a desire for the formal rewards of pay and security that are offered for contributing to that corporate success. For love, passion and desire to be directed to other than corporate ends is to threaten the managerial controls that are intended to achieve those ends. Any display of passion or desire on the part of organisational members for the bodies of other organisational members or for organisational clients is an especially powerful symbolic challenge to that control. We should not be surprised, therefore, that Jenny Elgin speaks of managers arguing emphatically that the workplace is 'no place for that sort of thing'. Indeed, most of us would see the point of their wanting to discourage shop workers spending time identifying which customers might be potential erotic magazine models or wanting to discourage office workers from having sexual intercourse at the window of their offices. However, Jenny and Hazel seem to be implying that a reasonable and sensitive manager would recognise that, while the sexuality of organisational employees may need to kept discreetly under control within the workplace, it is not something that can be completely suppressed. Sexuality may be expressed directly in the workplace through individuals courting each other or engaging in overtly sexual activities. Equally, it may be expressed indirectly through women expressing their femininity and men expressing their masculinity at work through the way they dress or through their style of relating to others. Either way, it is an aspect of the human spirit that will always present a possible challenge to managerial control.

Joking and humour can be seen, like sexuality, as expressions of the 'human spirit'. But humour, again like sex, is associated with pleasure rather than with work. Work organisations are meant to be serious places and not comedy clubs or sites for the pursuit of bodily pleasures. But both sex and humour are serious matters as well, it can be argued. This is partly because they are expressions of human 'spirit' and often express that spirit in the face of managerial attempts to harness human efforts to corporate ends. The office workers having sexual intercourse at the office window were not just finding an opportunity to express their love and desire for each other. They were also making a gesture of independence towards both their employer and the customers of the shop. The cabin crew cross-dressers can be seen as doing something similar with regard to the airline and to the passengers whom they had served. In each of these cases humour and sexuality were both involved in the expression of human autonomy. There was a serious aspect as well as a fun aspect to each of these two pieces of mischief. But the 'seriousness of humour' goes deeper than this (see Further Reading on humour in organisations, p. 162).

It might seem strange to talk about humour as a serious matter, but it can be understood as playing a seriously important role in the human construction of identities and the handling of existential anxieties. Earlier it was argued that narratives, stories, films, news stories, gossip and jokes all play a role in human culture of reassuring people in the face of the life's anxieties. It was pointed out how often these elements of culture lead us to contemplate the horrors of life – horrors ranging from being murdered or having an accident to a sexual partner's infidelity or the loss of one's job. Our engagement with fiction and non-fiction alike, with 'serious' stories as well as with comedy, frequently involves confronting the breakdown of order in our lives as we engage with the story we are reading or watching on a screen – before being reassuringly returned to order and reality as we close the book or leave the cinema. Humour, comedy and joking operate in a similar way. By making work-related jokes or transmitting funny stories about aspects of the work organisation, for instance, we challenge or question the normal order of the work organisation and its control apparatus – an order that is, however, left more or less intact after we have enjoyed 'the laugh' and returned to 'normal service'.

Activity 4.9

Look at the five 'messages from the underworld' (one picture and four documents) that have been collected from different work organisations and consider what role you think they might be playing in the lives of the employees of the organisations in which they were circulating.

Messages from the organisational underworld

Case 4.7

FIGURE 4.3 **Our company was recently in a boat race with two of our competitors. Guess which boat was ours!**

If you are unhappy

Once upon a time, there was a non-conforming swallow who decided not to fly south for the winter. However, soon the weather turned so cold that he reluctantly started to fly south. In a short time, ice began to form on his wings and he fell to earth in a barnyard, almost frozen. A cow passed by and crapped on the little swallow. The little bird thought it was the end. But, the manure warmed him and defrosted his wings. Warm and happy, able to breathe, he started to sing. Just then a large cat came by and, hearing the chirping, investigated the sounds. The cat cleared away the manure, found the chirping bird and promptly ate him.

There are three morals to this story. First, everyone who shits on you is not necessarily your enemy, second, everyone who gets you out of the shit is not necessarily your friend and, third, if you're warm and happy in a pile of shit, keep your mouth shut.

Job vacancy: Staffing and administration services sub-assistant

The pay is the market rate less 10% (but with a boredom compensation bonus).

We are a leading financial services company which is creeping into a very long period of unparalleled slow change.

If you are sure, predictable, pedantic and inflexible in your outlook, you could be just what we are looking for. Ideally aged exactly 42.5 years of age, a conservative dresser with at least 22 years' experience as the Personnel lady in a building society (or very similar environment) you are a play-it-safe procedure-follower who relishes plodding through long hours.

You will be administering pay and rations to our Head Office staff along with ensuring all paperwork is completed fully on staff movements.

Career prospects are excellent. Keep your nose clean and an increment each year can be yours. In as little as 15 years you could rise to be a Staff and Administration Services Assistant Officer with additional responsibility for sick pay.

Benefits are excellent: pay every month, holidays every year and your own desk and chair.

Interested applicants should apply in writing for a long application form from Major Gen. Horatio Flash-Blindly DSO (ret'd), Staffing and Administration Assistant Sub-General Manager, Newco Financial Services, Staid House, Oldtown.

We think we are an equal opportunities employer and believe this job would especially suit a nice lady.

In the beginning was the Plan

In the beginning was the Plan.
And then came the assumptions.
And the assumptions were without form.
And the Plan was completely without substance.
And darkness was upon the faces of the workers.
And they spake unto their Supervisors, saying
"It is a crock of crap and it stinketh".
And the Supervisors went unto the Section Heads and sayeth
"It is a pail of dung and none may abide the odour thereof".
And the Section Heads went unto their Managers and sayeth unto them
"It is a container of excrement and none may abide its strength".
And the Managers went unto their Directors and sayeth
"It contains that which aids plant growth and is very strong".
And the Managing Director went unto the Chairman, saying unto him
"It promoteth growth and is very powerful"
And the Chairman considered the Plan and sayeth unto the Board
"This powerful new Plan will actively promote the growth and efficiency of the Company".
And the Board looked upon the Plan.
And saw that it was good.
And the plan became policy.

Memorandum to all staff
From: the Board of Management
Subject: Retirement policy

As a result of the reduction of money budgeting for departmental areas, we are forced to cut down on the number of our personnel. Under the plan, older employees will be asked to go on early retirement, thus permitting the retention of younger people who represent our future.

Those being required to retire early may appeal to upper management. To make this possible there will be a Survey of Capabilities of Retired Early Workers (SCREW). The appeal process will be known as SHAFT (Scream to Higher Authority Following Termination). Under the terms of the new policy employees may be early retired once, SCREWED twice and SHAFTED as many times as the company deems appropriate.

If the employee follows the above procedures, he or she will be entitled to HERPES (Half Earnings for Retired Personnel's Early Severance). As HERPES is considered a benefit plan, any employee who has received HERPES will no long be SCREWED or SHAFTED by the company.

Management wishes to reassure the younger employees who remain on board, that the company will continue to see that they are well trained through our Special High Intensity Training known as SHIT. The company takes pride in the amount of SHIT our employees receive. We have given our employees more SHIT than any other company in the area. If any employee feels he or she does not receive enough SHIT on the job, see your immediate supervisor. Your supervisor is specially trained to make sure that you receive all the SHIT you can stand.

Each of these documents was widely circulated in the large organisations where they were collected by the researcher. The picture was collected in a hospital, the story of a swallow in a manufacturing company, the mock job advertisement in a building society, the 'In the beginning' text in a pharmaceutical company and the staff memorandum about early retirement in a retailing business. However, it is apparent that these same documents, sometimes in identical form, sometimes with local variations, can be found in one organisation after another. They circulate across societies, it would seem, as well as within organisations.

The documents mock or satirise aspects of the organisation and the way it is managed. They induce mirth by challenging the normal order of these organisations. The picture engages with the notion that the hospital has too many people giving orders (directing the boat), in relation to the numbers of people who are doing the real work (rowing the boat). The story of the swallow satirises those activities we have characterised as 'micropolitical' and implies that the workplace is a dangerous place in which it is difficult to know who is your friend and who is your enemy. The job advertisement apparently mocks the excessively bureaucratic nature of the building society and the poor career opportunities that staff are offered. Its satirical swipe at the employer's claim to be an equal opportunity employer suggests ignorance on the employer's part of the principles of equal opportunities (with the choice of the anachronistic and patronising term 'a nice lady'). It also portrays the management as hypocritical. Senior organisational managers seem to be the main target of 'In the beginning' piece and they are portrayed as plainly stupid, out of touch with common sense and prone to go along with any business nonsense as long as it can be dressed up in the language of planning, efficiency and growth. The workers and the section leaders can see that 'the plan' stinks. The managers, directors and the chairman, however, convince themselves that it is something worthwhile. And, with the retirement policy memorandum, another specific aspect of managerial language and discourse is mocked – the use of acronyms to give weight and importance to relatively routine managerial initiatives. But the document is, more seriously, an attack on what it implies are harsh, unfeeling and exploitative human resourcing policies being pursued by the company.

All of these documents, clearly intended to give employees 'a laugh', deal with serious matters that constitute threats both to employees and to the long-term survival of the organisations themselves (and hence, of course, to the job security of all employees). All comedy, as has been recognised by numerous theorists of humour from Aristotle onwards, deals with incongruity. It focuses upon the unexpected. It plays with the inappropriate. It turns normality on its head. The normal order of each of these organisations is made to look abnormal by being stretched and bent in the distorting mirror of the satirical document. This is exactly what was being done by the airline cabin crew exchanging clothes or by Jenny Elgin's colleagues altering her name badge. These documents and practical jokes distort normality so that we can laugh at and enjoy a temporary suspension of that normality before returning to our normal serious workplace demeanour and getting back to our work.

Workplace humour helps people adjust to aspects of work that they dislike or feel threatened by and it is always possible that some of the satirical intentions of comic interventions may be fulfilled. Mockery of individuals and practices can lead to changes in behaviour and procedures. But workplace humour and joking behaviour can be seen as playing a deeper role in people's lives too. It is part of the way we maintain our sanity. We often joke about the things that worry us most. At work for example, it is noticeable that people whose autonomy is most threatened by overbearing customers or managers will tend to make jokes about such customers or managers more often than those who do not experience such pressures. People whose jobs are the least secure tend to joke about 'getting the chop', 'getting the bullet' or receiving the 'little brown envelope' containing a redundancy notice than those who are relatively secure in their jobs. People doing the most dangerous jobs tend to be those who joke most about possible accidents. Those whose work in emergency services, hospitals and mortuaries involves them in matters of life and death, are the most prone to indulge in black humour and 'laugh in the face' of the death and mutilation that their jobs force them to confront. The joking here can be understood as a glimpse into the abyss. A glimpse into the abyss of disorder and madness, we might say, helps us retain our sanity in the light of the dangers that are seething down there and threatening to swallow us up. Much of our engagement with humour and comedy is like the tightrope walker in Figure 4.4 with his quick occasional glimpses down into the abyss over which he is walking.

To get across to the far side of the ravine, the tightrope walker must keep his eyes most of the time on the solid ground that he wants to reach. However, if he too casually or too confidently strides out in this direction, forgetting what horrors are seething beneath his feet, he is likely to slip from his rope. Equally,

FIGURE 4.4 Humour helps us over the existential abyss

though, if he looks down too intently into the cauldron below him, he will lose his balance and fall into the pit of horrors. When we move through our everyday lives, intent on our various life, work and family projects, we are like the tightrope walker looking to the solid ground that we wish to reach. But to remind ourselves of the precariousness of our situations, and to come to terms with everything that actually or potentially troubles us about the world, we glimpse into the abyss from time to time. We therefore laugh at the figure slipping over on the banana skin, we laugh at the stupidity of people from a neighbouring society, we laugh at the managers whose pretentiousness or incompetence threatens the security of our employment. Having laughed at what might otherwise frighten us into a loss of control in our lives (madness even), we return to our serious demeanour and travel onwards. When we bring sexuality and humour into the workplace, and when we indulge in the lavatory talk and sexually 'dirty' language of the 'underworld' documents reviewed earlier, we are reminding ourselves and those around us that we are not cogs in the corporate machine. We are demonstrating that we are also both creative human beings (who create jokes, write satires and make each other laugh) and recalcitrant biological animals (who copulate, excrete and refuse to be herded). Sexuality and humour thus play a part in the way each one of us struggles to control our lives and identity. It also plays its part, when it is mischievously brought into the workplace, in the struggle for control that goes on between people with varying degrees of power in the organisational pecking order.

We have concentrated in this chapter on various aspects of the informal and unofficial aspects of organisational life and looked at various challenges that are constantly being made to managerial efforts to shape and control work organisations. In the next chapter we turn to those aspects of the struggle for managerial control that are concerned with obtaining and maintaining 'human resources'.

Summary

In this chapter the following key points have been made:

- At the heart of the relationship between the employee and the employing organisation is an *implicit contract* whereby it is understood that the employee will make a particular set of contributions, at a particular level, to the organisation's work in return for a particular mix of rewards. This bargain has to be understood in light of both the life situation and projects of the employee and the strategic direction being followed by the organisation – it is thus central to the *strategic exchange* relationship between the individual and the organisation.
- The implicit contract, as it is understood by the employee, forms part of that employee's *orientation to work*, the meaning they attach to their employment and which influences the ways they act within that employment.

- Individuals' entry to work or to an organisation can be understood in terms of their *initial orientation to work*. This, however, is likely to change as both the organisational and the individual's circumstances (inside and outside work) change. The process of change continues as the individual's personal life and projects move on and as their employment career develops.
- Feelings and emotions play a central part in all work and organisational situations. They cannot be seen as incidental and peripheral to the rational task-based activities with which people are involved.
- In various kinds of work, service work and managerial work especially, there is an emotional dimension built into what is required of the worker. This *emotional labour* can be handled in different ways; by the worker choosing to engage in either 'deep' or 'surface' acting, for example.
- *Stress* is an emotionally related phenomenon. It involves an experience of distress which leads to an individual being incapable of performing the tasks that are required of them. It is not something that is inherent in either the individual or the work. It can only be understood by looking at how the circumstances of the individual interrelate with the organisational circumstances and pressures.
- People vary in how they cope with potentially stressing circumstances and the psychological, emotional and social resources that they can draw upon influence how well they cope.
- A variety of activities go on in every organisation which are not officially 'meant to happen' in the organisation. Examples of *organisational mischief* like fiddling, practical joking, sabotage and workplace sexual activity tend to challenge dominant modes of operating in organisations as well as helping people both to further and to defend their interests. They also enable people to protect their personal notions of 'self'. Managers and non-managers alike engage in organisational mischief.
- Sexuality and humour have a particular significance in the 'underlife' of the work organisation as they represent aspects of humanity (including the 'animal' aspects of humanity) that are especially unsusceptible to corporate or managerial control.
- Humour has a very important role in work situations in enabling people both to challenge and adjust to organisational controls and dominant interests. It also helps people control their lives generally and cope with the existential threats to sanity and a sense of order.

Recommended reading

The variety of ways in which matters of emotion arise within organisations is demonstrated by Steve Fineman in *Understanding Emotion at Work* (London: Sage, 2003) whilst David Wainwright and Michael Calnan provide a challengingly critical view of the way work stress has become such an important issue in recent times in their *Work Stress: The making of a modern epidemic* (Buckingham: Open University Press, 2002). The variety of forms of mischief that occurs in organisations is reflected upon by Steve Ackroyd and Paul Thompson in *Organisational Misbehaviour* (London: Sage, 1999) in a way which usefully complements the analysis in the present chapter. Humour plays a key part in this, as we have seen, and David Collinson shows us how attempts are increasingly being made in managerial circles to make humour 'work' for the organisation in his article, 'Managing humour' (*Journal of Management Studies*, 39(3): 269–288, 2002). And for more material on the role of sex in work and organisations see Jo Brewis and Steve Linstead's *Sex, Work and Sex Work: Eroticizing organization?* (London: Routledge, 2000).

Further reading

Further reading Work orientations, implicit and psychological contracts

Baldamus, W. (1961) *Efficiency and Effort*, London: Tavistock

Behrend, H. (1957) 'The effort bargain', *International Labor Relations Review*, 10: 503–515

Goldthorpe, J.H., Lockwood, D., Bechhofer, F. and Platt, J. (1968) *The Affluent Worker: Attitudes and behaviour*, Cambridge: Cambridge University Press

Guest, D. (1998) 'Is the psychological contract worth taking seriously?', *Journal of Organizational Behaviour*, 9: 649–664

Herriot, P., Manning, W.E.G. and Kidd, J.M. (1997) 'The content of the psychological contract', *British Journal of Management*, 8(2): 151–162

Kotter, J.P. (1973) 'The psychological contract', *California Management Review*, 15: 91–99

Levinson, H., Price, C., Munden, K. and Solley, C. (1966) *Men, Management and Mental Health*, Cambridge, MA: Harvard University Press

Noon, M. and Blyton, P. (2002) *The Realities of Work*, Basingstoke: Palgrave.

Robinson, S. and Rousseau, D.M. (1994) 'The psychological contract – not the exception but the norm', *Journal of Organisational Behavior*, 15(3): 245–259

Rousseau, D.M. (1995) *Psychological Contracts in Organisations: Understanding written and unwritten agreements*, Thousand Oaks, CA: Sage

Watson, T.J. (2003) *Sociology, Work and Industry*, Chapter 7, London: Routledge

Further reading Emotions and work

Albrow, M. (1997) *Do Organisations have feelings?*, London: Routledge

Damasio, A.R. (2000) *The Feeling of What Happened*, London: Heinemann

Fineman, S. (ed.) (1993) *Emotion in Organizations*, London: Sage

Fineman, S. (2003) *Understanding Emotion at Work*, London: Sage

Harré, R. and Finlay Jones, R. (eds) (1986) *The Social Construction of Emotions*, Oxford: Blackwell
Hochschild, A.R. (1985) *The Managed Heart: The commercialization of human feeling*, Berkeley, CA: University of California Press
Hopfl, H. and Linstead, S. (1993) 'Passion and performance: suffering and the carrying of organizational roles' in S. Fineman (ed.) *Emotion in Organizations*, London: Sage
Muchinsky, P.M. (2000) 'Emotions in the workplace: the neglect of organizational behaviour', *Journal of Organizational Behavior*, 21: 801–805
Putnam, L. and Mumby, D.K. (1993) 'Organizations, emotion and the myth of rationality' in S. Fineman (ed.) *Emotion in Organizations*, London: Sage
Taylor, S. (1998) 'Emotional labour and the new workplace' in P. Thompson and C. Warhurst (eds) *Workplaces of the Future*, London: Macmillan
Taylor, S. and Tylor, M. (2000) 'Emotional labour and sexual difference in the airline industry', *Work, Employment and Society*, 14(1): 77–95
Van Maanen, J. and Kunda, G. (1989) '"Real feelings": emotional expression and organizational culture', *Research in Organizational Behavior*, 11: 43–103
Wouters, C. (1989) 'The sociology of emotions and flight attendants: Hochschild's "managed heart"', *Theory, Culture and Society*, 6(1): 95–123

Further reading Work and stress

Cooper, C.L. (2000) *Theories of Organizational Stress*, Oxford: Oxford University Press
Cooper, C.L. and Sutherland, V.J. (1992) 'The stress of the executive lifestyle: trends in the 1990s', *Management Decision*, 30(6): 64–68
Cooper, C.L., Cooper, R.D. and Eaker, L. (1988) *Living With Stress*, Harmondsworth: Penguin
Newton, T., Handy, J. and Fineman, S. (eds) (1995) *Managing Stress: Emotion and power at work*, London: Sage
Wainwright, D. and Calnan, M. (2002) *Work Stress: The making of a modern epidemic*, Buckingham: Open University Press

Further reading Deviance and misbehaviour in organisations

Ackroyd, S. and Thompson, P. (1999) *Organisational Misbehaviour*, London: Sage
Adams, A. (1992) *Bullying at Work*, London: Virago
Collinson, D.L. (1992) *Managing the Shopfloor: Subjectivity, masculinity and workplace culture*, Berlin: de Gruyter
Collinson, D.L. (1994) 'Strategies of resistance: power, knowledge and subjectivity in the workplace' in J. Jermier, W. Nord and D. Knights (eds) *Resistance and Power in the Workplace*, London: Routledge
Dalton, M. (1948) 'The industrial rate buster', *Applied Anthropology*, 7(1): 5–23
Ditton, J. (1977a) *Part-time Crime: An ethnography of fiddling and pilferage*, London: Macmillan
Ditton, J. (1977b) 'Perks, pilferage and the fiddle: the historical structure of invisible wages', *Theory and Society*, 4(1): 39–71
Dubois, P. (1977) *Sabotage in Industry*, Harmondsworth: Penguin

Fine, G.A. (1988) 'Letting off steam: redefining a restaurant's work environment' in M.D. Moore and R.C. Snyder (eds) *Inside Organizations: Understanding the human dimension*, Newbury Park, CA: Sage, 119–128

Henry, S. (1987) *The Hidden Economy: The context and control of borderline crime*, Oxford: Martin Robertson

Jermier, J. (1988) 'Sabotage at work: the rational view', *The Sociology of Organisations*, 6: 101–134

Jermier, J., Knights, D. and Nord, W. (1994) *Resistance and Power in Organisations*, London: Routledge

Lee, D. (2000) 'An analysis of workplace bullying in the UK', *Personnel Review*, 29(5): 593–612

Mars, G. (1982) *Cheats at Work: An anthropology of workplace crime*, London: Counterpoint

Noon, M. and Delbridge, R. (1993) 'News from behind my hand: gossip in organisations', *Organisation Studies*, 14(1): 23–36

Punch, M. (1996) *Dirty Business: Exploring corporate misconduct: Analysis and cases*, London: Sage

Roy, D. (1952) 'Quota restriction and goldbricking in a machine shop', *American Journal of Sociology*, 57(5): 427–442

Roy, D. (1958) 'Banana time: job satisfaction and informal interaction', *Human Organisation*, 18(1): 158–161

Stockdale, M.S. (1996) *Sexual Harassment in the Workplace: Perspectives, frontiers and response strategies*, London: Sage

Thomas, A.M. and Kitzinger, C. (1994) 'It's just something that happens: the invisibility of sexual harassment in the workplace', *Gender, Work and Organisation*, 1(3): 151–161

Further reading Humour in organisations

Barsoux, J.-L. (1993) *Funny Business: Humour, management and business culture*, New York: Cassell

Boland, R.J. and Hoffman, R. (1983) 'Humour in a machine shop: an interpretation of symbolic action' in L.R. Pondy, P. Frost, G. Morgan and T. Dandridge (eds) (1983) *Organizational Symbolism*, Greenwich, CT: JAI Press

Bradney, P. (1957) 'The joking relationship in industry', *Human Relations*, 10(2): 179–187

Collinson, D.L. (1988) 'Engineering humour: masculinity, joking and conflict in shop floor relations', *Organization Studies*, 9(2): 181–199

Collinson, D.L. (2002) 'Managing humour', *Journal of Management Studies*, 39(3): 269–288

Davies, C. (1982) 'Ethnic jokes, moral values and social boundaries', *British Journal of Sociology*, 33(3): 383–403

Fox, S. (1990) 'The ethnography of humour and the problem of social reality', *Sociology*, 24(3): 431–446

Jacobson, H. (1997) *Seriously Funny: From the ridiculous to the sublime*, London: Viking

Linstead, S. (1985) 'Jokers wild: the importance of humour in the maintenance of organisational culture', *Sociological Review*, 33(4): 741–767

Mulkay, M. (1988) *On Humour*, Cambridge: Polity Press
Radcliffe-Brown, A.R. (1940) 'On joking relationships', *Africa*, 13: 195–210

Further reading Sexuality in organisations

Brewis, J. and Linstead, S. (2000) *Sex, Work and Sex Work: Eroticizing organization?*, London: Routledge
Burrell, G. (1992) 'Sex and organisations' in A.J. Mills and P. Tancred (eds) *Gendering Organisational Analysis*, London: Sage
Di Tomaso, N. (1989) 'Sexuality in the workplace: discrimination and harassment' in J. Hearn, D.L. Sheppard, P. Tancred-Sherrif and G. Burrell (eds) *The Sexuality of Organization*, London: Sage
Filby, M. (1992) 'The figures, the personality and the bums: service work and sexuality', *Work, Employment and Society*, 6(1): 23–42
Harlow, E., Hearn, J. and Parkin, W. (1992) 'Sexuality and social work organisations' in P. Carter, T. Jeffs and M. Smith (eds) *Changing Social Work and Welfare*, Buckingham: Open University Press
Hearn, J. and Parkin, W. (2001) *Gender, Sexuality and Violence in Organizations*, London: Sage
Roy, D. (1974) 'Sex in the factory: informal heterosexual relations between supervisors and workgroups' in C.D. Bryant (ed.) *Deviant Behavior*, Chicago, IL: Rand McNally

Week 12

Module Summary/Formative Assessment

Italic page numbers indicate figures and tables